Lecture Notes in Computer S   5804

Commenced Publication in 1973
Founding and Former Series Editors:
Gerhard Goos, Juris Hartmanis, and Jan van Leeuwen

Shlomi Dolev (Ed.)

Algorithmic Aspects of Wireless Sensor Networks

5th International Workshop, ALGOSENSORS 2009
Rhodes, Greece, July 10-11, 2009
Revised Selected Papers

 Springer

Volume Editor

Shlomi Dolev
Ben Gurion University of the Negev
Department of Computer Science
Beer-Sheva, Israel
E-mail: dolev@cs.bgu.ac.il

Library of Congress Control Number: 2009937645

CR Subject Classification (1998): F.2, G.1.2, G.2.2, I.2.9, C.1.3, D.2

LNCS Sublibrary: SL 5 – Computer Communication Networks and Telecommunications

ISSN   0302-9743
ISBN-10   3-642-05433-1 Springer Berlin Heidelberg New York
ISBN-13   978-3-642-05433-4 Springer Berlin Heidelberg New York

springer.com

© Springer-Verlag Berlin Heidelberg 2009
Printed in Germany

Typesetting: Camera-ready by author, data conversion by Scientific Publishing Services, Chennai, India
Printed on acid-free paper   SPIN: 12783946   06/3180   5 4 3 2 1 0

Preface

ALGOSENSORS, the International International Workshop on Algorithmic Aspects of Wireless Sensor Networks, is an annual forum for presentation of research on all algorithmic aspects of sensor networks, including the theory, design, analysis, implementation, and application of algorithms for sensor networks. The 5th edition of ALGOSENSORS was held during July 10–11, 2009, on Rhodes, Greece.

There were 41 extended abstracts submitted to ALGOSENSORS this year, and this volume contains the 21 contributions selected by the Program Committee. All submitted papers were read and evaluated by at least three Program Committee members, assisted by external reviewers. The final decision regarding every paper was taken following an electronic discussion.

The proceedings also include two two-page-long Brief Announcements (BA). These BAs are presentations of ongoing works for which full papers are not ready yet, or of recent results whose full description will soon be presented or has been recently presented in other conferences. Researchers use the BA track to quickly draw the attention of the community to their experiences, insights and results from ongoing distributed computing research and projects.

ALGOSENSORS 2009 was organized in cooperation with the EATCS and ICALP 2009. The support of Ben-Gurion University, the Foundations of Adaptive Networked Societies of Tiny Artefacts (FRONTS) project, and CTI is gratefully acknowledged.

August 2009   Shlomi Dolev

Organization

ALGOSENSORS, the International International Workshop on Algorithmic Aspects of Wireless Sensor Networks, is an annual forum for research presentations on all algoritmic facets of sensor networks. ALGOSENSORS 2009 was organized in cooperation with the EATCS and ICALP 2009.

Steering Committee

Josep Diaz	Technical University of Catalonia, Spain
Jan van Leeuwen	University of Utrecht, The Netherlands
Sotiris Nikoletseas	University of Patras and CTI, Greece (Chair)
Jose Rolim	University of Geneva, Switzerland
Paul Spirakis	University of Patras and CTI, Greece

Organizing Committee

Program Chair	Shlomi Dolev, Ben-Gurion University of the Negev, Israel
Web Chair	Konstantinos Marios Aggelopoulos, CTI, Greece

Program Committee

James Aspnes	Yale University
Chen Avin	Ben Gurion University
Ed Coffman	Columbia University
Shlomi Dolev	Ben Gurion University, (Program Chair)
Ted Herman	University of Iowa
Seth Gilbert	EPFL
Chryssis Georgiou	University of Cyprus
Mordecai Golin	Hong Kong UST
Maria Gradinariu Potop-Butucaru	University of Paris 6
Alex Kesselmen	Google
Darek Kowalski	University of Liverpool
Evangelos Kranakis	Carleton University
Danny Krizanc	Wesleyan

Limor Lahiani   Microsoft Israel R&D Center
Flaminia Luccio   Università Cà Foscari Venezia
Nancy Lynch   MIT
Thomas Moscibroda   Microsoft Research
Seffi Naor   Technion
Calvin Newport   MIT
Rafail Ostrovsky   UCLA
Marina Papatriantafilou   Chalmers University
Andrzej Pelc   University of Québec
Giuseppe Persiano   University Salerno
Jose Rolim   University of Geneva
Nicola Santoro   Carleton University
Elad Schiller   Chalmers University
Paul Spirakis   University of Patras and CTI
Eli Upfal   Brown University
Jennifer Welch   Texas A&M University
Moti Yung   Google

Sponsors

Referees

Zohir Bouzid   Zhang Fu   Yvonne-Anne Pignolet
Hyun-Chul Chung   Georgios Georgiadis   Giuseppe Prenice
Alex Cornejo   Niv Gilboa   Mariusz Rokicki
Devdatt Dubhashi   Kleoni Ioannidou   Srikanth Sastry
Amit Dvir   Amos Israeli   Hanan Shpungin
Moran Feldman   Maleq Khan   Roy Schwartz
Riccardo Focardi   Andreas Larsson   Saira Viqar
                        Gopal Pandurangan

Table of Contents

Invited Talks

Index

Invited Talk I
Actuator Nets: Folding, Reconfiguring and Deploying Sensors

Erik D. Demain

MIT CSAIL
32 Vassar St.
Cambridge, MA 02139
edemaine@mit.edu

Abstract. What happens when sensors can move around or otherwise change their geometry? When all sensors can move (a robot swarm), we would like to be able to determine and manipulate high-level properties, such as the boundary of the swarm or the connectivity of the communication network. When only a few sensors can move, we would like the mobile sensors to be able to deploy immobile sensors to improve or repair the network connectivity or coverage. When the sensors are attached to a connected substrate, and they can manipulate the substrate, we would like to be able to reconfigure the substrate into arbitrary shapes. I will describe several algorithmic projects to address all of these problems.

S. Dolev (Ed.): ALGOSENSORS 2009, LNCS 5804, p. 1, 2009.

Invited Talk II
The Power and Limitations of Simple Algorithms: A Partial Case Study of Greedy Mechanisim Design for Combinatorial Actions

Allan Borodin

Department of Computer Science
University of Toronto
10 Kings College Road
Toronto, OM, M5S 3G4
Canada
bor@cs.toronto.edu

Abstract. Given the diversity of computational problems, models of computation, solution concepts, and algorithmic approaches, it often seems a challenge to view computer science/informatik as a coherent discipline. Fortunately, various unifying ideas (e.g. NP-completeness) have brought significant perspective to a very complex and ever expanding field.

In a less ambitious program, I have been thinking about simple algorithmic approaches that arise frequently in approximation algorithms for combinatorial optimization. To be more specific, I am in interested in "greedy-like" algorithms and recently I am trying to understand the use of such algorithms in combinatorial auctions. I will discuss some precise models for simple greedy-like algorithms and how such algorithms can and cannot achieve desirable properties such a truthfulness, and convergence to "good" equilibria.

The ideas in this talk are based on recent work with Brendan Lucier and also relate to Yuli Ye's talk in ICALP.

S. Dolev (Ed.): ALGOSENSORS 2009, LNCS 5804, p. 2, 2009.
© Springer-Verlag Berlin Heidelberg 2009

Sensor Field: A Computational Model*

Carme Àlvarez, Amalia Duch, Joaquim Gabarro, and Maria Serna

ALBCOM Research Group, Universitat Politècnica de Catalunya
{alvarez,duch,gabarro,mjserna}@lsi.upc.edu

Abstract. We introduce a formal model of computation for networks of tiny artifacts, the static synchronous sensor field model (SSSF) which considers that the devices communicate through a fixed communication graph and interact with the environment through input/output data streams. We analyze the performance of SSSFs solving two sensing problems the **Average Monitoring** and the **Alerting** problems. For constant memory SSSFs we show that the set of recognized languages is contained in DSPACE($n + m$) where n is the number of nodes of the communication graph and m its number of edges. Finally we explore the capabilities of SSSFs having sensing and additional non-sensing constant memory devices.

1 Introduction

The use of networks of tiny artifacts is becoming a key ingredient in the technological development of XXI century societies. An example of those networks are the networks with sensors, where some of the artifacts have the ability of sensing the environment and communicate among themselves. There is no easy way to design a universal sensor network that acts properly in all possible situations. However, it is important to understand the computational process and behavior of the different types of artifact's networks, which will help in taking the maximum profit of those networks. In the particular case of networks with sensors several proposals (taxonomies and surveys) that elucidate the distinguishing features of sensor networks and their applications have been published ([1,5,12,14]). These proposals state clearly the need of formal models that capture the clue characteristics of sensor networks.

The general sensing setting can be described by two elements: the observers or end users and the phenomenon, the entity of interest to the observers that is monitored and analyzed by a network with sensors. The corresponding information is discretized in two ways: first the environment is sampled on a discrete set of locations (sensor positions), and second the measures taken by the sensors are digitalized to the corresponding precision. To analyze the correctness and performance of the system we are faced with a double task; on one side there

---

* Partially supported by the ICT Program of the EU under contract number 215270 (FRONTS). The first, third, and fourth authors were supported by MEC TIN-2007-66523 (FORMALISM) and the second author by MEC TIN2006-11345 (ALINEX-2).

S. Dolev (Ed.): ALGOSENSORS 2009, LNCS 5804, pp. 3–14, 2009.

is a computational problem to be solved by a particular network; on the other hand, it is necessary to assess whether computed solution is a valid observation of the phenomenon. Both tasks will require different analysis tools and we concentrate here on the first. The distinctive peculiarities of the computational system define new parameters to be evaluated in order to measure the performance of the system. Metrics are needed to allow us to estimate the suitability of an specific or generic network topology or the possibility of emergent behavior with pre-specified requirements.

The computational system can be modeled by combining the notion of graph automata [3] together with distributed data streams [6], a combination inspired in similar ideas developed in the context of concurrent programming [8]. Existing models coming from distributed systems [11], hybrid systems and ad-hoc networks [7,10] capture some of such networks. Models coming from the area of population protocol models [2,4] represent sensor networks, supposing that the corresponding sensing devices are extremely limited mobile agents (a finite state machine) that interact only in pairs by means of a communication graph.

We propose a general model capturing some characteristic differences of sensor networks. A sensor field is composed of a kind of devices that can communicate one to the other and also to the environment. We concentrate our initial study in the case in which the devices and the communication links do not appear and disappear during the computation. We also assume that those devices synchronize at barriers marking rounds, in a way similar to the BSP model [13]. During a computation round, a device access the received messages and data provided by the environment, performs some computation, and finally sends messages to its neighbors and to the environment. Those are the fundamental features of the *Static and Synchronous Sensor Field* (SSSF) model. The model allows the definition of complexity measures like latency, round duration, message number or message length among others. In this setting we can formulate a general and natural definition of sensing problems by means of input/output data streams.

We introduce the **Average Monitoring** and **Alerting** problems and, supposing that the sensor field has as many devices as input streams, we analyze solutions for several topologies. We obtain upper and lower bounds on the solutions to the problem and for some concrete topologies we propose optimal algorithms.

Our proposed model can be seen as a non-uniform computational model in the sense that it is easy to introduce constraints to all or some of the devices of the sensor field and relate it to classic complexity classes. By restricting their memory capacity to be constant, we show that the decisional version of the functions computed by this restricted SSSF belong to the class $\text{DSPACE}(n+m)$ where n is the number of nodes of the communication graph and m its number of edges. Finally, by restricting the memory capacity to be constant and by allowing the inclusion in the network of non-sensing devices we show that there is a SSSF of polynomial size, time and latency, solving the monitoring problem for a property which is computable in polynomial time.

The paper is organized as follows. In Section 2 we introduce the SSSF model as well as the sensing problems and the performance measures. In Section 3 we study SSSFs solving the Average Monitoring problem. The SSSF with restricted memory capacity of the devices (specifically supposing that it is logarithmic or constant), is analyzed in Section 4. We then extend the studied networks to include non sensing devices in Section 5. Finally, in Section 6 we post some conclusions and possibilities of future work.

Due to lack of space proofs and algorithms are just sketched, we refer the interested reader to the full version of the paper.

2   Static Synchronous Sensor Field: The Model

A *data stream* w is a sequence of data items $w = w^1 w^2 \ldots w^i \ldots$ that can be infinite. For any $i \geq 1$, $w[i]$ denotes the i-th element of w, i.e. $w[i] = w^i$. For any i, j, $1 \leq i \leq j$, $w[i,j]$ denotes the subsequence of w composed by all data items between the i-th and j-th positions, i.e. $w[i,j] = w^i \ldots w^j$. For any $n \geq 1$, an n-data stream $\mathbf{w}$ is an n-tuple of data streams, $\mathbf{w} = (w_1, \ldots, w_n)$. For any $i \geq 1$, $\mathbf{w}[i]$ denotes the n-tuple composed by all the i-th elements of each data stream, $\mathbf{w}[i] = (w_1[i], \ldots, w_n[i])$. For any i, j such that $1 \leq i \leq j$, $\mathbf{w}[i,j]$ denotes the n-tuple composed by the subsequences between the i-th and j-th positions of each data stream, $\mathbf{w}[i,j] = (w_1[i,j], \ldots w_n[i,j])$.

We use the standard graph notation. A *communication graph* is a directed graph $G = (N, E)$ where N is the set of nodes and E is the set of edges, $E \subseteq N \times N$. Unless explicitly stated we assume that N has n nodes that are enumerated from 1 to n and m edges. Each node k is associated to a device, let us say to device k, that has access to the k-th data stream. Each edge $(i,j) \in E$ specifies that device i can send messages to device j or what is the same, device j can receive messages from device i. Given a device k let us denote by $I(k) = \{i \mid (i,k) \in E\}$ the set of neighbors from which device k can receive data items and by $O(k) = \{j \mid (k,j) \in E\}$ the set of neighbors to which device k can send data. Let $in_k = |I(k)|$ and $out_k = |O(k)|$ be the in and out degrees of node k. Set $in_G = \max_{k \in N} in_k$ and $out_G = \max_{k \in N} out_k$. We use d_G to denote the diameter of the graph G.

A *Static Synchronous Sensor Field* consists of a *set of devices* and a *communication graph*. The communication graph specifies how the devices communicate one to the other. For the moment and without loose of generality, we assume that all devices are sensing devices that can receive information from the environment and send information to the environment. Since the model we consider is static we assume that the edges are the same during all the computation time. Moreover each device executes its own process, communicates with their neighbors (devices associated to adjacent nodes) and also with the environment. All the devices work in a synchronous way, at the begining of each round they receive data from their neighbors and from the environment, then they apply their own transition function changing in this way their actual configuration and finish the round sending data to their neighbors and to the environment. Let us describe in detail the main components of the Static Synchronous Sensor Field.

Static Synchronous Sensor Field $\mathcal{F}$ (SSSF $\mathcal{F}$): Formally we define a Static Synchronous Sensor Field $\mathcal{F}$ by a tuple $\mathcal{F} = (N, E, U, V, X, (Q_k, \delta_k)_{k \in N})$ where

- $G_{\mathcal{F}} = (N, E)$ is the communication graph.
- U is the alphabet of data items used to represent the input data streams that can be received from the environment.
- V is the alphabet of items used to represent the output data streams that can be send to the environment.
- X is the alphabet of items used to communicate each device to the other devices. Each $m \in X^*$ is called message or packet. $U, V \subseteq X$. We denote by data items the elements of alphabets U and V and by communication items (or items) the elements of X.
- (Q_k, δ_k) defines for each device associated to a node $k \in N$ (device k) its set of local states and its transition function, respectively.

The *local computation of each device k in $\mathcal{F}$* is defined by (Q_k, δ_k) and depends on the communication with its neighbors and with the environment. Q_k is a (potentially infinite) set of local states and δ_k is a transition function. A state codifies the values of some local set of variables (ordinary program variables, message buffers, program counters ...) and all what is needed to describe completely the instantaneous configuration of the local computation. The transition function δ_k that depends on its local state $q_k \in Q_k$ as well as on:

- the communication items received by device k from devices $i \in I(k)$,
- the data item that device k receives as input from the environment,
- the communication items sent by device k to devices $j \in O(k)$,
- and the data item that device k sends to the environment.

The transition function is defined as $\delta_k : Q_k \times (X^*)^{in_k} \times U \longrightarrow Q_k \times (X^*)^{out_k} \times V$. The meaning of $\delta_k(q_k, (x_{ik})_{i \in I(k)}, u_k) = (q'_k, (y_{kj})_{j \in O(k)}, v_k)$ is that if device k of $\mathcal{F}$ is in its local state $q_k \in Q_k$, receives $x_{ik} \in X^*$ from each of its neighbors $i \in I(k)$, and receives the input data item $u_k \in U$ from the environment, then in one computation step device k changes its local state to $q'_k \in Q_k$, sends $y_{kj} \in X^*$ to each of its neighbors $j \in O(k)$ and outputs $v_k \in V$ to the environment. In the case that device k does not send any value, we denote this 'no value' or 'does not care' by the special symbol $\perp$. For any device k, let q^0_k be the initial local state. For any $t \geq 1$, *the t-th computation round of device k* is described as follows: If the local state of device k is q^{t-1}_k, and it receives $(x^t_{ik})_{i \in I(k)}$ from its input neighbors, u^t_k from the environment and $\delta_k(q^{t-1}_k, (x^t_{ik})_{i \in I(k)}, u^t_k) = (q^t_k, (y^t_{kj})_{j \in O(k)}, v^t_k)$ then device k changes its local state from q^{t-1}_k to q^t_k, sends $(y^t_{kj})_{j \in O(k)}$ to its output neighbors and v^t_k to the environment.

A *computation* of $\mathcal{F}$ is a sequence $\mathbf{c}^0, \mathbf{d}^1, \mathbf{c}^1, \mathbf{d}^2, \ldots, \mathbf{c}^{t-1}, \mathbf{d}^t, \mathbf{c}^t, \ldots$, eventually infinite, where $\mathbf{c}^0 = (q^0_k)_{k \in N}$ is the n-tuple of the initial local states of the n

devices, and for each $t \geq 1$, $\mathbf{c}^t = (q_k^t)_{k \in N}$ is the n-tuple of the local states after t computation rounds. The tuple $\mathbf{d}^t = (d_k^t)_{k \in N}$ represents the input/output data of the t-th computation round (i.e. the transition from round $t - 1$ to round t). In particular, for device k the input/output data of the t-th round is represented by $d_k^t = ((x_{ik}^t)_{i \in I(k)}, u_k^t, (y_{kj}^t)_{j \in O(k)}, v_k^t)$. Note that device k receives $(x_{ik}^t)_{i \in I(k)}$ from its neighbors, $x_{ik}^t = y_{ki}^{t-1}$ receives u_k^t from the environment, changes its state from q_k^{t-1} to q_k^t, sends $(y_{kj}^t)_{j \in O(k)}$ to its neighbors and sends v_k^t to the environment.

The *stream behavior of a computation* $\mathbf{c}^0, \mathbf{d}^1, \mathbf{c}^1, \mathbf{d}^2, \dots, \mathbf{c}^{t-1}, \mathbf{d}^t, \mathbf{c}^t, \dots$ of $\mathcal{F}$ is defined as $(\mathbf{u}, \mathbf{v})$ where $\mathbf{u} = (u_k)_{k \in N}$ is the tuple composed by the input data streams of each device k, $u_k = u_k^1 u_k^2 \dots u_k^t \dots$ and $\mathbf{v} = (v_k)_{k \in N}$ is the tuple composed by the output data stream of each device $v_k = v_k^1 v_k^2 \dots v_k^t \dots$ Notice that this information can be extracted from the computation $\mathbf{c}^0, \mathbf{d}^1, \dots, \mathbf{c}^{t-1}, \mathbf{d}^t, \mathbf{c}^t,$ $\dots$. Thus the sensor field $\mathcal{F}$ outputs the tuple of output data streams $\mathbf{v} = (v_k)_{k \in N}$ given the tuple of input data streams $\mathbf{u} = (u_k)_{k \in N}$ or what is the same, $\mathbf{v}[1, t]$ given $\mathbf{u}[1, t]$ for each $t \geq 1$.

We define the function $f_{\mathcal{F}}$ associated to the stream behavior of $\mathcal{F}$ as follows: Given any pair of tuples of data streams $\mathbf{u}$ and $\mathbf{v}$ and any $t \geq 1$, $f_{\mathcal{F}}(\mathbf{u}[1, t]) = \mathbf{v}[1, t]$ if and only if the sensor field $\mathcal{F}$ computes $\mathbf{v}[1, t]$ given $\mathbf{u}[1, t]$.

Function computed by $\mathcal{F}$: A function f (defined on data streams) is *computed by a sensor field $\mathcal{F}$ with latency d* if for all (appropriate) tuple of data streams $\mathbf{u}$, and for all $t \geq 1$, $f_{\mathcal{F}}(\mathbf{u}[1, t + d])[t + d] = f(\mathbf{u}[1, t])[t]$. That is the SSSF outputs at time $t + d$ the t-th element of f. We say that f is *computed by a sensor field $\mathcal{F}$* if there exists d for which f is computed by $\mathcal{F}$ with latency at most d.

Note that $\mathbf{u}$ and $\mathbf{v}$ have in general infinite length. In order to express formally the behavior of a SSSF we consider all the finite prefixes of the input stream $(\mathbf{u}[1, t])$ and those of the output stream $(\mathbf{v}[1, t])$. However, take into account that each sensor will output only one data item $(\mathbf{v}[t])$ per round.

The computational resources used by a sensor to compute a function of this kind are the following. For each device and computation round we can measure

- *Time.* The number of operations performed in the given round of the device. This is a rough estimation of the "physical time" needed to input data, receive information from other sensor, compute, send information and output data.
- *Space.* The space used by the device in such computation round.
- *Message Length.* The maximum number of data items of a message sent by the device in such computation round.
- *Number of messages.* The maximum number of messages sent by the device in such round.

We consider the following worst case complexity measures taken over any device and computation round of a sensor field $\mathcal{F}$:

- *Size*: The number of nodes or devices of the communication graph G.
- *Time* $(\mathcal{T})$: The maximum time used by any device in any of its rounds.

- *Space* ($\mathcal{S}$): The maximum space used by any device of in any of its rounds.
- *MessageLength* ($\mathcal{L}$): The maximum message length of any device of in any of its rounds.
- *MessageNumber* ($\mathcal{M}$): The maximum number of messages sent by any device in any of its rounds.

In general we analyze these complexity measures with respect to the *Size* of the communication graph which usually will coincide with the number n of data streams, we denote by $\mathcal{T}(n)$ the *Time*, by $\mathcal{S}(n)$ the *Space*, by $\mathcal{L}(n)$ the *MessageLength* and by $\mathcal{M}(n)$ the *MessageNumber*.

Computational problems that are susceptible of being solved by sensor fields can be stated in the following way:

Sensing Problem Π: Given an n-tuple of data streams $\mathbf{u} = (u_k)_{1 \le k \le n}$ for some $n \ge 1$, compute an m-tuple of data streams $\mathbf{v} = (v_k)_{1 \le k \le m}$ for some $m \le n$ such that $R_\Pi(\mathbf{u}[1,t], \mathbf{v}[1,t])$ is satisfied for every $t \ge 1$. R_Π is the relation that output data streams have to satisfy given the input data streams, i.e. the property that defines the problem.

Problem Solved by $\mathcal{F}$: A sensor field $\mathcal{F}$ *solves problem* Π *with latency* d if for every pair of data streams $\mathbf{u}$ and $\mathbf{v}$, and every $t \ge 1$, if $f_\mathcal{F}(\mathbf{u}[1,t]) = \mathbf{v}[1,t]$ then $R_\Pi(\mathbf{u}[1,t], \mathbf{v}[1+d, t+d])$. A sensor field $\mathcal{F}$ *solves the problem* Π if there is a d such that $\mathcal{F}$ solves problem Π with latency d.

Let us post two examples of sensing problems. First we consider a problem in which it is needed to monitor continuously a wide area. This implies "sensing locally" and "informing locally" about a global environmental phenomena.

Average Monitoring: Given n data streams $(u_k)_{1 \le k \le n}$ for some $n \ge 1$, compute n data streams $(v_k)_{1 \le k \le n}$ such that $v_k[t] = (u_1[t] + \cdots + u_k[t])/n$.

The second example we consider is related to "fire detection alarm". In this case it is desired to detect the situation in which there is a high risk of fire. One element to be measured is the level of smoke in the air of such area and if this level is higher than a certain value then the alert has to be activated. A specific device (number 1 for instance) acts as a master and outputs the result.

Alerting: Given n data streams $(u_k)_{1 \le k \le n}$ for some $n \ge 1$, and threshold value A, device 1 has to compute a data stream v_1 such that

$$v_1[t] = \begin{cases} 1 & \text{if } \exists k : 1 \le k \le n : u_k[t] \ge A \\ \bot & \text{otherwise} \end{cases}$$

3   SSSFs Solving the Average Monitoring Problem

We study the requirements of a SSSF for solving the Average Monitoring problem. It is divided into two parts. We start by giving some lower bounds on the latency, the *MessageNumber*, and the *MessageLength*, required by some types of SSSF for solving the Average Monitoring. Later we provide optimal algorithms for the problem in particular topologies.

Lower Bounds. In order to be able to state lower bounds, we make an additional assumption: all the sent messages are formed only by tuples of input data items (without compression). An easy argument shows the following lower bound.

Lemma 1. *A SSSF $\mathcal{F}$ with communication graph G solving the Average Monitoring problem requires at least latency d_G.*

For the following results we assume, in addition, that along the whole computation the flow of packets from node i to node j, for any $i, j \in N$, follows a fixed path $p_{i,j}$. Thus the algorithm uses a fixed *communication pattern* $P = (p_{i,j})_{i,j \in N}$. We say that p_{ij} is a *diametral path* in P if it has length d_G. Let $\beta_P(k)$ be the out-degree of node k in the subgraph G' of G formed by the diametral paths in P that start at k. Set $\beta(G, P) = \max_{k \in N} \beta_P(k)$. Observe that those subgraphs are critical in terms of the delivery of packets in d_G rounds. It is easy to show the following lower bound on *MessageNumber*.

Lemma 2. *Let $\mathcal{F}$ be a SSSF, with communication graph G and communication pattern P, solving the Average Monitoring problem with latency d_G. It holds that for any round $t > d_G$, there is a device sending at least $\beta(G)$ packets simultaneously.*

Taking into account that the different communication flows must be pipelined along paths with critical length we can prove the following lower bound on *MessageLength*.

Lemma 3. *Let $\mathcal{F}$ be a SSSF, with communication graph G and communication pattern P, solving the Average Monitoring problem with latency d_G. Then, if $k_1, \ldots, k_{d_G+1}$ is the fixed communication path used by devices $k_1, \ldots, k_{d_G}$ to send their data to k_{d_G+1} in P and p is included in a diametral path in P, then there is a round $t_0 > d_G$ such that for any round $t > t_0$, there is a device receiving a message composed of at least d_G data items.*

Algorithms. We first propose a generic SSSF with optimal latency provided that the communication graph is strongly connected. In general, this algorithm is not optimal in *Space*, *MessageLength* and *MessageNumber*, we show that when the topology of the communication graph is known in advance, it is possible to obtain SSSF s with specific topologies that optimize such parameters. In what follows, we assume that every device in the SSSF is aware of the total number of devices n and the diameter d of the communication graph.

Lemma 4. *Let G be a strongly connected communication graph with n nodes. There is a SSSF $\mathcal{F}$ with communication graph G solving the Average Monitoring problem with latency d_G, $\mathcal{T}(n) = O(n\, d_G(in_G + out_G))$, $\mathcal{L}(n) = O(n\, d_G + \log n)$, $\mathcal{S}(n) = O(n\, d_G + \log n)$ and $\mathcal{M}(n) = out_G$.*

Proof Sketch. We consider the following flooding algorithm in which each sensors keeps a table M of size $d \times n$ of data items. The computation at each sensor is the following:

algorithm Generic Average Monitoring
   ▷ Initially
   $M[1 \ldots d] \times [1 \ldots n] = (\bot)_{d \times n}$
   $id =$ identifier of the node
   ▷ round
   // receive
   for $i \in I(k)$ {receive M_i from incoming neighbors; $M =$ update (M, M_i)}
   // compute
   $v = (M[d][1] + \ldots + M[d][n])/n$
   for $p = d, \ldots, 2$ {$M[p] = M[p-1]$}
   $M[1] = (\bot)_n$
   $M[1, id] = u$
   // send
   for $j \in O(k)$ flood M
   output v
end algorithm

In the generic algorithm, for any device k, table entry $M[\tau, i]$ at round t contains the value $u_i[t - \tau]$, provided that this data has arrived to the node k. The update of table M incorporates to M all the new values received from device i. Observe that, as $d = d_G$, the flooding guarantees that, when the data reaches the last row of M, all the data readings at time $t - d$ are present in the table. □

Algorithms with optimal latency. When the topology of the communication graph is known it is possible to improve the generic algorithm to obtain optimal algorithms provided latency is kept at its minimum. The lower bounds follow from Lemmas 1, 2, and 3 taking into account the considered topologies.

Theorem 1. *The* Average Monitoring *problem can be solved with latency d_G and optimal* MessageNumber *and* MessageLength *by* SSSFs *whose communication graph are bidirectional cliques, oriented rings or balanced binary trees, respectively.*

Improving the message length. By data aggregation and allowing a larger latency, it is possible to improve the *MessageLength*. In this case, messages are no longer tuples of data items but sums of data items. The synchronization needed to compute the right sums forces an increment on the latency.

Theorem 2. *The* Average Monitoring *problem can be solved with latency $2n - 1$, $\mathcal{T}(n) = \Theta(n)$, $\mathcal{S}(n) = \Theta(n \log n)$, $\mathcal{L}(n) = \Theta(\log n)$ and $\mathcal{M}(n) = \Theta(1)$ by a* SSSF *in which the communication network is an oriented ring.*

4 SSSFs of Devices with Constant Memory Capacity

Up to now we have not considered the possible memory restrictions of the *tiny* devices involved in a SSSF, but in applications, devices can have limited memory. The SSSF model can be adapted to take into account this fact, therefore we can consider devices with constant or bounded memory capacity. To this end, we also assume that each device has a buffer of limited size to store the data received from its neighbors. We assume that the communication graph might have any degree, but that a device cannot receive more packets in one round that those that can fit in the buffer. In the case that there are more incoming packets an arbitrary subset of them, filling the buffer, will be retrieved. In the opposite direction we assume that sending data to all the outgoing neighbors can be performed in constant time and space.

The Alerting problem can be solved in constant memory SSSF by the following algorithm. Initially all the nodes are in a non-alert state. At any round, if an unalerted device receives an alert message or reads a data that provokes an alert changes it state to alert and sends an alert message. An alerted device, different from device 1 does nothing. Device one upon achieving the alert state outputs 1 at each round. Thus we have the following.

Lemma 5. *Let G be a communication graph in which there is a path from any node to node 1. There is a SSSF $\mathcal{F}$ with communication graph G solving the Alerting problem with latency bounded by d_G, $\mathcal{T}(n) = \Theta(1)$, $\mathcal{S}(n) = \Theta(1)$, $\mathcal{L}(n) = \Theta(1)$ and $\mathcal{M}(n) = O(out_G)$.*

In general, we can say that by restricting the memory capacity of each device to be a constant w.r.t. the total number of devices then the kind of problems solved by these SSSFs are not more difficult than the ones in DSPACE($O(n+m)$) In order to prove it formally let us define the decisional version of $f_{\mathcal{F}}$.

Language associated to $\mathcal{F}$: Let $\mathcal{F}$ be a SSSF and let $f_{\mathcal{F}}$ be the function associated to the behavior of $\mathcal{F}$. We define the language associated to the behavior of $\mathcal{F}$, denoted by $L(\mathcal{F})$ as follows:

$$L(\mathcal{F}) = \{\langle \mathbf{u}[1], \mathbf{v}[1], \ldots, \mathbf{u}[t], \mathbf{v}[t]\rangle \mid t \geq 1 \text{ and } f_{\mathcal{F}}(\mathbf{u}[1, t]) = \mathbf{v}[1, t]\}.$$

Theorem 3. *Let $\mathcal{F}$ be a constant space SSSF. Then, the language $L(\mathcal{F}) \in DSPACE(O(n + m))$.*

Proof. We are going to present a deterministic Turing machine M that decides the language $L(\mathcal{F})$ in space $O(n+m)$. Since each device k has constant memory capacity, then the size of Q_k is also bounded by a constant as well as it is the number of items composing each sent or received packet. Recall that the behavior of $\mathcal{F}$ is described by a sequence $\mathbf{c}^0, \mathbf{d}^1, \mathbf{c}^1, \mathbf{d}^2, \ldots, \mathbf{c}^{i-1}, \mathbf{d}^i, \ldots$, eventually infinite, where $\mathbf{c}^0 = (q_k^0)_{k \in N}$ is the n-tuple of the initial local states of the n devices, and for each $i \geq 1$, $\mathbf{c}^i = (q_k^i)_{k \in N}$ is the n-tuple of the local states after i computation rounds. $\mathbf{d}^i = (d_k^i)_{k \in N}$ represents the input/output data and the sent/received messages of each device k in the transition from round $i - 1$ to round i. The Turing machine M on any input $\langle \mathbf{u}[1], \mathbf{v}[1], \ldots \mathbf{u}[t], \mathbf{v}[t]\rangle$ will compute such a sequence in the following way:

1. Initially M computes the initial configuration $\mathbf{c}^0$ and suppose that devices have neither received a message nor an input data item.

2. Simulates the i-th computation round computing $(\mathbf{c}^i, \mathbf{d}^{i+1})$ from $(\mathbf{c}^{i-1}, \mathbf{d}^i)$. In order to do this, for each device k, M applies δ_k considering that the input data item is given by $u_k[i]$ and verifies that the output data item is $v_k[i]$. If it is the case then M considers the next computation round $i + 1$; otherwise, M rejects.
3. Once M has consumed all its input word, it accepts.

M needs space $O(n + m)$ to decide $L(\mathcal{F})$. Note that in part 2 of the simulation M only needs to store the messages send/received, one for each edge of the communication graph, and it also needs the current state for each one of the nodes of the graph.   □

In [4] it is shown that all predicates stably computed in the model of Mediated Population Protocols are in the class of NSPACE($O(m)$). In this case the nondeterminism is required to verify that there exists a stable configuration reachable from the initial configuration.

5   Trading Space/Time for Size

In this section we analyze SSSFs with an additional amount of nodes in the communication graph in which the attached devices participate in the computation but do not play any active role in sensing. In such a network we have a communication graph with S nodes and we want to solve a problem that involves only $n < S$ input data streams.

Constant time: In a balanced communication tree we suppose that there are n sensing devices placed on the leaves of a balanced binary tree, edges to leaves are replaced by paths in such a way that all the leaves are at the same distance to the root. Thus, the tree has depth $O(\log n)$ and n leaves. In such a network we can consider an algorithm with two flows. In the bottom-up flow each node receives from its children the average of the data at the subtree leaves, together with the number of leaves, and computes its corresponding values to be sent to its parent. The top-down computation is initiated by the root that computes the average value which flows to the leaves. The analysis is summarized as follows.

Theorem 4. *Let G be a balanced communication tree whose n leaves are sensing devices with constant space and whose internal nodes are non-sensing devices with $O(\log n)$ space. There is a SSSF $\mathcal{F}$ with communication graph G solving the Average Monitoring problem with latency d_G, $\mathcal{S}(n) = \mathcal{L}(n) = O(\log n)$ and $\mathcal{T}(n) = \mathcal{M}(n) = O(1)$.*

In the algorithm described above the nodes in the communication tree require different levels of internal memory, ranging from constant at the leaves to $\log n$ in the upper levels. The following result shows that by increasing the number of auxiliary nodes we can solve sensing problems with constant memory components in an adequate topology within constant time.

Constant space devices: Let $\mathcal{P}$ be a property defined on U^n. We consider the following sensing problem:

Monitoring Problem for property $\mathcal{P}$: Given an n-tuple of data streams $u = (u_k)_{1 \le k \le n}$ for some $n \ge 1$, compute an n-tuple of data streams $v = (v_k)_{1 \le k \le m}$ such that $\mathbf{v}[t] = \mathcal{P}(\mathbf{u}[t])$ for every $t \ge 1$.

Any polynomially computable property can be decide by a uniform family of circuits with polynomial size. Furthermore those circuits can be assumed to be layered and to have bounded fan in and fan out by adding propagator gates. The communication network is formed by the circuit with sensors attached to the corresponding inputs together with a communication tree that flows the result to the inputs. As the circuit is layered we can guarantee the pipelined flow of partial computations with constant time and memory within latency equal to the circuit's depth plus the tree depth. Thus, we have polynomial in n.

Theorem 5. *Let $\mathcal{P}$ be a property defined on U^n computable in polynomial time. There is a constant space SSSF that solves the associated sensing problem in polynomial size and latency (with respect to n) with $\mathcal{S}(n) = \mathcal{T}(n) = \mathcal{L}(n) = \mathcal{M}(n) = O(1)$.*

6 Conclusions and Future Work

We have proposed a model for networks that abstracts some of the main characteristics of the problems that are expected to be solved on a network with sensors. In parallel we have introduced a prototypical family of sensing problems. The model has allowed us to analyze the complexity of some problems providing optimal SSSFs with respect to some performance measures. The analysis shows, as expected, that different sensing problems will require different sensor capabilities for storing data and message size. Our algorithms for the Average Monitoring problem can be easily adapted to solve the monitoring problem associated to other aggregation functions like: maximum, minimum, addition, median, etc, the complexity of the above algorithms differ depending on the structural properties of the aggregation function (see [9] for a classification) and the size of the aggregated data.

There is a clear trade-off between the internal memory allowed to each device and the number of additional computing units in the network as show in Lemma 5. It will be of interest to characterize those sensing problems that can be solved with logarithmic or constant space with no (or a small number of) additional nodes.

Although in the present paper the communication network has been assumed to be fixed, the model is flexible enough to allow the incorporation of a dynamic communication graph. Complexity measures and problem solving on such models will require additional effort.

On the other hand the hypothesis of fixed communication graphs models the idea of maintaining a virtual fixed topology, this topology will be maintained until the network task changes. In this situation the communication graph will be perceived as the same graph, although the devices taking care of one node might change over time. Our complexity analysis on fixed topologies should be combined with a study of the conditions that guarantee the existence, creation an maintenance of the virtual topology.

All through the paper we have not considered the energy consumption as a performance measure. For making an energy analysis we should have to incorporate a particular energy model to the sensor field. The performance measures taken in this paper proportionate the basic ingredients for analyzing energy consumption where sending/receiving a message has the same cost for all the nodes, like for example the unit disk graphs. It is of interest (and topic of future research) to consider energy models in which each link in the communication graph has different weights (or set of weights) representing the constants in the function that determines the cost of sending a message along the link.

Acknowledgments. We want to thank the anonymous referees for their careful reading and helpful comments.

References

1. Akyildiz, I.F., Su, W., Sankarasubramaniam, Y., Cayirci, E.: A Survey on Sensor Networks. IEEE Communications Magazine 40(8), 102–114 (2002)
2. Angluin, D., Aspnes, J., Diamadi, Z., Fischer, M.J., Peralta, R.: Computation in networks of passively mobile finite-state sensors. Distributed computing 18(4), 235–253 (2006)
3. Berstel, J.: Quelques applications des reseaux d'automates. Thèse de 3ème Cycle (1967)
4. Chatzigiannakis, I., Michail, O., Spirakis, P.G.: Mediated Population Protocols. In: Albers, et al. (eds.) ICALP 2009, Part II. LNCS, vol. 5556, pp. 363–374. Springer, Heidelberg (2009)
5. Estrin, D., Culler, D., Pister, K., Sukatme, G.: Connecting the Physical World with Pervasive Networks. Pervasive Computing 6(2), 59–69 (2002)
6. Gibbons, P.B., Tirthapura, S.: Estimating simple functions on the union of data streams. In: SPAA 2001, pp. 281–291 (2001)
7. Henzinger, T.A.: The Theory of Hybrid Automata. In: LICS 1996, pp. 278–292 (1996)
8. Hoare, C.A.R.: A calculus of total correctness for communicating processes. Sci. Comput. Program. 1(1-2), 49–72 (1981)
9. Karl, H., Willig, A.: Protocols and Architectures for Wireless Sensor Networks. John Wiley & Sons Ltd., Chichester (2005)
10. Lynch, N., Segala, R., Vaandrager, F.: Hybrid I/O Automata Revisited. In: Di Benedetto, M.D., Sangiovanni-Vincentelli, A.L. (eds.) HSCC 2001. LNCS, vol. 2034, pp. 403–417. Springer, Heidelberg (2001)
11. Peleg, D.: Distributed Computing. A Locality-Sensitive Approach, ch. 2. SIAM Monographs on Discrete Mathematics and Applications (2003)
12. Tilak, S., Abu-Ghazaleh, N.B., Heinzelman, W.: A Taxonomy of Wireless Micro-Sensor Network Models. Mobile Computing and Communications Review 6(2), 28–36 (2003)
13. Valiant, L.G.: A bridging model for parallel computation. Communications of the ACM 33(8), 103–111 (1990)
14. Vinyals, M., Rodriguez-Aguilar, J.A., Cerquides, J.: A Survey on Sensor Networks from a Multi-Agent Perspective. In: AAMAS 2008, pp. 1071–1078 (2008)

Near-Optimal Radio Use for Wireless Network Synchronization*

Milan Bradonjić[1], Eddie Kohler[2], and Rafail Ostrovsky[3],**

[1] Theoretical Division, and Center for Nonlinear Studies, Los Alamos National Laboratory, Los Alamos, NM 87545, USA
milan@lanl.gov
[2] Computer Science Department, University of California Los Angeles, CA 90095, USA
kohler@cs.ucla.edu
[3] Computer Science Department and Department of Mathematics, University of California Los Angeles, CA 90095, USA
rafail@cs.ucla.edu

Abstract. In this paper we consider the model of communication where wireless devices can either switch their radios off to save energy (and hence, can neither send nor receive messages), or switch their radios on and engage in communication. The problem has been extensively studied in practice, in the setting such as deployment and clock synchronization of wireless sensor networks – see, for example, [31,41,33,29,40]. The goal in these papers is different from the classic problem of radio broadcast, i.e. avoiding interference. Here, the goal is instead to minimize the use of the radio for both transmitting and receiving, and for most of the time to shut the radio down completely, as the radio even in listening mode consumes a lot of energy.

We distill a clean theoretical formulation of minimizing radio use and present near-optimal solutions. Our base model ignores issues of communication interference, although we also extend the model to handle this requirement. We assume that nodes intend to communicate periodically, or according to some time-based schedule. Clearly, perfectly synchronized devices could switch their radios on for exactly the minimum periods required by their joint schedules. The main challenge in the deployment of wireless networks is to *synchronize* the devices' schedules, given that their initial schedules may be offset relative to one another (even if their clocks run at the same speed). In this paper we study how frequently the devices must switch on their radios in order to both synchronize their clocks and communicate. In this setting, we significantly improve previous results, and show optimal use of the radio for two processors and near-optimal use of the radio for synchronization of an arbitrary number of processors. In particular, for two processors we prove **deterministic** matching $\Theta\left(\sqrt{n}\right)$ upper and lower bounds on the number of times the

---

* Full version of the paper is available on-line [8].
** The third author was supported in part by IBM Faculty Award, Xerox Innovation Group Award, NSF grants 0430254, 0716835, 0716389, 0830803 and U.C. MICRO grant.

S. Dolev (Ed.): ALGOSENSORS 2009, LNCS 5804, pp. 15–28, 2009.
© Springer-Verlag Berlin Heidelberg 2009

radio has to be on, where n is the discretized uncertainty period of the clock shift between the two processors. (In contrast, all previous results for two processors are randomized, e.g. [33], [29]). For $m = n^\beta$ processors (for any positive $\beta < 1$) we prove $\Omega(n^{(1-\beta)/2})$ is the lower bound on the number of times the radio has to be switched on (per processor), and show a nearly matching (in terms of the radio use) $\tilde{O}(n^{(1-\beta)/2})$ randomized upper bound per processor, (where $\tilde{O}$ notation hides *poly-log(n)* multiplicative term) with failure probability exponentially close to 0. For $\beta \geqslant 1$ our algorithm runs with at most *poly-log(n)* radio invocations per processor. Our bounds also hold in a radio-broadcast model where interference must be taken into account.

1   Introduction

MOTIVATION: Radios are inherently power-hungry. As the power costs of processing, memory, and other computing components drop, the lifetime of a battery-operated wireless network deployment comes to depend largely on how often a node's radio is left on. System designers therefore try to power down those radios as much as possible. This requires some form of *synchronization*, since successful communication requires that the sending and receiving nodes have their radios on at the same time. Synchronization is relatively easy to achieve in a wired, powered, and well-administered network, whose nodes can constantly listen for periodic heartbeats from a well-known server. In an ad hoc wireless network or wireless sensor network deployment, the problem becomes much more difficult. Nodes may be far away from any wired infrastructure; deployments are expected to run and even to initialize themselves autonomously (imagine sensors dropped over an area by plane); and environmental factors make sensors prone to failure and clock drift. Indeed there has been a lot of work in this area, see for example: [4,5,6,9,14,15,16,24,27,28,29,31,32,33,34,35,36,37,38,39,40]. Many distinct problems are considered in these papers, and it is beyond the scope of this paper to survey all these works, however most if these papers (among other issues) consider the following problem of radio-use consumption:

INFORMAL PROBLEM DESCRIPTION:
Consider two (or more) processors that can switch their radios on or off. The processors' clocks are not synchronized. That is, when a processor wakes up, each clock begins to count up from 0; however, processors may awake at different times. The maximum difference between the time when processors wake up is bounded by some positive integer parameter $n \in \mathbb{N}$. If processors within radio range have their radios on in the same step, they can hear each other and can synchronize their clocks. When a processor's radio is off, it saves energy, but can neither receive nor transmit. Initially, processors awaken with clock shifts that differ by at most n time units. The objective for all the processors is to synchronize their clocks while minimizing the use of radio (both transmitting and receiving). We count the maximum number of times any processor's radio has to be on in order to guarantee synchronization. Indeed, as argued in many papers referenced above, the total time duration during which the radio is on is

one of the critical parameters of energy consumption, and operating the radio for considerable time is far costlier than switching radio off and switching it back on. We assume that all the processors that have their radios on at the same time can communicate with each other. The goal of all processors is to synchronize their clocks, i.e. to figure out how much to add to their offset so that all processors wake up at the same time. (We also consider an extension that models radio *interference*, where if more then one processor is broadcasting at the same time, all receiving processors that have their radio switched on hear only noise.)

For multiple processors, we assume that all processors know the maximum drift n, otherwise the adversary can make the delay unbounded, It is also assumed that all processors know the total number of processors m, although, we also consider a more general setting where n is known for all processors, but m is not. In this setting, we relax the problem, and instead of requiring synchronization of all m processors, we instead require synchronization of an arbitrarily close to 1 constant fraction of all processors. In this relaxation of our model, we require that the radio usage guarantee holds only for those processors that eventually synchronize.

Furthermore, our model assumes that all processors are within radio range of each other, so that the link graph is complete. Our techniques can be thought of as establishing synchronization within completely connected single-hop regions. Clearly, single-hop synchronization is necessary for multi-hop synchronization. Our single-hop synchronization protocol, with simple changes, can synchronize a connected multi-hop network in the sense that (1) two directly connected nodes know one another's clock offsets, and (2) given any two nodes in the network v and w, there exists a path $v_0 = v, v_1, \ldots, v_n = w$ where each adjacent pair of nodes is connected and synchronized. Thus our central concern in this paper is on establishing lower bounds and constructing nearly optimal solutions for the single-hop case.

TOWARDS FORMALIZING THE ABSTRACT MODEL:
A NEW MODEL: To simplify our setting we wish to minimize both transmit and receive cost (i.e., all the times when the radio must be "on" either transmitting or receiving). We discretize time to units of the smallest possible interval that allows a processor to send a message to or receive a message from another processor within radio range. We normalize the cost of transmitting and receiving to 1 unit of energy per time step. (In practice, transmission can be about twice as expensive as receiving. We can easily re-scale our algorithms to accommodate this as well, but for clarity of exposition we make these costs equal.) We ignore the energy consumption needed to power the radio on and to power it off, which is at most comparable but in many cases insignificant compared to the energy consumption of having the radio active. This is the model considered, for example, in [31,29,5,6,37,42,12,34].

INFORMAL MODEL DESCRIPTION: For the purposes of analysis only, we assume that there is global time (mapped to positive integers). All clocks can run at different speeds, but we assume that clock drifts are bounded; i.e., there exists a global constant c, such that for any two clocks their relative speed ratio is bounded by c. Now, we define as a time "unit" the number of steps of the slowest clock, such that if two of the fastest processors' consecutive awake times overlap by at least a half of their length according to global time, then the number of steps of the slowest clock is sufficient time for any two processors to communicate with each other. This issue is elaborated in Section 7. In our report [8], that is, the full version of the paper, we give the Synchronization Algorithm. We now formalize the informal model description into the precise definition of our model.

OUR FORMAL MODEL AND PROBLEM STATEMENT:
Global time is expressed as a positive integer. m processors start at an arbitrary global time between 1 and n, where each processor starts with a local "clock" counter set to 0. The parameter n refers to the discretized uncertainty period, or equivalently, to the possible maximal clock difference, i.e., to the maximal offset between clocks; hence, we will use these terms interchangeably. Both global time and each started processor's clock counter increments by 1 each time unit. The global clock is for analysis only and is not accessible to any of the processors, but an upper bound on n is known to all processors. Each processor algorithm is synchronous, and can specify, at each time unit, if the processor is "awake" or "sleeping." (The "awake" period is assumed to be sufficiently long to ensure that the energy consumption of powering the radio on and then shutting it off at each time unit is far less than the energy expenditure to operate the radio even for a single time unit). All processors that are awake at the same time unit can communicate with each other. (Our interference model changes this so that exactly two awake processors can communicate with each other, but if three or more processors are simultaneously awake, none of them can communicate.) The algorithm can specify what information they exchange. The goal is for all m processors to adjust their local clocks to be equal to each other, at which point they should all terminate. The protocol is correct if this happens either always or if the protocol is randomized with probability of error that is negligible. The objective is to minimize, per processor, the total number of times its radio is awake.

We remark that the above model is sufficiently expressive to capture a more general case where clocks at different nodes run at somewhat different speeds, as long as the ratio of different speeds is bounded by a constant, which is formally proven in Section 7.

OUR RESULTS:
We develop algorithms for clock synchronization in radio networks that minimize radio use, both with and without modeling of interference. In particular, our results are the following.

1. For two processors we show a $\Omega(\sqrt{n})$ deterministic lower bound and a matching deterministic $O(\sqrt{n})$ upper bound for the number of time intervals a processor must switch its radio on to obtain one-hop synchronization.

2. For arbitrary $m = n^\beta$ processors, we prove $\Omega\left(n^{\frac{1-\beta}{2}}\right)$ is the lower bound on the number of time intervals the processor must switch its radio for any

deterministic protocol and show a nearly-matching (in terms of the number of times the radio is in use) $O\big(n^{\frac{1-\beta}{2}}\cdot\text{poly-log}(n)\big)$ randomized protocol, which fails to synchronize with probability of failure exponentially (in n) close to zero. Furthermore, our upper bound holds even if there is interference, i.e., if more than one processor is broadcasting, listening processors hear noise.

3. It is easy to see that processors cannot perform synchronization if n is unknown and unbounded, using a standard evasive argument. However, if n is known, we show that 8/9 (or any other constant fraction) of the processors can synchronize without knowing m, yet still using $O(n^{\frac{1-\beta}{2}}\cdot\text{poly-log}(n))$ radio send/receive steps, with probability of failure exponentially close to zero.

We stress that while the upper bound for two processors is simple, the matching lower bound is nontrivial. This (with some additional machinery) holds true for the multi-processor case as well.

COMPARISON WITH PREVIOUS (SYSTEMS) WORK:
Tiny, inexpensive embedded computers are now powerful enough to run complex software, store significant amounts of information in stable memory, sense wide varieties of environmental phenomena, and communicate with one another over wireless channels. Widespread deployments of such nodes promise to reveal previously unobservable phenomena with significant scientific and technological impact. Energy is a fundamental roadblock to the long-lived deployment of these nodes, however. The size and weight of energy sources like batteries and solar panels have not kept pace with comparable improvements to processors, and long-lived deployments must shepherd their energy resources carefully.

Wireless radio communication is a particularly important energy consumer. Already, communication is expensive in terms of energy usage, and this will only become worse in relative terms: the power cost of radio communication is fundamentally far higher than that of computation. In one example coming from sensor networks, a Mica2 sensor node's CC1000 radio consumes almost as much current while listening for messages as the node's CPU consumes in its most active state, and transmitting a message consumes up to 2.5 times more current than active CPU computation [36]. In typical wireless sensor networks, transmitting is about two times more expensive than listening, and about 1.5 times more expensive than receiving, but listening or transmitting is about 100 times more expensive as keeping the CPU idle and the radio switched off[1] (i.e., in a "sleep" state).

Network researchers have designed various techniques for minimizing power consumption [5,6,37]. For example, Low-Power Listening [34] trades more expensive transmission cost for lower listening cost. Every node turns on its radio for listening for a short interval τ once every interval $n > \tau$. If the channel is quiet, the node returns to sleep for another n; otherwise it receives whatever

---

[1] Example consumption costs: CPU idle with clock running and radio off ("standby mode"), 0.1–0.2 mA (milliamps); CPU on and radio listening, 10 mA; CPU on and radio receiving, 15 mA; CPU on and radio transmitting, 20–25 mA.

message is being transmitted. To transmit, a node sends a *preamble* of at least n time units long before the actual message. This ensures that no matter how clocks are offset, any node within range will hear some part of the preamble and stay awake for the message. A longer n means a lower relative receive cost (as τ/n is smaller), but also longer preambles, and therefore higher transmission cost.

A more efficient solution in terms of radio use was proposed by PalChaudhuri and Johnson [33], and further by Moscibroda, Von Rickenbach and Wattenhofer [29]. The idea is as follows. Notice that in the proposal of [34], the proposal was for a transmitting processor to broadcast continuously for n time units, while receiving processors switch their radios on once every n time units to listen. Even for two processors, this implies that total use of the radio is $n + 1$ time units (i.e., it is linear in n). The observation of [33,29] is that we can do substantially better by using randomization: if both processors wake their radios $O(\sqrt{n})$ time units at random (say both sending and receiving), then by birthday paradox with constant probability they will be awake at the same time and will be able to synchronize their clocks. As indicated before, we show instead a deterministic solution to this problem, its practical importance, and a matching lower bound.

Our results strengthen and generalize previous works that appeared in the literature [31,42,41,12]. See further comparisons in the relevant sections.

COMPARISON WITH RADIO BROADCAST:
Usually, in a broadcast setup, a node is able to receive a message if and only if it does not transmit, and there is one and only one of its neighbors that transmits, at that time. In the case when nodes are not able to detect collision, [3,2] showed randomized protocols. A deterministic broadcast algorithm, with work time $O(n^{11/6})$, has been given in [11]. The improvements of these algorithms have followed [25]: for undirected radio network graphs, with diameter *diam*, for randomized broadcast the expected work time has been $O(diam \cdot \log(n/diam) + \log^2 n)$, while for deterministic broadcast the expected work time has been $\Omega(n \log n / \log(n/diam))$. In [26], a faster algorithm for directed radio network graphs has provided running time $O(n \log n \log(diam))$. Additionally, other algorithms for broadcast [13,17,19,22,24] as well as for clock synchronization [32,35,14,4] have been proposed. The work of radio broadcast is different from the problem we address at this paper. However, as we mention in the technical description, once we resolve the problem of meeting times, we can easily combine our solutions with radio broadcast goal to avoid interference.

HIGH-LEVEL IDEAS OF OUR CONSTRUCTIONS AND PROOFS

- For the two processor upper bound, we prove that two carefully chosen affine functions will overlap no matter what the initial shift is. The only technically delicate part is that the shift is over the reals, and thus the proof must take this into account.

- For the two processor lower bound, we show that for any two strings with sufficiently low density (of 1's) there always exists a small shift such that none of the 1's overlap. This is done by a combinatorial counting argument.

- For multiple processors, the idea of the lower bound is to extend the previous combinatorial argument, while for the upper bound, the idea is to establish a "connected" graph of pairwise processor synchronization, and then show that this graph is an expander. The next idea is that instead of running global synchronization, we can repeat the same partial synchronization a logarithmic number of times (using the same randomness) to yield a communication graph which is an expander. We then use standard synchronization protocol over this "virtual" expander to reach global synchronization.
- For handling interference, we observe that standard "back-off" protocols [1,10] can be combined with previous machinery to achieve non-interference, costing only a poly-logarithmic multiplicative term.
- For the protocol that does not need to know m (recall that m is the total number of processors within radio-reach), we first observe that if $m > n$, by setting $m = n$ our protocol already achieves synchronization with near-optimal radio use. The technical challenge is thus to handle the case where $m < n$ but the value of m is unknown to the protocol. Our first observation is to show that processors can overestimate m, in which case the amount of energy needed is much smaller (per processor) than for smaller m, and then "check" if the synchronized component of nodes has reached current estimate on m. If it did not, than our current estimate of m can be reduced (by a constant factor) by all the processors. To assure that estimates are lowered by all the processors at about the same time, we divide the protocol into "epochs" which are big enough not to overlap even with a maximal clock drift (of n). Summing, the energy consumption is essentially dominated by the smallest estimate of m, which is within a constant factor of correct value of m, and all processors that detect it stop running subsequent (more expensive) "epochs".

2   Mathematical Preliminaries

Lemma 1 (Two-Color Birthday Problem). *For any absolute constant $C > \sqrt{1 - \ln 0.1} \approx 1.8173$ and any positive $s, t \in (0, 1)$, where $s + t = 1$, the following holds. Suppose $r = Cn^s$ identical red balls and $b = Cn^t$ identical blue balls are thrown independently and uniformly at random into n bins. Then, for sufficiently big n, the probability that there is a bin containing both red and blue balls is $\geqslant 0.8$.*

Proof. See the full version [8][2].   □

3   Lower Bounds

The problem of asynchronous wakeup, i.e., low-power asynchronous neighbors discovery, has already been known in the literature [31,42,41,12]. Its goal is to design an optimal wake-up schedule, i.e., to minimize the radio use for both

---

[2] For the proofs of all subsequent theorems, lemmas, and claims, see the full version [8].

transmitting and receiving. The techniques used, e.g., in the previously cited papers, vary from the birthday paradox in [31], block-design in [42], the quorum based protocol in [41] to an adaption of Chinese reminder theorem [20] in [12]. In our work, we firstly generalize the birthday paradox, obtaining the Two Color Birthday Problem (see Lemma 1). Next, we build the tools for our main analysis on the upper and lower bounds on the optimal radio use for wireless network synchronization. In particular, we start with Lemma 2, which is a stronger combinatorial bound compared to [42], and then generalize results in Lemma 3.

Recall that n is the maximum offset between processor starting times and $m = n^\beta$ is the number of processors. Assume that each processor runs for some time L. Its radio schedule can then be represented as a bit string of length L, where the ith bit is 1 if and only if the processor turned its radio on during that time unit. We first consider the two-processor case. Recall that in our model maximal assumed offset is at most n. If we take 2 bit strings corresponding to the two processors, the initial clock offset corresponds to a *shift* of one string against the other by at most n positions. Note that if we set $L \geqslant 4n$, the maximal shift is at most $n \leqslant L/4$.

Note. *In the next sections, without loss of generality we apply the ceiling function to any real number, e.g., L^α, L/C^2 are treated as $\lceil L^\alpha \rceil$, $\lceil L/C^2 \rceil$, respectively.*

To prove our lower bound, we need to prove the following: for any two L-bit strings with at most $\sqrt{L}/C$ ones in each string (for some constant $C > 1/\sqrt{2}$), there always exists a shift $< L/4$ of one string against another such that none of the ones after the shift in the first string align with any of the ones in the second string. In this case we say that the strings do not *overlap*. W.l.o.g., we make both strings (before the shift) identical. To see that this does not limit the generality, we note that if the two strings are not identical, we can make a new string by taking their bitwise OR, what we call the *"union"* of strings. If the distinct strings overlap at a given offset, then the "union" string will overlap with itself at the same offset.

Lemma 2 (Two Non-Colliding Strings). *For any absolute constant $C \geqslant 1/\sqrt{2}$, and for every L-bit string with $\ell \leqslant \frac{\sqrt{L}}{C}$ ones, there is at least one shift within $L/(2C^2)$ such that the string and its shifted copy do not overlap.*

Next, we want to prove a general lower bound for multiple strings. The high-level approach of our proof is as follows. We pick one string, and then upper bound the total number of ones possible in the "union" of all the remaining (potentially shifted) strings. If we can prove that assuming the density of all the strings is sufficiently small, and there always exists a shift of the first string that does not overlap the "union" of all the remaining strings, we are done. The "union" string is simply a new string with a higher density.

Lemma 3 (General Two Non-Colliding Strings with Different Densities). *Let $s, t > 0$ such that $s + t < 1$, and let $C > 1$. For two L-bit strings such that the number of ones in the first string is $a = L^s/C$, and the number of ones* in the second string is $b = L^t/C$, there is a shift within $L/C^2 + 1$ such that the first string and the shifted second string do not overlap.

Here, wlog, we considered only "left" shift. If we needed both left and right shift, then we would have an additional factor of 2. Using Lemma 3, the lower bounds immediately follow.

Theorem 1. *There exists an absolute constant $C > 1$, such that for any n^β strings of length L with at most $n^{(1-\beta)/2}$ ones in each string, there always exists a set of shifts for each string by at most $L/4$ such that no string's ones overlap any of the ones in all the other strings.*

4   Matching Upper Bound for Two Processors

We now show the upper bound. That is, we give the deterministic algorithm for two devices. In particular, for any initial offset of at most n, we show a schedule where two processors meet with probability equal to one inside a "time-window" of length $W = 2n + 4\sqrt{n} + 2$.

Theorem 2. *For any n, there exists a string of length $W = 2n + 4\sqrt{n} + 2$ with at most $4\sqrt{n} + 4$ ones such that this string will overlap itself for all shifts from 1 to n.*

We remark that the bound that we prove in the above section is in fact more general than the subsequent independent work of [12], which appeared after our report [8]. Note that our bound holds for all values of n, and in fact the two strings could be made identical by doubling the cost.

5   Upper Bound for m Processors

In this setting we have $m = n^\beta$ processors (and as before the maximum shift is at most n). We first state our theorem:

Theorem 3. *There exists a randomized protocol for n^β processors (which fails with probability at most $1/2^{O(n)}$) such that: (i) if $\beta < 1$ the protocol is using at most $O(n^{\frac{1-\beta}{2}} \cdot \text{poly-log}(n))$ radio steps per processor, and (ii) if $\beta \geqslant 1$ using at most $O(\text{poly-log}(n))$ radio steps per processor. Furthermore, the same bounds hold for the synchronization in the radio communication model, where a processor can hear a message if one (and strictly one) message is broadcasted.*

Next we give a high-level outline of the construction of our algorithm for $\beta \in [0, 1)$. For the case of $\beta \geqslant 1$ we only need Steps 4 and 5, see below. The formal analysis and proofs of the Main Algorithm are given in [8].

Outline of the Main Algorithm:

Step 1. We let each processor run for $L = 4n$ steps, waking up during this time $O\left(n^{\frac{1-\beta}{2}}\right)$ times uniformly at random. It is important to point out that each processor uses independent randomness. We view it as m-row and L ($L \geqslant W + n$) column matrix A (taking into account all the shifts), where $W = 2n + 4\sqrt{n} + 2$ is defined in Theorem 2. Fix any row of this matrix (say the first one). We say that this row "meets" some other row, if 1 in the first row also appears (after the shifts) in some other row. If this happens, the first processor can "communicate" with another processor. We show that for a fixed row, this happens with a constant probability.

Step 2. Each processor repeats Step 1 (using independent randomness) $O(\log m)$ times. Here, we show that a fixed row has at least $O(\log m)$ connections to other rows (not necessarily distinct) with probability greater than $1 - 1/\text{poly}(m)$.

Step 3. From Step 2. we conclude that the first row meets at least a constant number of *distinct* other rows with probability greater than $1 - 1/(2m)$.

Step 4. We use the union bound to conclude that *every* row meets at least constant number of distinct other rows with probability greater than $1/2$. If we repeat this process a logarithmic number of times, we show that we get an expander graph with overwhelming probability (for the definition of an expander see [30]). Thus, considering every row (i.e., every processor) as a node, this represents a random graph with degree of at least a constant number for each node, which is an expander with high probability.

Step 5. During the synchronization period, a particular processor will synchronize with some other processor, without collision, by attempting to communicate whenever it has a 1 in its row. (In the case of interference, the processor can communicate if only one other processor is up at this column, which we can achieve as well, using standard "back-off" protocols [1,10], costing only poly-logarithmic multiplicative term.)

Step 6. The processors can now communicate along the edges of the formed expander (which has logarithmic diameter) as follows. The main insight that we prove below is that if processors repeat *the same random choices* of Step 1 through Step 5, the communication pattern of the expander graph is preserved. Hence, the structure developed in Step 2 can be reused to establish a logarithmic-diameter (in m) spanning tree and synchronize nodes with poly-logarithmetic overhead (using known machinery over this "virtual" graph). We show in [8], by using standard methods, that communicating over the implicit expander graph to synchronize all nodes can be done in $diam + 2$ steps, where $diam$ is the diameter of the expander.

6   Protocol That Does Not Need to Know the Number of Processors

Suppose our processors know the offset n but not the number of all processors in the system, that is, m. The main observation here is that once we make a spanning tree of the graph, each node can also compute the number of nodes in its spanning tree. Hence, we can make an estimate of m and then check to see if this estimate is too big. Thus, until the right (within a constant factor) estimate is reached, all nodes will reject the estimate and continue. Adjusting constants appropriately, we can guarantee that an arbitrary constant fraction of the processors will terminate with the right estimate of m (within some fixed constant fraction). The algorithm for the estimation of m is as follows.

Algorithm: Estimation of m

E1. Set $i = 0$.
E2. Build a spanning tree using the Main Algorithm (from the previous section) for $m_i = n/2^i$ and count the number of nodes in the tree. If the number of the nodes in the tree is less than m_i then set $i := i + 1$ and go to step E2.
E3. Output m_i.

End of Algorithm: Estimation of m

Theorem 4. *Any constant fraction of the processors can synchronize without knowing m, yet still use $O(n^{\frac{1-\beta}{2}} poly\text{-}log(n))$ radio send/receive steps (with probability of failure exponentially close to zero). The bound on the radio use holds only for processors that synchronize.*

7   Our Model Can Handle Different Clocks' Speeds with Bounded Ratio

Here are the technical details that explain why our model is realistic even if processors have somewhat different clock speeds. For m processors, let their clock ticks be $\{\tau_1, \tau_2, \ldots, \tau_m\}$. Let τ_{min}, τ_{max} be minimum, maximum of the set $\{\tau_1, \tau_2, \ldots, \tau_m\}$, respectively. The clock ticks are in general different, but the ratio $\tau_{max}/\tau_{min} \leqslant c$ is bounded by some constant c, and each processor knows that upper bound c. Let τ_{trans} be the lower bound on the time necessary for the transmission, i.e., on the time necessary for communication and synchronization between two processors. It is also assumed that the lower bound on τ_{trans} is known to all processors. Now, knowing c and τ_{trans}, each processor i counts k_i clock ticks as a single *time step* s_i such that k_i is defined by $s_i = k_i \tau_i \geqslant 2\tau_{trans}$. In other words, each processor enables the condition necessary for the communication, making its time step $s_i \geqslant 2\tau_{trans}$. It follows that if two processors i and j overlap for a period of time $\geqslant \frac{1}{2} \min\{s_i, s_j\}$, then they can communicate. For further details see the full version.

Claim. If two processors i, j work within the same global time unit, then they can communicate and can synchronize.

8   Conclusions and Open Problems

In this paper, we have studied an important problem of power consumption in radio networks and completely resolved the deterministic case for two processors, showing matching upper and lower bound. For multiple processors, we were able to show a poly-logarithmic gap between our randomized protocol and our deterministic lower bound. However, this is not completely satisfactory. Our lower bound holds only for deterministic protocols, while our upper bound in multi-processor case is probabilistic (unlike the two-processor case, where our upper bound is deterministic as well). Closing this gap remains an interesting open problem.

Another interesting question is the following. It is important to note that in radio communication, conservation of power can be achieved in two different ways: one approach is to always broadcast the signal with the same intensity (or to power down radios completely in order to save energy); this is what we explored in this paper. The second approach is the ability for a radio to broadcast and receive signals at different intensity, the stronger the signal the further it reaches. In the case where all processors are at the same distance from each other, this is a non-issue (i.e., our single-hop networks, the main focus of this paper). However, for multi-hop networks the question of optimal power-consumption strategies with varying signal strength is still completely open.

References

1. Aldous, D.: Ultimate instability of exponential back-off protocol for acknowledgment-based transmission control of random access communication channels. IEEE Transactions on Information Theory 33(2), 219–223 (1987)
2. Alon, N., Bar-Noy, A., Linial, N., Peleg, D.: A lower bound for radio broadcast. Journal of Computer and System Sciences 43, 290–298 (1991)
3. Bar-Yehuda, R., Goldreich, O., Itai, A.: On the time complexity of broadcast in radio networks: an exponential gap between determinism and randomization. Journal of Computer and System Sciences 45, 104–126 (1992)
4. Blum, P., Meier, L., Thiele, L.: Improved interval-based clock synchronization in sensor networks. In: IPSN 2004: Proceedings of the third international symposium on Information processing in sensor networks, pp. 349–358 (2004)
5. Boulis, A., Srivastava, M.: Node-Level Energy Management for Sensor Networks in the Presence of Multiple Applications. Wireless Networks 10(6), 737–746 (2004)
6. Boulis, A., Ganeriwal, S., Srivastava, M.: Aggregation in sensor networks: an energy-accuracy trade-off. Ad Hoc Networks 1(2-3), 317–331 (2003)
7. Bollobas, B., de la Vega, W.F.: The diameter of random graphs. Combinatorica 2 (1982)
8. Bradonjić, M., Kohler, E., Ostrovsky, R.: Near-Optimal Radio Use For Wireless Network Synchronization (2008), http://arxiv.org/abs/0810.1756
9. Bush, S.F.: Low-energy sensor network time synchronization as an emergent property. In: Proc. 14th International Conference on Communications and Networks (ICCCN 2005), October 17-19, pp. 93–98 (2005)
10. Cali, F., Conti, M., Gregori, E.: IEEE 802.11 protocol: design and performance evaluation of an adaptive backoff mechanism. IEEE Journal on Selected Areas in Communications 18(9), 1774–1786 (2000)
11. Chlebus, B., Gasieniec, L., Gibbons, A., Pelc, A., Rytter, W.: Deterministic broadcasting in ad hoc radio networks. Distributed Computing 15(1), 27–38 (2002)

12. Dutta, P., Culler, D.: Practical asynchronous neighbor discovery and rendezvous for mobile sensing applications. In: Proceedings of the 6th ACM conference on Embedded network sensor systems (SenSys 2008), pp. 71–84 (2008)
13. Elkin, M.L., Kortsarz, G.: Polylogarithmic Inapproximability of the Radio Broadcast Problem. In: Proc. of 7th International Workshop on Approximation Algorithms for Combinatorial Optimization Problems, Cambridge, MA, pp. 105–114 (2004)
14. Elson, J., Römer, K.: Wireless sensor networks: a new regime for time synchronization. SIGCOMM. Comput. Commun. Rev. 33(1), 149–154 (2003)
15. Elson, J., Girod, L., Estrin, D.: Fine-Grained Network Time Synchronization using Reference Broadcasts. In: Proc. Fifth Symposium on Operating Systems Design and Implementation (OSDI 2002), vol. 36, pp. 147–163 (2002)
16. Fan, R., Chakraborty, I., Lynch, N.: Clock Synchronization for Wireless Networks. In: OPODIS 2004, pp. 400–414 (2004)
17. Gaber, I., Mansour, Y.: Centralized broadcast in multihop radio networks. Journal of Algorithms 46(1), 1–20 (2003)
18. Honda, N., Nishitani, Y.: The Firing Squad Synchronization Problem for Graphs. Theoretical Computer Sciences 14(1), 39–61 (1981)
19. Kesselman, A., Kowalski, D.: Fast distributed algorithm for convergecast in ad hoc geometric radio networks. In: Conference on Wireless on demand Network Systems and Services (2005)
20. Knuth, D.: The Art of Computer Programming. Seminumerical Algorithms, 3rd edn., vol. 2. Addison-Wesley, Reading (1997)
21. Kobayashi, K.: The Firing squad synchronization problem for a class of polyautomata networks. Journal of Computer and System Science 17, 300–318 (1978)
22. Koo, C.: Broadcast in Radio Networks Tolerating Byzantine Adversarial Behavior. In: Proceedings of 23rd ACM SIGACT-SIGOPS Symposium on Principles of Distributed Computing (PODC), pp. 275–282 (2004)
23. Kamath, A.P., Motwani, R., Palem, K., Spirakis, P.: Tail bounds for occupancy and the satisfiability threshold conjecture. Random Structures and Algorithms 7, 59–80 (1995)
24. Kothapalli, K., Onus, M., Richa, A., Scheideler, C.: Efficient Broadcasting and Gathering in Wireless Ad Hoc Networks. In: IEEE International Symposium on Parallel Architectures, Algorithms and Networks, ISPAN (2005)
25. Kowalski, D., Pelc, A.: Broadcasting in undirected ad hoc radio networks. In: Proceedings of the twenty-second annual symposium on Principles of distributed computing, pp. 73–82. ACM Press, New York (2003)
26. Kowalski, D., Pelc, A.: Faster deterministic broadcasting in ad hoc radio networks. In: Alt, H., Habib, M. (eds.) STACS 2003. LNCS, vol. 2607, pp. 109–120. Springer, Heidelberg (2003)
27. Kopetz, H., Ochsenreiter, w.: Global time in distributed real-time systems. Technical Report 15/89, Technische Universitat Wien, Wien Austria (1989)
28. Mills, D.L.: Internet time synchronization: the network time protocol. IEEE Transactions on Communications 39(10), 1482–1493 (1991)
29. Moscibroda, T., von Rickenbach, P., Wattenhofer, R.: Analyzing the Energy-Latency Trade-Off During the Deployment of Sensor Networks. In: INFOCOM 2006. 25th IEEE International Conference on Computer Communications. Proceedings, April 2006, pp. 1–13 (2006)
30. Motwani, R., Raghavan, P.: Randomized algorithms. Cambridge University Press, New York (1995)

31. McGlynn, M., Borbash, S.: Birthday protocols for low energy deployment and flexible neighbor discovery in ad hoc wireless networks. In: MobiHoc 2001: Proceedings of the 2nd ACM international symposium on Mobile ad hoc networking & computing, pp. 137–145 (2001)
32. Park, V., Corson, M.: A Highly Adaptive Distributed Routing Algorithm for Mobile Wireless Networks. In: INFOCOM 1997. Sixteenth Annual Joint Conference of the IEEE Computer and Communications Societies. Driving the Information Revolution (1997)
33. PalChaudhuri, S., Johnson, D.: Birthday paradox for energy conservation in sensor networks. In: Proceedings of the 5th Symposium of Operating Systems Design and Implementation (2002)
34. Polastre, J., Hill, J., Culler, D.: Versatile low power media access for wireless sensor networks. In: Proceedings of the 2nd international Conference on Embedded Networked Sensor Systems, SenSys 2004, Baltimore, MD, USA, November 03 - 05, pp. 95–107. ACM Press, New York (2004)
35. Sichitiu, M.L., Veerarittiphan, C.: Simple, accurate time synchronization for wireless sensor networks. In: 2003 IEEE Wireless Communications and Networking, 2003. WCNC 2003, March 16-20, vol. 2, pp. 1266–1273 (2003)
36. Shnayder, V., Hempstead, M., Chen, B., Allen, G., Welsh, M.: Simulating the power consumption of large-scale sensor network applications. In: SenSys 2004: Proceedings of the 2nd international conference on Embedded networked sensor systems, pp. 188–200. ACM Press, New York (2004)
37. Schurgers, C., Raghunathan, V., Srivastava, M.: Power management for energy-aware communication systems. ACM Trans. Embedded Comput. Syst. 2(3), 431–447 (2003)
38. Sivrikaya, F., Yener, B.: Time synchronization in sensor networks: a survey. IEEE Network 18(4), 45–50 (2004)
39. Sichitiu, M.L., Veerarittiphan, C.: Simple, Accurate Time Synchronization for Wireless Sensor Networks. In: Proc. IEEE Wireless Communications and Networking Conference (WCNC 2003), pp. 1266–1273 (2003)
40. Sundararaman, B., Buy, U., Kshemkalyani, A.D.: Clock synchronization for wireless sensor networks: a survey. Ad-hoc Networks 3(3), 281–323 (2005)
41. Tseng, Y.-C., Hsu, C.-S., Hsieh, T.-Y.: Power-saving protocols for IEEE 802.11-based multi-hop ad hoc networks. Comput. Netw. 43(3), 317–337 (2003)
42. Zheng, R., Hou, J., Sha, L.: Asynchronous wakeup for ad hoc networks. In: Proceedings of the 4th ACM international symposium on Mobile ad hoc networking & computing (MobiHoc 2003), pp. 35–45 (2003)

Approximating Barrier Resilience in Wireless Sensor Networks

Sergey Bereg[1] and David Kirkpatrick[2]

[1] Department of Computer Science, University of Texas at Dallas, USA
[2] Department of Computer Science, University of British Columbia, Canada

Abstract. Barrier coverage in a sensor network has the goal of ensuring that all paths through the surveillance domain joining points in some start region S to some target region T will intersect the coverage region associated with at least one sensor. In this paper, we revisit a notion of redundant barrier coverage known as k-barrier coverage.

We describe two different notions of width, or impermeability, of the barrier provided by the sensors in $\mathcal{A}$ to paths joining two arbitrary regions S to T. The first, what we refer to as the *thickness* of the barrier, counts the minimum number of sensor region intersections, over all paths from S to T. The second, what we refer to as the *resilience* of the barrier, counts the minimum number of sensors whose removal permits a path from S to T with no sensor region intersections. Of course, a configuration of sensors with resilience k has thickness at least k and constitutes a k-barrier for S and T.

Our result demonstrates that any (Euclidean) shortest path from S to T that intersects a fixed number of distinct sensors, never intersects any one sensor more than three times. It follows that the resilience of $\mathcal{A}$ (with respect to S and T) is at least one-third the thickness of $\mathcal{A}$ (with respect to S and T). (Furthermore, if points in S and T are moderately separated (relative to the radius of individual sensor coverage) then no shortest path intersects any one sensor more than two times, and hence the resilience of $\mathcal{A}$ is at least one-half the thickness of $\mathcal{A}$.)

A second result, which we are only able to sketch here, shows that the approximation bounds can be tightened (to 1.666 in the case of moderately separated S and T) by exploiting topological properties of simple paths that make double visits to a collection of disks.

1 Introduction

Various notions of *coverage* provided by wireless sensor networks have attracted considerable attention over the past few years. (D.W. Gage [6] initiated the formal study of sensor coverage, and the recent survey papers of Meguerdichian *et al.* [16] and Cardei and Wu [1], as well as the Ph.D. thesis of S. Kumar [10] provide comprehensive overviews of work on the topic). A fundamental concern is the design of networks that achieve high quality of coverage. Central to this endeavor is the evaluation of the quality of coverage of a given sensor network.

S. Dolev (Ed.): ALGOSENSORS 2009, LNCS 5804, pp. 29–40, 2009.

In general, coverage can be expressed geometrically, by relating the positions, and associated *coverage regions*, of individual sensors to some underlying surveillance domain. However, different applications motivate different notions of coverage. Three concepts that have received a significant amount of study are *area coverage*, where the goal is to achieve coverage for *all points* in the surveillance domain by a static collection of sensors, *sweep coverage*, where the goal is to ensure that any point moving continuously within the surveillance domain will be detected at some point in time by a collection of moving sensors, and *barrier coverage*, where the goal is to ensure that all paths through the surveillance domain joining points in some start region S to some target region T will intersect the coverage region associated with at least one member of some static collection of sensors.

Barrier coverage has the attractive feature of guaranteeing the absence of undetected transitions between critical subsets of the surveillance domain (for example, between unsecured entry and exit points) without the high (and in many cases, unwarranted) cost of full area coverage. However, as has been observed in several papers, barrier coverage, in its simplest formulation, does not adequately capture the robustness requirements of typical applications; for example, a configuration of sensors could provide a barrier cover between S and T which, on the failure of even a single sensor would disintegrate into something that does not even provide a reasonable approximation to barrier coverage.

Several proposals have been made to increase the robustness of the barrier coverage concept. Some [14,13] are based on probabilistic assumptions about the distribution of sensors or paths. Other proposals retain the deterministic/worst-case nature of basic barrier coverage. Meguerdichian *et al.* [16,15] suggest measuring the quality of barrier coverage in terms of what they call *maximal breach paths* (paths that maximize the distance to their closest sensor) and *minimum exposure paths* (paths that minimize the total degree of exposure to sensors, measured in terms of both proximity and duration). Jiang and Chen [8] consider double barrier coverage, which holds when every path from S to T must, at some point, be simultaneously covered by at least two distinct sensors. Kumar *et al.* [11,12] introduce a different notion of multiple coverage for paths connecting certain highly constrained regions S and T. Specifically, they define a configuration of sensors to provide k-barrier coverage if every path joining a point in S to a point in T must intersect at least k distinct sensor regions. Most recently, Chen *et al.* [3,4] have studied *localized* notions of k-barrier coverage that constrain the space of feasible paths that need to be covered.

In this paper, we revisit the notion of k-barrier coverage in a more general context than has been previously studied. Specifically, we consider an arbitrary arrangement $\mathcal{A}$ of sensors and two arbitrary regions S and T within the surveillance domain. We describe two different notions of impermeability of the barrier provided by the sensors to paths from S to T. The first, what we refer to as the *thickness* of the barrier, counts the minimum number of sensor region intersections, over all paths from S to T. The second, what we refer to as the *resilience* of the barrier, counts the minimum number of sensors whose removal permits a path from S to T with no sensor region intersections. The critical distinction between these notions is the fact that thickness counts multiple encounters of the same sensor, while resilience counts only the first encounter. It follows that any arrangement of sensors with resilience k has thickness at least k, and constitutes a k-barrier for S and T.

Figure 1 illustrates an arrangement $\mathcal{A}$ of *disk sensors* (sensors whose coverage regions are unit disks) and a path joining a point $s \in S$ to a point $t \in T$. The dual of $\mathcal{A}$, denoted $\hat{\mathcal{A}}$ is a directed graph whose vertices are the faces of $\mathcal{A}$ and whose arcs connect vertices corresponding to adjacent faces in $\mathcal{A}$. If we assign weight 1 to arcs that correspond to a transition entering a disk region, and weight 0 to arcs that correspond to a transition exiting a disk region, then it is easy to see that geometric paths that intersect k (non-necessarily distinct) sensor regions while traversing the arrangement $\mathcal{A}$ correspond to combinatorial paths in the dual graph $\hat{\mathcal{A}}$ with path length k. Thus, the thickness of $\mathcal{A}$ with respect to the points s and t corresponds to the length of the shortest path from the face containing s to the face containing t in $\hat{\mathcal{A}}$. (Of course, such a path can be computed efficiently using standard graph algorithms). Note that the same reduction extends to arbitrary regions S and T. (It suffices to add an artificial source node s^* with an edge (s^*, f) to every face f that intersects S, with weight equal to the number of disks that cover f). The exact resilience of $\mathcal{A}$ seems much more difficult to compute in general.

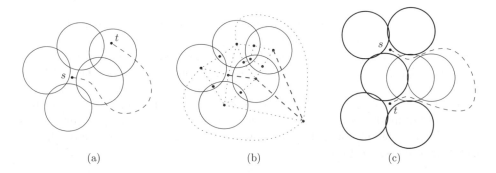

(a)   (b)   (c)

Fig. 1. (a) An st-path in a disk arrangement $\mathcal{A}$. (b) Dual of $\mathcal{A}$ with corresponding path highlighted. (c) An arrangement with thickness 2 and resilience 1 (bold disks correspond to double sensors).

Our motivation is to extend the analysis of what we call barrier resilience beyond the restricted contexts (regions separated by either open or closed belts) examined by Kumar *et al.* [12]. While there is evidence to suggest that determining the exact resilience of an arbitrary sensor configuration with arbitrary regions S and T is hard, we show that for configurations of sensors with identical disk coverage regions there is a close relationship between thickness and resilience. Since, as we have seen, thickness can be computed efficiently, it follows that there is an efficient algorithm to approximate thickness.

Arrangements with thickness one are exactly the same as those with resilience one (for all types of sensor coverage regions). However, for arrangements of disk sensors with thickness greater than one, the relationship between thickness and resilience is non-trivial. We note that for line-sensors (sensors whose coverage regions are unbounded lines) the notions of thickness and resilience coincide (since paths need never intersect a line-sensor more than once). On the other hand, for line-segment-sensors (sensors whose coverage regions are unit length line segments) – as studied by Kloder and Hutchinson [9], among others – there are sensor arrangements whose thickness is arbitrarily larger than their resilience.

We show, in section 3, that for an arbitrary arrangement $\mathcal{A}$ of unit disk sensors, and arbitrary points s and t in $\mathcal{A}$, any (Euclidean) shortest path from s to t that intersects a fixed number of distinct sensors, never intersects any one sensor more than three times. Furthermore, if s and t are moderately separated, more specifically if they do not co-reside on the fringe of some disk of $\mathcal{A}$, then any (Euclidean) shortest path from s to t that intersects a fixed number of distinct sensors, never intersects any one sensor more than two times. (Both of these bounds are tight, in the worst case.)

It follows immediately that the resilience of $\mathcal{A}$ (with respect to s and t) is at least one-third of the thickness of $\mathcal{A}$ (with respect to s and t). Furthermore, if s and t are moderately separated (as above) then the resilience of $\mathcal{A}$ is at least one-half of the thickness of $\mathcal{A}$. Thus any algorithm that computes the thickness of $\mathcal{A}$ provides a 3-approximation (or, under mild restrictions, a 2-approximation) of the resilience of $\mathcal{A}$.

It is natural to ask if these approximation bounds can be tightened by somehow recognizing when a path in the dual graph $\hat{\mathcal{A}}$ re-enters a sensor disk (and can thus have its length discounted). In the next section we recall some related work that shows that such a discounting scheme, operating in polynomial time, is unlikely to exist for general graphs, even if one is only looking for a partial discount. Despite this, we are able to tighten the approximation bound (to 1.666 in the case of moderately separated s and t) by exploiting topological properties of simple paths that make double visits to a collection of disks. These results are sketched briefly in section 4.

2   Background and Related Work

2.1 k-Barrier Coverage of Belt Regions

Kumar et al. [11,12] introduced the notions of k-coverage of paths and k-barrier coverage of belt regions. Belt regions are defined by two uniformly separated boundaries and are either open, in which case the boundaries define the opposite sides of a strip in the plane, or closed, in which case they form the sides of a fixed width ring. In either case, the deployment of sensors within the belt is intended to cover all possible paths joining one boundary to the other.

Kumar et al. showed that the problem of determining if a given configuration of sensors provides a k-barrier cover for an open belt region can be reduced to the problem of determining if a given graph admits k vertex-disjoint paths between two specified vertices. Their reduction represents the sensor configuration by its intersection graph IG and exploits a well-known result in graph theory (Menger's theorem) to relate the size of minimum separating sets and maximum sets of vertex disjoint paths. Since efficient algorithms (based on maximum flows) exist for determining the existence of a maximum set of vertex disjoint paths between two specified vertices, the k-barrier question is essentially settled in this instance.

In the preliminary version [11] of their work Kumar *et al.* claimed that similar results hold for closed belts, based on the existence of non-contractable cycles in IG. This claim was subsequently retracted [12] and, consequently, the k-barrier question, even for this constrained setting, remains open.

2.2 The Minimum Colour Single Path Problem

We described a reduction of the problem of determining the thickness of a sensor arrangement $\mathcal{A}$ with respect to the points s and t to that of determining the length of the shortest path between two specified faces in $\hat{\mathcal{A}}$. It is natural to ask if a similar reduction might hold for the problem of determining the resilience of $\mathcal{A}$. A promising approach in this direction is choose unique colours for each sensor and then colour the directed edges of the $\hat{\mathcal{A}}$ with colour i if that edge corresponds to a crossing into the region covered by sensor i. With this coloured-dual representation of $\mathcal{A}$ the problem of determining the resilience of $\mathcal{A}$ with respect to the points s and t reduces to that of finding a path from s to t, in this coloured dual, that uses the minimum number of distinct colours.

This *minimum colour single path problem*, for general edge-coloured graphs, was apparently first mentioned in [7]. Unfortunately, it has been shown to be NP-hard in general [2,17]. In fact, the NP-hardness of Yuan *et al.* [17], which describes a simple reduction from the well-known set cover problem, can be easily strengthened to show that the minimum colour single path problem remains NP-hard even if the underlying graph is planar and no colour appears on more than two edges.

Since the minimum set cover problem is hard to approximate to within a logarithmic factor [5], it follows from the reduction of Yuan *et al.* that the minimum colour single path problem is also hard to approximate to within a logarithmic factor. (Of course, if no colour is used more than d times then there is an obvious d-approximation algorithm.)

3   Relating Resilience and Thickness for Unit Disk Sensors

In this section we establish a close connection between resilience and thickness for arrangements of disk sensors by proving that minimum (Euclidean) length paths, among all s, t paths that intersect at most k sensors, have the property that they intersect any fixed sensor at most a small constant number of times. The intuition behind the result is quite straightforward: (i) if a path π visits some disk D too many times then there must exist a shortcut; (ii) the absence of a shortcut would require that D be intersected by a large number of other pairwise-disjoint disks, whose avoidance is what forces π to repeatedly intersect D; and (iii) the existence of such a collection of disks is impossible, by standard packing arguments. Unfortunately, the details are lengthy and somewhat intricate, especially if one wants to produce the tightest possible bounds.

Let π be any s, t path through $\mathcal{A}$. We find it useful to consider the entire family $\mathcal{P}_\pi$ of s, t paths that avoid all of the sensors avoided by π. We can think of such paths as geometric paths that avoid a fixed set of disk obstacles corresponding to the avoided sensors. Clearly, there is nothing lost by restricting attention to minimum (Euclidean) length paths in $\mathcal{P}_\pi$. Thus, we begin by establishing some properties of Euclidean shortest disk-obstacle-avoiding paths.

3.1 Shortest Paths Avoiding Disk Obstacles

Given a collection of unit disk obstacles $D_1, \ldots, D_n$ and two points s and t in the plane, we say that a path from s to t is *legal* if it avoids the interior of every obstacle. Any shortest legal path has the property that it is a sequence where (i) each element is either a straight line segment or an arc of the boundary of an obstacle, and (ii) successive elements have common tangent and direction at the common endpoint. As is common in the bounded-curvature motion planning literature, we refer to such paths as *Dubins paths*.

Dubins paths have have many interesting local properties, some of which we develop in this section. Our broader goal, however, is to establish the following global property.

Lemma 1. *Let D be an arbitrary unit disk that does not contain either s or t. Any shortest legal st-path π crosses the boundary of D at most six times. Furthermore if either s or t has distance at least $\sqrt{3} - 1$ from the boundary of D then the path π crosses the boundary of D at most four times.*

Since it is straightforward to account for coverage of the endpoints s and t, the following theorem is an immediate consequence:

Theorem 1. *Let $\mathcal{A}$ be an arrangement of disks and s and t be two points in the plane. If s and t are well-separated then the resilience of $\mathcal{A}$ is at least one-half of the thickness of $\mathcal{A}$. For general s and t the resilience of $\mathcal{A}$ is at least one-third of the thickness of $\mathcal{A}$.*

As indicated above, we begin by developing some structural properties of shortest legal paths.

Lemma 2. *Let a and b be two points on the boundary of a unit disk D. If there exists a legal path from a to b lying entirely within D, then the shortest legal path from a to b lies entirely within D.*

Proof. Let π_1 be a path from a to b outside D and let π_2 be the shortest path from a to b within D. Let $\widehat{ab}$ be the shortest arc of D with endpoints a and b. π_1 is not shorter than $\widehat{ab}$. It suffices to prove that $\widehat{ab}$ is not shorter that π_2. Let

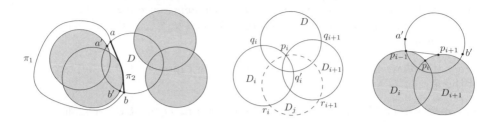

Fig. 2. Illustrations for the proof of Lemma 2

R be the region between $\widehat{ab}$ and π_2. Let $\hat{D}$ be the union of disks intersecting R. Let C be any connected component of $R \cap \hat{D}$. The boundary of C consists of two parts $\overline{C}_{\text{ext}}$, an arc joining two points a' and b' on the boundary of D. and the remainder $\overline{C}_{\text{int}}$. It suffices to prove that the length of $\overline{C}_{\text{ext}}$ is no less than the length of $\overline{C}_{\text{int}}$.

Fix any k and consider a set of k obstacles such that the length of $\overline{C}_{\text{int}}$ is largest among all sets of k obstacles. Let $p_0, p_1, p_2, \ldots, p_m$ (where $p_0 = a'$ and $p_m = b'$) be the endpoints of arcs on $\overline{C}_{\text{ext}}$. Let D_i be the obstacle with arc $p_{i-1}p_i$ on its boundary. Let $S = \{D_1, \ldots, D_{m-1}\}$.

First we show that every $p_i, i = 1, \ldots, m - 1$ lies on the boundary of only two obstacles from S. Suppose to the contrary that p_i lies on the boundary of some other disk D_j from S. We specify circular arcs by their endpoints with the assumption that the arc is traced counterclockwise from its first to its second endpoint. The length of arc p_iq_i is at most the length of arc $q_i'q_i$ which is less than π (since the length of arc $a'b'$ is less than π). However the arc p_ir_i on D_i must have length greater than π (since it is outer arc of $D_i \cup D_j$). Similarly r_{i+1} is not in D. It follows that $D_j - (D_i \cup D_{i+1})$ is disjoint from D contradicting that $D_j \in S$.

If all p_i lie on the boundary of D then it is obvious that the sum of arc lengths is the same as the length of $\overline{C}_{\text{ext}}$ Otherwise, suppose that p_i is the first point that does not lie on the boundary of D. In this case we show that the disks D_i and D_{i+1} can be perturbed to increase the length of internal boundary contradicting our maximality assumption. Rotate D_i about p_{i-1} and D_{i+1} about p_{i+1} in such a way that the intersection point p_i moves perpendicular to and away from the line $p_{i-1}p_{i+1}$. Since p_i is not on the boundary of other disks there must be a sufficiently small such motion that preserves the structure of the internal boundary while increasing the length of both $p_{i-1}p_i$ and p_ip_{i+1} (both line segments and arcs). The lemma follows.   □

It follows from lemma 2 that no three successive crossing points on the boundary of D can be joined by legal paths within D. Obstacles that together block any legal path within D joining two successive boundary crossing points a to b form what we call an *obstruction* for a and b. Obstructions consisting of just two disks are called *2-obstructions* for a and b.

Lemma 3. *Let a and b be two points on the boundary of a unit disk D. If there does not exist a legal path from a to b within D, then there must be a 2-obstruction for a and b.*

Proof. It follows from the fact that every unit disk intersecting D intersects one of the arcs of D with endpoints a and b.   □

The next lemma shows that every 2-obstruction in D must cover at least half of the boundary of D. It follows that no disk D contains two disjoint 2-obstructions.

Lemma 4. *Let D be a unit disk and $\hat{D} = A \cup B$ be the union of two unit disks that form a 2-obstruction for points a and b on the boundary of D. Then at least half of the boundary of D lies inside $\hat{D}$.*

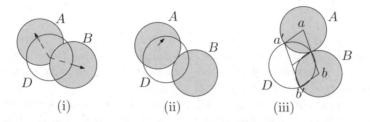

Fig. 3. Illustrations for Lemma 4

Proof. We move disks A and B such that the total length of the boundary of D inside $\hat{D}$ decreases: (i) move A and B away from D until A and B are tangent, (ii) rotate A about center of B, so that the distance between centers of A and D increases, until (iii) the tangent point of A and B lies on the boundary of D. Then $\hat{D}$ covers half of the boundary of D since $abb'a'$ is a parallelogram, see Fig. 3.   □

We exploit the bounded curvature of Dubins paths to show that if path π approaches disk D by passing between two obstacles D_1 and D_2 that intersect D then either (i) π terminates in or near D, or (ii) π is constrained in terms of the depth of its approach to D.

Lemma 5 (Access lemma). *Let D_1, D_2 be unit disks such that D properly intersects both D_1 and D_2. Assume that the centers of D_1 and D_2 are on the x-axis as in Figure 4. Let D' be the unit disc tangent to both D_1 and D_2 and with center below x-axis. If a Dubins path does not cross the top arc of D then it crosses the top arc of D' at most once.*

Proof (See Figure 4.). Suppose a Dubins path π' crosses the top arc of D' twice. Consider the highest point a of π' between these two crossings. We can place a unit disk A tangent to π' at a. π' cannot cross the top arc of A without crossing the horizontal line through the center of A. Then the top arc of A acts as a

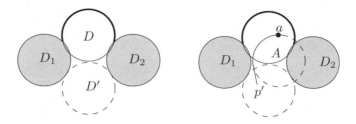

Fig. 4. The top arc of D (bold) is an obstacle

barrier for π'. Any way of placing of that barrier must intersect either D_1, D_2 or the top arc of D. Consequently it is impossible either to reach a from the first crossing point or continue from a to the second crossing point.   □

We are now prepared to prove the main result of this section.

3.2   Proof of Lemma 1

Suppose that π crosses the boundary of D k times. For any two crossing points a and b, if there is a legal ab-path within D then a and b are set to be D-*connected*; otherwise they are D-*obstructed*. Crossing points partition the boundary of D into k arcs. By Lemma 2 if two crossing points a and b are D-connected then we can assume that π contains the shortest legal ab-path within D as a subpath. It follows that any crossing point a is D-connected to at most one other crossing point; otherwise π is not a shortest legal st-path.

Let a and b be D-connected crossing points and let π' be the subpath of π connecting a and b. One of the arcs with endpoints a and b must be free of crossing points. Suppose otherwise. Then there must exist two crossing points c and d on either side of π' that are both D-obstructed from a. By Lemma 3 there are two obstructions for pairs a, c and a, d. These obstructions are disjoint within D since they do not obstruct π'. By Lemma 3 two obstructions cover the entire boundary length of D, a contradiction.

Suppose that s, t are not in D. The crossings of the boundary of D by π form successive pairs. Consider any 3 such pairs. The associated 6 crossings must be connected in D as shown in Fig. 5 (a). Consider disks intersecting the 3 arcs between connections. Each connection corresponds to an arc on the boundary of D. There two types of arcs: narrowly exposed and widely exposed arcs, see Fig. 5 (b). An arc is *widely exposed* if we can place a unit circle tangent to D and disjoint from obstacles.

We first show that only one arc can be widely exposed. Suppose that there are two widely exposed arcs. We assume that the third arc is narrowly exposed. We use capital letters for disks and small letters for their centers. Let E, F be the disks corresponding to the widely exposed arcs. By Lemma 3 there are two different D-obstructions. One exposed arc corresponds to two disks of these D-obstructions. By pushing them toward D (rotation about e or f), we assume that they coincide. Let A, B, C be the three disks in the obstructions.

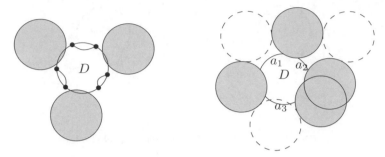

Fig. 5. (a) D-connections. (b) Narrowly exposed arcs a_1 and a_2 and widely exposed arc a_3.

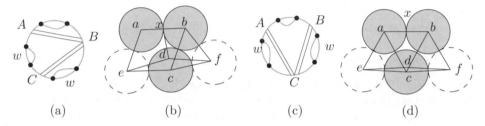

(a)   (b)   (c)   (d)

Fig. 6. Two widely exposed arcs are labeled w. D-obstructions are shown by straight line segments.

Case 1. The narrowly exposed arc is obstructed by A and B as in Fig. 6 (a). ec is parallel to df in parallelogram $ecfd$. If A is tangent to both B and E as shown in Fig. 6 (b), then ab, ec and df are parallel and $|ad| = 2$ in parallelogram $abfd$. Let x be the tangent point of A and B. Then $|xd| > |ad| - |ax| = 1$ (since a, x and d are not collinear). If A rotates clockwise about e then the top crossing point x of A and B rotates about b clockwise increasing the distance $|xd|$. Thus $|xd| > 1$ in any case. It contradicts the condition that $A \cap B \subseteq D$.

Case 2. D-obstructions and widely exposed arcs are as in Fig. 6 (c). If disks A and B intersect in D then it is Case 1. They also do not intersect outside D (then the exposed arc is trapped). Rotate disk A about c clockwise until A and B are tangent, see Fig. 6 (d). We assume that ef is horizontal and c is below ef. Since $|ac| \leq 2$ then slope of ab is larger than slope of cf (in quadrilateral $abfc$). On the other hand slope of ab is smaller than slope of ec (in quadrilateral $abce$). Contradiction.

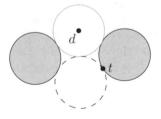

Fig. 7. Narrow pocket

It follows from Lemma 5 that if π intersects a narrowly exposed arc then one of its endpoints must be in a pocket bounded by disk D'. Thus, at most two arcs can be narrowly exposed. It follows that there are at most 6 crossings in total and, if there are exactly 6 crossings, then both s and t are nearby d. The longest distance from d to t (or s) in a narrow pocket is $\sqrt{3}$, see Fig. 7. Thus if D has three crossings by π both endpoints of π must lie within distance $\sqrt{3}$ of the center of D.

4   Tightening the Approximation Factor

The algorithm implicit in the last section computes an approximation of the resilience of the sensor arrangement $\mathcal{A}$ by simply finding a shortest path π in the dual graph $\hat{\mathcal{A}}$. In this section we describe how the approximation factor for any path π' can be improved by identifying a large collection of subpaths of π' whose individual subpath lengths all overcount the number of distinct sensor intersections. We record these subpaths as *shortcut* edges and combine as many shortcuts as possible to provide a discounted path length (and hence a tighter resilience estimate) for the pair s, t.

The details of this refined algorithm, particularly its analysis, are quite involved. First we develop two types of easily identifiable shortcut edges. Next we argue that we can find, among these shortcut edges, one edge associated with each doubly visited disk, that together form a *weakly compatible* set. Finally, we show that any weakly compatible set S of shortcut edges has a subset of size at least $|S|/3$ that forms a *strongly compatible* set. Since the discount achieved by our algorithm equals or exceeds the size of the largest strongly compatible subset of shortcut edges, it follows that if the minimum resilience path π' makes double visits to d disks (i.e. its resilience estimate provided by the unmodified shortest path algorithm exceeds its true resilience by d) then our modified algorithm provides a resilience estimate that exceeds the true value by at most $2d/3$.

5   Extensions

As we explained in the introduction, our results rely heavily on the assumption that the sensor regions associated with individual sensors are disks. However total congruence of sensor regions is not essential. Although it would result in weaker bounds, our arguments could still be applied if coverage regions were disks with radius between r_0 and r_1.

In general, it might be of interest to model physical obstacles, either to paths or sensor coverage, in trying to more accurately evaluate the barrier resilience of sensor networks. Of course, if obstacles can be expressed as the union of disks then it is straightforward to extend our existing results. More generally, obstacles can have a significant impact on our multiple visitation bounds. It is not hard to construct examples in which long thin obstacles force multiple crossings of one sensor.

Acknowledgment

The authors wish to acknoledge the support of the MITACS Facility Location project and in particular the very helpful discussions with our colleagues Binay Bhattacharya, Yuzhuang Hu, Hossein Maserrat, and Qiaosheng Shi.

References

1. Cardei, M., Wu, J.: Coverage in wireless sensor networks. In: Ilyas, M., Mahgoub, I. (eds.) Handbook of Sensor Networks: Compact Wireless and Wired Sensing Systems, ch. 19, pp. 432–446. CRC Press, Boca Raton (2005)
2. Carr, R.D., Doddi, S., Konjevod, G., Marathe, M.: On the red-blue set cover problem. In: Proc. 11th ACM-SIAM Symp. on Discr. Algor., pp. 345–353 (2000)
3. Chen, A., Kumar, S., Lai, T.H.: Designing localized algorithms for barrier coverage. In: Proc. of the 13th Annual ACM International Conference on Mobile Computing and Networking (MobiCom 2007), pp. 63–74 (2007)
4. Chen, A., Lai, T.H., Xuan, D.: Measuring and guaranteeing quality of barrier-coverage in wireless sensor networks. In: MobiHoc 2008: Proceedings of the 9th ACM international symposium on Mobile ad hoc networking and computing, pp. 421–430. ACM, New York (2008)
5. Feige, U.: A threshold of $\ln n$ for approximating set cover. J. ACM 45(4), 634–652 (1998)
6. Gage, D.W.: Command control for many-robot systems. In: Proc. 19th Annu. AUVS Tech. Symp., AUVS 1992, Hunstville AL, pp. 28–34 (1992)
7. Jacob, R., Koniedov, G., Krumke, S., Marathe, M., Ravi, R., Wirth, H.: The minimum label path problem. In: Unpublished manuscript, Los Alamos National Laboratory (1999)
8. Jiang, C.-D., Chen, G.-L.: Double barrier coverage in dense sensor networks. J. Comput. Sci. and Tech. 23(1), 154–165 (2008)
9. Kloder, S., Hutchinson, S.: Barrier coverage for variable bounded-range line-of-sight guards. In: Proc. of IEEE International Conference on Robotics and Automation (ICRA 2007), pp. 391–396 (2007)
10. Kumar, S.: Foundations of coverage in wireless sensor networks. PhD thesis, Columbus, OH, USA, Adviser-Lai, Ten H (2006)
11. Kumar, S., Lai, T.H., Arora, A.: Barrier coverage with wireless sensors. In: Proc. of the 11th Annual International Conference on Mobile Computing and Networking (MobiCom 2005), pp. 284–298 (2005)
12. Kumar, S., Lai, T.H., Arora, A.: Barrier coverage with wireless sensors. Wireless Networks 13(6) (2007)
13. Lazos, L., Poovendran, R., Ritcey, J.A.: Probabilistic detection of mobile targets in heterogeneous sensor networks. In: IPSN 2007: Proceedings of the 6th international conference on Information processing in sensor networks, pp. 519–528. ACM, New York (2007)
14. Liu, B., Dousse, O., Wang, J., Saipulla, A.: Strong barrier coverage of wireless sensor networks. In: MobiHoc 2008: Proceedings of the 9th ACM international symposium on Mobile ad hoc networking and computing, pp. 411–420. ACM, New York (2008)
15. Meguerdichian, A., Koushanfar, F., Qu, G., Potkonjak, N.: Exposure in wireless ad-hoc sensor networks. In: Proc. of the 7th Annual International Conference on Mobile Computing and Networking (MobiCom 2001), pp. 139–150 (2001)
16. Meguerdichian, S., Koushanfar, F., Potkonjak, M., Srivastava, M.: Coverage problems in wireless ad-hoc sensor networks. In: Proc. of the 20th Annual Joint Conference of the IEEE Conference on Computer and Communications (INFOCOM 2001), vol. 3, pp. 1380–1387 (2001)
17. Yuan, S., Vannat, S., Juex, J.P.: Minimum-color path problems for reliability in mesh networks. In: Proc. 24th Annu. Joint Conf. of the IEEE Computer and Communications Societies (INFOCOM 2005), vol. 4, pp. 2658–2669 (2005)

Improved Approximation Algorithms for Maximum Lifetime Problems in Wireless Networks

Zeev Nutov[1] and Michael Segal[2]

[1] Dept. of Computer Science, The Open University of Israel
nutov@openu.ac.il
[2] Dept. of Communication Systems Engineering
Beer-Sheva 84105, Israel
segal@cse.bgu.ac.il

Abstract. A wireless ad-hoc network is a collection of transceivers positioned in the plane. Each transceiver is equipped with a limited battery charge. The battery charge is then reduced after each transmission, depending on the transmission distance. One of the major problems in wireless network design is to route network traffic efficiently so as to maximize the *network lifetime*, i.e., the number of successful transmissions. In this paper we consider **Rooted Maximum Lifetime Broadcast/Convergecast** problems in wireless settings. The instance consists of a directed graph $G = (V, E)$ with edge-weights $\{w(e) : e \in E\}$, node capacities $\{b(v) : v \in V\}$, and a root r. The goal is to find a maximum size collection $\{T_1, \ldots, T_k\}$ of Broadcast/Convergecast trees rooted at r so that $\sum_{i=1}^{k} w(\delta_{T_i}(v)) \leq b(v)$, where $\delta_T(v)$ is the set of edges leaving v in T. In the Single Topology version all the Broadcast/Convergecast trees T_i are identical. We present a number of polynomial time algorithms giving constant ratio approximation for various broadcast and convergecast problems, improving previously known result of $\Omega(\lfloor 1/\log n \rfloor)$-approximation by [1]. We also consider a generalized **Rooted Maximum Lifetime Mixedcast** problem, where we are also given an integer $\gamma \geq 0$, and the goal is to find the maximum integer k so that k Broadcast and γk Convergecast rounds can be performed.

1   Introduction

Wireless ad-hoc networks received a lot of attention in recent years due to massive use in a large variety of domains, from life threatening situations, such as battlefield or rescue operations, to more civil applications, like environmental data gathering for forecast prediction. The network is composed of nodes located in the plane, communicating by radio. A transmission between two nodes is possible if the receiver is within the transmission range of the transmitter. The underlying physical topology of the network depends on the distribution of the nodes as well as the transmission power assignment of each node. Since the nodes have only a limited initial power charge, energy efficiency becomes a crucial factor in wireless networks design.

S. Dolev (Ed.): ALGOSENSORS 2009, LNCS 5804, pp. 41–51, 2009.
© Springer-Verlag Berlin Heidelberg 2009

The transmission range of node v is determined by the power $p(v)$ assigned to that node. It is customary to assume that the minimal transmission power required to transmit to distance d is d^ϕ, where the *distance-power gradient* ϕ is usually taken to be in the interval $[2, 4]$ (see [2]). Thus, node v receives transmissions from u if $p(u) \geq d(u, v)^\phi$, where $d(u, v)$ is the Euclidean distance between u and v. There are two possible models: symmetric and asymmetric. In the symmetric model, also referred to as the undirected model, there is an undirected communication link between two nodes $u, v \in T$, if $p(u) \geq d(u, v)^\phi$ and $p(v) \geq d(v, u)^\phi$, that is if u and v can reach each other. The asymmetric variant allows directed (one way) communication links between two nodes. Krumke et al. [3] argued that the asymmetric version is harder than the symmetric one. This paper addresses the asymmetric model.

Ramanathan and Hain [4] initiated the formal study of controlling the network topology by adjusting the transmission range of the nodes. Increasing the transmission range allows more distant nodes to receive transmissions but leads to faster battery exhaustion, which results in a shorter network lifetime. We are interested in maximizing the network lifetime under two basic transmission protocols, data broadcasting and data gathering (or convergecast). *Broadcasting* is a network task when a source node r wishes to transmit a message to all the other nodes in the network. In *convergecast* there is a destination node r, and all the other nodes wish to transmit a message to it. Here we consider convergecast *with aggregation*, meaning that a node uses aggregation mechanism to encode the data available at that node before forwarding it to the destination. We consider the case of unidirectional antennas, hence the message is transmitted to every node separately. Each node v, has an initial battery charge $b(v)$. The battery charge decreases with each transmission. The network lifetime is the number of rounds performed from network initialization to the first node failure due to battery depletion.

We assume that all the nodes share the same frequency band, and time is divided into equal size slots that are grouped into frames. Thus, our MAC layer is based on TDMA scheduling [5,6,7], such that collisions and interferences do not occur.

Many papers considered *fractional* version of the problem when splitting of packets into fractional portions is allowed. This versions admits an easy polynomial time algorithm via linear programming, c.f., [8,9,10,11,12,13]. As data packets are usually quite small, there are situations where splitting of packets into fractional ones is neither desirable nor practical. We consider a model where data packets are considered as units that cannot be split, i.e., when the packet flows are of *integral* values only. This discrete version was introduced by Sahni and Park [14].

In many *Network Design* problems one seeks a subgraph H with prescribed properties that minimizes/maximizes a certain objective function. Such problems are vastly studied in Combinatorial Optimization and Approximation Algorithms. Some known examples are Max-Flow, Min-Cost k-Flow, Maximum b-Matching, Minimum Spanning/Steiner Tree, and many others. See, e.g., [15,16].

Formally, we obtain the following problem, which is the "wireless variant" of the classic arborescence packing problems. An *out-arborescence*, or simply an *arborescence*, is a directed tree that has a path from a root s to every node; an *in-arborescence* is a directed tree that has a path from every node to s. For a graph $H = (V, I)$ and a node $v \in V$, let $\delta_H(v) = \delta_I(v)$ denote the set of edges leaving v in H, and let $\delta_H^{in}(v) = \delta_I^{in}(v)$ denote the set of edges entering v in H. We look at variants of the following problem:

Rooted Maximum Lifetime Broadcast

Instance: A directed graph $G = (V, E)$ with edge-weights $\{w(e) : e \in E\}$, battery capacities $\{b(v) : v \in V\}$, and a root $r \in V$.

Objective: Find a maximum size collection $\mathcal{T} = \{T_1, \ldots, T_k\}$ of out-arborescences in G rooted at r that satisfies the *energy constraints*

$$\sum_{i=1}^{k} w(\delta_{T_i}(v)) \leq b(v) \quad \text{for all } v \in V . \tag{1}$$

In the **Rooted Maximum Lifetime Convergecast** we seek a maximum size collection of in-arborescences, that are directed to r. In the **Rooted Maximum Lifetime Mixedcast**, we are also given an integer $\gamma \geq 0$, and the goal is to find the maximum integer k so that k Convergecast and γk Broadcast rounds can be performed. We observe that the problem is APX-hard, and the broadcast version is hard even for unit weights (however, Convergcast version with unit weights is polynomially solvable). In fact, for Broadcast, even determining whether $k \geq 1$ is NP-complete [1]. Hence it seems that an approximation ratio of the type $\lfloor k/\rho \rfloor$ is the best one can expect. We give algorithms when ρ is a constant, improving the ratio $\rho = O(\log n)$ established in [1].

More generally, we characterize the class of **Maximum Network Lifetime** problems as follows. In these problems, every node v has a limited battery capacity $b(v)$, and a transmission energy $w(vu)$ to any other node u is known. In transmission round i, we choose a subnetwork H_i with given properties, and every node transmits one message to each one of its neighbors in H_i; in many applications, each H_i is an arborescence (see [1]). The goal is to maximize the *lifetime* of the network, that is to find a maximum length feasible sequence $H_1, H_2, \ldots, H_k$ of subnetworks; feasibility means that every graph H_i satisfies the required properties, and that for every node v the total transmission energy during all rounds is at most $b(v)$. This is the *Multiple Topology* version of the problem. In the *Single Topology* variant, all the networks H_i are identical, c.f., [1] for more details. We note that in [17] was given a constant ratio approximation algorithm for the case when each H_i should be an st-path, for given $s, t \in V$. Here we consider the case when each H_i is an arborescence rooted from/to the root r.

In a more general setting, we might also be given a *cost-function* c on the edges, which can be distinct from the *weight-function* w, and wish to minimize the total cost $\sum_{i=1}^{k} c(H_i)$ of the communication subnetworks. We call this variant **Min-Cost Maximum Network Lifetime**.

While most of the problems considered in this paper deal with the case of convergecast with aggregation, we also deal with the problem Partial Level Aggregation Convergecast where we want to find a tree T of G directed towards the root node r that satisfies the energy constraints $\sum w(\delta_T(v)) \leq \frac{b(v)}{level(v)}$ for all $v \in V$, where $level(v)$ is the length of the longest path between v and its descendant in T.

1.1   Previous Work

The authors in [18] show that for Broadcast, the problem is NP-Hard in the case of Single Source/Single Topology and has a polynomial solution for fractional version in the case of Single Source/Multiple Topology. They also show that it is NP-Hard in both of these cases for multicast. Segal [19] improved the running time of the solution for the Broadcast protocol and also showed an optimal polynomial time algorithm for the integral version of Single Topology Convergecast; the latter algorithm simply finds, using binary search, the largest integer k so that the graph $G - \{vu \in E : w(vu) > b(v)/k\}$ contains an arborescence directed to the root. For Multiple Topology Convergecast fractional version Kalpakis et al. [11] does have a polynomial solution in $O(n^{15} \log n)$ time. To counter the slowness of the algorithm, Stanford and Tongngam [20] proposed a $(1 - \varepsilon)$-approximation in $O(n^3 \frac{1}{\varepsilon} \log_{1+\varepsilon} n)$ time based on the algorithm of Garg and Könemann [21] for packing linear programs. Elkin et al. [1] gave an $\Omega(\lfloor 1/\log n \rfloor)$-approximation for the discrete version of Multiple Topology Convergecast problem. Regarding the case without aggregation, some partial results were given in [22], [23] and [24]. The paper [22] considered the conditional aggregation where data from one node can be compressed in the presence of data from other nodes. Liang and Liu [24] present a number of heuristics for different types of aggregation problems. Buragohain et al. [23] proved the hardness of optimal routing tree problem for non-aggregate queries.

1.2   Our Results

We give the first constant ratio approximation algorithm for Rooted Maximum Lifetime Broadcast/Convergecast/Mixedcast.

Theorem 1. Rooted Maximum Network Lifetime *admits a polynomial time algorithm that finds a solution of value $\ell \geq \lfloor k/\beta^2 \rfloor$ where:*

Single Topology: $\beta = 1$ *for Convergecast, $\beta = 5$ for Broadcast and $\beta = 6$ for Mixedcast.*
Multiple Topology: $\beta = 4$ for Convergecast, $\beta = 6$ for Broadcast, and $\beta = 10$ for Mixedcast.

Furthermore, for Min-Cost Maximum Network Lifetime *the algorithm computes $\ell \geq \lfloor k/\beta^2 \rfloor$ arborescences so that their total cost is at most the total cost of k optimal arborescences.*

For Broadcast, even checking whether $k \geq 1$ is NP-complete [1]. Thus we cannot guarantee any approximation ratio for such a problem, and an approximation of the form $\lfloor k/\rho \rfloor$ is the best one can expect. However, as Single Topology Convergecast is in P [19], for Multiple Topology Convergecast checking whether $k \geq 1$ can be done in polynomial time. This implies:

Corollary 1. *Multiple Topology Convergecast version of* Maximum Network Lifetime *admits a* $1/31$-*approximation algorithm.*

The following table summarizes the ratios for variants of Maximum Network Lifetime.

Table 1. Summary of the ratios for variants of Maximum Network Lifetime. Except the polynomial solvability of the Single Topology Convergecast that was proved in [19], the other ratios are proved in this paper.

Single Topology			Multiple Topology		
Convergecast	*Broadcast*	*Mixedcast*	*Convergecast*	*Broadcast*	*Mixedcast*
k	$\lfloor k/25 \rfloor$	$\lfloor k/36 \rfloor$	$\max\{\lfloor k/16 \rfloor, 1\}$	$\lfloor k/36 \rfloor$	$\lfloor k/100 \rfloor$

A related problem for which we can give a constant ratio approximation is minimizing the battery capacity b so that for $b(v) = b$ for all $v \in V$ at least k rounds of communications can be performed. Formally, this problem can be stated as follows:

Minimum Battery Rooted Lifetime k-Convergecast/Broadcast/Mixedcast
Instance: A directed graph $G = (V, E)$ with edge-weights $\{w(e) : e \in E\}$, a root $r \in V$, and an integer k.
Objective: Find a minimum battery capacity b so that if $b(v) = b$ for all $v \in V$, then there exists a collection $\mathcal{T} = \{T_1, \ldots, T_k\}$ of k out/in-arborescences in G rooted at r so that (1) holds.

Theorem 2. Minimum Battery Rooted Lifetime k-Broadcast/Convergecast/ Mixedcast *admits a* β-*approximation algorithm, where* β *is as in Theorem 1.*

For Partial Level Aggregation Convergecast we gave a number of optimal and approximate solutions and discuss the possibilities to extend them to more general case.

2   Weighted Degree Constrained Network Design

Our results are based on a recent result due to Nutov [25] for directed Weighted Degree Constrained Network Design problems with intersecting supermodular demands. Lewin-Eytan et al. [26] were first to introduce the problem in context of Steiner trees. In Degree Constrained Network Design problems (without weights) one seeks the cheapest subgraph H of a given graph G that satisfies both prescribed connectivity requirements and degree constraints. One such type of problems are the Matching/Edge-Cover problems, which are solvable in polynomial time, c.f., [15]. For other degree constrained problems, even checking whether there exists a feasible solution is NP-complete, hence one considers bicriteria approximation when the degree constraints are relaxed.

The connectivity requirements can be specified by a set function f on V, as follows.

Definition 1. *For an edge set of a graph H and node set S let $\delta_H(S)$ $(\delta_H^{in}(S))$ denote the set of edges in H leaving (entering) S. Given a set-function f on subsets of V and a graph $H = (V, F)$, we say that H is f-connected if*

$$|\delta_H^{in}(S)| \geq f(S) \quad \text{for all } S \subseteq V. \tag{2}$$

Several types of f are considered in the literature, among them the following known one:

Definition 2. *A set function f on V is* intersecting supermodular *if for any $X, Y \subseteq V$, $X \cap Y \neq \emptyset$*

$$f(X) + f(Y) \leq f(X \cap Y) + f(X \cup Y) . \tag{3}$$

In [25] are considered network design problems with *weighted-degree* constraints. The *weighted degree* of a node v in a graph H with edge-weights $\{w(e) : e \in F\}$ is $w(\delta_H(v)) = \sum_{e \in \delta_H(v)} w(e)$.

Directed Weighted Degree Constrained Network (DWDCN)
Instance: A directed graph $G = (V, E)$ with edge-costs $\{c(e) : e \in E\}$ and edge-weights $\{w(e) : e \in E\}$, a set-function f on V, and degree bounds $\{b(v) : v \in V\}$.
Objective: Find a minimum cost f-connected subgraph H of G that satisfies the *weighted degree constraints*

$$w(\delta_H(v)) \leq b(v) \quad \text{for all } v \in V . \tag{4}$$

The function f is usually not given explicitly, but is assumed to admit an evaluation oracle (or other relevant oracles). Since for most functions f even checking whether DWDCN has a feasible solution is NP-complete, one considers bicriteria approximation algorithms. An (α, β)-approximation algorithm for DWDCN either computes an f-connected subgraph $H = (V, F)$ of G of cost $\leq \alpha \cdot \mathsf{opt}$ that satisfies $w(\delta_H(v)) \leq \beta \cdot b(v)$ for all $v \in V$, or correctly determines that the problem has no feasible solution. Note that even if the problem does not have a feasible solution, the algorithm may still return a subgraph that violates the degree constraints (4) by a factor of β.

Let opt denote the optimal value of the following natural LP-relaxation for DWDCN that seeks to minimize $c \cdot x$ over the following polytope P_f:

$$x(\delta_E^{in}(S)) \geq f(S) \qquad \text{for all } S \subset V \qquad \text{(Cut Constraints)}$$

$$\sum_{e \in \delta_E(v)} x(e)w(e) \leq b(v) \qquad \text{for all } v \in V \qquad \text{(Weighted Degree Constraints)}$$

$$0 \leq x(e) \leq 1 \qquad \text{for all } e \in E$$

Similarly, we may consider the version of DWDCN where the Cut Constraints are on edges leaving S, namely we have $x(\delta_E(S)) \geq f(S)$ for all $S \subset V$. We assume that f is intersecting supermodular. For an edge set I, let $x(I) = \sum_{e \in I} x(e)$. Let us fix parameters α and β as follows:

- Single Topology Convergecast, or DWDCN with Cut Constraint on the edges entering S and $0, 1$-valued f:
  $\alpha = \beta = 1$.
- Single Topology Broadcast, or DWDCN with Cut Constraint on the edges leaving S and $0, 1$-valued f:
  $\alpha = 2$ and $\beta = 5$.
- Multiple Topology Convergecast, or DWDCN with Cut Constraint on the edges entering S:
  $\alpha = 1$ and $\beta = 4$.
- Multiple Topology Broadcast, or DWDCN with Cut Constraint on the edges leaving S:
  $\alpha = 3$ and $\beta = 6$.

The following result has been proved in [25].

Theorem 3. *[25] DWDCN with intersecting supermodular f admits a polynomial time algorithm that computes an f-connected graph H of cost $\leq \alpha \cdot$ opt so that the weighted degree of every $v \in H$ is at most $\beta b(v)$.*

3   Proof of Theorems 1 and 2

A graph H is k-*edge-outconnected from* r if it has k-edge-disjoint paths from r to any other node; H is k-*edge-inconnected from* r if it has k-edge-disjoint paths from every node to r. DWDCN problem includes as a special case the Weighted Degree Constrained k-Outconnected Subgraph problem, by setting $f(S) = k$ for all $\emptyset \neq S \subseteq V \setminus \{r\}$, and $f(S) = 0$ otherwise. For $k = 1$ we get the Weighted Degree Constrained Arborescence problem. Our problems are equivalent to the problem of packing maximum number k of edge-disjoint trees rooted at r so that their union H satisfies (4). By Edmond's Theorem [27], this is equivalent to requiring that H is k-edge-outconnected from r (or k-edge in-connected to r, in the case of convergecast) and satisfies (4). This gives the following problem:

Weighted-Degree Constrained k-Outconnected Subgraph
Instance: A directed graph $G = (V, E)$ with edge-costs $\{c(e) : e \in E\}$, edge-weights $\{w(e) : e \in E\}$, degree bounds $\{b(v) : v \in V\}$, and a root $r \in V$.
Objective: Find a k-edge-outconnected from r spanning subgraph H of G that satisfies the weighted degree constraints (4) so that k is maximum.

In the Weighted-Degree Constrained k-Inconnected Subgraph problem, we require that H is k-edge-inconnected to r.

The following is the natural LP-relaxation for Weighted-Degree Constrained k-Outconnected Subgraph that seeks to minimize $c \cdot x$ over the following polytope P_k:

$$x(\delta_E^{in}(S)) \geq k \qquad \text{for all } \emptyset \neq S \subseteq V \setminus \{r\} \text{ (Cut Constraints)}$$

$$\sum_{e \in \delta_E(v)} x(e)w(e) \leq b(v) \quad \text{for all } v \in V \qquad \qquad \text{(Weighted Degree Constraints)}$$

$$0 \leq x(e) \leq 1 \qquad \text{for all } e \in E$$

Namely, $P_k = P_f$ for

$$f(S) = \begin{cases} k & \text{if } \emptyset \neq S \subseteq V \setminus \{r\} \\ 0 & \text{otherwise} \end{cases}$$

In the Convergecast case the Cut Constraints are on edges leaving S, namely we have $x(\delta_E(S)) \geq f(S)$ for all $S \subset V$, with f as defined above. In both cases, the function f is intersecting supermodular, hence Theorem 3 applies.

We now explain how Weighted-Degree Constrained k-Outconnected/k-Inconnected Subgraph is related to our problem. We may assume that we know the maximum number k of trees, by applying binary search in the range $0, \ldots, nq$ where

$$q = \max_{v \in V} \frac{b(v)}{\min\{w(e) : e \in \delta_E(v), w(e) > 0\}} .$$

Indeed, if G contains an arborescence of weight 0, then k is infinite. Otherwise, every arborescence contains a node v that uses an edge $e \in \delta_G(v)$ with $w(e) > 0$. As there are n nodes, this implies the bound $k \leq nq$. As an edge of G may be used several times, add $k - 1$ copies of each edge of G. Equivalently, we may assign to every edge capacity k, and consider the corresponding "capacitated" problems; this will give a polynomial algorithm, rather than a pseudo-polynomial one. For simplicity of exposition, we will present the algorithm in terms of multigraphs, but it can be easily adjusted to capacited graphs.

As has been mentioned, for the Convergecast case checking whether $k \geq 1$ can be done in polynomial time [19]. Now we observe that Theorem 3 implies Theorem 2, as well as a "pseudo-approximation" algorithm for Weighted-Degree Constrained k-Outconnected/k-Inconnected Subgraph:

Corollary 2. *For* Weighted-Degree Constrained k-Outconnected/k-Inconnected Subgraph *there exists a polynomial time algorithm that either correctly establishes that the polytope P_k is empty, or finds a k-outconnected subgraph H that violates the energy constraints by a factor at most β, namely*

$$\sum_{e \in \delta_H(v)} w(e) \leq \beta \cdot b(v) \quad \text{for all } v \in V . \tag{5}$$

The above corollary immediately implies Theorem 2. We show how to derive from it also Theorem 1. Assuming we know k (binary search), The algorithm as in Theorem 1 is as follows:

1. Set $b(v) \leftarrow b(v)/\beta$ for all $v \in V$, where β is as in Corollary 2.
2. Compute a k-outconnected from r in the case of broadcast, and k-inconnected to r in the case of convergecast, spanning subgraph H of G using the algorithm as in Corollary 2.

   In the case of Mixedcast, H is the union of a k-inconnected to r and γk-outconnected from r spanning subgraphs H_{in} and H_{out}.

For the approximation ratio, all we need to prove is that if the original instance admits a k-outconnected/k-inconnected subgraph, then the new instance with weighted-degree bounds $b(v)/\beta$ admits an ℓ-outconnected/ℓ-inconnected spanning subgraph with $\ell = \lfloor k/\beta^2 \rfloor$, and is of low cost. This is achieved via the following lemma.

Lemma 1. *Let $H_k = (V, F)$ be a k-outconnected from r (k-inconnected to r) directed graph with costs $\{c(e) : e \in F\}$ and weights $\{w(e) : e \in F\}$. Then for any $\ell \leq k$ the graph H_k contains an ℓ-outconnected from r (an ℓ-inconnected to r) spanning subgraph H_ℓ so that $c(H_\ell) \leq c(H_k) \cdot (\alpha\ell/k)$ and so that $w(\delta_{H_\ell}(v)) \leq w(\delta_{H_k}(v)) \cdot (\beta\ell/k)$ for all $v \in V$.*

Substituting $\ell = \lfloor k/\beta^2 \rfloor$ in Lemma 1 and observing that $\alpha \cdot \lfloor k/\beta^2 \rfloor/k \leq 1$ in all cases, we obtain:

Corollary 3. *Let H be a k-outconnected from r (k-inconnected to r) directed graph with edge weights $\{w(e) : e \in F\}$. Then H contains a subgraph H' so that H' is $\lfloor k/\beta^2 \rfloor$-outconnected from r ($\lfloor k/\beta^2 \rfloor$-inconnected to r), $c(H') \leq c(H)$, and $w(\delta_{H'}(v)) \leq w(\delta_H(v))/\beta$ for all $v \in V$.*

Except the Mixedcast part, Theorem 1 is easily deduced from Corollaries 2 and 3. For Mixedcast, note that $\beta = \beta_{in} + \beta_{out}$, where β_{in} and β_{out} are the parameters in Theorem 1 for Convergecast and Broadcast, respectively. From Lemma 1, we obtain that if H_k is k-outconnected from r and γk-inconnected to r, then H_k contains two spanning subgraphs: H_{out} that is ℓ-outconnected from r and H_{in} that is $\gamma\ell$-inconnected to r satisfying:

$$w(\delta_{H_{in}}(v)) + w(\delta_{H_{out}}(v)) \leq w(\delta_H(v)) \cdot \beta_{out} \cdot (\ell/k) + w(\delta_H(v)) \cdot \beta_{in} \cdot (\gamma\ell/\gamma k)$$
$$= w(\delta_H(v)) \cdot (\ell/k) \cdot (\beta_{out} + \beta_{in}) = w(\delta_H(v)) \cdot (\beta\ell/k) .$$

Then, similarly to Corollary 3, we deduce that if H is k-outconnected from r and γk-inconnected to r, then H contains a subgraph H' so that H' is $\lfloor k/\beta^2 \rfloor$-outconnected from r and $\lfloor \gamma k/\beta^2 \rfloor$-inconnected to r, $c(H') \leq c(H)$, and $w(\delta_{H'}(v)) \leq w(\delta_H(v))/\beta$ for all $v \in V$.

4   Partial Level Aggregation Convergecast

In the problem of Partial Level Aggregation Convergecast we want to find a tree T of G directed towards the root node r that satisfies the energy constraints $\sum w(\delta_T(v)) \leq \frac{b(v)}{level(v)}$ for all $v \in V$, where $level(v)$ is the length of the longest path between v and its descendant in T. We consider the following cases.

- **Uniform initial batteries.** In this case, we note that the optimal solution is achieved by the tree of minimal depth (in regard to tree's root). We can find such tree by choosing every vertex to serve as the root, building the BFS tree starting at the chosen vertex, and picking up the tree of minimal depth. The total time complexity of the proposed algorithm is $O(|V|(|V| + |E|))$. Notice, that the problem becomes NP-complete when we are aiming to find the tree of maximal depth (HAMILTONIAN PATH).

- **Arbitrary initial batteries.** The simplest way to do is to use the above mentioned algorithm and to obtain $B_{\max}/B_{\min}$ approximate solution, where $B_{\max} = \max_{v \in V} b(v)$ and $B_{\min} = \min_{v \in V} b(v)$. We mention that for the case of complete graph, the optimal solution is the star, rooted at the node with minimal battery charge.

We can slightly change the definition of the problem in order to introduce the notion of weighted edges. To reflect this change, we transform the energy constraint to be $\sum w(\delta_T(v)) \leq \frac{b(v)}{w(e_1)+w(e_2)+...+w(e_h)}$, where $w(e_i)$ is the weight of the edge e_i located on the most energy consumed path between v and its descendant in T. For arbitrary initial batteries and arbitrary edge weights we will use the construction based on Hamiltonian circuit and presented at Elkin et al. [1] where G is the complete graph. The authors at [1] have shown how to construct a spanning tree T of G that has a bounded hop-diameter of $O(n/\rho + \log \rho)$ with $w(e_T^*) = O(\rho^2 w(e^*))$, where e_T^* and e^* are the longest edges in T and the MST of G, respectively. The tightness of the tradeoff has been also established in [1]. Following this, the best approximation factor that can be given for this problem is $\Omega(n)$ which is achieved by $\rho = 1$.

References

1. Elkin, M., Lando, Y., Nutov, Z., Segal, M., Shpungin, H.: Novel algorithms for the network lifetime problem in wireless settings. In: ADHOC-NOW, pp. 425–438 (2008)
2. Pahlavan, K., Levesque, A.H.: Wireless information networks. Wiley-Interscience, Hoboken (1995)
3. Krumke, S.O., Liu, R., Lloyd, E.L., Marathe, M.V., Ramanathan, R., Ravi, S.S.: Topology control problems under symmetric and asymmetric power thresholds. In: Pierre, S., Barbeau, M., Kranakis, E. (eds.) ADHOC-NOW 2003. LNCS, vol. 2865, pp. 187–198. Springer, Heidelberg (2003)
4. Ramanathan, R., Hain, R.: Topology control of multihop wireless networks using transmit power adjustment. In: INFOCOM 2000, pp. 404–413 (2000)
5. Deb, B., Nath, B.: On the node-scheduling approach to topology control in ad hoc networks. In: ACM MOBIHOC, pp. 14–26 (2005)
6. ElBatt, T.A., Ephremides, A.: Joint scheduling and power control for wireless ad-hoc networks. In: IEEE INFOCOM, pp. 976–984 (2002)
7. Wieselthier, J.E., Nguyen, G.D., Ephremides, A.: Algorithms for energy-effcient multicasting in static ad hoc wireless networks. ACM MONET 6(3), 251–263 (2001)
8. Chang, J., Tassiulas, L.: Maximum lifetime routing in wireless sensor networks. IEEE/ACM Transaction on Networking 12(4), 609–619 (2004)
9. Floréen, P., Kaski, P., Kohonen, J., Orponen, P.: Exact and approximate balanced data gathering in energy-constrained sensor networks. Theor. Comp. Sci. 344(1), 30–46 (2005)
10. Hong, B., Prasanna, V.K.: Maximum lifetime data sensing and extraction in energy constrained networked sensor systems. J. Parallel and Distributed Computing 66(4), 566–577 (2006)
11. Kalpakis, K., Dasgupta, K., Namjoshi, P.: Efficient algorithms for maximum lifetime data gathering and aggregation in wireless sensor networks. Computer Networks 42(6), 697–716 (2003)

12. Ordonez, F., Krishnamachari, B.: Optimal information extraction in energy-limited wireless sensor networks. IEEE Journal on Selected Areas in Communications 22(6), 1121–1129 (2004)
13. Xue, Y., Cui, Y., Nahrstedt, K.: Maximizing lifetime for data aggregation in wireless sensor networks. Mobile Networks and Applications 10, 853–864 (2005)
14. Park, J., Sahni, S.: Maximum lifetime broadcasting in wireless networks. IEEE Transactions on Computers 54(9), 1081–1090 (2005)
15. Schrijver, A.: Combinatorial Optimization Polyhedra and Efficiency. Springer, Heidelberg (2004)
16. Gonzalez, T.F. (ed.): Handbook on Approximation Algorithms and Metaheuristics. Chapman & Hall/CRC, Boca Raton (2007)
17. Nutov, Z.: Approximating maximum integral flows in wireless sensor networks via weighted-degree constrained k-flows. In: DIALM-POMC, pp. 29–34 (2008)
18. Orda, A., Yassour, B.A.: Maximum-lifetime routing algorithms for networks with omnidirectional and directional antennas. In: MobiHoc 2005, pp. 426–437 (2005)
19. Segal, M.: Fast algorithm for multicast and data gathering in wireless networks. Information Processing Letters 107(1), 29–33 (2008)
20. Stanford, J., Tongngam, S.: Approximation algorithm for maximum lifetime in wireless sensor networks with data aggregation. In: SNPD 2006, pp. 273–277 (2006)
21. Garg, N., Könemann, J.: Faster and simpler algorithms for multicommodity flow and other fractional packing problems. In: FOCS 1998, pp. 300–309 (1998)
22. von Rickenbach, P., Wattenhofer, R.: Gathering correlated data in sensor networks. In: DIALM-POMC, pp. 60–66 (2004)
23. Buragohain, C., Agrawal, D., Suri, S.: Power aware routing for sensor databases. In: INFOCOM, pp. 1747–1757 (2005)
24. Liang, W., Liu, Y.: Online data gathering for maximizing network lifetime in sensor networks. IEEE Transactions on Mobile Computing 6(1), 2–11 (2007)
25. Nutov, Z.: Approximating directed weighted-degree constrained networks. In: APPROX, pp. 219–232 (2008)
26. Lewin-Eytan, L.J., Naor, (Seffi) J., Orda, A.: Maximum-lifetime routing: system optimization & game-theoretic perspectives. In: ACM Mobihoc, pp. 160–169 (2007)
27. Edmonds, J.: Matroid intersection. Annals of discrete Mathematics 4, 185–204 (1979)

On Active Attacks on Sensor Network Key Distribution Schemes

Stefan Dziembowski*, Alessandro Mei**, and Alessandro Panconesi***

University of Rome *La Sapienza*

Abstract. This paper concerns sensor network key distribution schemes (KDS) based on symmetric-key techniques. We analyze the problem of active attacks against such schemes. By active attacks we mean those attacks, where the adversary can maliciously disturb the communication between the sensors. We observe that the active adversary that captured even a small number of sensors, can anyway get a full control over the network, no matter how strong the KDS is. Therefore we conclude that the best scheme in this context is the one based on the method of Blöm (1984) (which guarantees perfect secrecy of the keys, as long as the number of corrupted sensors is small).

1 Introduction

Wireless sensor networks (WSNs) are a new promising technology that emerged a few years ago. A WSN consist of a large number of intelligent nodes which are low-cost, low-power and small. Their goal is to produce globally meaningful information from local data obtained by individual nodes. A typical node is equipped with a sensing unit (for temperature, light, sound, vibration, stress, weight, pressure, humidity, etc., depending on the application), a weak wireless link and processor with a small amount of memory. It is powered by a small battery that will usually not be replaced when it gets exhausted. WSNs have one or more points of control called *base stations*, which are nodes that are orders of magnitude more powerful and often serve as an interface to some other networks. In a typical application the sensors connect to each other to communicate the outcomes of their measurements. Later they may send some statistics about these values to the base station (this is called *in-network processing* [7]), or perform some actions depending on the messages that he received (this is called *in-network control* [14]). The principal characteristics of the WSNs, that make them different from the other types of networks, are: (1) *low computing power*: the total amount of processor cycles that a given sensor can use during its lifetime is severely constrained (because the computation costs energy); hence the sensors are not able to perform a large number of cryptographic public-key operations (like public-key encryption, or digital signatures);

---

* Supported by the European Research Council *Starting Grant*, Project Number: 207908. Part of this work was done when this author was receiving a Marie-Curie Fellowship 2006-024300-CRYPTOSENSORS.

** Partially funded by the FP7 EU project "SENSEI, Integrating the Physical with the Digital World of the Network of the Future", Grant Agreement Number 215923, www.ict-sensei.org.

*** Supported by *Progetto FIRB Italia-Israele*.

S. Dolev (Ed.): ALGOSENSORS 2009, LNCS 5804, pp. 52–63, 2009.

(2) *limited communication capability*: since transmitting information costs energy also the total amount of data that the sensor can send during its lifetime is small; (3) *limited transmission range*: since each sensor's wireless link has range that covers only a limited number of other nodes, the sensors can communicate with each other only if the distance between them is small, and therefore every sensor has only few neighbors in the network; (4) *small memory*: in order to keep the prices of the sensors low, the manufacturers usually equip it only with small memory; (5) *lack of tamper-resistance*: since tamper resistant hardware is expensive to construct, the sensor are usually easy to reverse-engineer, i.e., anybody who captures a sensor may get a full information about its internal state; (6) *mobility and unknown topology*: in many cases the sensors frequently change their physical positions, moreover, even if the network is static, its topology may be unknown at the moment of the deployment (the sensor may be even distributed in a random way: e.g. they may be dropped from an airplane).

In many cases sensor networks have to be designed with security in mind. In particular, one often has to guarantee that the messages exchanged between the sensors remain *secret* even if the adversary eavesdrops on the communication between the nodes. In practice, however, we usually have to deal with stronger attacks in which the adversary may also be able disturb the behavior of the network by introducing fake messages, or modifying the legitimate ones. In many applications guaranteeing integrity of the output produced by the network is actually more important than its secrecy. This is especially true when the data that the network collects is anyway available publicly (like e.g. the temperature, or air pressure), and the main goal of the adversary may be to alter the outcome of the measurement.

Some papers already considered the problem of active attacks. In particular, some of them [4,13] proposed schemes that included mechanisms for message authentication- which is a technique that allows a node in the network to ensure that a given message M, that supposedly originates from some other node P_i, really comes from P_i. However, up to our knowledge, none of them fully analyzed the problem of active attacks. This is quite unfortunate, since in general security against an active adversary is trickier and harder to analyze than the one against the passive (eavesdropping only) adversary. In this paper we discuss the problem of active attacks against the sensor-network key distribution schemes (focusing on the problem of message authentication), and we evaluate security of the existing protocols. Our conclusion is that, when the active attacks are considered, the most appropriate scheme is the scheme of Blöm [2].

Organization of the paper. In the next section we provide a short introduction to the key distribution in sensor networks. Then, in Sect. 3, we describe informally the security issues related to the active attacks on the key distribution schemes, and we argue that the scheme of Blöm is more suitable when such attacks are considered. The formal definitions are provided in Sect. 4, and the scheme (based on the one of Blöm) is constructed in Sect. 5.

2   Key Distribution in Sensor Networks

Any secure communication requires a secret cryptographic key. Of course, one cannot simply equip all the sensors (in a given network) with the same key S, since the sensors are not tamper-proof, and therefore by capturing and reverse-engineering one sensor the adversary could learn S. Going to the other extreme, one could give to each sensor P_i a separate key $S_{i,j}$ to communicate with each P_j, but this would be impractical, since it would require each sensor to store large amounts of data, linear in the number of all sensors in the network. Therefore usually a more sophisticated *key distribution scheme (KDS)* is needed. Unfortunately, the standard key-distribution schemes used for other types of networks either require interaction between the nodes and a trusted center (see e.g. [10]), which is too expensive to be implemented on low-powered devices, or rely on energy-consuming public key-techniques, and therefore cannot be used on typical sensors.

The problem of designing key-distribution schemes for the sensor networks attracted a lot of attention over the last couple of years. We will later define the notion of a key-distribution scheme more formally, but for now let us assume that such a scheme consists of (1) a method for distributing the key material between the sensor (a key material of each sensor P_i is called its *key ring*, and denoted S_i), and (2) a protocol that allows pairs (P_i, P_j) of sensors to establish a common secret key $S_{i,j}$ (since we are interested only in symmetric cryptography we will always have $S_{i,j} = S_{j,i}$). In principle, such a protocol could involve a number of steps in which P_i and P_j exchange messages. In this paper, however, for the sake of simplicity, we will assume that (unless explicitly stated otherwise) all the schemes are *non-interactive*, i.e. P_i can compute $S_{i,j}$ just from his key-ring and the identity of P_j. This can be done without loss of generality for the following reasons: (1) most of the interactive schemes can be easily converted to the non-interactive ones (for example in [13,11] it is shown how to remove the need of interaction from the scheme of [6]), and (2) in practical applications, for the efficiency reasons, one would probably anyway consider only the non-interactive schemes. Schemes in which every pair of sensors is able to establish such a common key will be called *complete*. We will say that a scheme is *t-resilient* if each key $S_{i,j}$ remains secret even if an adversary captured less than t sensor and learned their key rings (of course, we have to assume that he did not capture P_i and P_j).

In general, the existing approaches for constructing the KDS's can be divided in two classes. The first class originates from a method proposed in a different context in [2] and relies on simple linear-algebraic tools. For any parameter t it allows to construct a complete t-resilient scheme in which the key ring of each sensor is of a size $\alpha \cdot t$, where α is the length of each $S_{i,j}$ (all $S_{i,j}$'s are of equal length). If the adversary captures t sensors then the security of the [2] scheme breaks down entirely, as from the key rings of any t sensors one can compute the key rings of all the remaining ones. In [1] it was shown that the scheme of [2] is optimal in the class of complete schemes, in the following sense: in every complete t-resilient key KDS the size of the key ring needs to be at least $\alpha \cdot t$.

The second class of such methods derives from the first paper that explicitly considered the problem of key distribution in sensor networks [6]. The key idea is to relax the requirement of *completeness* and *t-resiliency*, so that the lower bound of [1] does not hold. More precisely, [6], and the follow-up papers [3,15,13] construct *β-incomplete γ-partially-resilient* schemes, where *β-incompleteness* means that for a randomly chosen pair (P_i, P_j) of distinct sensors the probability that P_i and P_j can establish a common key $S_{i,j}$ is equal to β (which may be less than 1), and γ-*partial-resiliency* means that for a randomly chosen pair (P_i, P_j) of distinct sensors the probability that P_i and P_j can establish a common key $S_{i,j}$ *and* this key remains secret for the adversary, is equal to γ, which, of course, is usually a function $\gamma(x)$ of the number x of captured sensors.

The scheme of [2] can be viewed as a special case of such a generalized notion, if we set $\beta := 1$, and $\gamma(x)$ equal to

$$\gamma_{\mathsf{Blom}}^t(x) := \begin{cases} 1 \text{ if } x < t \\ 0 \text{ otherwise.} \end{cases} \tag{1}$$

In [6] it is shown how to construct a scheme with $\beta \in (0, 1)$ and γ being some function, slowly decreasing to 0. Let us now compare the scheme of [6] with a t-resilient scheme of [2]. Clearly, as long as the number x of captured sensors is below the the threshold t, the scheme of [2] is better than the one of [6]. However, for $x \geq t$ the scheme of [6] beats [2], as it can still offer a certain degree of security, while [2] is broken completely. It was argued in [6] that the problem of the incompleteness of the scheme can be bypassed by the routing techniques: if two sensors are not able to establish a common key they can always ask some other sensors to route the messages for them.

Encryption. Of course, key distribution is just a first step in constructing cryptographic protocols in which the $S_{i,j}$'s are used. For example, $S_{i,j}$'s may be treated as keys for symmetric encryption—in this case we can define an *encryption-key distribution scheme* (denoted *Enc-KDS*) as a functionality that consists of the following procedures:

1. a procedure for distributing key material among the sensors (let S_i denote the key material of a sensor P_i), and
2. for a pair (P_i, P_j) of sensors a procedure $Enc_{i,j}$ that, given a key ring S_i of P_i and any message M, produces a ciphertext $C = Enc_{i,j}(S_i, M)$. This procedure is executed by P_i. The ciphertext C can later be decrypted by sensor P_j using a procedure $Dec_{i,j}$. We should always have $Dec_{i,j}(S_j, C) = M$.
   In case of the incomplete schemes such a procedure may exist only for certain subset of the set of all the pairs of sensors.

Typically, Enc-KDS is constructed on top of a KDS scheme in a following straight-forward way. Let Θ be a KDS and let (E, D) be some standard symmetric encryption scheme, where $C = E_K(M)$ denotes a result of encrypting M with a key K, and $D_K(C)$ denotes the result of decrypting C with key K. Then, one can construct an Enc-KDS, where (1) the key material $S_1, \ldots, S_w$ is distributed in the same way as in Θ; (2) in order to compute $Enc_{i,j}(S_i, M)$ the sensor P_i first calculates $S_{i,j}$ (as in Θ) and then sets $Enc_{i,j}(S_i, M) := E_{S_{i,j}}(M)$; and (3) in order to compute $Dec_{i,j}(S_j, C)$ the sensor P_j calculates $S_{i,j}$ and then sets $Dec_{i,j}(S_j, C) = D_{S_{i,j}}(C)$.

Authentication. It was suggested in some papers [4,13] that in a similar way one can achieve message authentication, by combining a KDS with a *message authentication code* (MAC) scheme. Recall that MAC is a scheme that consists of (1) a procedure Auth that, given a secret key K and a message M produces a *tag* $T = \mathsf{Auth}_K(M)$, and (2) a procedure Ver that given a key K, a message M and a tag T verifies if T is a valid tag for M under the key K (see [9], or [5] for a formal definition). Obviously the keys $S_{i,j}$ distributed in the KDS can be used as keys for a MAC. A resulting scheme will be called a *MAC-key distribution scheme*. Formal security definition of a MAC-KDS appears in Sect. 4.

3   Active vs. Passive Security of the Key Distribution Schemes

So far we did not say anything about the security of the Enc- and MAC-KDS schemes. To reason formally about it we use a notion of an *adversary* that attacks the scheme and we define what is his goal and what he is allowed to do in order to achieve it, i.e. what is the attack model. We will provide such a definition in Sect. 4. For now, let us just discuss it informally. First, for the purpose of this discussion, assume that the goal of the adversary is simply to guess as many keys $S_{i,j}$ as he can: clearly if the adversary knows $S_{i,j}$ then he can decrypt the messages sent between P_i and P_j (if $S_{i,j}$ is used for encryption), or fabricate messages (if $S_{i,j}$ is used for authentication), although of course there may also exist other (than just guessing the keys) ways of breaking the protocol. The definition of the attack model depends on the type of a scheme whose security we are considering. When defining security of the Enc-KDS schemes we can restrict ourselves to an adversary that is only *passive*, i.e. he is only allowed to:

1. selectively capture some sensors, and learn all their internal data, including their key material, and the entire history of the execution (we will also say that a sensor was *corrupted* by the adversary, and otherwise we will call him *honest*),
2. eavesdrop all the messages sent by the sensors.

In case of the MAC-KDS schemes we should consider an adversary that is *active*, i.e., besides of capturing some sensors, and passively listening to the messages sent between the remaining ones, he has also the ability to interfere with the transmission. In other words, additionally to what is described in Points 1 and 2 above, he can

3. prevent some messages from arriving, and
4. fabricate new messages, send them to the honest sensors.

Note, that such an adversary can simulate also other attacks that are not explicitly mentioned above. For example, our adversary can alter any message M sent between two sensors (P_0 and P_1, say) in the following way. Suppose that his goal is to modify M by transforming it into some $\xi(M)$. He can achieve it by (a) intercepting M (he can do it by Point 2 above), (b) preventing M from arriving to P_1 (see Point 3), and (c) fabricating $M' := \xi(M)$ and sending it to P_1 (Point 4).

As another example consider an attack in which the adversary "takes control over some sensor P_i". This can be simulated as follows. First, the adversary captures P_i (Point 1). Then, he starts blocking all the messages that P_i may send (Point 3). At the same time he starts simulating P_i, controlling his execution in an arbitrary way. Observe that (by Point 2) he can eavesdrop all the messages that are sent to P_i, and forward them to his simulated copy of P_i. He can also fabricate messages claiming that they come from P_i (Point 4).

Our approach is different from the one used in the practitioners' community, where it is common to design protocols that are secure against one particular class of active attacks. One example of such a class are the so-called *Sybil attacks*, where a single node may present multiple identities to the other sensors in the network (such additional identities are called the *Sybil nodes*). Other types of active attacks that were considered in the literature include the *sinkhole attacks*, *wormhole attacks*, *replay attacks*, etc. (see e.g. [8]) All of these attacks can be easily simulated by our adversary.

Our, more general approach has the following advantages. First, Points 2–4 correspond to a real-life attack scenario where an adversary is equipped with a laptop and an antenna (such an attack was already described in [8]). Using this tools he may easily eavesdrop and disturb the communication in the network by inserting new messages, or preventing the legitimate ones from arriving to the destination by jamming the communication. Hence, we follow a good tradition in cryptography of being prudent by granting the adversary in the formal model as much power as he can realistically obtain in real life.

Moreover, a formal security framework allows us to give a precise evaluation of the protocols that we construct. Many previous papers in this area used just informal descriptions of the threat model, which in some cases led to ad-hoc constructions without precise security properties. Consider e.g. the idea of [11] to use random key predistribution to protect against the Sybil attacks. In the protocol of [11] some subset of the sensors jointly verify the identity of another sensor P_i by testing if he knows certain keys from the key pool (call these sensors the *verifiers*). The problem with the solution presented in [11] is that it does not take into account that some of the verifiers may actually also be controlled by the adversary. Such "corrupted verifiers" could e.g. falsely confirm that P_i passed the test, or, which may be even worse, accuse the honest sensors of being the Sybil nodes. Whether this attack is legitimate or not is not clear from the model of [11].

3.1 The Power of Active Attacks

One may wonder what is the additional power of the active attacks. We now argue that active security significantly differs from the passive one. First, observe that if the active attacks are considered, then some of the ideas that were valid in passive scenario break down completely. Consider e.g. the suggestion of [6] to route the messages between sensors that cannot establish a key, via some other sensors. An active adversary can simply capture a small number of sensors, make virtual copies of them (in his laptop, say), and then, by impersonating the captured sensors, volunteer to route the messages between any two parties that are not able to establish a key. Clearly, we can assume that the attacker has a more powerful antenna then the sensors, so he is able to jam messages from any legitimate sensors that may also want to do routing. In this way the system becomes completely broken. Of course the fact that the simple routing does not work in this context does not mean that the entire approach based on [6] fails, as there may exist applications that do not require the network to be complete. It is however unclear how to create them without using public-key cryptography. The second difference is more fundamental. We describe it below.

How Many Corruptions Can We Tolerate? Let $\mathcal{P}$ be the set of all sensors in the network, and let w be the degree of every node in the network (for simplicity assume that the network graph is regular). Suppose we use the strongest KDS possible, i.e. every sensor P_i is simply equipped with a separate key $S_{i,j}$ to communicate with any other sensor P_j (call it: a *perfect* KDS). As we argued in Sect. 2 such a scheme is too memory-consuming to be practical, but assume for a moment that we use it, just for the sake of this argument. Now, assume that the adversary corrupted some random set $\mathcal{P}'$ of sensors (let $x := |\mathcal{P}'|$). Thus, the adversary knows the keys $\mathcal{S}' = \{S_{i,j}$ such that $P_i \in \mathcal{P}'$ and $P_j \in \mathcal{P}\}$. Of course if the adversary is passive then the only damage that he can do is that he can decrypt the messages encrypted with the keys in $\mathcal{S}'$, which he trivially knows anyway (since he corrupted the sensors that know this values).

The situation in case of the *active* security is very different. Suppose, e.g., that the sensors connect to their neighbors in order to learn the output of their measurements. Now, assume that the keys $S_{i,j}$ are used for the message authentication. Let P_{i_0} be some sensor, and let $\mathcal{W}$ be the set of its neighbors. The active adversary can simply create "virtual copies" of the sensors from $\mathcal{P}'$, pretend that they are the "new" neighbors of P_{i_0}, and start sending arbitrary messages from them to P_{i_0}, authenticating them with appropriate keys from $\mathcal{S}'$. Moreover, since he fully controls the communication he can jam the messages coming from the "legitimate" neighbors (i.e. those in $\mathcal{W}$). Therefore if $x \geq w$, then the adversary can completely substitute the set of neighbors of P_{i_0}, by the "virtual" sensors that he controls. Of course the adversary may simultaneously perform the same attack against many other honest sensors, not just against P_{i_0}, and hence he may take a total control over the network! Let us now look at some possible remedies for this problem and discuss why in most of the cases they fail.

Detection of the change of neighbors. One natural idea may be to instruct the sensors to take special actions when the set of their neighbors changes rapidly. This idea may work in some cases, however it breaks down completely in case of the mobile networks, where the neighbors change frequently. Also, the adversary may choose to slowly substitute the legitimate neighbors with the "virtual" ones. Since the sensors are anyway expected to die at some point, because of the battery exhaustion, this will not raise any alarm.

Node replication detection. One could also think about introducing a mechanism in which the honest sensors jointly detect if a given sensor does not claim to be a neighbor of too many of them at the same time. This is called *node replication detection*, and there exist techniques for achieving it [11,12]. Unfortunately the techniques of [11] (see Sect. 2.2) assume that the sensors can connect to the trusted center (which would trivialize the problem of key distribution), and the techniques of [12] rely on the public-key cryptography, and it is questionable if they can be built just using the symmetric-key cryptography. The main difficulty is that the adversary (that controls some corrupted sensors) may insert false "accusations" against some honest sensors, and it is unclear how to resolve such disputes. Note also that the centralized solutions (e.g. reporting the set of neighbors to the base station) do not work here, since we are interested in schemes that do not rely on the interaction with the base station.

Location-dependent KDS. Another idea that one could consider is to make the key-rings dependent on the geographic location of the sensor. In this way, a corrupted sensor could claim to be a neighbor of only those sensors that are physically close to him. This of course would require the network to be completely static and the positions of the sensors would need to be known before the network is deployed. In such a case, however, much simpler solutions exist: instead of inventing a sophisticated key distribution scheme just give to each sensor a separate key to communicate to each of its neighbors (which are known beforehand).

In Sect. 3 we argued that the assumption that the adversary fully controls the communication corresponds to a practical attack when the attacker is equipped with a laptop and an antenna. Hence, one could consider the following countermeasure against the attack described above: let each sensor listen to all the messages he can hear, and verify that the sensor that claims to be his neighbor does not claim to be a neighbor of too many other sensors in the network. Of course, the need of receiving and analyzing the messages would increase the energy consumption. Moreover, this countermeasure works only if the adversary has just one static antenna that is used for broadcasting messages to all the sensors in the network. This method fails if the adversary can change the physical location of his antenna and decrease the strength of the signal, so that only the sensor that are close can hear it. He may also use several weaker antennas, or he can distribute his own sensors that would serve as "relay stations". This should be quite economical, as it is believed that the main advantage of the sensor networks will actually be the low prices of the sensors.

So far, we assumed that the scheme that we use is perfect (i.e. every sensor P_i knows an independent key $S_{i,j}$ to communicate with each P_j). In this paper we are interested in schemes that are not perfect, and hence may be partially resilient and incomplete. Clearly, partial resiliency may only help the adversary, and therefore the attack described above remains valid (actually, as we show in the next section partial resiliency causes even some additional problems). Let us now assume that the scheme is β-incomplete. This means that, in particular, each sensor P_{i_0} can establish a connection with (on average) $\beta \cdot w$ of its neighbors. On the other hand, also (on average) $\beta \cdot x$ sensors, out of x sensors that the adversary corrupted, can establish a connection with P_{i_0}. Thus if $\beta \cdot x \geq \beta \cdot w$ (which is trivially equivalent to $x \geq w$), then again the adversary can substitute the honest neighbors of P_{i_0} with the sensors controlled by him. Hence we get the following.

Moral 1. *In case of active security it makes sense to consider only adversaries that corrupt less than w sensors.*

A Problem with Partial Resiliency. In this section we argue that in case of the partially resilient incomplete schemes the situation gets even worse than what was described in Sect. 3.1. Suppose we have some γ-partially-resilient β-incomplete KDS, and assume that the adversary corrupted some number x of sensors. The difference $\beta - \gamma(x)$ corresponds to a probability that a link between two sensors exists and it is broken, and, of course, the smaller it is, the better for us. Let now ask the following question: how large difference between β and $\gamma(x)$ can we tolerate? We now argue that the answer is very different for the passive and for the active security.

Clearly in case of a passive adversary even large values of $\beta - \gamma(x)$ can still be tolerated. For example if $\beta = 60\%$ and $\gamma(x) = 40\%$ then the adversary can eavesdrop on average only on $(\beta - \gamma(x))/\beta = 1/3$ links, which for some applications may be still be acceptable.

Now, let us examine the case of active security. Again, consider some sensor P_{i_0}, let $\mathcal{W}$ be the set of its neighbors, and let $w = |\mathcal{W}|$. Clearly P_{i_0} can directly communicate with $\beta \cdot w$ sensors (on average). However, the set of sensors that could potentially communicate with P_{i_0}, if they were its neighbors, is much larger, and on average equal to $\beta \cdot n$. Out of this set, there are on average $(\beta - \gamma(x)) \cdot n$ sensors P_j that can communicate with P_{i_0}, *but* the adversary knows the key S_{j,i_0}. Hence the adversary can do the following.

1. Determine[1] the set $\mathcal{P}''$ of sensors such that for every $P_j \in \mathcal{P}''$ the adversary knows S_{j,i_0}. As we argued before the expected size of $\mathcal{P}''$ is $(\beta - \gamma(x)) \cdot n$.
2. For each $P_j \in \mathcal{P}''$ create a "virtual copy" of it, and claim to P_{i_0} that it is his new neighbor. Since the adversary knows S_{j,i_0} he can easily impersonate P_j, and send (in his name) to P_{i_0} any message he wants. He can also jam the communication of P_{i_0} with the legitimate neighbors.

Hence, if $(\beta - \gamma(x)) \cdot n \geq \beta \cdot w$ then the adversary can replace all the honest neighbors of P_{i_0} with the sensors controlled by him. Of course, as in Sect. 3.1, he can perform the same attack not just against not just against P_{i_0}, but against all the sensors in the network. Thus we conclude with the following.

Moral 2. *In case of active security it makes sense to consider only adversaries that corrupt such a number x of sensors that $\gamma(x) \cdot n$ is smaller than $(\beta - \gamma(x)) \cdot w$.*

For example suppose that $n = 10.000, w = 100$ and $\beta = 50\%$. Even if $\gamma(x)$ is very close to β, say: $\gamma(x) = 49\%$, then the security is broken, since $\beta \cdot w = 50$ and $(\beta - \gamma(x)) \cdot n = 100$. In the full version of this paper [5] we provide an analysis of some of the schemes existing in the literature, showing that, for the realistic values of the parameters the value of $(\beta - \gamma(x)) \cdot n$ is much larger than w.

The bottom-line is that as long as the active security is considered, the right choice of a KDS is simply the original scheme of [2] (see Sect. 2). By setting $t = w$ (where w is the typical number of neighbors of a sensor) we get a scheme that is resilient against an adversary that corrupted less than w sensors (and where the key-ring of each sensor is $w \cdot \alpha$). This should suffice, as, by Moral 1, if the adversary corrupts w sensors then anyway he can take a full control over the network. Hence, no matter how strong our KDS is, the security is in this case completely broken anyway. Of course storing $w \cdot \alpha$ bits may be expensive for larger values of w. However, in most of the applications the size of the sensor's memory needs to be anyway linear in w, since the sensor most likely needs to store some information about each of the neighbors with which it connects.

In the next section we formally define the authentication-key distribution schemes. Then, in Sect. 5 we construct a scheme, based on the method of [2], that is secure in this framework. As we remarked above, we believe that this is the right choice of a MAC-KDS. In the full version of this paper [5] we also analyze possibility of constructing a secure authentication scheme basing on the approach of [6].

---

[1] Clearly, the adversary can compute $\mathcal{P}''$ in polynomial time, unless some special intractability assumptions are introduced.

4   Definition

In this section we give a formal definition of a MAC-KDS. A similar definition was already proposed in [4], however we belive that our approach is slightly simpler. We start with a functional definition. Consider a group of *sensors* $\mathcal{P} = \{P_1, \ldots, P_n\}$. A *MAC-key distribution scheme (MAC-KDS) for* $\mathcal{P}$ is a tuple of algorithms $\Phi = (\text{Distr}, \text{Auth}, \text{Ver})$, where:

- Distr is a randomized algorithm that outputs a sequence $(S_1, \ldots, S_n)$, where each $S_i \in \{0, 1\}^*$ is interpreted as a key ring of P_i.
- Auth is a deterministic algorithm that takes as input a tuple (P_i, P_j, S_i, M) (where $P_i, P_j \in \mathcal{P}$ and $M \in \{0, 1\}^*$) and outputs a *tag* $T \in \{0, 1\}^*$, or a special symbol $\perp$. We will always have that either $\text{Auth}(P_i, P_j, S_i, M) \neq \perp$ for every M, in which case we say that *a link between P_i and P_j exists*, or that $\text{Auth}(P_i, P_j, S_i, M) = \perp$ for every M, in which case we say that a *a link between P_i and P_j does not exist*. Moreover, we require that a link between P_i and P_j exists if and only in a link between P_j and P_i exists.
- Ver is a deterministic algorithm that takes as input a pair (P_i, P_j, S_j, M, T) and outputs OK or $\overline{\text{OK}}$. We require that if a link between P_i and P_j exists, then it always holds that $\text{Ver}(P_i, P_j, S_j, M, T) = \text{OK}$, where $T = \text{Auth}(P_i, P_j, S_i, M)$.

Additionally, the above algorithms take as input a *security parameter* α. We say that Φ is β-incomplete, if the probability that a link between any two distinct sensors exists is equal to β.

The security of KDS was already informally discussed in Sect. 3. In our definitions we will be as pessimistic as we can—i.e. in order to make our definitions stronger, we will give to the adversary as much power as possible. We will be also very generous in defining what counts as the success of the adversary. Our definition will follow a common style in cryptography, namely we will define a game between a polynomial-time (in α) Turing machine $\mathcal{A}$, called an *adversary* and an oracle Υ_Φ. The oracle will internally simulate the execution of the key-distribution scheme Φ. First, the oracle runs Distr to obtain the key-rings $(S_1, \ldots, S_w)$. Then, the adversary attacks the scheme by issuing requests to the oracle. Below we describe the requests that the adversary can issue.

Corruption requests ("*corrupt*"). The adversary can issue less than t requests denoted $corrupt(P_i)$ (where P_i is any sensor). The meaning of this request is that the adversary wants learn the internal state of P_i. The oracle Υ_Φ replies with S_i. This requests can be chosen adaptively, i.e. they can depend on what $\mathcal{A}$ has seen so far.

Authentication request ("*auth*"). As described in Sect. 3 we grant to the adversary power to fully control the communication. To be realistic we should also assume that he can influence the contents of the messages that are sent, e.g. by causing a certain event on which the sensors are supposed to react. To capture this we assume that the adversary may simply perform a *chosen-message attack*, i.e. he may choose the messages that are sent by the honest sensors. Since we can also assume that the adversary can prevent some messages from arriving to destination, when analyzing security we can just restrict ourselves to the messages that the adversary has chosen. We will model this attack by giving the adversary a right to issue a request $auth(P_i, P_j, M)$, to which the oracle replies with $\mathsf{Auth}(P_i, P_j, S_i, M)$.

Testing requests ("_try_"). The adversary is allowed to fabricate any message that he wants, and send it some sensor P_j. By observing the reaction of P_j he may obtain some information about its private data. We model this by allowing $\mathcal{A}$ to issue a request of $try(P_i, P_j, M, T)$ whose meaning is "the adversary wants to know if P_j accepts T as a tag on a message M coming from P_i". The oracle replies with $\mathsf{Ver}(P_i, P_j, S_j, M, T)$. In practical scenarios the adversary may get this information e.g. by sending (M, T) to P_j (claiming it comes from P_i), observing the actions of P_j, and checking if P_j replies with some error message.

Consider some execution of $\mathcal{A}$ against an oracle Υ_Φ. We will say that a link between P_i and P_j is _broken_ if the adversary managed to fabricate _at least one_ message that P_j accepts as originating from P_i, i.e. if he at least once issues a request $try(P_i, P_j, M, T)$ such that the oracle replied OK. To exclude trivial ways of achieving this goal, we require that the adversary never issued any of the following requests: $auth(P_i, P_j, M)$, $auth(P_j, P_i, M)$, $corrupt(P_i)$, and $corrupt(P_j)$. We will say that the scheme is γ-_partially-secure_ if for every x, and for every polynomial-time adversary $\mathcal{A}$ that corrupts less than x sensors we have that

$$P\left(\text{the number of links that exist and are not broken is at most } \gamma(x) \cdot \tfrac{n(n-1)}{2}\right) \quad (2)$$

is negligible[2] in α. We have chosen to multiply $\gamma(x)$ by $\frac{n(n-1)}{2}$ to remain consistent with the notation used in Sect. 2.

5   The Construction Based on the Scheme of [2]

In this section we construct a MAC-KDS scheme Φ^t_{Blom} that is γ^t_{Blom}-secure, where γ^t_{Blom} was defined in Eq. (1). Our construction is based on the scheme of Blöm [2]. The main building blocks are: a _message authentication code_ scheme $\mathsf{MAC} = (\mathsf{MAC.Auth}, \mathsf{Mac.Verify})$ and a hash function H, which will be modeled as a random oracle (this concepts are defined in [9], see also [5]). Let F be a Galois Field $\mathrm{GF}(2^\alpha)$, and let V be an $w \times m$ Vandermonde matrix, over F, i.e.:

$$V = \begin{bmatrix} V_1 \\ \vdots \\ V_w \end{bmatrix} := \begin{bmatrix} 1^0 \; 1^1 \; \cdots \; 1^{m-1} \\ \vdots \\ w^0 \; w^1 \; \cdots \; w^{m-1} \end{bmatrix}$$

The scheme $\Phi_{Blom} = (\mathsf{Blom.Gen}, \mathsf{Blom.Auth}, \mathsf{Blom.Ver})$ is defined as follows.

- The Blom.Gen algorithm first chooses a random symmetric $m \times m$-matrix D with entries in F. Then, it sets $U = (U_1^T, \ldots, U_w^T) := (V \cdot D)^T$. The share of each P_i is U_i.

---

[2] A function μ is negligible if for every $c > 0$ there exists x_0 such that for every $x > x_0$ we have $|\mu(x)| < x^{-c}$.

- The Blom.Auth(P_i, P_j, S_i, M) algorithm first computes $S_{i,j} := U_i \cdot V_i$. Then it outputs MAC.Auth($H(S_{i,j}), M$).
- The Blom.Ver(P_i, P_j, S_j, M, T) algorithm computes $S_{j,i} = U_j \cdot V_j$ and outputs Mac.Verify($H(S_{j,i}), M, T$).

Denote $S := U \cdot V$. Clearly S is symmetric. Hence $S_{i,j} = S_{j,i}$ and the output of Blom.Ver is always OK on the legitimate tags. The original scheme of [2] did not require hashing the key. This is needed in our case, since we use the values $S_{i,j}$ as keys for the MAC, and without hashing our protocol would be vulnerable to the *related key attacks*, sice the keys $S_{i,j}$ would not be independent.

Lemma 1. *The scheme Φ_{Blom} constructed above is γ_{Blom}-secure.*

The proof appears in the full version of this paper [5].

References

1. Bellare, M., Desai, A., Jokipii, E., Rogaway, P.: A concrete security treatment of symmetric encryption. In: FOCS 1997, p. 394 (1997)
2. Blom, R.: An optimal class of symmetric key generation systems. In: Beth, T., Cot, N., Ingemarsson, I. (eds.) EUROCRYPT 1984. LNCS, vol. 209, pp. 335–338. Springer, Heidelberg (1985)
3. Chan, H., Perrig, A., Song, D.: Random key predistribution schemes for sensor networks. In: IEEE Symposium on Security and Privacy (May 2003)
4. Du, W., Deng, J., Han, Y.S., Varshney, P.K., Katz, J., Khalili, A.: A pairwise key predistribution scheme for wireless sensor networks. ACM Transactions on Information and System Security 8(2), 228–258 (2005)
5. Dziembowski, S., Mei, A., Panconesi, A.: On active attacks on sensor network key distribution schemes. full version of this paper (to appear)
6. Eschenauer, L., Gligor, V.D.: A key-management scheme for distributed sensor networks. In: ACM CCS 2002, pp. 41–47 (2002)
7. Heidemann, J., Silva, F., Intanagonwiwat, C., Govindan, R., Estrin, D., Ganesan, D.: Building efficient wireless sensor networks with low-level naming. In: SOSP 2001, pp. 146–159. ACM, New York (2001)
8. Karlof, C., Wagner, D.: Secure routing in wireless sensor networks: attacks and countermeasures. Ad Hoc Networks 1(2-3), 293–315 (2003)
9. Katz, J., Lindell, Y.: Introduction to Modern Cryptography. Chapman & Hall/Crc Cryptography and Network Security Series. Chapman & Hall/ CRC (2007)
10. Neuman, B.C., Ts'o, T.: Kerberos: An authentication service for computer networks. IEEE Communications 32(9), 33–38 (1994)
11. Newsome, J., Shi, E., Song, D., Perrig, A.: The sybil attack in sensor networks: analysis & defenses. In: IPSN 2004, pp. 259–268. ACM, New York (2004)
12. Parno, B., Perrig, A., Gligor, V.: Distributed detection of node replication attacks in sensor networks. In: IEEE Symposium on Security and Privacy, pp. 49–63 (2005)
13. Pietro, R.D., Mancini, L.V., Mei, A.: Energy efficient node-to-node authentication and communication confidentiality in wireless sensor networks. Wirel. Netw. 12(6), 709–721 (2006)
14. Silberstein, A., Yang, J.: Many-to-many aggregation for sensor networks. In: IEEE 23rd International Conference on Data Engineering, 2007. ICDE 2007, pp. 986–995 (2007)
15. Zhu, S., Xu, S., Setia, S., Jajodia, S.: Establishing pairwise keys for secure communication in ad hoc networks: A probabilistic approach. In: ICNP 2003, p. 326 (2003)

Key Levels and Securing Key Predistribution against Node Captures*

Jacek Cichoń, Jarosław Grząślewicz, and Mirosław Kutyłowski

Institute of Mathematics and Computer Science, Wrocław University of Technology, Poland
{jacek.cichon,miroslaw.kutylowski}@pwr.wroc.pl

Abstract. We consider key predistribution schemes deployed for securing communication in ad hoc networks of tiny devices. As node captures are inevitable in these networks and the devices are likely non tamper-proof, an adversary can collect the keys and decrypt some transmissions.

We propose and analyze *key levels* technique that can be used on top of most key predistribution schemes in order to reduce chances of an adversary. The modification does not increase the number of keys loaded into a device, while it increases the computational cost in an insignificant way. Also, it composes well into a framework of adaptive key management allowing to refresh the keys without causing incompatibility problems with the devices holding the old keys. Finally, we show how to reduce the number of keys in a device for random key predistribution by an appropriate construction of the pool of keys.

Keywords: key management, node capture, random key predistribution.

1 Introduction

In this paper we consider securing communication between devices in ad hoc networks. Due to lack of physical protection of radio communication the only way to secure transmissions is to encrypt the messages sent. So each session is started with establishing a session key used throughout the session for encryption.

We assume that the devices are too weak to use asymmetric methods (like Diffie-Hellman or Shamir scheme) and therefore we have to use only computationally weak methods. Since there is no symmetric counterpart of the methods like Diffie-Hellman, either the first transmission between devices is insecure, or some keys are preinstalled and when two devices establish a communication link, they use shared preinstalled keys to derive the session key.

Installing the same keys in all devices is risky, since reverse engineering a single device gives access to the whole communication in the network. In their seminal work [1] Eschenauer and Gligor propose to preinstall a subset of keys in each device:

- There is a pool $\mathcal{K}$ of keys selected at random from the key space.
- Before deploying a device, it receives a random subset of keys from the pool $\mathcal{K}$.
- When two devices wish to establish a secure communication link, they exchange the identifiers of the keys known by them. If they share at least one key from $\mathcal{K}$, they derive a session key from the shared keys.

* Partially supported by EU within the 7th Framework Programme, contract 215270 (FRONTS).

This method reduces security problems that arise due to capture of devices that, by definition, are not tamper resistant. An adversary gets only a subset of keys from the pool from each device and breaking the system takes more time and money.

Chan, Perrig and Song [2] proposed two mechanisms for random key predistribution to address the problem of an adversary capturing nodes: q-composite random key predistribution and connection via multiple paths. The first method works as follows:

- increase the size of subsets of key preinstalled in the devices;
- establish a session key for two devices, only if they share at least q keys from the pool $\mathcal{K}$, the session key must depend on all shared keys.

For a small scale attack it becomes harder to have all q keys at once than a one key. However, if the adversary launches a large scale attack, the situation becomes even worse. This effect is due to the fact that the adversary collects substantially more keys from each corrupted device.

In the second method they propose to use q intermediate devices: nodes A and B find nodes $R_1, \ldots, R_q$ in their neighborhood and establish communication paths: A to R_1 and R_1 to B, then A to R_2 and R_2 to B, $\ldots$, and finally A to R_q and R_q to B. On each of these paths A and B establish a key independently from the other paths. All these keys are XOR-ed in order to get the final session key between A and B. In this case the adversary can break security of the link between A and B if and only if it can break security of all paths. The main disadvantage of this solution is necessity of a certain density of the network, as well as a higher communication volume.

Situation is much easier when locations of the nodes are known in advance (at least approximately). Then one can assign a key only to certain nodes in the area assigned to this key. In such a case a key compromise is only a local problem and does not affect any node outside the key area. On the other hand, this helps to decrease the number of keys held by each device. For some details see for instance [3,4]. One can also try to divide the devices into (intersecting) groups so that the communication will be always within a certain group. Both approaches fail in case of mobility and unsupervised systems.

One can also design predistribution schemes where the keys are assigned not at random, but using sophisticated schemes. The goal is to improve the probability of sharing a key by two nodes (see e.g. the scheme [5] based on Blom's idea [6]) – and thereby reduce the number of key in a device. Further improvements can be achieved when we take into account that we may build a specific infrastructure from the nodes of the network in order to facilitate key establishment (see e.g. [7]).

Problem Statement and Results. Our goal is to improve security of the previous key predistribution schemes without increasing communication volume as well as size of the subsets of the keys held by the devices. We get the following results:

- We present a generic *key levels* and *tree construction* methods that can be used on top of almost all mechanisms designed so far improving them in a cheap way.
- We show that with key levels technique it is easy to include adaptiveness in random key predistribution, so that an adversary is forced to capture the devices continuously in order to compromise communication in the network.
- We show how to reduce the number of keys held by a device for random key predistribution by an appropriate construction of the pool of keys (*zigzag construction*).

2   Key Layers Scheme

Our first idea is that each key K from the pool $\mathcal{K}$ corresponds to multiple variants of K. Namely, instead of K we use keys $K_1, K_2, \ldots$, where

$$K_1 = K \quad \text{and} \quad K_{i+1} = G(K_i) \quad \text{for } i = 2, 3, \ldots \qquad (1)$$

and G is a secure one-way function (see [8]). The key K_i is called then the i-level version of K. Also, we may use a trap-door function G such as encryption with a public key (provided that encryption is computationally easy). The later method is suited for dynamic solutions as discussed in Sect. 6, where we need a trap-door to derive K_i from K_{i+1}.

The Key Layers Scheme uses a pool $\mathcal{K}$ of n keys, each of them is a key of level 1. The Key Layers Scheme is a L-level scheme, if we use L levels of each of these keys.

Key Predistribution. For each device A we install the keys in the following way:

– choose a subset $S_A \subset \mathcal{K}$ of cardinality m at random;
– for each $K \in S_A$ choose $l \in \{1, \ldots, L\}$ according to some probability distribution $\mathcal{P}$ independently of the choices made for the other keys. Then install K_l in A.

Establishing a Shared Key for Devices A and B. The following steps are executed:

1. for each key K_i held by A, device A sends to B the identifier of K and level index i; device B behaves in the same way,
2. if A and B have versions of the same key K, say K_i and K_j, then both A and B insert $K_{\max(i,j)}$ into a list J of shared keys,
3. A and B determine the session key as $H(J, A, B, I)$, where H is a secure hash function and I is a session identifier.

Note that if A holds K_i, B holds K_j and $j > i$, then A can compute K_j using equality (1), while on the other hand B is unable to derive K_i, since it would mean inverting a one-way function.

Also note that i need not to be sent in clear: instead of sending i station A can send some leading bits of $H(K_i, A, B)$, where H is a secure hash function. Then B can try to find it on the list of leading bits of $H(K_j, A, B)$, $H(K_{j+1}, A, B)$, $\ldots$. The index $j + \delta$, where there is such a coincidence indicates with high probability that $i = j + \delta$. If there is no coincidence, then $j = \max\{i, j\}$.

Main Idea. Enhancing security is based on the following simple trick. Assume that the number of levels is 2 and A and B both know K_1. If the adversary captures a device containing K_1, then A and B are exposed to the adversary. However, the adversary might be unlucky and capture a device with version K_2 of the key K. So with the same number of keys held by each device, the adversary may be unable to break some links.

3   Single Key Case

First we consider the case when a connection is based on a single key from the pool $\mathcal{K}$ shared by devices A and B, and that $L = 2$, i.e. each key occurs on two levels. Assume that during predistribution key levels are chosen according to distribution $\mathcal{P}$, i.e. $\Pr(K_1) = p$ and $\Pr(K_2) = 1 - p$ for a key K.

Assume that A, B and the adversary Mallet get a version of the same key K, but the choice of levels is independent. In this case Mallet is unable to break encryption of the link established by A and B if and only if A and B use K_1 and Mallet has got K_2. This occurs with probability $f(p) = p^2(1 - p)$. It is easy to see that the maximum of this function is reached for $p = \frac{2}{3}$. Note that $f(\frac{1}{2}) = \frac{1}{8}$ and $f(\frac{2}{3}) = \frac{4}{27}$. So we indeed improve upon the uniform distribution, but the improvement is moderate.

Below we consider the number of key levels higher than 2. Let $S_{k,L,\mathcal{P}}$ denote probability that the adversary cannot decode a link established between A and B when the number of key levels is L, the number of shared keys necessary to derive the session key is k, the adversary gets access to one level key of each of the L keys used to establish the link, and the level is chosen according to the probability distribution $\mathcal{P}$. By $S_{k,L}$ we mean $S_{k,L,\mathcal{P}}$ for the optimal probability distribution $\mathcal{P}$ (i.e. the probability that minimizes the chances of the adversary).

Continuous Case and a Lower Bound. Assume that the number of key levels is very large, with each key indexed by a number from the interval $[0, 1]$ and infinitesimal differences between indexes describing consecutive key levels. Intuitively, this is the most advantageous situation, for which we can achieve the best resilience to an adversary. We shall see that it is true, but still the advantage is moderate.

We model key choices of Alice Bob and adversary Mallet as independent random variables A, B and M with values in the the interval $[0, 1]$ with the same probability density d. Notice that the probability that the link between A and B remains secure equals $\Pr[M > \max\{A, B\}]$. Let $S_{1,\infty,d}$ denote this probability. First let us make the following technical observation:

Lemma 1. *Suppose that X, Y, Z are independent random variables with the same density probability function. Then* $\Pr[Z > \max\{X, Y\}] = \frac{1}{3}$ *regardless of the density function.*

Proof. Since X, Y, Z have density probability functions, $\Pr[X = Y] = \Pr[Y = Z] = \Pr[X = Z] = 0$ and we may assume that X, Y, Z have pairwise different values. There are 6 different configurations of these random variables: $X < Y < Z, Y < X < Z$, $X < Z < Y, Y < Z < X, Z < X < Y, Z < Y < Z$ and each of them has the same probability. Only for the first two configurations we have $Z > \max\{X, Y\}$, so $\Pr[Z > \max\{X, Y\}] = \frac{2}{6}$.   □

So we obtain a somewhat surprising result:

Corollary 1. $S_{1,\infty,d} = \frac{1}{3}$ *no matter which probability density function d is used.*

This result seems to contradict our observations for $L = 2$, where the choice of probabilities really counts. However, this is not the case as we shall see after proving the next theorem:

Theorem 1. $S_{1,L,\mathcal{P}} \leq \frac{1}{3}$ for any L and any probability distribution $\mathcal{P}$.

Proof. Let A, B, M be independent random variables with values in $\{1, \ldots, L\}$ according to the probability distribution $\mathcal{P}$. Let $p_i = \Pr[K_i]$ for $i = 1, \ldots, L$ and distribution $\mathcal{P}$. Then

$$\Pr[M > \max\{A, B\}] = \sum_{i=1}^{L} \Pr[M > \max\{A, B\}|M = i] \cdot \Pr[M = i] =$$

$$\sum_{i=1}^{L} \Pr[i > \max\{A, B\}] \cdot p_i = \sum_{i=2}^{L} (p_1 + \ldots + p_{i-1})^2 \cdot p_i \ .$$

Let $q_0 = 0$ and $q_i = p_1 + \ldots + p_i$ for $i = 1, \ldots, L$. Let us split interval $[0, 1]$ into subintervals $I_i = [q_{i-1}, q_i)$. Then $|I_i| = p_i$ and

$$\tfrac{1}{3} = \int_0^1 x^2 dx \geq \sum_{i=1}^{L} \inf_{x \in I_i}(x^2) \cdot |I_i| = \sum_{i=2}^{L} (p_1 + \ldots + p_{i-1})^2 \cdot p_i = S_{1,L,\mathcal{P}} \ \square$$

Determining Optimal Probabilities. For each L finding the optimal probability distribution on the set $\{K_1, \ldots, K_L\}$ of variants of the key K is equivalent to maximizing

$$\sum_{i=2}^{L} (p_1 + \ldots + p_{i-1})^2 \cdot p_i \tag{2}$$

on the simplex $\{(p_1, \ldots, p_L) : \sum_i p_i = 1 \land (\forall i)(p_i \geq 0)\}$. For example, $S_{1,4} = \frac{1119364}{4785507} \approx 0.2339$ and the optimal probabilities of K_1, K_2, K_3, K_4 are, respectively, 0.437055, 0.218527, 0.182106, and 0.162312.

Now we show a recursive formula for finding $S_{1,L}$. Let us recall that $S_{1,1} = 0$ and that $S_{1,2} = \frac{4}{27}$. Let us assume that $S_{1,L}$ is known and consider the case of $K_1, \ldots, K_{L+1}$, variants of a key K. Let q denote the probability of choosing the first L levels; our goal is to find the optimal q. The probability of adversary's failure equals

$$P(q, p) = q^2 \cdot (1 - q) + q^3 \cdot p = q^2(1 + q(p - 1)) \tag{3}$$

where p is the probability of adversary's failure conditioned on the event that the level of the shared key is within the first L levels for the users as well as for the adversary. The probability p is maximized when the conditional probabilities are such as for the optimal choice of L levels, i.e. $p = S_{1,L}$. The expression $P(q, p)$ is maximized for $\frac{dP(q,p)}{dq} = 0$, i.e. for $2q + 3q^2(p - 1) = 0$ or

$$q = \frac{2}{3(1 - p)} \ . \tag{4}$$

By substituting q in (3) we get

$$S_{1,L+1} = q^2 \big(1 + q(p-1)\big) = \frac{4}{9} \cdot \frac{1}{(1-p)^2} \cdot \Big(1 + \frac{2}{3(1-p)}(p-1)\Big) = \frac{4}{27} \cdot \frac{1}{(1 - S_{1,L})^2} \ .$$

So finally: $(p_1^2, p_2^2) = (\frac{2}{3}, \frac{1}{3})$ for $L = 2$, and for $L > 2$ we get the recurrence:

$$(p_1^{L+1}, \ldots, p_{L+1}^{L+1}) = \frac{2}{3(1 - S_{1,L})} \left(p_1^L, \ldots, p_L^L, \frac{1}{2} \right) \ .$$

Theorem 2. *The sequence $S_{1,n}$ is increasing and* $S_{1,n} = \frac{1}{3} - \frac{4}{9} \cdot \frac{1}{n} + \frac{4}{81} \cdot \frac{\ln n}{n^2} + o\left(\frac{\ln n}{n^2}\right)$.

Proof. Let $h(x) = \frac{4}{27}(1-x)^{-2}$. Then $S_{1,L+1} = h(S_{1,L})$ for each $L \geq 0$. The function h is increasing in the interval $[0,1]$ and $h(\frac{1}{3}) = \frac{1}{3}$. Therefore $h : [0,\frac{1}{3}] \rightarrow [0,\frac{1}{3}]$. Moreover, $h(x) > x$ for $x \in [0,\frac{1}{3})$. Since h is continuous in $[0,\frac{1}{3})$, the sequence $S_{1,L}$ is increasing and $\lim_L S_{1,L} = \frac{1}{3}$.

Let $g(x) = \frac{1}{3} - h(\frac{1}{3} - x)$, $m_1 = \frac{1}{3}$ and $m_{n+1} = g(m_n)$. Then it is easy to prove by induction that $S_{1,L} = \frac{1}{3} - m_L$ for $L \geq 2$. Taking Taylor series for g we get $g(x) = x - \frac{9}{4}x^2 + \frac{9}{2}x^3 + O(x^4)$. By Theorem 1 from [9] we finally get $m_n = \frac{4}{9} \cdot \frac{1}{n} - \frac{4}{81} \cdot \frac{\ln n}{n^2} + o(\frac{\ln n}{n^2})$. $\square$

Let $U_{1,L}$ denotes the probability that the adversary cannot decode a link established between A and B when the number of key levels is L, a single shared key is used to establish the session key, and the key levels are chosen according to the uniform distribution. From Equation (2) we easily deduce that $U_{1,L} = \frac{1}{3} - \frac{1}{2L} + \frac{1}{6L^2}$. So for large L the uniform distribution has very similar properties to the optimal one and that the probability of adversary failure is very close to the bound established in Theorem 1.

4   Expected Time of Adversary Attack

Suppose that the intersection of two sets of keys $\mathcal{K}_A$ and $\mathcal{K}_B$ has cardinality m. An adversary tries to compromise the connection between nodes A and B based on the intersection $\mathcal{K}_A \cap \mathcal{K}_B$.

Suppose that in one *step* adversary Mallet is able to get precisely one random element from the intersection $\mathcal{K}_A \cap \mathcal{K}_B$ (for this purpose Mallet has to retrieve keys from a number of devices). If there are no key levels, then this is equivalent to the Coupon Collector Problem, and takes in average $m \cdot H_m$ steps, where H_m denotes the mth harmonic number.

Two Level Case. Let us consider the schema with two levels of each key. Let p denote the probability of choosing the first level of a key.

Let $\mathcal{M} = \mathcal{K}_A \cap \mathcal{K}_B$, $|\mathcal{M}| = m$. Moreover, let $E \subseteq \mathcal{M}$ be the set of all keys K such that one of the devices holding $\mathcal{K}_A$ and $\mathcal{K}_B$ keeps K_2 (so K_2 is used for deriving the session key). Let $D = \mathcal{M} \setminus E$ (for $K \in D$ Mallet *must* get K_1). Let $|D| = a$ and $|E| = b$. The process of collecting the keys by Mallet can be described as a process of throwing balls at random into urns. There are three groups of urns: U_1 and U_2 have a urns each, while U_3 has b urns. U_1 and U_2 correspond to choosing, respectively, the keys from D of level 1 and 2. An urn from U_3 corresponds to choosing a key from E (regardless of its level). So we model getting a key by Mallet by throwing a ball to the urns so that: the probability to hit a given urn from U_1 is p/m, the probability to hit a given urn from U_2 is $(1-p)/m$, and the probability to hit a given urn from U_3 is $1/m$.

We are interested in the expected number of steps for filling all urns from $U_1 \cup U_3$. In the final calculus we must consider all possible configurations of a and b when $m = a + b$ is fixed.

Theorem 3. *Let $L_{m,p}$ denote the number of steps after which adversary collects all keys for compromising connection based on m shared keys. Then*

$$E[L_{m,p}] = \int_0^\infty \left(1 - \frac{H(t)}{e^t}\right) dt \ , \tag{5}$$

where $H(z) = \left(e^{z/m} - 1 - p^2(e^{qz/m} - 1)\right)^m$ and $q = 1 - p$.

Proof. Let x indicate the number of occupied urns from U_1, let y indicate the number of occupied urns from U_3 and z indicate the total number o balls thrown. Then

$$F(x, y, z) = (1 + x(e^{pz/m} - 1))^a (1 + y(e^{z/m} - 1))^b (e^{qz/m})^a \ ,$$

where $m = a + b$ and $q = 1 - p$ is the generating function of the probabilities modeling the described above process, i.e. $[x^\alpha][y^\beta][z^\gamma]F(x, y, z)$ is the probability that after throwing γth ball α urns from the group U_1 and β urns from U_2 are occupied (see e.g. [10] for details on generating functions technique).

Since we are interested in finding the probability of filling all urns marked by variables x and y we must extract the coefficients $[x^a][y^b]F(x, y, z)$. One can easily see that

$$[x^a][y^b]F(x, y, z) = (e^{pz/m} - 1)^a (e^{z/m} - 1)^b (e^{qz/m})^a \ .$$

Let us finally sum up over all possible configurations of pairs (a, b) with the fixed sum $a + b = m$. Notice that the probability that the intersection of two sets of keys has the configuration (a, b) conditioned on event $a + b = m$ equals $\binom{m}{a}(p^2)^a(1 - p^2)^b$. It is easy to check that

$$\sum_{a=0}^m \binom{m}{a}(p^2)^a(1 - p^2)^{m-a}[x^a][y^{m-a}]F(x, y, z) = H(z) \ ,$$

where $H(z) = (e^{z/m} - 1 - p^2(e^{(1-p)z/m} - 1))^m$. Moreover

$$H(z) = \sum_{n \geq 0} \left(\sum_{i=0}^n q_i\right)\frac{z^n}{n!} \ ,$$

where q_i is the probability that all urns in $U_1 \cup U_3$ become filled precisely in the ith step. Since $\sum_{i=0}^\infty q_i = 1$, we get

$$e^z - H(z) = \sum_{n \geq 0} \left(\sum_{i=n+1}^\infty q_i\right)\frac{z^n}{n!} \ .$$

In order to remove coefficients $1/n!$ from this formula, we use the Borel transform (see [11] for details) to the function $e^z - H(z)$:

$$\int_0^\infty (e^{zt} - H(zt))e^{-t}dt = \sum_{n \geq 0}\left(\sum_{i>n}^\infty q_i\right)z^n \ .$$

Notice that $\sum_{n \geq 0} n q_n = \sum_{n \geq 0}\sum_{i>n} q_i$, so, after putting $z = 1$, we finally get

$$E[L_{m,p}] = \int_0^\infty \left(1 - \frac{H(t)}{e^t}\right) dt \ . \qquad \square$$

Formula (5) is well suited for fast numerical calculations. For $m = 1$ the optimal value of p is 0.5; in this case $E[L_m] = 1.25$. If $m = 10$, then the optimal p is 0.32164; in this case $E[L_m] = 40.9724$, so $E[L_m] = 1.39887 \cdot m \cdot H_m$, where H_m denotes, as before, the mth harmonic number. So the actual cost of breaking the transmission is increased by almost 40% compared to the scheme with no key levels.

Continuous Limit Case. Let us consider now the limit case with an infinite number of key levels (compare Sect. 3). Let L_∞ denote the number of steps after which adversary collects all keys for compromising connection based on m common keys. Then

$$E[L_\infty] = \tfrac{3}{2} \cdot m \cdot H_m ,$$

where H_m denotes, as before, the mth harmonic number. Indeed, assume, like in Sect. 3, that the distribution of key levels has a density function d concentrated in $[0, 1]$. Let $\mathcal{M} = \mathcal{K}_A \cap \mathcal{K}_B$ and $|\mathcal{M}| = m$. Assume that an adversary randomly and independently chooses a key from the set $\mathcal{M}$ according to the density d. That is, he first chooses uniformly at random an element $x \in \mathcal{M}$ and next he selects a version of the key x according to the density d. By Corollary 1 each single step will succeed with probability $\tfrac{2}{3}$. Therefore, again by the Coupon Collector Problem, $E[L_\infty] = \tfrac{3}{2} \cdot m \cdot H_m$. So by increasing the number of levels we increase the cost for the adversary to break the links. The ultimate achievable increase is 50%, so for the ease of operation one can reduce the number of levels to a reasonable values such as $m = 10$. The previous subsections provides all necessary information to make a decision.

Even if the above result may sound somewhat pessimistically, one should also be aware of the fact that the chances to break a link after getting a bounded number of keys drop dramatically if key levels are used.

5   Key Trees

In this section we present an alternative approach to linear ordering of levels. Assume that we have a family $\mathcal{H}$ of trapdoor functions (see [12]) with the following properties:

- for each $H_i \in \mathcal{H}$ there is a trapdoor secret S_i,
- for a given x and $y = H_i(x)$ it is infeasible to compute x or any $x' \neq x$ such that $y = H_i(x')$,
- given y and the trapdoor secret S_i for H_i, it is easy to find x, x' such that $y = H_i(x) = H_i(x')$ while it is infeasible to compute x from x' (x' from x) given H_i only,

Now assume that a key K belongs to the pool of keys. Instead of using key levels with $K_0 = K$, the system provider derives the following keys:

$$\hat{K} = H_i(K), \quad \text{and} \quad K' \text{ such that } K' \neq K \text{ and } H_i(K') = \hat{K}.$$

For this purpose, the system provider chooses $H_i \in \mathcal{H}$ and keeps the trapdoor secret S_i before generating the keys from the pool. H_i is published.

During initialization of a device, instead of a key K the provider assigns either K or K' to the device, each with probability $\tfrac{1}{2}$.

In order to derive the session key nodes A and B use the following shared key:

1. if A and B share either K or K', they use it for calculating the session key,
2. if one of A and B holds K and the other one holds K', they use $\hat{K}$.

Advantages. For the two-level scheme discussed in Sect. 3, the adversary fails to break a link with probability $\frac{4}{27} \approx 0.148$ even if he has a version of the appropriate key. However, there no improvement if at least one of the communicating parties has level 2 key. On the other hand, the solution described here offers much more:

- probability of success of protecting the link is 0.25 (instead of $0.148..$),
- neither K nor K' is privileged from the point of view of the adversary. So in particular, the users will not complain about getting "weak keys" (as it might be the case for K_2 for 2-level design).

There is also a disadvantage: using more complex functions H_i, which might be too hard for the simplest devices.

Tree Architecture. Instead of a single key K or a chain of keys $K_0, K_1 \ldots$, we can construct the following tree $T_{\hat{K}}$ of keys:

- each node of the tree is labeled with a key, the root is labeled with $\hat{K}$,
- if a node is labeled with key K, then its parent is labeled with $H_i(K)$ (i is the child index).

During a predistribution phase:

- first some number of trees is chosen for a device,
- for each tree $T_{\hat{K}}$ chosen, a single leaf is chosen uniformly at random, the key labeling this leaf is loaded into the device.

Assume that A and B determine their session key. If A has a key K_a and B has a key K_b from the same tree T, then they use the key K labeling the first common ancestor of the leaves holding K_a and K_b. Obviously, A and B can compute K by applying H_i appropriate number of times to, respectively, K_a and K_b.

Resilience to Key Collection. Assume that an adversary as well as A and B are holding keys from a tree T, say the keys K_{ad}, K_A and K_B labeling the leaves P_{ad}, P_A and P_B. When establishing a communication link, A and B look for the first ancestor P of P_A and P_B and compute a key K corresponding to this node. The adversary can compute K if and only if P is the ancestor of P_{ad}. It is easy to see that the probability of the opposite case equals $(\frac{1}{2})^2 + (\frac{1}{4})^2 + (\frac{1}{8})^2 + \ldots$ (the number of terms in this expression equals the depth of the tree). Since $\sum_{i=1}^{\infty} 1/(2^i)^2 = \frac{1}{4} \cdot \frac{1}{1-1/4} = \frac{1}{3}$ the best we can achieve with deep trees is the same as with a large number of key levels. However, there are some advantages: the number of operations for finding the shared key is reduced and there are no "weak keys".

6   Evolving Keys

In this section we sketch a simple proactive application architecture based on key levels, where we enhance security by refreshing the keys by lowering their levels. In fact this technique is remotely related to [13].

In the proposed scheme each key K from the pool has an infinite number of versions: K_i for $i = -1, -2, \ldots$ satisfying the formula (1). Here G is an encryption function with a public key encryption key and a secret decryption key, and where encryption is easy, while decryption might be very hard. So the keys can be derived in case of need from any K_i by the system provider holding the public and the secret key.

The lifespan of the system is divided into epochs with potentially unlimited number of epochs. During epoch j the devices get the keys of levels from the interval $[-j \cdot k, -(j-1) \cdot k - 1]$. The key element of the scheme is the *Update Procedure* during which a device may upload versions of its keys from the current epoch:

– a device D appears at a trusted service point P run by the system provider (a kiosk that has got *recent* keys from HSM run by the system provider).
– P checks identity of D (and its holder) in some strong way (i.e. not with the keys from the pool),
– if authentication succeeds, P uploads to D new versions of the keys: if D already holds a key K_t, then P replaces K_t by some version of K_t with the level corresponding to the current epoch.

There is no necessity to update the keys during each epoch - communication between two devices can be secured by their shared keys just as described in Sect. 2.

One nice feature is that a holder of a device can adopt its security level - if the keys are updated more frequently, the device can establish a link with the fresh keys, probably still uncorrupted by the adversary. According to its policy a device may refuse to establish a connection with too old keys. An adversary may still collect keys, but breaking secured links becomes a never ending game: the adversary has to continue capturing devices. Since holders of the devices may be checked during the upload procedure, it becomes risky to appear at the upload stations with stolen or cloned devices.

7   Zigzag Key Predistribution

Now we sketch a technique which can be used to reduce the number of keys held by a device or to increase the probability of successful key establishment. By reducing the number of keys in each device we also increase the cost of the adversary to break the system by collecting the keys (at least for some transmissions). The idea is to modify the generation of the keys in the pool $\mathcal{K} = \{K_1, \ldots, K_n\}$. Instead of a random generation of keys from $\mathcal{K}$, the system provider generates them as follows:

1. choose functions HL and HR as in Sect. 5 (in fact, HR requires no trapdoor),
2. choose a key K_1 at random,
3. for $i = 1$ to $n - 1$ perform the following steps:
    – assign $U_i := HR(K_i)$,
    – using a trapdoor secret S find $K_{i+1} \neq K_i$ such that $HL(K_{i+1}) = U_i$,
4. output HL, HR and $\mathcal{K} = \{K_1, \ldots, K_n\}$.

Assigning the Keys to a Device via Random Predistribution. If we have to choose a subset of m keys, then we choose at random a subset of m keys C such that if $K_i, K_j \in C$, then $|i - j| \geq 2$.

Establishing a Connection. If A and B wish to derive a session key, they use not only the keys they share, but also the neighboring keys. More precisely, if A holds K_i and B holds K_{i+1}, then they use U_i: A computes $U_i := HR(K_i)$ while B computes $U_i := HL(K_{i+1})$.

Parameter Choice. In order to guarantee connection with probability at least $1 - p$ for random key predistribution and a pool of size N we look for a k such that

for two random subsets $C_1, C_2 \subseteq \mathcal{K}$ of size k with probability at least $1 - p$ there are $K_i \in C_1$ and $K_j \in C_2$ such that $|i - j| \leq 1$.

Note that for a standard key predistribution as described in [1] the corresponding condition would be $|i - j| \leq 0$.

In order to compare the regular key predistribution with the zigzag method we have to examine properties of the later scheme. Let $\mathcal{C}_{n,m}$ be the class of all sets $A \subseteq \{1, \ldots, n\}$ of cardinality m such that the distance between each two points from A is at least 2. Let $\mathcal{C}_{n,m,1} = \{A \in \mathcal{C}_{n,m} : n \notin A\}$ and $\mathcal{C}_{n,m,2} = \{A \in \mathcal{C}_{n,m} : n \in A\}$.

There is a one-to-one correspondence between members of the class $\mathcal{C}_{n,m,1}$ and the class of all subsets of the set $\{1, \ldots, n - m\}$ of cardinality m. Namely, for this purpose for each $A \in \mathcal{C}_{n,m,1}$, we remove from $\{1, \ldots, n\}$ all points of the form $a + 1$, where $a \in A$, and then we re-index the numbers: the ith remaining number becomes index i. Therefore $|\mathcal{C}_{n,m,1}| = \binom{n-m}{m}$. Similarly, there is a one-to-one correspondence between members of the class $\mathcal{C}_{n,m,2}$ and the class of all subsets of the set $\{1, \ldots, n - m - 1\}$ of cardinality $m - 1$. Therefore $|\mathcal{C}_{n,m,2}| = \binom{n-m}{m-1}$ and $|\mathcal{C}_{n,m}| = \binom{n-m}{m} + \binom{n-m}{m-1}$.

Let us consider $A, B \in \mathcal{C}_{n,m}$ such that the distances between each two points $a \in A$ and $b \in B$ is at least 2. Let us observe that then $A \cup B \in \mathcal{C}_{n,2m}$. Conversely, if we take any set $C \in \mathcal{C}_{n,2m}$ the we may split this set into $\binom{2k}{m}$ pairs $(A, B) \in \mathcal{C}_{n,m} \times \mathcal{C}_{n,m}$ such that $A \cup B = C$. Therefore there are $|\mathcal{C}_{n,2m}| \cdot \binom{2m}{m}$ pairs (A, B) in $\mathcal{C}_{n,m} \times \mathcal{C}_{n,m}$ such that the distances between each two points $a \in A$ and $b \in B$ is at least 2.

Let $D(m, n)$ denote probability of the event "$(A, B) \in \mathcal{C}_{n,m} \times \mathcal{C}_{n,m}$ and there are $a \in A$, $b \in B$ such that $|a - b| \leq 1$". From the above discussion we deduce that

$$D(n, m) = 1 - \frac{\left(\binom{n-2m}{2m} + \binom{n-2m}{2m-1} \right) \binom{2m}{m}}{\left(\binom{n-m}{m} + \binom{n-m}{m-1} \right)^2} .$$

After some simple transformations we get

$$D(n, m) = 1 - \frac{\binom{2m}{m} \binom{1-2m+n}{2m}}{\binom{1-m+n}{m}^2} .$$

By using this formula one can check, for example, that

1. $D(n, \sqrt{n \log n}) \geq 1 - \frac{1}{10^{11}}$, for $n > 80$,
2. $D(n, 2\sqrt{n}) \geq 1 - \frac{1}{10^6}$ for $n \leq 10^4$.

Fig. 1 presents a diagram on which we compare behavior of the random key predistribution as defined in [1] and the zigzag construction. One can see that the zigzag construction can be used to reduce substantially the number of keys in each device.

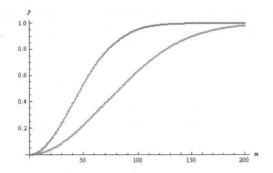

Fig. 1. probability of establishing a connection with at least one shared keys for $n = 10^4$ and different values of parameter m denoting the number of keys assigned to a device; the lower curve describes the probabilities for random key predistribution, the upper curve depicts the probabilities for the zigzag construction

References

1. Eschenauer, L., Gligor, V.D.: A key management scheme for distributed sensor networks. In: 9th ACM Conference on Computer and Communication Security (CCS 2002), pp. 41–47. ACM, New York (2002)
2. Chan, H., Perrig, A., Song, D.: Random key predistribution schemes for sensor networks. In: IEEE Symp. Security Privacy, pp. 197–213. IEEE, Los Alamitos (2003)
3. Liu, D., Ning, P.: Improving key predistribution with deployment knowledge in static sensor networks. TOSN 1(2), 204–239 (2005)
4. Du, W., Deng, J., Han, Y.S., Varshney, P.K.: A key predistribution scheme for sensor networks using deployment knowledge. IEEE Trans. Dependable Sec. Comput. 3(1), 62–77 (2006)
5. Du, W., Deng, J., Han, Y.S., Varshney, P.K., Katz, J., Khalili, A.: A pairwise key predistribution scheme for wireless sensor networks. ACM Trans. Inf. Syst. Secur. 8(2), 228–258 (2005)
6. Blom, R.: An optimal class of symmetric key generation systems. In: Beth, T., Cot, N., Ingemarsson, I. (eds.) EUROCRYPT 1984. LNCS, vol. 209, pp. 335–338. Springer, Heidelberg (1985)
7. Traynor, P., Kumar, R., Choi, H., Cao, G., Zhu, S., Porta, T.F.L.: Efficient hybrid security mechanisms for heterogeneous sensor networks. IEEE Trans. Mob. Comput. 6(6), 663–677 (2007)
8. Bellare, M., Yee, B.S.: Forward-security in private-key cryptography. In: Joye, M. (ed.) CT-RSA 2003. LNCS, vol. 2612, pp. 1–18. Springer, Heidelberg (2003)
9. Stević, S.: Asymptotic behavior of a sequence defined by iteration. Matematicki Vesnik 48(3-4), 99–105 (1966)
10. Gardy, D.: Occupancy urn models in the analysis of algorithms. Journal of Statistical Planning and Inference 101(1), 95–105 (2002)
11. Szpankowski, W.: Average Case Analysis of Algorithms on Sequences. John Wiley and Sons, Chichester (2001)
12. Krawczyk, H., Rabin, T.: Chameleon signatures, pp. 143–154 (2000)
13. Ren, M., Kanti Das, T., Zhou, J.: Diverging keys in wireless sensor networks. In: Katsikas, S.K., López, J., Backes, M., Gritzalis, S., Preneel, B. (eds.) ISC 2006. LNCS, vol. 4176, pp. 257–269. Springer, Heidelberg (2006)

Revisiting DoS Attacks and Privacy in RFID-Enabled Networks

Paolo D'Arco, Alessandra Scafuro, and Ivan Visconti

University of Salerno, Italy
{paodar,visconti}@dia.unisa.it, alescafu@gmail.com

Abstract. Vaudenay presented in [ASIACRYPT 2007] a general RFID security and privacy model that abstracts some previous works in a single, concise, and much more understandable framework. He introduced eight distinct notions of privacy, corresponding to adversaries of different strength, and proved some possibility and impossibility results for such privacy notions. However, some interesting problems as: 1) achieving *stronger privacy using low-cost tags* (i.e., tags that usually can not perform public-key cryptography), 2) achieving *stronger privacy in presence of side-channel attacks* (e.g., DoS attacks, detection of the outputs of identification protocols), and 3) achieving *stronger privacy under standard complexity-theoretic assumptions*, are still left open.

In this paper, we address the above problems and give two contributions.

First of all we show that Vaudenay's privacy notions are *impossible to achieve* in presence of DoS attacks. Therefore, we extend the model to better reflect the real-world scenario, where these attacks are easy to mount (e.g., by physically destroying/making inactive tags). More precisely, we refine Vaudenay's privacy model to deal with DoS and DoS-like attacks, and introduce an additional privacy notion, referred to as *semi-destructive* privacy, which takes into account hardware features of some real-world tags. Then, we show an *efficient RFID protocol* that, by only using symmetric-key cryptography, satisfies the notion of semi-destructive privacy, *under standard complexity-theoretic assumptions*.

1 Introduction

RFID technology. Radio frequency identification (RFID) enables *readers* to perform wireless identification of objects labeled with RFID *tags*. It is well known that the pervasive use of this technology introduces various privacy threats (e.g, tracking of users, profiling, linking activities). Unfortunately, RFID tags have often very restricted computational and storage capabilities. Therefore, privacy so far has been addressed with lower priority with respect to other critical requirements as *authentication* (which prevents an adversary from impersonating tags) and *efficiency* (e.g., suitability for low-cost tags).

Privacy models. The design of a secure and privacy-preserving RFID system requires an appropriate security and privacy model to enable a careful analysis of the system. However, existing security and privacy models for RFID

S. Dolev (Ed.): ALGOSENSORS 2009, LNCS 5804, pp. 76–87, 2009.

(e.g., [1,2,3,4]) suffer from various shortcomings. Indeed, they do not consider important aspects like adversaries with access to side-channel information (e.g., information on whether the identification of a tag was successful or not) or the privacy of corrupted tags (i.e., whose secrets have been disclosed).

Vaudenay's model. Given the various and in some cases incomparable privacy models defined before, Vaudenay presented in [5] a general model that abstracts some previous works in a single, concise and more understandable framework. Indeed, he introduced eight privacy notions which correspond to adversaries of different strength (the security definition is equivalent to the one given in [3]). In [6] the eight privacy classes of [5] have been reduced to three privacy classes, under some restrictions on the power of the adversary. According to [5], the first four notions (i.e., weak, forward, destructive, and strong privacy) allow the adversary to obtain, as side-channel information, the result of an interaction between tag and reader. The other four notions (narrow-weak, narrow-forward, narrow-destructive and narrow-strong privacy) instead do not consider the side-channel information about the successful identification of a tag with a reader. Unfortunately the only non-narrow privacy notions achieved in [5] are forward and weak privacy. Moreover, forward privacy is obtained by using public-key cryptography (not implemented yet in currently available low-cost tags). On the other hand, concerning with the narrow privacy notions, narrow-strong privacy is obtained by using public-key cryptography and narrow-destructive privacy is obtained in the controversial random oracle model [7]. In a recent work [8] following up some ideas discussed in [9], narrow-forward privacy has been obtained with symmetric-key operations only on the tags, but extending the model with anonymizers.

DoS attacks and privacy in RFID systems. In [5] a narrow-destructive RFID protocol, secure in the random oracle model, was proposed. Moreover, it was showed how a DoS attack can be mounted by the adversary to desynchronize a tag from a reader. This attack has the consequence that the tag is not able to succeed anymore in the identification with the reader. It was also pointed out how the adversary can use the desynchronization attack, along with side channel information, to succeed in the *privacy experiment*, which is used to model the privacy notion. More specifically, the desynchronization attack is turned into a privacy attack. Finally, building on that, it was shown that the narrow-destructive scheme does not even enjoy weak privacy.

Our results. In this paper, we give two contributions. First of all, we revisit Vaudenay's model by considering DoS attacks. We show that an adversary that is able to stop the activities of a tag is *always successful* in winning the privacy experiment, regardless of the privacy level considered (i.e., even achieving narrow-weak privacy would be impossible). DoS attacks are not included in Vaudenay's model and we show that, unfortunately, the model results to be inadequate in measuring privacy notions when such attacks can occur. However, since in the real world a DoS attack is *semantically different from a privacy violation*, we consider the possibility of refining the adversarial model, so that privacy notions are still achievable and make sense even when DoS attacks are possible. To this aim, we present a formal framework for privacy-preserving RFID systems, which builds on top of the security and privacy model of [5] and includes DoS attacks. In our new model, security and privacy are achievable (meaningfully) even when the adversary is allowed to mount DoS attacks.

Then, we focus on the design of an RFID protocol that improves on previous constructions. We concentrate on achieving simultaneously: *efficiency, security* and *a satisfying privacy notion*. We introduce a new notion of privacy, referred to as *semi-destructive* privacy, that can be appropriate for currently available low-cost tags, and show a privacy-preserving RFID protocol that achieves the notion. The protocol that we propose, which is the main contribution of the work, enjoys several appealing features that were not simultaneously achieved by previous proposals. Indeed, our protocol 1) has computational and storage requirements that are suitable for low-cost tags (i.e., they will have to perform only minimal symmetric-key computations); 2) enjoys a seemingly better privacy notion, i.e. semi-destructive privacy, which allows the adversary to corrupt tags, to play at a protocol level with non-corrupted tags and access to side channel information; 3) is proved secure under standard complexity theoretic assumptions (i.e, we do not resort to any random oracle). Due to the separation we introduce between DoS attacks and privacy attacks, our protocol only cares about privacy (and actually the reader can easily check that DoS attacks are immediate to mount against our protocol).

2   RFID Security and Privacy Model

An RFID system consists of three types of players: issuer I, reader R, and tag T. I creates tags. In [5], I and R are assumed to be trusted, thus they always follow the prescribed protocols. Moreover, there exists a database that receives additional information from I upon each tag creation. R is allowed to read and update the database during the execution of the identification protocol. R has typically sufficient computational and storage capabilities for performing public-key cryptography and can handle multiple instances of the tag identification protocol with different tags in parallel.

Reflecting the real-world scenario, where different tags are available, T can be violated by the adversary, depending on the privacy notions. The greatest part of available tags are passive devices, which become active when powered by the electromagnetic field of R. Usually such tags are limited in computational and storage capabilities (i.e., they can store a few Kbytes and perform at most symmetric-key cryptographic tasks).

RFID schemes. According to [5] (which follows up [10]), an RFID scheme is defined by the following procedures:

SetupReader(1^n) $\rightarrow$ (sk_R, pk_R) on input a security parameter n, this procedure creates a public parameter pk_R, known to all players, and a secret parameter sk_R, known only to R. It also creates a database that 1) can be read and updated by R during the execution of an identification protocol; 2) might receive an update by I during the creation of a new tag; 3) can not be read and updated by any other player.

SetupTag$_{pk_R}$(ID) $\rightarrow$ (K, S) on input pk_R and ID, I runs this procedure and outputs two strings K and S that correspond to the creation of a tag T with identifier ID. T is initialized with the state S, whereas the pair (ID, K) is sent to the database.

IdentTag[T$_{ID}$(S) $\leftrightarrow$ R(sk_R, pk_R)] $\rightarrow$ out is a (potentially interactive) protocol between T with identifier ID and R. The goal of this protocol is to identify T and to verify if it is legitimate (i.e., if the identifier ID of tag T belongs to the database). The output out corresponds to the identity of the tag in case of successful identification or to $\perp$ otherwise.

Adversary. The privacy and security definitions of [5] are based on *security experiments* where a polynomially bounded adversary can interact with a *set of oracles* through the following *oracle queries*.

CreateTag^b(ID) allows the adversary to create a tag with a unique tag identifier ID, which can be chosen by the adversary. This oracle internally calls SetupTag$_{pk_R}$(ID) to create (K, S) for tag ID. If input $b = 1$, the adversary chooses the tag to be legitimate, which means that (ID, K) is sent to the database. For input $b = 0$, the pair (ID, K) is not added to the database (and thus the created tag is not legitimate). This oracle query models the capability an adversary has in obtaining (e.g., buying) legitimate tags and in creating forged ones that then circulate in the system.

DrawTag(Δ) $\rightarrow$ (vtag$_1$, b_1, . . . , vtag$_m$, b_m). Initially, the adversary can not interact with any tag. The adversary can only get access to a set of tags that are chosen from the set of free tags, according to a given distribution Δ, by querying the DrawTag oracle. This oracle query models the real-world setting, where the adversary can only interact with tags which lie in its reading range. The oracle returns an array of temporary identifiers vtag$_1$, . . . , vtag$_m$ of the tags the adversary is given access to (e.g., vtag may be a temporary identifier the tag uses for only one single protocol session). For tags already drawn or not existing ones the oracle returns $\perp$. The DrawTag oracle manages a secret look-up table $\mathcal{T}$ to keep track of the real identifier ID$_i$, associated to the temporary identifier vtag$_i$, i.e., $\mathcal{T}$(vtag$_i$) = ID$_i$. Moreover, the DrawTag oracle also provides the adversary information on whether the corresponding tags are legitimate ($b_i = 1$) or not ($b_i = 0$).

FreeTag(vtag). On the other hand, the FreeTag oracle makes a tag vtag inaccessible to the adversary, which means that the adversary can not interact with the tag vtag any longer until it is made accessible again (under a new temporary identifier vtag$'$) by another DrawTag query. This oracle query models the possibility that a tag can get out of the reading range of the adversary.

Launch() $\rightarrow$ π_R asks the reader to start a new instance π_R of the IdentTag protocol (where π_R is a random session identifier). This oracle query allows the adversary to start different parallel IdentTag protocol instances with the reader R.

SendTag(m, vtag) $\rightarrow m'$ sends a message m to the tag T, known as vtag to the adversary. Tag T responds with message m'. This oracle call allows the adversary to perform active attacks against T.

SendReader(m, π_R) $\rightarrow m'$ sends a message m to the instance π_R of the IdentTag protocol, executed by the reader R. The reader R responds with message m'. This oracle query allows the adversary to perform active attacks against R.

Execute (vtag) $\rightarrow (\pi, \tau)$ executes in turn one Launch query with SendReader and SendTag queries, in order to execute a complete protocol between vtag and reader R. The oracle returns the transcript containing the protocol messages and the protocol identifier π.

Result(π_R) returns 0 if the instance π_R of the IdentTag protocol has been completed but the tag T that participated in the protocol has not been accepted by the reader R (i.e., $out = \perp$). In case R identified a legitimate tag, Result returns 1. This oracle query allows the adversary to obtain side channel information on whether the authentication of T was successful or not.

CorruptTag(vtag) $\rightarrow S$ returns the current state S of the tag T that is known as vtag to the adversary. This oracle query models (physical) attacks on the tags that disclose the current state of the tag.

The notions of privacy for an RFID scheme are defined in [5] through *restrictions* imposed to the adversary in the use of the oracle queries. This corresponds in the real-world to adversaries and tags of different strengths.

Weak privacy. The weakest notion of privacy is referred to as *weak*, and does not allow any tag corruption. This notion makes sense if one can obtain an RFID system based on tags whose internal states can not be violated (e.g., due to tamper-resistant hardware). This is a quite strong requirement that does not seem to be applicable to currently available low-cost tags.

Forward privacy. This notion requires that, once the adversary has called a corrupt query, then the only next queries that it can still make are corruption queries. The above restriction makes sense in the real world only in case the adversary can violate tags when the system is already over. Forward privacy still does not correspond to the large part of real-world systems.

Destructive privacy. This notion requires that, once a corrupt query for a given tag has been asked, then the adversary can not ask further queries for the same tag. Still the system is up and the adversary can use all oracle queries but with respect to other tags only. Such a privacy notions makes sense to model real-life systems where tags have their states in a protected area that can be accessed by the adversary but at the price of making the tag unusable. Low-cost tags can typically achieve such requirements. Indeed the location of the memory in the tag can easily be embedded in other components (e.g., circuit, antenna), thus any external access to the memory would make the tag unusable.

Moreover, tamper-evident hardware is much easier to produce than tamper-proof hardware. Therefore, this privacy notion makes sense for many real-life applications of RFID.

Strong privacy. This is the strongest notion of privacy and basically does not assume any restriction on the power of the adversary in using oracle queries. Therefore, according to this notion, even a tag already violated can circulate again in the system, and thus can be again observed by the adversary. This privacy notion can in theory be of interest for many real-life systems since the hardware requirement for tags is minimal (i.e., no protected area is required). Unfortunately, in [5] it has been shown that this privacy notion is impossible to achieve.

Four more privacy notions have been defined in [5] by relaxing each of the previous notion. From a technical point of view the relaxation consists in removing side-channel information from the view of the adversary. More precisely, it is not able to use the query Result, which means that in the real world it is not able to detect if a tag has been accepted by the reader or not. This is an important limitation and therefore these relaxed variants of privacy notions, which are referred to as *narrow-weak, narrow-forward, narrow-destructive* and *narrow-strong* seem to be able to model only a restricted part of real-world RFID applications. Notice that, in [6] it has been showed that the above eight privacy notions collapse to three if the protocols we focus our attention on 1) do not use *correlated keys*, 2) are correct and do not produce *false negatives* (i.e., legitimate tags are correctly identified) and 3) the adversary is a *wise* adversary which, loosely speaking, means that it does not use the Result query when he already knows the answer. Under such assumptions, the Result query is rarely useful (and used). However, at the state of current knowledge, we do not know how much the subset of wise adversaries is representative of the set of adversaries.

To summarize, given the impossibility of achieving strong privacy, the most challenging and concretely useful notion to achieve is destructive privacy. In this paper we will show how to achieve a slightly relaxed notion, that we refer to as semi-destructive privacy, with a protocol that is suitable for low-cost tags and secure under standard complexity-theoretic assumptions.

Correctness. The definition of correctness requires that, with overwhelming probability, R returns ID when it runs the protocol with T, correctly created by I with ID as input; while R returns $\perp$ otherwise. Therefore, correctness could fail in case of 1) *false negative*: T with identifier ID has been correctly created by I but R outputs $\perp$; 2) *false positive*: T has not been created by I and R outputs *out* $\neq \perp$; 3) *incorrect identification*: T with identifier ID has been created by I but the output of R is *out* $\notin \{$ID$, \perp\}$.

Security. The definition of security given in [5] focuses on showing that the adversary is not able to succeed in a security experiment where R outputs ID, the tag T associated to ID has not been corrupted, and the adversary has not simply played as a proxy between T and R (thus R receives messages computed at least in part by the adversary). We will refer to a transcript played by T and R (until the last message sent by T) as *matching conversation*. The definition of [5] says that security is a critical property and therefore it must be preserved even against the strongest possible adversary, that can use all oracle queries without any restriction.

Privacy. The definition of privacy given in [5] depends on the power of the adversary involved in the experiment (see Sec. 2). The crucial requirement for each privacy definition is the existence of a polynomial-time algorithm $\mathcal{B}$, called Blinder, that without carrying any secret is able to simulate the work of T and R. $\mathcal{B}$ has no special access to the adversary, it can only observe the input/output to/from oracle queries that the adversary asks for. The definition of privacy therefore requires that the success probability of the adversary does not (non-negligibly) deviates when $\mathcal{B}$ replaces the oracles Launch, SendReader, SendTag and Result.

3   DoS-Resilient Privacy Notions for RFID

A DoS attack basically enables an adversary to make tags unusable. In this section we discuss DoS attacks and their impact on the privacy model of [5], described in Section 2. Indeed, in [5], Vaudenay, in presenting the properties of the narrow-destructive protocol secure in the random oracle model, pointed out how an adversary can make unusable a tag at a protocol level through a DoS attack. Then, he showed how this attack can be used to prove that the protocol does not enjoy even the notion of weak privacy.

Our first observation is that, in the real-world, an adversary can *easily physically destroy/make inactive/render unusable an RFID tag*. Such operations can be seen as a sort of "extreme" DoS attack. For example, sometimes, a tag can be made inactive through the use of strong electromagnetic fields, without physically touching the tag at all. Hereafter, we refer to such attacks with the generic term of DoS-like attacks.

Privacy and DoS attacks in [5]. Vaudenay showed a narrow destructive scheme where R sends a random challenge, T sends an answer and both update respectively the corresponding entry in the database and the state of the tag, so that consistency is maintained for the next identification. Then, he showed a weak adversary who breaks the privacy of the narrow-destructive scheme through a DoS attack. Indeed, the DoS attack breaks the synchronization between T and R making T no longer identifiable (i.e., during the attack T updates its key, while the database still contains the old key). In our opinion, such an attack shows that the relation between DoS-like attacks and privacy notions deserves further investigation. As we have already mentioned, in the real world an adversary can very often easily mount a sort of DoS attack, by making tags not identifiable anymore. From the above discussion, in order to model the real world, an oracle describing the action of making inactive a tag has to be provided, otherwise a notion of privacy in the considered model would not say anything about privacy when the protocol is used in the real world. Unfortunately, such an oracle is not included in the model of [5]. So we extend the model with it. The next theorem shows that DoS attacks are very harmful for privacy. Indeed, there is a simple adversary which does not even corrupt tags but is always successful with respect to any of the eight notions of privacy. Let us define MakeInactive as the oracle used by the adversary to make silent a tag.

Theorem 1. *In the model of [5], if an adversary is allowed to query the MakeInactive oracle, then no privacy is achievable.*

The proof can be found in the full version of this paper [11]. The main idea consists in showing an adversary that draws two tags, makes inactive one of them, and later when it will draw a tag, it will recognize the previous tag from the fact that no answer is received when querying it.

The previous theorem shows an impossibility for obtaining any form of privacy in the above model and such a result correctly matches the real-world, where an adversary that makes inactive a tag can easily trace it by noticing that the tag does not work anymore. Moreover, we observe that, in the real world, privacy attacks often consist in distinguishing the tag that has been used to access a service, among the set of tags that actually *can* access the service. Hence, inactive tags should not be still part of the privacy game run by the adversary since they can not be used to access a service anymore. Therefore, the direction of investigation that we follow consists in considering a tag *usable* as long as it can be identified by the reader (i.e., only usable tags should be drawn).

One can argue that the capability of making inactive tags was already included in the adversaries that can corrupt tags. However, the use of the corrupt query for such purposes fails in modelling real-world DoS-like attacks for several reasons. First of all [5] showed that there exist protocols that are private against narrow-strong adversaries (that can corrupt tags), while the above theorem shows that no privacy notions is achievable when MakeInactive is used. Second, a privacy notion as weak privacy does not allow any tag corruption because, for example, one assumes that the state of the tag is protected by a tamper-proof area. However, tamper-proof areas can always be physically destroyed (along with data they store), so a different oracle query is needed anyway.

We now give in details the definitions of MakeInactive and DrawTag oracles that represent our extension to the model of [5].

Definition 1. MakeInactive (vtag): *makes* vtag *unusable. It moves* vtag *from the set of usable tags (i.e., the ones that can be drawn) to the set of unusable tags (i.e., tags that can not be drawn). This oracle is queried by the adversary for making inactive a tag. It can be also called by a tag on itself (e.g., upon detecting an adversarial attack) and by the blinder when answering to a* SendTag *query.*

Notice that actually a tag can easily make inactive itself by calling the *kill* function that is already built in currently available low-cost tags. On the other hand, the need for such a MakeInactive oracle call also by the blinder is necessary to make the real experiment consistent with the simulated experiment. Indeed, the former can see tags that make inactive themselves, while the latter would never see such an event since tags are never activated and the blinder replaces their work. Access to the MakeInactive oracle for the blinder is therefore necessary to have in the simulated world a comparable number of usable tags (i.e., tags that can be drawn) in the system with respect to the real world.

The redefinition of the DrawTag oracle also considers the property of a tag of being still usable or not.

Definition 2. DrawTag(Δ) $\rightarrow$ (vtag$_1$, b_1, ..., vtag$_m$, b_m): *the adversary can only get access to a set of tags by querying the DrawTag oracle. This oracle selects tags according to the input distribution Δ, from the set of free tags that are still* usable. *Such a query models the real setting, where the adversary can only interact with tags that are in its reading range and that have not been made inactive. The oracle returns an array of temporary identifiers* vtag$_1$, ..., vtag$_m$ *of the tags which adversary is given access to (e.g.,* vtag *may be a temporary identifier the tag uses for only one single protocol session). For tags already drawn, not existing or unusable, the oracle returns $\perp$. The DrawTag oracle manages a secret look-up table T that keeps track of the real identifier* ID$_i$ *that is associated with the temporary identifier* vtag$_i$, *i.e.,* T(vtag$_i$) = ID$_i$. *Moreover, the DrawTag oracle also provides the adversary with information on whether the corresponding tags are legitimate ($b_i = 1$) or not ($b_i = 0$).*

4   Semi-destructive Privacy: Definition and Construction

We introduce the class of *semi-destructive* adversaries, which essentially have the *same oracle access* of the destructive ones but with a small restriction on the corrupt query. Then, we describe a *protocol* that enjoys privacy w.r.t. such a class of adversaries, which is *secure under standard complexity-theoretic assumptions* and only needs basic symmetric-key computations on the tag's side.

Semi-destructive privacy. Privacy classes are distinguished according to the adversary's access to the CorruptTag oracle. The adversary's corruption power can be viewed as the inverse of the tag's capability to make its state inaccessible. We concentrate on the challenging notion of a destructive adversary. Such an adversary, in [5], can query the CorruptTag oracle at *any time*, with the consequence that later on the tag is not usable anymore. The destructive privacy notion was introduced motivated by the existence of tags that, once violated, can not work anymore (i.e., forcing an elementary tamper-proof area allows the adversary to read the state at the price of destroying the tag).

Let us now consider *the instant* in which the CorruptTag oracle and the MakeInactive oracle queries are asked for, and let us look at the case in which a tag is corrupted/deactivated *while it is powered on* (i.e., under an electromagnetic field that gives it sufficient power to do computations). In this case, we assume that the tag is able to detect that some tentative state violation is happening. In other words, the tag's state is protected against this violation attempt, and the tag activates a computation that basically kills the tag (e.g., erases the state). Note that such an hardware requirement is still under the profile of a low-cost tag and thus it makes sense for real world applications.

Hence, we consider a notion of semi-destructive privacy that requires tags with an additional hardware feature with respect to the one required by the destructive privacy notion of [5]. We however point out that the resulting tags would be much simpler and cheap than tags able to perform public-key cryptographic computations.

Finally notice that our new privacy notion is slightly weaker than the notion of destructive privacy of [5] but it is not directly comparable to the notion of forward privacy. Indeed, with respect to forward privacy, our new notion gives to the adversary essentially more power, but a forward adversary can make corrupt queries even during a protocol execution.

Definition 3. *A* semi-destructive adversary *is a destructive adversary such that when tag* vtag *has been activated by a* SendTag$(\cdot, \text{vtag})$ *query and it is still waiting for another* SendTag$(\cdot, \text{vtag})$ *query to complete the protocol, then a* CorruptTag *or a* MakeInactive *query erases the state of the tag and makes it inactive.*

We directly have the new notion of *semi-destructive* privacy, where the privacy experiment is played by semi-destructive adversaries.

4.1   Semi-destructive Privacy for Low-Cost Tags

In this section we present a semi-destructive RFID protocol that is suitable for low-cost tags and is secure under standard complexity-theoretic assumptions.

In our scheme we use as subprotocol a symmetric encryption scheme which satisfies a sort of *authenticity* of the encryption. Such a notion has been studied and formalized in [12]. The notion of authenticity of a symmetric encryption scheme we need can be specified using another game, the INT-CTXT game. An adversary $\mathcal{A}_{\text{ctxt}}$ for the INT-CTXT game first has access to an oracle $\mathcal{O}$ which computed encryptions and decryptions under a given secret key K as answers to encryption and decryption queries of $\mathcal{A}_{\text{ctxt}}$. $\mathcal{A}_{\text{ctxt}}$ wins if it then outputs a ciphertext c still under the same secret key K that has not been previously returned by $\mathcal{O}$. We refer to [12] for details and relations among security notions. Notice that such encryption schemes can be constructed on top of any IND-CPA encryption scheme and a scheme for secure message authentication codes (MAC). We now describe the procedures of our system.

SetupReader$(1^n) \rightarrow (sk_{\text{R}}, pk_{\text{R}})$ on input the security parameter generates an empty database DB and outputs $(sk_{\text{R}} = \perp, pk_{\text{R}} = 1^n)$. SetupTag$_{pk_{\text{R}}=1^n}(\text{ID}) \rightarrow (K, S)$ randomly selects an n-bit string K, and outputs the pair $(K, S) = (K, (K, b = 0^n))$. S is stored in the state of the tag, while the database DB will have a unique entry indexed by ID. This entry will have K as associated value. IdentTag$[\text{T}_{\text{ID}}(S) \leftrightarrow \text{R}(sk_{\text{R}}, pk_{\text{R}})] \rightarrow out$ is the actual identification protocol, we show a graphical illustration in Fig. 1, while a rigorous description of the procedures of T and R (and of their counterpart in the ideal model) is given in the full version of this paper [11].

High-level overview. Let us shortly describe the protocol and give intuitions about the enjoyed properties. The protocol is a three-round protocol. The reader

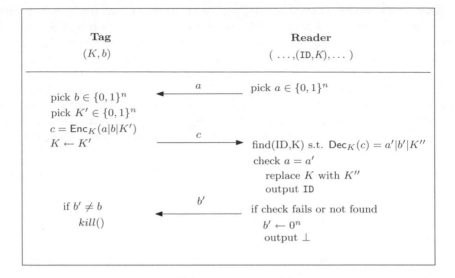

Fig. 1. Semi-Destructive RFID

R starts by sending a random challenge a to tag T. Then, the tag T chooses a random value b and a new encryption key K', computes $c = \mathsf{Enc}_K(a|b|K')$, updates K with K' and sends c to R. The reader R checks whether there exists a pair (ID, K) such that the encryption is authentic and that the plaintext is equal to $a|\cdot|\cdot$. In such a case, R sends $b' = b$ back to T, and updates its encryption key K with K'. Otherwise, it sends to T a string $b' = 0^n$. On the other hand, T, if receives b' different from b, it erases its state. An extra activity of T consists in erasing its state in the following cases.

1. The protocol is not concluded; this is useful in case the adversary later draws again the same tag and immediately corrupts it.
2. An invasive attack is detected; this is useful in case the adversaries tries to read the state of the tag or tries to make it inactive.

Intuitively, the protocol is correct and secure due to the properties of the encryption scheme: indeed, it uses a form of *authenticated encryption* [12]. It is easy to check that false negatives are impossible. Moreover, only the legitimate T can produce the required encryption of the challenge. Indeed, the INT-CTXT property of the encryption scheme guarantees that no adversary is able to produce an authentic ciphertext, and it also guarantees the integrity of the corresponding plaintext (see Thm 3.1 of [12]). Finally, it is semi-destructive private because, the messages sent in the first and last rounds are truly random strings, while the message sent by T, due to the IND-CPA property of the encryption scheme, looks like an encryption of a random message to an adversary. Moreover, the secret keys it gets through corrupt queries are truly random values, never used for encrypting messages (but perhaps part of a plaintext).

Theorem 2. *The scheme depicted in Fig. 1 is* correct, secure *and* semi-destructive *private if the underlying encryption scheme is IND-CPA and INT-CTXT secure.*

Acknowledgments. We wish to thank Ahmad-Reza Sadeghi and Christian Wachsmann for several useful discussions about RFID privacy notions. This work has been supported by the European Commission through the FP7 ICT program, under Contract FET-215270 FRONTS and by the European Commission through the EU ICT program under Contract ICT-2007-216646 ECRYPT II.

References

1. Avoine, G.: Adversarial model for radio frequency identification. Cryptology ePrint Archive, Report 2005/049 (2005), http://eprint.iacr.org/2005/049
2. Juels, A., Weis, S.A.: Defining strong privacy for RFID. Cryptology ePrint Archive, Report 2006/137 (2006), http://eprint.iacr.org/2006/137
3. Damgård, I., Østergaard, M.: RFID security: Tradeoffs between security and efficiency. In: RSA Conference, Cryptographers' Track, pp. 318–332 (2008)
4. Burmester, M., van Le, T., de Medeiros, B.: Provably secure ubiquitous systems: Universally composable RFID authentication protocols. In: Proceedings of Second International Conference on Security and Privacy in Communication Networks (SecureComm), pp. 1–9. IEEE Computer Society, Los Alamitos (2006)
5. Vaudenay, S.: On privacy models for RFID. In: Kurosawa, K. (ed.) ASIACRYPT 2007. LNCS, vol. 4833, pp. 68–87. Springer, Heidelberg (2007)
6. Ng, C.Y., Susilo, W., Mu, Y., Safavi-Naini, R.: RFID privacy models revisited. In: Jajodia, S., Lopez, J. (eds.) ESORICS 2008. LNCS, vol. 5283, pp. 251–266. Springer, Heidelberg (2008)
7. Bellare, M., Rogaway, P.: Random oracles are practical: A paradigm for designing efficient protocols. In: Proceedings of the Annual Conference on Computer and Communications Security, CCS (1994)
8. Sadeghi, A., Visconti, I., Wachsmann, C.: Anonymizer-enabled security and privacy for rfid. In: Conference on RFID Security 2009, Leuven, Belgium (2009)
9. Sadeghi, A., Visconti, I., Wachsmann, C.: User privacy in transport systems based on RFID e-tickets. In: International Workshop on Privacy in Location-Based Applications (PiLBA), Malaga, Spain, October 9 (2008)
10. Bocchetti, S.: Security and privacy in rfid protocols, master thesis (2006)
11. D'Arco, P., Scafuro, A., Visconti, I.: Revisiting DoS Attacks and Privacy in RFID-Enabled Networks. Full version
12. Bellare, M., Namprempre, C.: Authenticated encryption: Relations among notions and analysis of the generic composition paradigm. In: Okamoto, T. (ed.) ASIACRYPT 2000. LNCS, vol. 1976, p. 531. Springer, Heidelberg (2000)

Link Reversal: How to Play Better to Work Less

Bernadette Charron-Bost[1,2], Jennifer L. Welch[3,*], and Josef Widder[2,4,**]

[1] CNRS, France
[2] Ecole polytechnique, France
[3] Texas A&M University, USA
[4] TU Wien, Embedded Computing Systems Group E182/2, Austria

Abstract. Sensor networks, with their ad hoc deployments, node mobility, and wireless communication, pose serious challenges for developing provably correct and efficient applications. A popular algorithm design technique for such systems is link reversal, first proposed by Gafni and Bertsekas [1] for routing, and subsequently employed in algorithms for, e.g., partition-tolerant routing [2], mutual exclusion [3], and leader election [4,5,6]. Gafni and Bertsekas [1] considered the problem of assigning virtual directions to network links to ensure that the network is loop-free and that every node in the network has a (directed) path to a destination node. They proposed two algorithms, full reversal (FR) and partial reversal (PR), together with an implementation of each based on associating an unbounded value with each node in the graph.

In this paper, we consider a generalization, called $\mathcal{LR}$, of these two algorithms, which was proposed and analyzed in a previous paper [7]. The key to the generalization is to associate a binary label with each link of the graph instead of an unbounded label with each node. In the $\mathcal{LR}$ formalism, initial labelings form a continuum with FR and PR at opposite ends. We previously showed that the number of steps a node takes until convergence — that is, the cost associated to a node — depends only on the initial labeling of the graph. In this paper, we compare the work complexity of labelings in which all incoming links of a given node i are labeled with the same binary value μ_i. Finding initial labelings that induce good work complexity can be considered as a game in which to each node i a player is associated who has strategy μ_i. In this game, one tries to minimize the cost, i.e., the work complexity. Expressing the initial labelings in a natural way as a game allows us to compare the work complexity of FR and PR in a way that, *for the first time, provides a rigorous basis for the intuition that PR is better than FR*.

1 Introduction

Sensor networks, with their ad hoc deployments, node mobility, and wireless communication, pose serious challenges for developing provably correct and efficient applications. A popular algorithm design technique for such systems is link

* Supported in part by NSF grant 0500265 and Texas Higher Education Coordinating Board grants ARP 000512-0130-2007 and ARP 000512-0007-2006.
** Partially supported by the Austrian FWF projects P20529 and P18264.

S. Dolev (Ed.): ALGOSENSORS 2009, LNCS 5804, pp. 88–101, 2009.
© Springer-Verlag Berlin Heidelberg 2009

reversal, first proposed by Gafni and Bertsekas [1] for routing, and subsequently employed in algorithms for partition-tolerant routing [2], mutual exclusion [3], leader election [4,5,6], etc.

Gafni and Bertsekas [1] introduced two algorithms which achieve loop-free routes in a network. Both algorithms start with a directed acyclic graph and reverse the direction of some links, resulting in a graph with a path from each node to a special destination node D; such a graph is called D-oriented. In acyclic graphs, D-orientation is equivalent to the property that there is no node other than D that is a sink (without outgoing links). Gafni and Bertsekas employed a natural policy: if a node other than D is a sink, it reverses the direction of some of its incident links. Two such algorithms are presented in [1], namely full reversal (FR) and partial reversal (PR). In the algorithm FR, every node that becomes a sink reverses *all* of its incident links; in contrast, in the algorithm PR, a node that becomes a sink only reverses those incident links that have not been reversed since the last time the node was a sink. To describe the algorithms formally, and to prove their correctness, Gafni and Bertsekas introduced a formalism based on totally ordered labels — called *heights* — on the *nodes* of an undirected graph: the heights of two neighbors induce a virtual direction on the link from the node with the greater height to the one with smaller height. The problem of D-orientation is thus reduced to achieving a labeling where D is the only local minimum. Gafni and Bertsekas then expressed FR and PR by employing increasing heights which are represented by pairs and triples of integers, respectively. A node other than D that becomes a local minimum increases its height so that it is no longer a local minimum.[1] Using this representation, the correctness was proven, i.e., the convergence of the algorithms and that they achieve D-orientation. Later, Busch *et al.* [8,9] established bounds on the complexities of these algorithms using the same formalism.

In [7], we introduced a simpler formalism, based on directed graphs whose *links* are labeled with 0 or 1. We presented the algorithm $\mathcal{LR}$, which always converges and whose executions coincide with FR if all links are initially labeled with 1, and with PR if they are all initially labeled with 0. We provided a sufficient condition (AC) on the initial link labeling which permanently guarantees acyclicity of the graph during the whole execution, and so, as explained above, also ensures D-orientation. In such a way, we obtain a continuum between FR and PR that correspond to the two globally uniform link labelings. Moreover, for every execution starting with a directed graph where the link labeling satisfies (AC), we established formulae for the *exact* number of steps a node takes during an execution, called the *work* done by the node. As pointed out by Gafni and Bertsekas [1], there are graphs for which FR is better than PR, and there are graphs for which PR is better than FR, with respect to the *global work* (defined as the sum of the work over all nodes). Our formulae help to find such graphs, but they give no direct insight for explaining why PR seems to be a better strategy than FR in practice.

---

[1] It makes its height larger than the heights of an appropriately chosen subset of its neighbors (e.g., all neighbors in the case of FR).

Interestingly, we also provided in [7] a policy for initial link labels, called the *locally uniform* policy (LU, for short), which ensures (AC) and which can be locally implemented: for each node i, all the *incoming* links of i are initially labeled with the same value $\mu_i \in \{0, 1\}$. In this policy, FR corresponds to the uniform labeling 1 (for each i, $\mu_i = 1$) and PR to the uniform labeling 0 (for each i, $\mu_i = 0$). In such a way, LU specializes the continuum between FR and PR provided by (AC).

In this paper, we compare the work done in executions starting with graphs labeled according to LU using game theory. As LU is a local policy (each node may be responsible for the labeling of its incoming links), it is natural to associate to each node a player with the two (pure[2]) strategies 0 and 1. Then a strategy profile — consisting of a strategy for each player — corresponds to a (initial) labeled graph. The cost of each player i is then the work done by i in an execution starting from the initial labeled graph. In the same way, the social cost of a given strategy profile is defined as the global work (the sum of the work over all nodes). The main contribution of the paper is to show how the game theory approach allows us to analyze the different initial labelings with LU in a rigorous manner. In particular it allows us to compare FR and PR, both with respect to the individual work done by the nodes, and to the global work.

After presenting the algorithm $\mathcal{L}R$ and recalling the result regarding its complexity [7], we study in Section 2 the influence of the labelings on the work. We start by investigating the influence of i's choice on its own work as well as on the work of the others.

In Section 3, we formally define the game we consider, and briefly recall the required concepts from game theory. Then, we give a characterization of Nash equilibrium from which we conclude that there always exists a Nash equilibrium, namely the profile corresponding to FR. We show that in terms of social cost (global work complexity), this profile is the worst Nash equilibrium. Moreover, the social cost of FR may be larger than the optimal social cost by some factor which depends on the topology and the size of the graph, and so there is no constant bound on the price of anarchy [10].

In contrast, the profile corresponding to PR is not necessarily a Nash equilibrium. However, we show that its social cost is at most twice the optimal social cost. Hence, even if not optimum, PR is never a disastrous strategy compared to others, and seems "less risky" than FR with this respect. We complement the study of PR by assessing its social cost when D-orientation is lost by the removal of a few links, a common practical situation: we show that the social cost of PR is quite limited, contrary to FR that may perform badly in this case. Thus the two latter points both establish that PR is a better strategy than FR.

Finally, we consider the *mixed* [11] version of the game, in which each player i's mixed strategy μ_i^* is the probability that μ_i is set to 1, and the cost is the expected work. In such a way, we can model random initialization of the link-labeled graph according to LU as a mixed game. We provide a characterization of mixed Nash equilibria, and show that there are no interesting mixed Nash

---

[2] That is, deterministic. We omit the word "pure" when it is clear from the context.

equilibria different from the pure ones, and randomization does not help to find more efficient initial link labelings under the LU policy.

2   The LR Algorithm

2.1   Definitions and Work Complexity

Let G be a directed, connected, and acyclic graph with a special node D. The set of nodes other than D is denoted by V, and $N = |V|$. For convenience, we denote $V = \{1, 2, \cdots N\}$.[3] Let E be the set of links in G. A node with a path to D is called *good* and otherwise is called *bad*.

The algorithm works on G where each link has a *binary* label: let $\phi : E \to \{0, 1\}$ be a binary labeling of links in G, and consider the resulting link-labeled directed graph $G^\dagger$. If $\phi(e) = 1$, we say e is marked; otherwise it is said to be unmarked.

For each node $i \in V \cup \{D\}$, let In_i and Out_i denote the sets of incoming and outgoing links incident to i. In In_i, we distinguish the subset of marked incoming links In_i^1 from the subset of unmarked incoming links In_i^0. Then, the $\mathcal{LR}$ algorithm is described with the two following transition rules executed by any *sink* node i other than D:

LR1. If $In_i^0 \neq \emptyset$, then i reverses the directions of all the links in In_i^0, and marks them; moreover i unmarks all the links in In_i^1.

LR2. Otherwise (i.e., if $In_i^0 = \emptyset$), i reverses the direction of all its incident links and the labels remain unchanged.

As observed in [7], $\mathcal{LR}$ coincides with FR if initially all labels are equal to 1, and with PR if all labels are initially 0. In [7], we showed that for any initial link-labeled graph $G^\dagger$, this algorithm converges to a directed graph which only depends on $G^\dagger$. Moreover, we provided a sufficient condition (AC) on the initial link-labeling which ensures that the resulting graph has a sole sink D and is acyclic, and thus is D-oriented (cf. Section 1). More precisely, condition (AC) restricts the manner in which links in each circuit are labeled (for a more detailed discussion, the reader is referred to [7]).

The complexity measure that is usually considered for link reversal algorithms is the *work complexity* measure [8]. The work complexity of a node is the number of reversals performed by that node, that is to say, the number of LR1 and LR2 transitions. The *global work complexity* is the sum, over all nodes, of the work complexity of each node. In [7], we established the exact formula of the work by each node as a function of the initial link-labeled directed graph when the latter satisfies the (AC) condition. To make this function explicit, we now introduce some notation. A *chain* in G is a sequence of nodes $i_0, \cdots, i_k$ such that for any j, $0 \leq j \leq k - 1$, either (i_j, i_{j+1}) or (i_{j+1}, i_j) is a link of G. Since the initial graph $G^\dagger$ is connected, for any node i, there is a chain connecting D and i.

---

[3] We do not need to assume that nodes are uniquely labeled in a ordered set.

Such a chain C is naturally oriented from i to D and is called a D-*chain from* i. Let $C^\dagger$ denote the corresponding D-chain when its links are equipped with the binary link labels in $G^\dagger$. We consider the numbers of marked links in $C^\dagger$ which are oriented according to and against the orientation. These two numbers are denoted $\ell^1(C^\dagger)$ and $r^1(C^\dagger)$, respectively. Let $s^0(C^\dagger)$ be the number of nodes in $C^\dagger$ which have two distinct incoming unmarked links *relative to* $C^\dagger$. We define the *residue* $Res(C^\dagger)$ to be 1 if the first link (with respect to the natural orientation towards D) in $C^\dagger$ is unmarked and against the orientation, and 0 otherwise. Further we denote by $\mathcal{C}(i, G^\dagger)$ the non-empty set of D-chains from i with the link directions and the link labels inherited from $G^\dagger$. Moreover, we introduced the partitioning of V into three disjoint subsets: $\mathcal{S}(G^\dagger)$ is the set of nodes all of whose incident links are unmarked and incoming, $\mathcal{N}(G^\dagger)$ is the set of nodes with no unmarked incoming link, and $\mathcal{O}(G^\dagger)$ consists of the remaining nodes.

Theorem 1 ([7]). *If the initial link-labeled directed graph $G^\dagger$ satisfies the condition (AC), the number of link reversals made by node i is*

$$\min_{C^\dagger \in \mathcal{C}(i, G^\dagger)} \left(r^1(C^\dagger) + s^0(C^\dagger) + Res(C^\dagger) \right) \text{ if } i \in \mathcal{S}(G^\dagger) \cup \mathcal{N}(G^\dagger)$$

and

$$\min_{C^\dagger \in \mathcal{C}(i, G^\dagger)} \left(2r^1(C^\dagger) + 2s^0(C^\dagger) + Res(C^\dagger) \right) \text{ if } i \in \mathcal{O}(G^\dagger).$$

From Theorem 1, we derived the work complexity of $\mathcal{LR}$ in the two particular cases of uniform link labelings, i.e., for FR and PR. For that, we specialize the notation introduced above for the particular cases of 0 and 1 uniform labelings. For any node i, we denote the set of all D-chains from i by $\mathcal{C}(i, G)$; for any $C \in \mathcal{C}(i, G)$, let $r(C)$ be the number of links in C that are directed away from D and $s(C)$ be the number of nodes in C which have two distinct incoming links relative to C. We also define $Res(C)$, the residue of C, to be 1 if and only if the first link of C is directed toward i. Note that in the case of the 1 uniform labeling (FR), both $\mathcal{S}$ and $\mathcal{O}$ are empty, and so $\mathcal{N}$ contains all the nodes other than D. As for the 0 uniform labeling (PR), $\mathcal{S}$ and $\mathcal{N}$ consist of all the sinks and all the sources, respectively.

Corollary 1. *The number of reversals made by node i in an execution of FR is $\min_{C \in \mathcal{C}(i, G)} (r(C))$. The number of reversals made by node i in an execution of PR is $\min_{C \in \mathcal{C}(i, G)} (s(C) + Res(C))$, if i is a sink or a source in G, or $\min_{C \in \mathcal{C}(i, G)} (2s(C) + Res(C))$, otherwise.*

2.2   Locally Uniform Link Labelings

As observed in [7], condition (AC) naturally leads to the link labeling policy where each node i is allowed to choose $\mu_i \in \{0, 1\}$ for the initial labels of all its *incoming* links. With such a policy, condition (AC) is ensured when the directed graph G is acyclic. Note that the above policy, which we denote by LU, can be easily implemented with a distributed scheme. Besides, FR and PR correspond to the globally uniform choices $\mu_i = 1$ and $\mu_i = 0$, respectively. The LU policy thus encapsulates and establishes a continuum between FR and PR. In fact, this policy provides 2^N possible link-labeling initializations that we are going to compare in the following using game theory.

Consider the set of vectors $S = \{0, 1\}^N$. Let $\vec{0}$ and $\vec{1}$ denote the vectors in S whose components all are 0 and 1, respectively. For any vector $\vec{\mu} \in S$, let $\vec{\mu}_i$ denote its ith component. The link-labeled directed acyclic graph in which for each node $i \in V$, all incoming links of i are labeled with $\vec{\mu}_i$ is denoted by $G^{\vec{\mu}}$. Similarly, let $C^{\vec{\mu}}$ denote the labeled D-chain from some node i in $G^{\vec{\mu}}$ when C is a D-chain from i.

As $G^{\vec{\mu}}$ satisfies (AC), Theorem 1 provides node i's work in $\mathcal{LR}$ starting with $G^{\vec{\mu}}$, denoted by $\sigma_i(\vec{\mu})$.

We now discuss the impact of the choice $\vec{\mu}_i$ on the dynamics of $\mathcal{LR}$. Considering the two rules of $\mathcal{LR}$, we observe that whenever a link e is reversed, e is marked after the reversal. If node i is a sink or a source in the initial graph, then for any initial labeling, all of i's incident links will be marked whenever i becomes a sink. Consequently, i always executes LR2, that is, i reverses all its incident links. Let us now consider a node i with incoming and outgoing links in the initial graph: if $\vec{\mu}_i = 1$, the links that are initially incoming to i are initially marked, due to LU. Whenever i becomes a sink, all of its incident links are marked, and so i always reverses all incident links, using LR2. If $\vec{\mu}_i = 0$, all its incoming links are initially unmarked. When i becomes a sink, i has both marked and unmarked incoming links, and therefore uses LR1 to reverse the unmarked links and unmark the marked ones.

For nodes with incoming and outgoing links, the choice of $\vec{\mu}_i$ thus determines whether node i makes a full reversal at every step (LR2) or whether i reverses only some links (LR1). In particular, if $\vec{\mu} = \vec{1}$, the resulting execution corresponds to FR, and if $\vec{\mu} = \vec{0}$, the execution corresponds to PR.

2.3   Labelings and Work

In the following propositions, we investigate the influence of i's choice for $\vec{\mu}_i$ first on its own work, and then on the work of the other nodes. We denote by $(\vec{\mu}_{-i}, s)$ the vector in S which results from replacing the ith component of $\vec{\mu}$ by s.

First, observe that for every node i and any vector $\vec{\mu} \in S$, we have $i \in \mathcal{N}(G^{(\vec{\mu}_{-i}, 1)})$. Moreover, if i is neither a sink nor a source, then $i \in \mathcal{O}(G^{(\vec{\mu}_{-i}, 0)})$. Combining this remark with Theorem 1, we easily show the following proposition which formally establishes that, from an egoistic viewpoint, it is in the interest of i to choose $\vec{\mu}_i = 1$.

Proposition 1. *For every node $i \in V$, and any vector $\vec{\mu} \in S$, we have*

$$\sigma_i(\vec{\mu}_{-i}, 0) \geq \sigma_i(\vec{\mu}_{-i}, 1).$$

Further, if i is a sink or a source, then

$$\sigma_i(\vec{\mu}_{-i}, 0) = \sigma_i(\vec{\mu}_{-i}, 1).$$

However, the damage caused by the choice of $\vec{\mu}_i = 0$ on the work of i is limited by the factor 2.

Proposition 2. *For every node $i \in V$, and any vector $\vec{\mu} \in S$:*

$$\sigma_i(\vec{\mu}_{-i}, 0) \leq 2 \cdot \sigma_i(\vec{\mu}_{-i}, 1).$$

On the contrary, the next proposition states that if another node j changes its incoming labels from 0 to 1, the work performed by i stays the same, or increases.

Proposition 3. *For any two different nodes i and j, and any vector $\vec{\mu} \in S$:*

$$\sigma_i(\vec{\mu}_{-j}, 0) \leq \sigma_i(\vec{\mu}_{-j}, 1).$$

Repeated application of Proposition 3 leads to the following corollary.

Corollary 2. *For every node $i \in V$, and any two vectors $\vec{\mu}$ and $\vec{\nu}$ in S such that for all $j \in V$, $\vec{\mu}_j \leq \vec{\nu}_j$ and $\vec{\mu}_i = \vec{\nu}_i$, it holds that $\sigma_i(\vec{\mu}) \leq \sigma_i(\vec{\nu})$.*

Finally, we show that when using the LU policy, whether a node has to perform reversals *solely* depends on the initial directed graph G (and not on $G^{\vec{\mu}}$). In particular, if there is a labeling in S for which node i performs no reversal, then for every labeling in S, i makes no reversal.

Proposition 4. *For each node $i \in V$, the following statements are equivalent:*

(1) $\forall \vec{\mu} \in S : \sigma_i(\vec{\mu}) = 0$.
(2) $\exists \vec{\mu} \in S : \sigma_i(\vec{\mu}) = 0$.
(3) i is a good node (i.e., there is a path from i to D).

3   The LU Policy as a Game

We now interpret the LU policy as a game where to each node i, we associate a player who may choose a value in $\{0, 1\}$ for $\vec{\mu}_i$. The cost for player i is naturally given by the work. This interpretation gives us a tool to precisely analyze the LU policy, and compare different initial LU labelings. Game-theoretic analysis allows us to manage the contradictory interests of the players that appear in Propositions 1 and 3. From a distributed algorithmic viewpoint, our results provide a rigorous comparison of FR and PR, which correspond to the special cases $\vec{1}$ and $\vec{0}$, respectively. From the sole viewpoint of game theory, we find that the game has interesting properties on its own.

3.1   Game-Theoretic Definitions

The LU game consists of the set V of N *players*. Each player i has two possible *(pure) strategies* 0 and 1 to label its incoming links. To play the game LU, each player i selects a strategy $\vec{\mu}_i \in \{0, 1\}$. We use the vector $\vec{\mu} = (\vec{\mu}_1, \vec{\mu}_2, \cdots \vec{\mu}_N)$, called a *profile*, selected by the players. As explained above, the profile $\vec{\mu}$ selected by the players entirely determines the work for each player/node. Naturally, we consider for each player i, the *cost* $\sigma_i(\vec{\mu})$ which is the work that i has to perform in $\mathcal{LR}$ starting from $G^{\vec{\mu}}$.

We now recall basic notions from game theory [12,13]. A Nash equilibrium is a profile $\vec{\mu}$ of the game where no player prefers a different strategy, if the current strategies of the other players are fixed:

$$\forall i \in V, \forall s \in \{0,1\} : \ \sigma_i(\vec{\mu}_{-i}, s) \geq \sigma_i(\vec{\mu}).$$

A Nash equilibrium thus represents a profile where from a local and selfish viewpoint, each player i has no motivation to change its strategy. A Nash equilibrium is based on local conditions and so is not necessarily the best possible profile in an absolute way, in the sense that all players have minimal cost. Such a best profile $\vec{\mu}$ is called a *global optimum*:

$$\forall i \in V, \forall \vec{\nu} \in S : \sigma_i(\vec{\mu}) \leq \sigma_i(\vec{\nu}).$$

A game does not necessarily contain a global optimum and further a game does not necessarily contain a Nash equilibrium.

To evaluate the overall quality of a profile $\vec{\mu}$, we consider the *social cost* which is the sum of all players' costs:

$$SC(\vec{\mu}) = \sum_{i \in V} \sigma_i(\vec{\mu}).$$

Clearly, $SC(\vec{\mu})$ is the global work complexity of the $\mathcal{LR}$ algorithm starting from $G^{\vec{\mu}}$. While a global optimum does not necessarily exist, there is always a profile with minimal social cost among all profiles. However, the minimal social cost is reached by any global optimum if it exists.

Further, we are interested in measuring the increase in the social cost when the profiles result from egoistic players' strategies choices — that is, Nash equilibria — instead of when the profiles are established centrally, and for the common good (that is, with minimal social cost). Koutsoupias and Papadimitriou [10] introduced the *price of anarchy* which captures this notion: it is defined as the ratio between the worst social cost of a Nash equilibrium and the minimal social cost among all profiles.

In Section 2.3, we saw that FR corresponds to egoistic strategy choices, and in the following section we show that, with respect to the social cost, FR corresponds to the worst Nash equilibrium. For our game, finding the price of anarchy thus coincides with showing how much worse FR is than a profile with minimal social cost.

3.2   Properties of Strategy Profiles: The FR Strategy

In this section, we first show that the LU game has the remarkable property that it always contains a Nash equilibrium. In particular, the profile $\vec{1}$, which corresponds to FR, is always a Nash equilibrium. We commence with the exact characterization of Nash equilibria in the LU game.

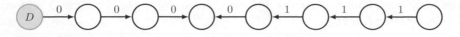

Fig. 1. A global optimum other than $\vec{0}$ and $\vec{1}$

Theorem 2. *The profile $\vec{\mu}$ is a Nash equilibrium iff for all nodes i it holds that i is a sink, or i is a source, or $\vec{\mu}_i = 1$, or $\sigma_i(\vec{\mu}) \leq 1$.*

The conditions in Theorem 2 are rather different in nature: whether some node is a sink or a source solely depends on the graph and not on the strategy. On the contrary, the condition $\vec{\mu}_i = 1$ is independent of the graph. The final condition $\sigma_i(\vec{\mu}) \leq 1$ is hybrid: Proposition 4 shows that good nodes never take steps independently of the profile and thus always satisfy $\sigma_i(\vec{\mu}) = 0$. Further, Theorem 1 shows that under LU, a bad node which is a neighbor of a good node always has a cost equal to 1. Such nodes thus satisfy this condition for any $\vec{\mu}$. Other nodes may satisfy the latter condition, but this depends on both the directed graph and the strategies of the other players (as exemplified in Figure 1 where each node makes exactly 1 reversal).

Theorem 2 implies that for the graph given in Figure 1, the indicated labeling is a Nash equilibrium. In fact, it is a global optimum (as for each node i, $\sigma_i(\vec{\mu}) = 1$). Figure 1 thus provides an example of a graph for which neither FR nor PR is the best strategy. More generally, determining the best strategies requires knowing the topology of the whole graph. Since no such global knowledge is available at each node, the LU strategies other than FR and PR are not interesting in a distributed setting. However, we will show in the following how these strategies and the continuum that they form between FR and PR play a key role in the analysis and comparison of FR and PR.

As an immediate consequence of the theorem, we obtain that FR is always a Nash equilibrium.[4]

Corollary 3. *The profile $\vec{1}$ is a Nash equilibrium.*

Conversely, $\vec{0}$ is not necessarily a Nash equilibrium: for instance, consider the directed graph in Figure 1 with the labeling $\vec{0}$. The second node (from the right) may reduce its work from 2 to 1 by changing its strategy from 0 to 1. However, from a global viewpoint, i.e., with respect to the social cost, $\vec{0}$ has advantageous properties compared to $\vec{1}$. We start by showing that the social cost of $\vec{1}$ may be very bad, and in particular it is the worst among all Nash equilibria.

Theorem 3. *If the profile $\vec{\mu}$ is a Nash equilibrium then for all nodes i:*

$$\sigma_i(\vec{\mu}) \leq \sigma_i(\vec{1}).$$

Corollary 4. *If the profile $\vec{\mu}$ is a Nash equilibrium then $SC(\vec{\mu}) \leq SC(\vec{1})$.*

---

[4] The existence of a (pure) Nash equilibrium for any directed acyclic graph is not a triviality since the LU game is not a potential game [14], as can be easily proved.

We have thus established that $\vec{\mathbb{1}}$ is the worst Nash equilibrium (with respect to the global work complexity). Moreover, we are going to bound the ratio between the social cost of $\vec{\mathbb{1}}$ and the social cost of any profile. Combining the two latter results, we derive an upper bound on the price of anarchy which will be proved to be tight in the next section.

First, let us introduce additional notation. Let B be the number of bad nodes, and let R denote the maximum of the work of any node in $\vec{\mathbb{1}}$. Let us recall that Corollary 1 gives R as the following function of the topology of the graph:

$$R = \max_{i \in V} \left(\min_{C \in \mathcal{C}(i,G)} (r(C)) \right).$$

Theorem 4. *For all $\vec{\mu} \in S$ it holds that*

$$\frac{SC(\vec{\mathbb{1}})}{SC(\vec{\mu})} \le R \cdot \left(1 - \frac{R-1}{2B} \right).$$

By Corollary 4, $\vec{\mathbb{1}}$ has the worst social cost among all Nash equilibria, and we consequently obtain:

Corollary 5. *The price of anarchy is less than or equal to $R \cdot \left(1 - \frac{R-1}{2B} \right)$.*

3.3 The *PR* Strategy: A Socially Conscious Choice

Now, we focus especially on the profile $\vec{\mathbb{0}}$ (*PR*) in the *LU* game. First, we establish that when $\vec{\mathbb{0}}$ is a Nash equilibrium, it is a global optimum and consequently it has minimal social cost. As a result, we prove that the bound on the price of anarchy in Corollary 5 is actually tight. Then, we show that the social cost of $\vec{\mathbb{0}}$ is at most twice the optimal social cost. Finally, we complement the study of $\vec{\mathbb{0}}$ by assessing its social cost absolutely, when the graph results from the removal of k links.

Theorem 5. *If $\vec{\mathbb{0}}$ is a Nash equilibrium, then $\vec{\mathbb{0}}$ is a global optimum.*

Consider a graph which is a chain with D as an end node and all links are oriented away from D. From Theorem 1, we obtain $SC(\vec{\mathbb{1}}) = \frac{N \cdot (N+1)}{2}$ while $SC(\vec{\mathbb{0}}) = N$. Observe that for this chain, $\vec{\mathbb{0}}$ is a Nash equilibrium since for each node i, $\sigma_i(\vec{\mathbb{0}}) = 1$. Theorem 5 ensures that $\vec{\mathbb{0}}$ achieves the minimal social cost, and the price of anarchy in this example is thus equal to $\frac{N+1}{2}$. This shows that the bound in Corollary 5 is tight since we have $N = B = R$ in this case, and so $R \cdot \left(1 - \frac{R-1}{2B} \right) = \frac{N+1}{2}$.

Hence the social cost of $\vec{\mathbb{1}}$ (*FR*) may be worse than $\vec{\mathbb{0}}$ (*PR*) by some factor which depends on the graph. In [7], we gave an example of a graph where *PR* behaves worse than *FR*. However, the social cost of *PR* in this example is less than twice the social cost of *FR*. Using the properties of the *LU* game, we are now in position to prove that, in fact, this holds for any graph:

Theorem 6. *For any node $i \in V$ and any $\vec{\mu} \in S$,*

$$\sigma_i(\vec{\mathbb{0}}) \le 2 \cdot \sigma_i(\vec{\mu}).$$

Corollary 6. *For all $\vec{\mu} \in S$ it holds that $SC(\vec{0}) \leq 2 \cdot SC(\vec{\mu})$.*

As already discussed in Section 2.2, initially labeling the incoming links of some node i (which is neither source nor sink) with 0 has the effect that i only uses LR1, every time it is a sink. Therefore, choosing $\vec{\mu}_i = 0$ can be seen as the lazy approach to link reversal, since it guarantees only some links are reversed in each reversal. Corollary 6 thus shows that the *price of laziness* is bounded by 2 with link reversal.

From this corollary, we further derive that the social cost of PR is at most twice the social cost of FR. We have already seen in this section that the social cost of FR may be up to $\frac{N+1}{2}$ times greater than the one of PR. Consequently, there are graphs where FR is much worse than PR while for all graphs, PR may be worse than FR at most by a factor of 2. Contrary to the FR strategy, PR is never a disastrous strategy even if not optimum, and so appears as "less risky" than FR.

We now give another argument in favor of the PR strategy: when removing a few links from a D-oriented graph (a frequent situation in practice), PR's social cost is quite limited, contrary to FR which may be very bad in this case.

Theorem 7. *If $G = (V \cup \{D\}, E)$ is a connected, directed and acyclic graph which is obtained by removing k links from a D-oriented, directed and acyclic graph G', then for all $i \in V$, $\sigma_i(\vec{0}) \leq 2k$. Consequently,*

$$SC(\vec{0}) \leq 2kB$$

where B is the number of bad nodes.

Hence, each bad node makes at most 2 reversals with the $\vec{0}$ profile when removing a single link. The same link removal with profile $\vec{1}$ (FR) can cause some node to make $N - 1$ steps, where N is the number of nodes in G other than D: consider the circuit G' in which the links incident to D are oriented toward D and all other links are oriented in one direction o. Removing the link incident to D in G' that is oriented according to o leads to a graph G which is a chain in which all links except the one incident to D are oriented away from D. The first node i in this chain has $\sigma_i(\vec{1}) = N - 1$. Moreover, the social cost for $\vec{1}$ is $\frac{N \cdot (N-1)}{2}$, while that of $\vec{0}$ is $N - 1$ in this example.

The previous theorem shows one common situation in which PR performs very well. This may explain *a posteriori* why several link reversal algorithms (e.g., [2,4]) are based on the PR strategy since they are usually analyzed in the context of a D-oriented graph from which one link is removed.

3.4   Properties of Mixed Strategy Profiles

Until now, we have studied deterministic strategies in order to compare the work complexity of different initial link-labelings. A natural question is whether random link-labelings have interesting properties. To investigate this, we consider the mixed version of the LU game: by assigning a probability to each pure strategy of a player, one obtains a *mixed strategy*, and considers the expected cost of this profile.

More precisely, each player i selects a mixed strategy $\vec{\mu}_i^* \in [0,1]$ in the sense that strategy 1 is chosen with probability $\vec{\mu}_i^*$. The vector $\vec{\mu}^* = (\vec{\mu}_1^*, \vec{\mu}_2^*, \cdots \vec{\mu}_N^*)$ is called a *mixed profile*. We denote by S^* the set of all mixed strategy profiles. Let $\bar{\sigma}_i(\vec{\mu}^*)$ denote the expected cost of player i in the mixed profile $\vec{\mu}^*$ which is obtained by weighting each of i's pure strategy profile costs by the probability that this profile occurs in $\vec{\mu}^*$; further $\bar{\sigma} = (\bar{\sigma}_1(\vec{\mu}^*), \bar{\sigma}_2(\vec{\mu}^*), \cdots \bar{\sigma}_N(\vec{\mu}^*))$. Then, $\vec{\mu}^*$ is a *mixed Nash equilibrium* if

$$\forall i \in V, \forall p \in [0,1] : \bar{\sigma}_i(\vec{\mu}_{-i}^*, p) \geq \bar{\sigma}_i(\vec{\mu}^*).$$

Nash [11] showed that every finite mixed game has an equilibrium. As shown above, the LU game has always a pure Nash equilibrium, and a natural question at this point is to study whether there are mixed Nash equilibria that are different from pure ones, that is, mixed equilibria $\vec{\mu}^*$ in which $\vec{\mu}_i^*$ is in the open interval $]0,1[$ for some player i. To answer this question, consider sinks: from Proposition 1, we see that, if the other strategies are fixed, the cost for sinks is the same for both pure strategies.

Further, if some sink j is on some D-chain from i, then setting $\vec{\mu}_j = 0$ augments s^0, while setting $\vec{\mu}_j = 1$, the link directed to i augments r^1, and consequently, i's choice has no influence on the cost of others by Theorem 1. Consequently, if $\vec{\mu}$ is a pure Nash equilibrium such that j is a sink and $\vec{\mu}_j = 1$, then also $(\vec{\mu}_{-j}, 0)$ is a pure Nash equilibrium. Moreover, it is obvious that when fixing the other strategies, any choice of $\vec{\mu}_j^* \in]0,1[$ also leads to a mixed equilibrium. However, such additional equilibria are not particularly interesting as they provide additional favorable choices for players whose choices do not influence the work. We now show that generally all mixed equilibria that are different from pure ones are not interesting and that therefore randomization does not help here.

As the cost for player i in a mixed profile is the weighted strategy profile costs of player i, we directly obtain from Proposition 1:

Proposition 5. *For any node i, and any mixed profile $\vec{\mu}^* \in S^*$:*

$$\bar{\sigma}_i(\vec{\mu}_{-i}^*, 0) \geq \bar{\sigma}_i(\vec{\mu}_{-i}^*, 1).$$

Using this corollary, we can prove the following theorem which characterizes the nature of the mixed Nash equilibria in this game.

Theorem 8. *If $\vec{\mu}^*$ is a mixed Nash equilibrium and there is some $i \in V$ with $\vec{\mu}_i^* \in]0,1[$, then for any $p \in [0,1]$, $(\vec{\mu}_{-i}^*, p)$ is a mixed Nash equilibrium.*

4 Conclusions

Link reversal is an important technique that appears in a variety of algorithms for sensor networks. *FR* and *PR* were originally presented in a way hinting that superior performance could be obtained from *PR*. However, the only analyses done until now did not support this intuition, and instead showed that the work complexity of the two algorithms is asymptotically the same. By applying game theory to the study of our generalized version of link reversal, we have been able to provide in this paper for the first time a rigorous basis for the intuition that *PR* is better than *FR*.

The approach taken in this paper should not be confused with a different approach to analyzing distributed algorithms using game theory [15]: often, the problem—in our case this would be achieving *D*-orientation—is modeled as a game in which the strategies are steps a node may choose to execute at a given point during the execution. For instance, upon becoming a sink, a node may choose the subset of its incident links it reverses. Such an approach is operational, as strategies are chosen during the execution and the choice may thus depend on (parts of) the current global state.

In contrast, we have used game theory in this paper solely to analyze the impact of the choice of initial labelings that nodes can apply to their incoming links. Our main findings are that *FR* is a Nash equilibrium, but has the worst social cost among all Nash equilibria. In fact, the price of anarchy (determined by the social cost of *FR*) is proportional to the number of nodes in the graph. On the other hand, although *PR* is not necessarily a Nash equilibrium, its social cost is never more than twice the optimal; furthermore, in response to the loss of some links, the number of reversals performed on average by each bad node is proportional to the number of lost links. Game theory thus provides us with a formal basis to understand the discrepancy between *FR* and *PR*.

Finally, we showed that randomized assignment of uniform labels to links does not provide any advantage over deterministic strategies.

Acknowledgments. We are grateful to Olivier Bournez and Johanne Cohen for introducing us to the joy of game theory and for very helpful advice.

References

1. Gafni, E.M., Bertsekas, D.P.: Distributed algorithms for generating loop-free routes in networks with frequently changing topology. IEEE Transactions on Communications 29, 11–18 (1981)
2. Park, V.D., Corson, M.S.: A highly adaptive distributed routing algorithm for mobile wireless networks. In: IEEE Infocom 1997 - 16th Conference on Computer Communications, pp. 1405–1413. IEEE, Los Alamitos (1997)
3. Walter, J.E., Welch, J.L., Vaidya, N.H.: A mutual exclusion algorithm for ad hoc mobile networks. Wireless Networks 7, 585–600 (2001)
4. Malpani, N., Welch, J.L., Vaidya, N.: Leader Election Algorithms for Mobile Ad Hoc Networks. In: Proceedings of the 4th international workshop on Discrete algorithms and methods for mobile computing and communication (2000)
5. Ingram, R., Shields, P., Walter, J.E., Welch, J.L.: An asynchronous leader election algorithm for dynamic networks. In: Proc. of the IEEE International Parallel & Distributed Processing Symposium (to appear, 2009)
6. Derhab, A., Badache, N.: A self-stabilizing leader election algorithm in highly dynamic ad hoc mobile networks. IEEE Trans. Parallel Distrib. Syst. 19, 926–939 (2008)

7. Charron-Bost, B., Gaillard, A., Welch, J.L., Widder, J.: Routing without ordering. In: Proceedings of the 21st ACM Symposium on Parallelism in Algorithms and Architectures, SPAA (to appear, 2009)
8. Busch, C., Surapaneni, S., Tirthapura, S.: Analysis of link reversal routing algorithms for mobile ad hoc networks. In: Proceedings of the 15th ACM Symposium on Parallelism in Algorithms and Architectures (SPAA), pp. 210–219 (2003)
9. Busch, C., Tirthapura, S.: Analysis of link reversal routing algorithms. SIAM Journal on Computing 35, 305–326 (2005)
10. Koutsoupias, E., Papadimitriou, C.H.: Worst-case equilibria. In: 16th Annual Symposium on Theoretical Aspects of Computer Science (STACS), pp. 404–413 (1999)
11. Nash, J.: Non-cooperative games. The Annals of Mathematics 54, 286–295 (1951)
12. Osborne, M.J.: An Introduction to Game Theory. Oxford University Press, Oxford (2003)
13. Nisan, N., Roughgarden, T., Tardos, E., Vazirani, V.V. (eds.): Algorithmic Game Theory. Cambridge University Press, Cambridge (2007)
14. Monderer, D., Shapley, L.S.: Potential games. Games and Economic Behavior 14, 124–143 (1996)
15. Halpern, J.Y.: Beyond Nash equilibrium: solution concepts for the 21st century. In: Twenty-Seventh Annual ACM Symposium on Principles of Distributed Computing (PODC), pp. 1–10 (2008)

Early Obstacle Detection and Avoidance for All to All Traffic Pattern in Wireless Sensor Networks*

Florian Huc[1], Aubin Jarry[1], Pierre Leone[1], Luminita Moraru[1],
Sotiris Nikoletseas[2], and Jose Rolim[1]

[1] Computer Science Department
University of Geneva
1211 Geneva 4, Switzerland
[2] University of Patras and CTI
26500 Patras, Greece

Abstract. This paper deals with early obstacles recognition in wireless sensor networks under various traffic patterns. In the presence of obstacles, the efficiency of routing algorithms is increased by voluntarily avoiding some regions in the vicinity of obstacles, areas which we call dead-ends. In this paper, we first propose a fast convergent routing algorithm with proactive dead-end detection together with a formal definition and description of dead-ends. Secondly, we present a generalization of this algorithm which improves performances in all to many and all to all traffic patterns. In a third part we prove that this algorithm produces paths that are optimal up to a constant factor of $2\pi + 1$. In a fourth part we consider the reactive version of the algorithm which is an extension of a previously known early obstacle detection algorithm. Finally we give experimental results to illustrate the efficiency of our algorithms in different scenarios.

1 Introduction

In this paper, we study the problem of routing messages in sensor networks. Due to the specificity of such networks, routing algorithms need to make computations based on local information. Numerous algorithms have been proposed for this problem. For a class of them which is called geographic routing algorithms, it is assumed that the sensors know their geographic position e.g. by using a GPS or by other localization techniques [BJ05]. The algorithms we propose in this paper belong to this class.

Geographic routing algorithms differ in the way they avoid obstacles (Definition 1). Indeed, the strategy of these algorithms is mainly to greedily progress towards the destination (whose position is supposed to be known). To do so, coordinates are used to compute the Euclidean distance to the destination, and the greedy strategy consists in choosing a node whose Euclidean distance is smaller.

---

* Research partially funded by FP6-015964 AEOLUS and FRONTS 215270.

S. Dolev (Ed.): ALGOSENSORS 2009, LNCS 5804, pp. 102–115, 2009.

Since obstacles block greedy progressions in a local minima, several techniques have been introduced to get out of local minima; for instance, GRIC follows the obstacles' borders while introducing some inertia; Face Routing routes along the faces of a planarized network. These algorithms do not use other information than the coordinates of the nodes and their efficiency is usually estimated according to the communication overhead at each node and the length of the path discovered. The algorithm presented in [KWZ08] discovers a path whose length is at most $O(d^2)$, where d is the Euclidean distance from the source to the destination. Moreover, it is shown that no memoryless algorithm can guarantee a better result.

Some other algorithms using extra node memory have been proposed. This is the case of the early detection algorithm proposed in [MLNR07]. We investigate this direction further by proposing a class of proactive obstacle detection algorithms (ODA). The algorithm proposed in [MLNR07] considers networks containing only one base station, with a *all to one* data traffic pattern. In this paper we propose a faster convergent algorithm which works under the same hypothesis but also in the case of all to many and all to all traffic pattern hypothesis. We then propose an extension that improves its performances in the case of *all to many* and *all to all* traffic pattern.

These algorithms mark the nodes in the vicinity of obstacles while routing messages, and favor the non marked ones. One of the performance parameters of ODA is the time of convergence - the time needed to acknowledge the presence of obstacles in their vicinities. An important contribution of this paper is a significant improvement of the convergence time in comparison to [MLNR07]. Furthermore, we prove that this algorithm computes a path whose length is at most a constant times the length of the shortest path (and hence optimal up to a constant factor) under the hypothesis that the plane is covered uniformly by sensor except on the obstacles ; this situation being an approximation of a dense sensor network. To do so, we describe and give a formal definition of the marked areas, also called dead-ends.

The paper is organized as follow: Section 2 introduces the current state of the art in geographic routing, with emphasis on obstacle avoidance algorithms. Section 3 contains the description of our fast convergent and proactive algorithm for all to one traffic pattern (remarks that this algorithm also work under other traffic patterns). Section 4 describes improvements of this algorithm for all to many and all to all traffic patterns. Section 5 is an analysis of dead-ends (or marked) areas and it includes the proof that our algorithm computes a path whose length is at most $(2\pi + 1)d$, where d the Euclidean distance from the source to the destination. In Section 6, we propose the reactive version of the algorithm. In Section 7, we compare the performances of our algorithms with the state of the art. The conclusions are presented in the last section.

2   State of the Art

We address the problem of finding near optimal paths in sensor networks using geographic routing. We suppose that all nodes know their position and that obstacles are present in the network. Considering this framework, several scenarios can be considered : *all to one*, when any node in the network can be the originator of a message whose destination is a unique Base Station; *all to many* when several Base Stations are present in the network ; *all to all* when any node can be destination of a message.

By default, geographic routing algorithms greedily route the messages towards the destination [KSU99], [Fin87], [MM96], [CNS05]. When the greedy forwarding technique fails, the algorithms enter a recovery mode, used until the greedy forwarding technique is again feasible. The solutions are divided in the following categories[CV07]: flood based, planar graph based, spanning tree based and geometric based.

Flooding based techniques [SL01],[JPS99] broadcast the message if it reaches a local minima. Although the complexity is low, the overhead is high. And, even if they guarantee delivery, path optimality is not a concern. An alternative to flooding is multicast. [CDNS06] proposes a redundant multipath delivery scheme that uses probabilistic choices to achieve an optimal trade-off between efficiency and cost; while this method indeed copes well in sparse networks, it fails to bypass big obstacles.

[BCN06] is a protocol combining greedy routing and adaptation of the transmission range to bypass obstacles. It manages to "jump over" obstacles, but the routing path created is not optimal and the energy cost can become high.

Planar graph traversal techniques [KK00], [HBBW04], [BMSU01], [DSW02] are used since they were proved to guarantee delivery if a path exists. Planar graph based obstacle avoidance strategies use greedy as long as a node has a neighbor closer to the destination. Otherwise, one of the existing planar graph traversal algorithms [Urr02], [KWZ03], [KWZZ03] is used. Since the representation of the network is not always a planar graph, this class of strategies needs to use a distributed planarization algorithm. This can be done at the network level, in the network setup phase, or it can be done on demand, only for the set of nodes where greedy forwarding cannot be used.

The performances of these strategies depend on two factors: the performances of graph traversal algorithm and of the distributed planarization algorithm [KGKS05], [GS69], [Tou91]. Most of the algorithms are concerned with improving the planar graph traversal algorithms. In [KWZ08], the authors propose a variant of [KK00] which computes paths whose length is $O(d^2)$, where d is the length of the shortest paths to the destination. Furthermore, they prove that no algorithm not using sensors's memories can guarantee a better approximation ratio.

Spanning tree based techniques build a spanning tree when a message is blocked at a node. In [RRR+99] they are forwarded using flooding, while in [LLM06] the locations covered by subtrees are aggregated using convex hulls to decide which direction in the tree is closer to the destination. The disadvantage of the method is the overhead needed to transmit the information several hops away.

Geometric based techniques use memories of sensors to capture geometric properties of the network in order to improve performances. For instance, a geometric obstacle avoidance algorithm is proposed in [FGG06]. It uses the geometric properties of a node (position of its neighbours) to determine if a message can be blocked at that node. The objective is to find obstacles of the network, which are areas of the network bounded by nodes at which messages are blocked. This technique needs angle computation and hence the sensors are supposed to have specific equipment. Furthermore, the obstacle detection is done during an initialisation phase and hence decrease the available energy of all nodes, even the one that are not in a local minima.

Other existing early obstacle detection techniques using geographic routing where concerned with the all to one scenario, i.e. when all the traffic was directed towards a single base station. They are based on the detection, and marking of nodes close to obstacles in a reactive manner. This way it avoids the use of energy at nodes which are not local minima.

The algorithms proposed in [MLNR07, MLNR08] are based on two modes, the greedy mode and the perimeter mode. In greedy mode, the node which has to send a message choose among its optimal (see bellow) neighbours the one that decrease the most the euclidien distance towards the destination. When a node is in perimeter mode, it means that the message is currently following the border of an obstacle in some direction. The node sends the message so that it keeps following the border of the obstacle in the same direction, until it is completely avoided, see [KK00] for a precise description of this mode.

The difference between the two algorithms differ in the way to mark optimal or non optimal nodes. Initially all nodes are marked as optimal. The method [MLNR07]: *behavior based routing* evaluates the ratio between the total number of times greedy or perimeter routing were previously used by a node. If the ratio is in favour of perimeter, the node is marked as non optimal. In the second method [MLNR08]: *neighborhood based routing*, a node on a routing path tags itself based on the outcome of a node optimality evaluation method - the evaluation is optimal if a node has at least one neighbor tagged as optimal and which is closer to the destination. If a node is non-optimal, then we consider that any path towards the destination using it will be as well non-optimal. These protocols gradually evaluates the performance of a path, detecting reactively the nodes around obstacles, and progressively redefining the routing paths. Each node is evaluating itself and spreads locally information about its performances. Once the non optimal nodes are detected and advertised, each node in greedy routing mode will avoid to choose non optimal neighbors for forwarding, thus redirecting the message outside the non optimal area. There are two main disadvantages of these methods. First, the convergence time is slow since several paths needs to be routed through non optimal areas before they are detected. Second, it lacks generality. Indeed, if there are several base stations in the network, then the paths could be even longer than with the classical algorithms (e.g. GPG).

3   Single Destination Routing and *Dead-Ends* Detection

To avoid *local minima*, a solution consisting in marking nodes with optimal and non-optimal reputations has been developed in [MLNR07]: non-optimal nodes lead to *local minima* and should be avoided, whereas nodes marked as optimal can be safely used for greedy routing.

Similarly, in this paper we will consider marking nodes as optimal or non-optimal. Our marking bears important differences as it is done proactively whenever a local minima is detected.

Initially, all nodes are marked as optimal. Then the following algorithm is run, in which *current node* stands for any node that has a message to send.

Algorithm 1. Algorithm Dead-End

Input : A node and the destination of its message.
Output : A node to which to forward the message.
The current node proceeds to a dead-end evaluation process;
if The current node is optimal **then**
   it chooses the next node using a greedy mode;
else
   it chooses the next node using an escape mode.
end if

Dead-End Evaluation Process. The current node checks if it would find a node to which to send the message if it uses the greedy mode, i.e. it checks if it is a local minima towards the destination. If it is not a local minima, it makes nothing, otherwise it means it has no neighbors closer to the destination. In this case, it marks itself as non-optimal and broadcasts this information to all its neighbors. Each node which receives such a message checks if it has *optimal* neighbors closer to the destination than itself. If not, it marks itself as non-optimal and broadcast it. The same process repeats recursively until a whole area is marked as non-optimal. We call such an area a *dead-end.*

At this point, an exit is computed for the messages originated at non-optimal nodes. A node receiving a message that one of its neighbours is marked as non-optimal, but which does not mark itself as non-optimal, advertises that it is a potential exit from the dead-end. Then a non-optimal node knowing an exit, advertises itself as an exit recursively. Each non-optimal node chooses as exit the first neighbor advertised as exit.

Overhead. This algorithm induces communications only in dead-ends. Hence any node outside a dead-end will NOT waste energy. Also nodes in dead-ends use energy at this point to mark themselves so that not to be contacted later on. Finally, the overhead is of exactly two broadcasts per node in the dead-end and one for the nodes adjacent to one in the dead-end. Hence this algorithm would be efficient in large sensor network.

Greedy Mode. Good nodes function in greedy mode. They route received messages greedily, i.e., they send the message to the optimal node among their neighbors which is the closest to the destination.

Escape Mode. Bad nodes function in escape mode. They know (cf dead-end process above) one of their neighbors as a direction towards the exit of the *dead-end*, so they send messages to this node.

Algorithm Convergence. we say that the algorithm converges when the number of non-optimal nodes does not increase anymore. It means, that a message sent by an optimal node will be entirely routed greedily, avoiding any *dead-ends*. A message sent by a non-optimal node will first escape the dead-end until it reaches an optimal node, after what it will be routed greedily.

4   Multiple Directions Routing and *Dead-Ends* Detection

The previous algorithm detects the presence of obstacles towards the destination of a message, and marks nodes accordingly. It increases the performances of the routing algorithm for messages sent to this destination, but, if there are multiple destinations, it can decrease the performances for a message directed to another destination. We are aiming at finding efficient paths regardless of the destination of the message. A solution is to divide the communication area reached by the node in several directions and to keep track of the optimality for each direction. A parameter *directions* is chosen accordingly to the number of destinations, if there are several base station for instance, or accordingly to the shape of the obstacles if they are known. Otherwise, an arbitrary size can be chosen (heuristically height works well). To each node is associated an array of size *directions*, which indicates if the node is optimal for a specific direction or not.

Given a node n, and a message that it has to send, n computes in which direction i the destination is. For example, if there are four directions, a node n, split the networks into the four geometrical quadrants.

The algorithm is an adaption of the one of the previous section:

Algorithm 2. Algorithm Directional Dead-End

Input : A node and the destination of its message.
Output : A node to which to forward the message.
The current node computes in which direction is the destination;
The current node proceeds to a dead-end evaluation process for this direction;
if The current node is an optimal node for this direction **then**
    it chooses the next node using a greedy mode;
else
    it chooses the next node using an escape mode.
end if

Each of the *greedy mode*, *escape mode* and *dead-end process* that we compared are described in the following.

Greedy Mode. If node n is optimal for direction i, it chooses among all its neighbors that are closer to the destination and marked as optimal for the direction of the destination, the closest to the destination (notice that from the neighbor point of view, the direction towards the destination is not necessary i).

Escape Mode. As in the algorithm of Section 3, if a node is non-optimal, it has precomputed a neighbor which he knows to be an exit for the *dead-end* in direction i. So the node sends the message to this precomputed node. The dead-end exit is relative to a direction and hence can be different for each direction.

Dead-End Evaluation Process. This process verifies locally if a greedy routing would find an optimal node. If so it does nothing, otherwise it do what is described in section 3, except that the notion of optimal and non-optimal node is relative to the direction of the destination, let say i. To summarize, the process is the following: the current node marks itself as non-optimal for direction i and broadcast the information to all its neighbors. Any other node that marks itself as non-optimal also broadcast the information and the process is repeated recursively until it stops. When this process end, the exit of the dead-end area is computed, c.f. Section 3. And a node is marked as non-optimal for the direction of the destination i, if all its neighbors closer to the destination are non-optimal for this direction i.

5   Dead-End Analysis

This section aims at describing from a theoretical point of view the behaviour of our algorithms using the *recursive execution of the dead-end evaluation process*. We indicate which areas (called *dead-ends*) need to be marked such that a message routed greedily avoid all local minima.

We concentrate ourselves in the case of all to one routing pattern as this analyse extends to the all to many routing pattern.

To describe which part of the network is marked as non-optimal, we use a *continuous model*. We suppose that the plane is completely covered by sensors except on some regions called obstacles (definition 1 below), that prevent direct communications between nodes. *Each point of the plan that is not an obstacle represent a node that can transmit a message.*

Theorem 1 describes the minimum part of the plane that will be marked as a dead-end area when there is a single destination D.

Definition 1 (obstacle). *An obstacle p is a position in the plane such that for any pair of nodes (x_1, x_2) at positions p_1 and p_2, if $p \in [p_1, p_2]$ then x_2 is not a neighbor of x_1.*

We use polar coordinates with origin the destination D, to describe the positions of nodes in the network.

Theorem 1. *If there is a continuous line of obstacles $\{(f(\alpha), \alpha)\}_{\alpha \in [\beta, \gamma]}$ such that $f : [\beta, \gamma] \to \mathbb{R}$ is a continuous function, then the dead-end area contains at least all the sensors at position (ρ, α) such that $\alpha \in [\beta, \gamma]$ and $f(\alpha) < \rho \leq \min(f(\beta), f(\gamma))$.*

Proof. Let x_1 be a sensor that is not in a dead-end area. There is a sequence of nodes $x_2, \ldots x_n$ such that $x_n = O$, and $\forall 0 < i < n$ x_i is a neighbor of x_{i+1} and x_{i+1} is closer to the destination than x_i.

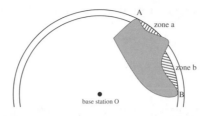

Fig. 1. A line of obstacles from A to B creates dead-ends: zone a and zone b

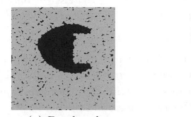

(a) Dead-end   (b) Obstacle

Fig. 2. Simulations show Dead-ends

Suppose that x_1 is at position (ρ_1, α_1) with $\alpha_1 \in [\beta, \gamma]$ and $f(\alpha_1) < \rho_1 \leq \min(f(\beta), f(\gamma))$. Then there is a node x_i at position (ρ_i, α_i) such that

- $\alpha_i \in [\beta, \gamma]$ and
- $f(\alpha_i) < \rho_i \leq \min(f(\beta), f(\gamma))$ and
- x_{i+1} is at position $(\rho_{i+1}, \alpha_{i+1})$ with
  - $\min(f(\beta), f(\gamma)) < \rho_{i+1}$ or
  - $\alpha_{i+1} \notin [\beta, \gamma]$ or
  - $\rho_{i+1} \leq f(\alpha_{i+1})$.

Since x_{i+1} is closer to D than x_i, we have $\rho_{i+1} < \rho_i$, and therefore $\rho_{i+1} \leq \min(f(\beta), f(\gamma))$. If $\alpha_{i+1} \notin [\beta, \gamma]$ or if $\rho_{i+1} \leq f(\alpha_{i+1})$, then $[(\rho_i, \alpha_i), (\rho_{i+1}, alpha_{i+1})]$ intersects the line $\{(f(\alpha), \alpha)\}_{\alpha \in [\beta, \gamma]}$ and x_{i+1} can not be a neighbor of x_i.

Remark 1. The analysis works similarly if we consider several directions. The difference is that there is multiple dead-ends, each being associated to a given direction. A node can be in as many dead-ends as there are directions.

Approximation Ratio

In this section we consider a network with a single obstacle, however there is no hypothesis on the shape and size of the obstacle.

We consider a message whose origin and destination are outside the obstacle and dead-ends. Our objective is to prove that, in a continuous model, the path produced by our algorithm is at most a constant times longer than the Euclidean distance between its source and its destination., and therefore optimal up to a constant factor.

Definition 2. *Given a point O and an obstacle, the apparent angle of the obstacle is the angle of the smallest circular sector originating in O and containing the obstacle.*

Theorem 2. *Given a network with a single obstacle under the continuous model assumption and a message with source s and destination t, when the corresponding dead-ends are marked and if s is not situated in the dead-ends, calling α the apparent angle of the obstacle from t, if $\alpha < 2\pi$, then the length of the path computed by the algorithm is at most $(\alpha+1)d$, where d is the Euclidean distance from s to t.*

Proof. The dead-ends are described by Theorem 1. The algorithm does not enter dead-ends by definition. Instead, it follows their border. The worst case happens when the computed path bypass the obstacle from the other side than the shortest path. In this case, the computed path will turn around the whole obstacle following the dead-ends border (Notice that the distance to the destination may not increase since we are in greedy mode). The path will at most turn around the obstacle for an angle of α ,the apparent angle of the obstacle from t, before finding a straight line to the destination ($\alpha < 2\pi$ by hypothesis). Hence the computed path has length at most $(\alpha + 1)d(s,t)$, where $d(s,t)$ is the distance between s and t.

6   Reactive Dead-End Discovery

In this section, we propose reactive variants of the algorithm proposed in Section 4 : Directional Dead-End. By reactive, we mean that only the node forwarding the message computes wether it is optimal or non-optimal. This algorithm combines the multiple marking according to a number of chosen directions, and the caracteristics of the algorithms presented in [MLNR07, MLNR08]. They converge slower than the one proposed in Sections 3 and 4 but the global overhead is reduced.

As before, there are two modes, the greedy mode during which the next node is chosen greedily among the optimal neighbors, and the perimeter mode.

perimeter mode: This is the routing mode inside dead-ends. We use GPSR, it works on a planarized graph of the network and routes the message around a face towards the destination. This algorithm is explained in the introduction.

When constructing a path to route a message, nodes along the path are evaluated. The current node design the node which currently has the message to send. In this Section, only the current node is evaluated at each time step.

We compare two ways to determine whether a node is optimal or non-optimal.

greedy neighborhood evaluation: In this evaluation, we consider all the neighbors closer to the destination than the current node. A node marks itself as non-optimal for the direction in which is the destination if all of them are non-optimal for this direction and optimal for this direction otherwise. Notice that

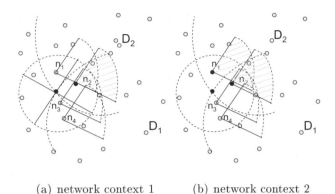

(a) network context 1   (b) network context 2

Fig. 3. Example

the number of non-optimal node may either increase or decrease in the network as we consider traffic towards multiple directions, this is illustrated by figure 3.

First we describe the fig. 3. The current node is situated at the center of the circle and it has to send messages towards the two destination d_1 and d_2. For the sake of simplicity the area covered by the node is divided in only four directions. For each neighbor only the direction towards the destination is taken into account for this evaluation. The directions used for the evaluation are marked in the two pictures. We use an empty segment for optimal nodes and a segment with stripes for non-optimal nods: n_1 and n_2 in the first picture and n_2 in the second picture. There are two greedy nodes, n_1 and n_2 towards d_2 and three greedy nodes, n_2,n_3,n_4 towards d_1.

In this example, the greedy neighborhood evaluation works as follow : in the first picture, the current node contains optimal neighbors closer to both destination (n_3 for d_1, and n_1 for d_2), therefore it will be marked as optimal for this direction. In the second picture, all neighbors closer to d_2 are supposed to be non-optimal, so the current node will mark itself as non-optimal for this direction. However, if an evaluation is made towards d_1, which is in the same direction, the current node will mark itself as optimal, whatever is previous mark was.

one flip evaluation: A drawback of the previous method is that nodes will often change their mark, depending on the message destination. This will trigger additional traffic in the network. In one flip evaluation, we keep non-optimal nodes. In other words, once a node is marked as non-optimal, it remains non-optimal. In this evaluation method, the number of non-optimal nodes can only increase.

In the second example of fig. 3, once the current node has been evaluated towards d_2, it is marked as non-optimal and remains non-optimal, even if it routes a message towards d_1.

7   Simulation Results

The measurements are made with a network of 50x50 with a single obstacle. The network traffic is from left to right. We are using different network densities, from 20 to 40 neighbors in average.

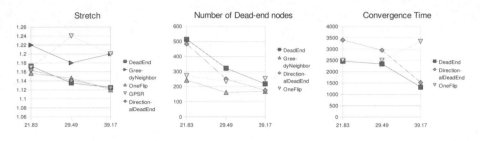

Fig. 4. Simulation results : path stretch, number of dead-end nodes and convergence time

7.1   Stretch

In this section, we compare the average ratio between the path computed by various algorithms and the distance between the source and the destination. The algorithm compared are GPSR which serves as point of comparison with existing work, Dead-End, Directional Dead-End, greedy neighbor evaluation and one flip evaluation.

The obstacle is a half moon situated in the middle of the network, the network traffic is all to all.

We observe that the algorithms Dead-End, Directional Dead-End and one flip evaluation perform well and computes close to optimal path in terms of path length. The improvement consisting in marking nodes using a direction is not significant (Dead-End performs as well as the two others), especially when compared with the increased complexity : it needs more computation at each steps and more memories at each nodes.

7.2   Dead-End Nodes

The number of dead-end nodes decrease when the density of the network increases. This can be explained by the fact that when the density increase, the dead-ends converge to the dead-ends described in Section 5. The area covered by dead-end nodes decreases more rapidly than the density increases.

7.3   Convergence Time

We compare the convergence time of the various algorithms. For Dead-end and Directional Dead-end, fig. 4 indicates the time after which no more nodes have been marked during 400 steps. One flip evaluation does not converge in this sense, however, fig. 4 indicates the time after which no more nodes have been marked during 200 steps ; although, if the number of non-optimal node after this time is not stable, it does not change much. Greedy neighbor evaluation is not convergent even in this sense.

So in terms of convergence, Dead-end and Directional Dead-end are more efficient.

The convergence time decreases when the density increase, this corroborates the decreasing number of dead-end nodes when the density increases. Indeed it takes less time to mark all of them.

8 Conclusion

In this paper we introduced several improvements to the obstacle detection and avoidance routing algorithms and compare them together. We showed that our dead-end recursive evaluation technique outperform previous algorithms in terms of convergence time. The algorithms proposed all do well in terms of path stretch. The main contribution is a theoretical guaranty that, in a continuous network, the algorithm Dead-End computes a path whose length is at most $\pi + 1$ times bigger than the length of the shortest path. This result is interesting since it is optimal up to a constant factor and that, without using memories, the best distributed algorithm cannot guarantee to compute a path whose length is smaller than the square of the distance.

However, the algorithms we proposed are designed for static networks. It would be interesting to extend them to the dynamic case in the hope of getting theoretical guaranties on the computed path under some hypothesis on the dynamicity of the system. An approach may consist in checking the non-optimality of non-optimal nodes after a certain time.

References

[BCN06]   Boukerche, A., Chatzigiannakis, I., Nikoletseas, S.E.: A new energy efficient and fault-tolerant protocol for data propagation in smart dust networks using varying transmission range. Computer Communications 29(4), 477–489 (2006)

[BJ05]   Biaz, S., Ji, Y.: A survey and comparison on localisation algorithms for wireless ad hoc networks. International Journal of Mobile Communications 3(4), 374–410 (2005)

[BMSU01]   Bose, P., Morin, P., Stojmenovi, I., Urrutia, J.: Routing with guaranteed delivery in ad hoc wireless networks. Wireless Networks 7(6), 609–616 (2001)

[CDNS06]   Chatzigiannakis, I., Dimitriou, T., Nikoletseas, S.E., Spirakis, P.G.: A probabilistic algorithm for efficient and robust data propagation in wireless sensor networks. Ad Hoc Networks 4(5), 621–635 (2006)

[CNS05]   Chatzigiannakis, I., Nikoletseas, S.E., Spirakis, P.G.: Efficient and robust protocols for local detection and propagation in smart dust networks. MONET 10(1-2), 133–149 (2005)

[CV07]   Chen, D., Varshney, P.K.: A survey of void handling techniques for geographic routing in wireless networks. IEEE Communications Surveys and Tutorials 9(1-4), 50–67 (2007)

[DSW02]   Datta, S., Stojmenovic, I., Wu, J.: Internal node and shortcut based routing with guaranteed delivery in wireless networks. Cluster Computing 5(2), 169–178 (2002)

[FGG06]   Fang, Q., Gao, J., Guibas, L.J.: Locating and bypassing holes in sensor networks. MONET 11(2), 187–200 (2006)

[Fin87]   Finn, G.G.: Routing and addressing problems in large metropolitan-scale internetworks. Technical Report RR-87-180, University of Southern California, Marina del Rey, Information Sciences Institut (March 1987)

[GS69]   Gabriel, K.R., Sokal, R.R.: A new statistical approach to geographic variation analysis (1969)

[HBBW04]   Heissenbüttel, M., Braun, T., Bernoulli, T., Wälchli, M.: Blr: beacon-less routing algorithm for mobile ad hoc networks. Computer Communications 27(11), 1076–1086 (2004)

[JPS99]   Jain, R., Puri, A., Sengupta, R.: Geographical routing using partial information for wireless ad hoc networks (1999)

[KGKS05]   Kim, Y.-J., Govindan, R., Karp, B., Shenker, S.: Geographic routing made practical. In: NSDI 2005: Proceedings of the 2nd conference on Symposium on Networked Systems Design & Implementation, Berkeley, CA, USA, pp. 217–230. USENIX (2005)

[KK00]   Karp, B., Kung, H.T.: Gpsr: greedy perimeter stateless routing for wireless networks. In: MobiCom 2000: Proceedings of the 6th annual international conference on Mobile computing and networking, pp. 243–254. ACM Press, New York (2000)

[KSU99]   Kranakis, E., Singh, H., Urrutia, J.: Compass routing on geometric networks. In: Proc. 11 th Canadian Conference on Computational Geometry, Vancouver, August 1999, pp. 51–54 (1999)

[KWZ03]   Kuhn, F., Wattenhofer, R., Zollinger, A.: Worst-Case Optimal and Average-Case Efficient Geometric Ad-Hoc Routing. In: Proc. 4th ACM Int. Symposium on Mobile Ad-Hoc Networking and Computing, MobiHoc (2003)

[KWZ08]   Kuhn, F., Wattenhofer, R., Zollinger, A.: An algorithmic approach to geographic routing in ad hoc and sensor networks. IEEE/ACM Transactions on Networking 16(1), 51–62 (2008)

[KWZZ03]   Kuhn, F., Wattenhofer, R., Zhang, Y., Zollinger, A.: Geometric ad-hoc routing: of theory and practice. In: PODC 2003: Proceedings of the twenty-second annual symposium on Principles of distributed computing, pp. 63–72. ACM Press, New York (2003)

[LLM06]   Leong, B., Liskov, B., Morris, R.: Geographic routing without planarization. In: NSDI 2006: Proceedings of the 3rd conference on 3rd Symposium on Networked Systems Design & Implementation, Berkeley, CA, USA, pp. 25–25. USENIX Association (2006)

[MLNR07]   Moraru, L., Leone, P., Nikoletseas, S., Rolim, J.D.P.: Near optimal geographic routing with obstacle avoidance in wireless sensor networks by fast-converging trust-based algorithms. In: Q2SWinet 2007: Proceedings of the 3rd ACM Workshop on QoS and security for wireless and mobile networks, pp. 31–38. ACM, New York (2007)

[MLNR08]   Moraru, L., Leone, P., Nikoletseas, S., Rolim, J.: Geographic Routing with Early Obstacles Detection and Avoidance in Dense Wireless Sensor Networks. In: Coudert, D., Simplot-Ryl, D., Stojmenovic, I. (eds.) ADHOC-NOW 2008. LNCS, vol. 5198, pp. 148–161. Springer, Heidelberg (2008)

[MM96]   Mathar, R., Mattfeldt, J.: Optimal transmission ranges for mobile communication in linear multihop packet radio networks. Wirel. Netw. 2(4), 329–342 (1996)

[RRR+99]   Radhakrishnan, S., Rao, N., Racherla, G., Sekharan, C., Batsell, S.: Dst
            - a routing protocol for ad hoc networks using distributed spanning trees.
            In: IEEE Wireless Communications and Networking Conference, pp. 100–
            104 (1999)
[SL01]   Stojmenovic, I., Lin, X.: Loop-free hybrid single-path/flooding routing
            algorithms with guaranteed delivery for wireless networks. IEEE Trans.
            Parallel Distrib. Syst. 12(10), 1023–1032 (2001)
[Tou91]   Toussaint, G.: Some unsolved problems on proximity graphs (1991)
[Urr02]   Urrutia, J.: Routing with guaranteed delivery in geometric and wireless
            networks. pp. 393–406 (2002)

A Note on Uniform Power Connectivity in the SINR Model[*]

Chen Avin[1], Zvi Lotker[1], Francesco Pasquale[2], and Yvonne-Anne Pignolet[3]

[1] Ben Gurion University of the Negev, Israel
[2] University of Salerno, Italy
[3] ETH Zurich, Switzerland
{avin,zvilo}@cse.bgu.ac.il, pasquale@dia.unisa.it,
pignolet@tik.ee.ethz.ch

Abstract. In this paper we study the connectivity problem for wireless networks under the Signal to Interference plus Noise Ratio (SINR) model. Given a set of radio transmitters distributed in some area, we seek to build a directed strongly connected communication graph, and compute an edge coloring of this graph such that the transmitter-receiver pairs in each color class can communicate simultaneously. Depending on the interference model, more or less colors, corresponding to the number of frequencies or time slots, are necessary. We consider the SINR model that compares the received power of a signal at a receiver to the sum of the strength of other signals plus ambient noise . The strength of a signal is assumed to fade polynomially with the distance from the sender, depending on the so-called path-loss exponent α.

We show that, when all transmitters use the same power, the number of colors needed is constant in one-dimensional grids if $\alpha > 1$ as well as in two-dimensional grids if $\alpha > 2$. For smaller path-loss exponents and two-dimensional grids we prove upper and lower bounds in the order of $\mathcal{O}(\log n)$ and $\Omega(\log n / \log \log n)$ for $\alpha = 2$ and $\Theta(n^{2/\alpha-1})$ for $\alpha < 2$ respectively. If nodes are distributed uniformly at random on the interval $[0, 1]$, a *regular* coloring of $\mathcal{O}(\log n)$ colors guarantees connectivity, while $\Omega(\log \log n)$ colors are required for any coloring.

1 Introduction

The performance of wireless networks depends on the coordination of the timing and frequency bands of broadcasting nodes. This is due to the fact that if two nodes close to each other transmit concurrently, the chances are that neither of their signals can be received correctly because of interference. Thus, choosing an appropriate interference model is critical. The most popular models can be divided into two classes: graph-based models (protocol models) and fading channel models. Graph-based models, such as the unit disk graph (UDG) model [4], describe interference as a binary property by a set of interference edges.

---

[*] Zvi Lotker and Francesco Pasquale were partially supported by a gift from Cisco Reseach Center.

S. Dolev (Ed.): ALGOSENSORS 2009, LNCS 5804, pp. 116–127, 2009.

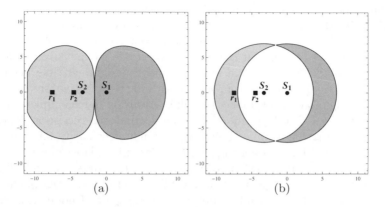

Fig. 1. Reception diagrams for scenario with two links, $l_1 = (s_1, r_1)$ and $l_2 = (s_2, r_2)$. The shaded areas denote where the signal of a sender can be decoded (the area in the lighter gray belongs to sender s_2), white indicates that the received signal power is too weak for reception. *(a)* SINR model: only node r_2 receives a message from its sender, the interference is too high at r_1. *(b)* Unit Disk Graph model: neither r_1 nor r_2 receive a message from their corresponding senders.

The existence of an edge between two communication pairs, usually based on the distance between nodes, implies that the two pairs cannot transmit successfully at the same time (or on the same frequency). Such models, serving as a simple abstraction of wireless networks, have been very useful for the design of efficient distributed algorithms. Nevertheless, graph-based models bear the limitation of representing interference as a local property. In reality, the interference of several concurrent senders accumulates and can interrupt the reception at a far-away receiver. Therefore, the focus of the algorithmic networking community has recently shifted from graph-based models to the more realistic fading channel models, such as the physical Signal to Noise plus Interference (SINR) model [9] that we use in this paper. In this model, a message is received successfully if the ratio between the strength of the sender signal at the receiving location and the sum of interferences created by all other simultaneous senders plus ambient noise is larger than some hardware-defined threshold. Interference is modeled as a continuous property, decreasing polynomially with the distance from the sender, according to the value of the so-called path-loss exponent α. More formally, a receiver r_i receives a sender s_i's transmission if and only if

$$\frac{\frac{P(s_i)}{d(s_i, r_i)^\alpha}}{N + \sum_{j \neq i} \frac{P(s_j)}{d(s_j, r_i)^\alpha}} \geq \beta,$$

where $P(s_k)$ denotes the transmission power of sender s_k, $d(s_k, r_i)$ is the distance between sender s_k and receiver r_i, N denotes the ambient noise power level and β is the minimum SINR required for the successful reception of a message.

In this paper we focus on the uniform power assignment, where every node transmits with the same power. This strategy has several important advantages due to its simplicity. While the benefits of power control are obvious, wireless devices that always transmit at the same power are less expensive and less complicated to build. Therefore, the uniform power assignment has been widely adopted in practical systems. From the algorithmic perspective, the lack of freedom in choosing power levels makes reaching a decision much simpler. Moreover, recently a study of *SINR diagrams*[1] [1] showed that the reception zones of all senders are *convex* for a uniform scheme but not necessarily for non-uniform power assignments. This finding suggests that designing algorithms may be much simpler for uniform networks than for non-uniform networks. Figure 1 illustrates a setting with uniform power levels in the SINR and in the UDG model.

In any network, it is typically required that any pair of nodes can exchange message via relay nodes. In other words, the nodes have to be connected by a communication backbone, e.g., a spanning tree or a connected dominating set. In this paper, we investigate how many colors (time slots / frequencies) are necessary to guarantee that the resulting links (node pairs that can communicate) form a connected graph. [15] was the first to explore this question in the physical interference model. The authors suggest an algorithm that constructs a spanning tree, and assigns power levels and time slots to each link of the tree. This algorithm guarantees that at most $\mathcal{O}(\log^4 n)$ colors suffice for all transmissions to be received correctly, i.e., even in worse-case networks, the scheduling complexity of a strongly-connected topology is polylogarithmic in n and such topologies can thus be scheduled efficiently. The algorithm assigns many different power levels to the links and does not lend itself to a distributed implementation. As we discussed earlier, the study of the uniform case is still worthwhile, thanks to its simplicity and the way cheap commercial hardware is built. Therefore we aim at shedding light on the connectivity problem for uniform power assignments in this paper. More precisely, given a coloring we can construct a *SINR graph*, that represents which nodes can communicate concurrently. We examine the number of colors are necessary such that a strongly connected SINR graph can be built. We show that the number of colors needed is constant in one-dimensional grids if $\alpha > 1$ as well as in two-dimensional grids if $\alpha > 2$. For smaller path-loss exponents, more colors are necessary. If $\alpha = 2$ (i.e., the signal propagation in the vacuum), the upper and lower bounds for the number of colors are in the order of $\mathcal{O}(\log n)$ and $\Omega(\log n / \log \log n)$ respectively. Even smaller values of α have been measured for indoor propagation [18]. For $\alpha < 2$ we provide a tight bound of $\Theta(n^{2/\alpha-1})$. For the special case of $\alpha = 2$ we examined the connectivity of nodes distributed uniformly at random on the interval [0,1]. In this setting, a regular coloring of $\Theta(\log n)$ colors guarantees connectivity.

---

[1] The SINR diagram of a set of transmitters divides the plane into $n + 1$ *regions* or reception zones, one region for each transmitter that indicates the set of locations in which it can be heard successfully, and one more region that indicates the set of locations in which no sender can be heard. This concept is perhaps analogous to the role played by Voronoi diagrams in computational geometry.

2   Related Work

The seminal work of Gupta and Kumar [9] initiated the study of the capacity of wireless networks. The authors bounded the throughput capacity in the best-case (i.e., optimal configurations) for the protocol and the physical models for $\alpha > 2$.

For both model classes, many scheduling algorithms have been suggested. E.g., [10,13,19] analyze algorithms in graph-based models. Typically, these algorithms employ a coloring strategy, which neglects the aggregated interference of nodes located further away. The resulting inefficiency of graph-based scheduling protocols in practice is well documented, both theoretically and by simulation [8,16] as well as experimentally [17]. Recently, Lebhar et al. [14] consider the case of $\alpha > 2$ and senders that are deployed uniformly at random in the area. They showed how a UDG protocol can be emulated when the network operates under the SINR model. Their emulation cost factor is $\mathcal{O}(\log^3 n)$. The fact that interference is continuous and accumulative as well as the geometric constraints lead to an increased difficulty of the scheduling task in the SINR model, even if the transmission power of the nodes is fixed. Two scheduling problems are shown to be NP-complete in the physical SINR model in [7]. Goussevskaia et al. propose in [6] a scheduling algorithm with an approximation guarantee independent of the network's topology. Their algorithm gives a constant approximation for the problem of maximizing the number of simultaneously feasible links and leads to a $\mathcal{O}(\log n)$ approximation for the problem of minimizing the number of time slots to schedule a given set of requests. Furthermore, in [12], the problem is shown to be in APX, thus precluding a PTAS and the authors propose an improved algorithm leading to a constant approximation. Yet another line of research investigates static properties under the SINR model, e.g., the maximum achievable signal-to-interference-plus-noise ratio [20] or the shape of reception zones of nodes in a network [1].

Non-uniform power assignments can clearly outperform a uniform assignment [17,16] and increase the capacity of the network, therefore the majority of the work on capacity and scheduling addressed non-uniform power. Recent work [3] compares the uniform power assignment with power control when the area where nodes, whereas [5,11] give upper and lower bounds for power-controlled oblivious scheduling. As mentioned in the introduction, Moscibroda et al. [15] were the first to raise the question of the complexity of connectivity in the SINR model. While their work applies for networks with devices that can adjust their transmission power, we address networks composed of devices that transmit with the same power.

3   Model

Let (M, d) be a metric space and $V \subseteq M$ a finite set of $n = |V|$ *nodes*. A node v_j successfully receives a message from node v_i depending on the set of concurrently transmitting nodes and the applied interference model. A standard interference model that captures some of the key characteristics of wireless communication and is sufficiently concise for rigorous reasoning is the physical SINR model [9]. In this model, the successful reception of a transmission depends on the strength of the received signal, the interference caused by nodes transmitting simultaneously, and the ambient noise level. The received power $P_{r_i}(s_i)$ of a signal transmitted by a sender s_i at an intended receiver r_i is $P_{r_i}(s_i) = P(s_i) \cdot g(s_i, r_i)$, where $P(s_i)$ is the transmission power of s_i and $g(s_i, r_i)$ is the propagation attenuation (link gain) modeled as $g(s_i, r_i) = d(s_i, r_i)^{-\alpha}$. The *path-loss exponent* $\alpha \geq 1$ is a constant typically between 1.6 and 6. The exact value of α depends on external conditions of the medium (humidity, obstacles, etc.) and on the exact sender-receiver distance. Measurements for indoor and outdoor path-loss exponents can be found in [18].

Given a sender and a receiver pair $l_i = (s_i, r_i)$, we use the notation $I_{r_i}(s_j) = P_{r_i}(s_j)$ for any other sender s_j concurrent to s_i in order to emphasize that the signal power transmitted by s_j is perceived at r_i as interference. The *total interference* $I_{r_i}(L)$ experienced by a receiver r_i is the sum of the interference power values created by the set L of nodes transmitting simultaneously (except the intending sender s_i), i.e., , $I_{r_i}(L) := \sum_{l_j \in L \setminus \{l_i\}} I_{r_i}(s_j)$. Finally, let N denote the ambient noise power level. Then, r_i receives s_i's transmission if and only if

$$\mathrm{SINR}(l_i) = \frac{P_{r_i}(s_i)}{N + I_{r_i}(L)} = \frac{P(s_i)g(s_i, r_i)}{N + \sum_{j \neq i} P(s_j)g(s_j, r_i)} = \frac{\frac{P(s_i)}{d(s_i, r_i)^\alpha}}{N + \sum_{j \neq i} \frac{P(s_j)}{d(s_j, r_i)^\alpha}} \geq \beta,$$

where $\beta \geq 1$ is the minimum SINR required for a successful message reception. For the sake of simplicity, we set $N = 0$ and ignore the influence of noise in the calculation of the SINR. However, this has no significant effect on the results: by scaling the power of all senders, the influence of ambience noise can be made arbitrarily small. Observe that for real scenarios with upper bounds on the maximum transmission power this is not possible, however, for our asymptotic calculations we can neglect this term. We assume that every node can listen/send on all available frequencies simultaneously.

The *scheduling complexity*, introduced in [15], describes the number of time slots or frequencies necessary to successfully transmit messages over a given set of communication links. More formally, we are given a network with a set of directed links representing communication requests. For each such link we assign a color (time slot/frequency) and a power level such that all simultaneous transmissions are successful, i.e., not violating the signal-to-interference plus noise ratio at any receiver.

The *connectivity problem* of a given set V of nodes located in the Euclidean plane is the scheduling complexity of a connected communication graph of V, i.e., an assignment of power levels and colors to each link of the directed strongly connected graph such all transmissions are received correctly.

In this paper, we investigate the uniform connectivity problem, i.e., the connectivity problem for a set V when only uniform power assignments are allowed. We give a formal definition of the graph we examine the connectivity of:

Definition 1 ((Uniform) SINR graph). *Let (M, d) be a metric space, $V \subseteq M$ be a finite set of* nodes, $c : V \to [k]$ *be a coloring of the nodes, and $E \subseteq V^2$ be the set defined as follows*

$$E = \left\{ (u, v) \in V^2 \ : \ \frac{1/d(u, v)^\alpha}{\sum_{w \in V \setminus \{u\} \ : \ c(w) = c(u)} 1/d(w, v)^\alpha} \geqslant \beta \right\} \tag{1}$$

We will refer to the directed graph $G = (V, E)$ as the (uniform) SINR graph.

In other words, the definition of the graph says that a node v can *decode* a message coming from node u (i.e. there is an edge from u to v) if and only if the ratio between the *power* (i.e. $1/d(u, v)^\alpha$) at which v receives the message from u and the sum of the powers from the other *interfering* nodes (nodes w that use the same *frequency* or transmit in the same time slot, i.e. $c(w) = c(u)$) is at least some fixed constant β.

The question we want to answer is the following: Given the metric space (M, d) and the set of nodes $V \subseteq M$, how many colors k do we need in order to be sure that a coloring $c : V \to [k]$ exists such that the resulting graph G is strongly connected?

In this paper, the set of nodes V will be located in $\mathbb{R}$ or in $\mathbb{R}^2$ and d will always denote the Euclidean distance.

4   Connectivity in Grids

4.1   One-Dimensional Grid

Let $V = \{p_1, \ldots, p_n\} \subseteq \mathbb{R}$ be a set of n nodes with $p_1 < p_2 < \cdots < p_n$. We say that V is a *one-dimensional grid* if the nodes are equally spaced, i.e. $d(p_i, p_{i+1})$ is the same for every $i = 1, \ldots, n$ (without loss of generality, we will assume $p_i = i$ for every i).

We say that a coloring $c : V \to [k]$ is a *regular k-coloring* if the points are colored in a *Round Robin* way, i.e. if $c(p_i) = (i \mod k) + 1$ for $i = 1, \ldots, n$.

Theorem 1. *Let $V = \{p_1, \ldots, p_n\}$ be a one-dimensional grid with $p_i = i$ for every $i = 1, \ldots, n$. For any $\alpha > 1$ a constant k and a coloring $c : V \to [k]$ exist such that the corresponding SINR graph is strongly connected.*

Proof. Consider a regular k-coloring, where k is a sufficiently large constant that we will choose later. Now we show that, for every $i = 1, \ldots, n - 1$, there is a directed edge from node p_i to node p_{i+1} in the SINR graph . According to the definition of the SINR graph, we must show that

$$\frac{1/d(p_i, p_{i+1})^\alpha}{\sum_{j \in [n] \setminus \{i\} \ : \ c(p_j) = c(p_i)} 1/d(p_j, p_{i+1})^\alpha} \geqslant \beta \tag{2}$$

For the numerator, we have $1/d(p_i, p_{i+1})^\alpha = 1$ for any α. For the denominator, observe that the nodes with the same color of p_i are $\{ \ldots p_{i-2k}, \ p_{i-k}, \ p_{i+k}, \ p_{i+2k},$

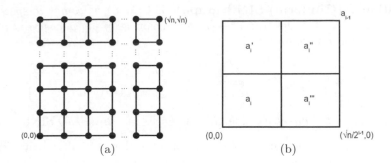

Fig. 2. (a) Two dimensional grid topology. (b) Grid division for the lower bound.

...}. Thus, for any $j = 1, \ldots, n$, we have at most 2 nodes at distance at least $j(k-1)$ from node p_i, hence

$$\sum_{j \in [n] \setminus \{i\} \,:\, c(p_j) = c(p_i)} \frac{1}{d(p_j, p_{i+1})^\alpha} \leqslant \sum_{j=1}^{n} \frac{2}{(j(k-1))^\alpha} = \frac{2}{(k-1)^\alpha} \sum_{j=1}^{n} \frac{1}{j^\alpha} < \frac{2}{(k-1)^\alpha} g(\alpha)$$

where we named $g(\alpha) = \sum_{j=1}^{\infty} j^{-\alpha}$. Observe that $g(\alpha) = \mathcal{O}(1)$ for any constant $\alpha > 1$. In order to satisfy (2) it is sufficient to choose $k \geqslant 1 + (2\beta g(\alpha))^{1/\alpha}$.

In exactly the same way we can show that for every $i = 2, \ldots, n$, there is a directed edge from node p_i to node p_{i-1}, hence the the SINR graph is strongly connected.   □

4.2   Two-Dimensional Grid

Consider the following two dimensional grid topology of n nodes. An array of $\sqrt{n}$ arrays containing $\sqrt{n}$ nodes each, where the left bottom corner node is denoted by (0,0), see Fig. 2 (a).

A *regular k^2-coloring* partitions the nodes into k^2 sets such that the closest distance between any two nodes of the same color is k. In other words, each set forms another grid with distance k. If α exceeds two, the number of colors required for connectivity is constant.

Theorem 2 (Bound 2D grids, $\alpha > 2$). *Let $V = \{p_1, \ldots, p_n\} \subseteq [0, \sqrt{n}]^2$ be a two-dimensional grid. For any $\alpha > 2$ a constant k and a coloring $c : V \to [k]$ exist such that the corresponding SINR graph is strongly connected.*

Proof. Consider a regular k^2-coloring for a grid consisting of n nodes. Let the node v at (0,0) belong to color j. Without loss of generality we can assume that v is connected to the node at (0,1) in the corresponding interference graph. We now explore the interference accrued at node (0,1) if all nodes of color j transmit simultaneously. In this case the total interference at (0,1) is

$$I_{(0,1)} < \sum_{i=1}^{\sqrt{n}} \frac{2i+1}{(ki-1)^\alpha} < \frac{3}{(k/2)^\alpha} \sum_{i=1}^{\sqrt{n}} \frac{1}{i^{\alpha-1}} < \frac{3 \cdot 2^\alpha (\alpha-1)}{2k^\alpha(\alpha-2)},$$

for $\alpha > 2$ due to a standard bound for Rieman's zeta-function. This level of interference needs to be below $1/\beta$, hence the distance k has to satisfy the following inequality: $k > \left(3 \cdot 2^{\alpha-1}\beta(\alpha - 1)/(\alpha - 2)\right)^{1/\alpha}$.

Note that the node in the center of the grid faces at most four times the amount of interference that the node at $(0,1)$ is exposed to. Thus this procedure can be repeated to bound the interference at any node in the grid. In other words, a regular $\left(6 \cdot 2^{\alpha}\beta(\alpha - 1)/(\alpha - 2)\right)^{2/\alpha}$-coloring ensures connectivity in a constant number of rounds.   □

Observe that this result holds for infinite grids as well. In addition, it coincides with the UDG interference model, where a constant number of colors suffices as well. The situation changes dramatically if α is less than or equal to two. If $\alpha = 2$, the number of necessary colors increases logarithmically in the number of nodes.

Theorem 3 (Upper bound 2D grids, $\alpha = 2$). *Let $V = \{p_1, \ldots, p_n\} \subseteq [0, \sqrt{n}]^2$ be a two-dimensional grid. For $\alpha = 2$ a regular $\mathcal{O}(\log n)$-coloring ensures that the corresponding SINR graph is strongly connected.*

Proof. We start similarly to the proof for $\alpha > 2$ and sum up the interference accumulated at node $(0,1)$ under a regular k^2-coloring. In this case the total interference at $(0,1)$ is less than

$$I_{(0,1)} < \sum_{i=1}^{\sqrt{n}} \frac{2i+1}{(ki-1)^{\alpha}} < \frac{3}{(k/2)^{\alpha}} \sum_{i=1}^{\sqrt{n}} \frac{1}{i^{\alpha-1}} = \frac{6 \log n}{k^2}.$$

Moreover, the total interference at $(0,1)$ exceeds

$$I_{(0,1)} > \sum_{i=1}^{\sqrt{n}} \frac{2i+1}{(\sqrt{2}ki)^{\alpha}} > \frac{\sqrt{2}^{\alpha}}{d^{\alpha}} \sum_{i=1}^{\sqrt{n}} \frac{1}{i^{\alpha-1}} = \frac{2 \log n}{k^2}.$$

Note that the node in the center of the grid faces at most four times the amount of interference that the node at $(0,1)$ is exposed to.

β being a constant entails that k^2 has to be in the order of $\Omega(\log n)$ if we want that a message from the node at $(0,0)$ can be decoded at $(0,1)$. There are $\mathcal{O}(k^2)$ nodes at a radius of k around $(0,1)$, consequently, we need $\Omega(\log n)$ frequencies if $\alpha = 2$ and we want all nodes to be able to send concurrently and form a connected structure. We achieve this goal by partitioning the existing grid into $\log n$ grids that send with distinct frequencies.   □

Theorem 4 (Lower bound 2D grids, $\alpha = 2$). *Let $V = \{p_1, \ldots, p_n\} \subseteq [0, \sqrt{n}]^2$ be a two-dimensional grid and $\alpha = 2$. Let $c : V \rightarrow [k]$ be a coloring. If the corresponding SINR graph is strongly connected, then the number of colors is $k = \Omega\left(\frac{\log n}{\log \log n}\right)$.*

Proof. For the lower bound, we show that no matter how we distribute the colors on the grid, we need $\Omega(\frac{\log n}{\log \log n})$ colors to ensure connectivity. More precisely, we show that in whatever way we position the nodes, we can always find a node where the interference experienced is at least as high as at $(0,0)$ in the grid situation.

Let us start by demonstrating the minimum interference accumulated at any node if we use three colors. Without loss of generality, there is at least one color j that is assigned to at least $\frac{n}{3}$ nodes. In the following, we will only consider this color j. Let us divide the grid into 4 parts $(a_1, a_1', a_1'', a_1''')$ of equal size. Among these, there is at least one square with at least $n/12$ nodes with color j, because there would not be $\frac{n}{3}$ nodes of color j together with the other squares otherwise. Without loss of generality we can assume that this is the square a_1 anchored in $(0,0)$ and we denote the number of nodes in a_1 by $|a_1|$. We now want to compute the minimal interference that one of the nodes in a_1 experiences. To this end we assume that there are exactly $\frac{n}{3}$ nodes with color j and exactly $\frac{n}{12}$ nodes in a_1 (otherwise the interference for nodes in a_1 increases. By positioning all $\frac{n}{3} - |a_1| = \frac{n}{4}$ nodes that are not in a_1 into the corner $(\sqrt{n}, \sqrt{n})$, i.e. the corner with the largest distance from $(0,0)$, the minimal interference any node in a_1 experiences exceeds $\frac{n}{4} \cdot \frac{1}{2n} = \frac{1}{8}$ because the largest distance between a point in a_1 and $(\sqrt{n}, \sqrt{n})$ is $\sqrt{2n}$. Let us now consider the interference the nodes in a_1 cause among themselves. We proceed as before by dividing the square a_1 into four squares $(a_2, a_2', a_2'', a_2''')$ of side length $\frac{\sqrt{n}}{4}$ each. Using the same arguments we know that one of them, let us say, a_2 contains at least $\frac{n}{48}$ nodes of color j and to minimize the interference within a_2 we look at the case where $|a_2|$ is $\frac{n}{48}$ and anchored at $(0,0)$. We can now compute the minimal amount of interference caused by the $\frac{n}{12} - \frac{n}{48} = \frac{n}{16}$ nodes in a_1 at $(0,0)$ to be at least $\frac{n}{16} \cdot \frac{2}{n} = 1/8$ because the maximal distance within a_1 is $\frac{\sqrt{n}}{\sqrt{2}}$. If we repeat these steps, it holds that in step i we have $\frac{n}{4^i}$ nodes in distance $\frac{\sqrt{2n}}{2^{i-1}}$ responsible for a sum of interference of $\frac{n}{4^i} \cdot \frac{4^{i-1}}{2n} = 1/8$ (see Fig. 2 (b)). After $\lfloor \log_4 n \rfloor$ steps there is only one node left in a_i and we stop. The total interference is thus in $\Omega(\log n)$.

We can generalize this approach to more than three colors. If we use k colors and partition the square with most nodes into $k+1$ squares and proceed recursively, the number of nodes in a_{i-1} outside a_i is in the order of $\frac{n}{(k+1)^i}$, where a_i is the square with most nodes in the ith step. These nodes are at most in distance $\frac{\sqrt{2n}}{(k+1)^{(i-1)/2}}$ from the nodes in a_i and thus cause interference of $\frac{n}{(k+1)^i} \cdot \frac{(k+1)^{i-1}}{2n} = \frac{1}{2(k+1)}$. The maximal number of recursions is $\lfloor \frac{\log n}{\log k} \rfloor$. Consequently, all the nodes are responsible for $\Omega(\frac{\log n}{k \log k})$ interference at $(0,0)$.

Typically the SINR threshold β that guarantees the reception of a message is a small constant. Hence, a neighbor on the grid (at distance 1) can receive our message if and only if the total interference is at most $1/\beta$. Now observe that, if $k < \frac{\log n}{c \log \log n}$ for some positive constant c, then we have that

$$\frac{\log n}{k \log k} > \frac{\log n}{\frac{\log n}{c \log \log n} (\log \log n - \log(c \log \log n))} > c$$

Thus, for any constant β, a large enough constant c exists such that, if $k < \frac{\log n}{c \log \log n}$, then the interference ratio is larger than β. $\qquad\square$

Corollary 1 (Upper and lower bound 2D grids, $1 \le \alpha < 2$). *Let $V = \{p_1, \ldots, p_n\} \subseteq [0, \sqrt{n}]^2$ be a two-dimensional grid and $1 \le \alpha < 2$. Let $c : V \to [k]$ be a coloring. If the corresponding SINR graph is strongly connected, then the number of colors is $k = \Theta\left(n^{2/\alpha - 1}\right)$.*

5   Connectivity for Random Instances: The One-Dimensional Case

In this section, we consider a set V of n nodes thrown independently and uniformly at random in $[0, 1]$, the unit interval.[2] We assume the path-loss exponent to be $\alpha = 2$. Due to lack of space, we omit all the proofs. They can be found in the full version [2] that is available on the web.

Our first result shows that $\mathcal{O}(\log n)$ colors are enough to guarantee strong connectivity of the corresponding SINR graph.

Theorem 5 (Upper bound). *Let $V = \{p_1, \ldots, p_n\} \subseteq [0, 1]$ where $p_1, \ldots p_n$ are independent random variables uniformly distributed in $[0, 1]$. Then a coloring $c : V \to [k]$ that uses $k \in \mathcal{O}(\log n)$ colors and guarantees that the corresponding SINR graph is strongly connected exists*

> *Idea of the proof.* Consider a *regular* coloring of $c \log n$ colors, with a sufficiently large constant c, so we can partition the interval $[0, 1]$ in subintervals of length $\Theta(\log n/n)$, each one of them containing (i) $\Theta(\log n)$ nodes w.h.p. and (ii) no more than one node for each color w.h.p.
>
> For any node p, we can take an interval of length $\Theta(\log n/n)$ containing $\Theta(\log n)$ nodes and such that every node in that interval is an out-neighbor of node p. Indeed, for any node q in that interval, the power at which q receives the signal from p is $\Omega(n^2/\log^2 n)$. For the nodes *interfering* with p, we have that for any h there are $\mathcal{O}(1)$ interfering nodes at distance $\Omega(h \log n/n)$ from q, hence the total *interfering power* at node q is $\mathcal{O}(n^2/\log^2 n)$. By choosing the constant c appropiately, the resulting ratio between the power at which q receives the signal from p and the interfering power is an arbitrary large constant. $\qquad\square$

The previous theorem shows that, with a regular $\mathcal{O}(\log n)$-coloring, the resulting SINR graph is strongly connected w.h.p. The next theorem proves that this is the best we can achieve with regular colorings.

---

[2] In contrast to the grid, where we set the minimal distance between two nodes to be one, we consider the unit interval for the random case because of its direct correspondence to probability.

Theorem 6 (Lower Bound for regular colorings). *Let* $V = \{p_1, \ldots, p_n\} \subseteq$ $[0, 1]$ *where* $p_1, \ldots p_n$ *are independent random variables uniformly distributed in* $[0, 1]$, *and let* $c : V \rightarrow [k]$ *be a regular coloring. If the corresponding SINR graph is strongly connected w.h.p., then the number of colors is* $k = \Omega(\log n)$.

In Theorem 5 we showed that, using a regular coloring with $\mathcal{O}(\log n)$ colors, we can make the SINR graph strongly connected. In Therorem 6 we proved that, if we restrict ourselves to regular colorings, we cannot use asymptotically less colors. An interesting open question is whether or not we can find a *non-regular* coloring with $o(\log n)$ colors that makes the SINR strongly connected. The next theorem states that, in any case, we must use at least $\Omega(\log \log n)$ colors.

Theorem 7 (Lower Bound for arbitrary colorings). *Let* $V = \{p_1, \ldots, p_n\}$ $\subseteq [0, 1]$ *where* $p_1, \ldots p_n$ *are independent random variables uniformly distributed in* $[0, 1]$, *and let* $c : V \rightarrow [k]$ *be any coloring. If the corresponding SINR graph is strongly connected w.h.p., then the number of colors is* $k = \Omega(\log \log n)$.

6   Conclusions and Open Problems

In this paper we initiate the study of connectivity in the uniform power SINR model. Clearly we can not achieve connectivity in the SINR model if we use only one frequency, since the SINR diagram is a partition of the plane. To overcome this problem we can either use a sophisticated scheduling algorithm or we can increase the number of frequencies. However those two actions are equivalent i.e., any schedule can be translated into a choice of frequencies and any frequency assignment can be translated into a schedule. Therefore we can defined the connectivity problem in the SINR model as the minimal number of frequency the network needs to use to maintain connectivity (the scheduling complexity of connectivity).

We provided upper and lower bounds for the number of time slots or frequencies to build a strongly connected graph of communication edges. We focused on nodes arranged in a regular grid or uniformly at random on the unit interval. We proved that if the nodes are located on a regular grid the number of frequencies needed to maintain connectivity is a function of the dimension of the grid and the path-loss exponent α. Apart from the special case $\alpha = 2$ these bounds are asymptotically tight. In contrast, when transmitters are located uniformly at random on the interval $[0, 1]$ there is a big gap between the upper bound $\mathcal{O}(\log n)$ in Theorem 5 and the lower bound $\Omega(\log \log n)$ in Theorem 7. A natural open question is to close this gap. Other intriguing problems include determining upper and lower bounds for general colorings in the random two-dimensional case, or algorithms computing the uniform power complexity of connectivity of arbitrarily positioned nodes.

References

1. Avin, C., Emek, Y., Kantor, E., Lotker, Z., Peleg, D., Roditty, L.: SINR Diagrams: Towards Algorithmically Usable SINR Models of Wireless Networks. In: Proc. 28th Ann. Symp. on Principles of Distributed Computing, PODC (2009)

2. Avin, C., Lotker, Z., Pasquale, F., Pignolet, Y.A.: A note on uniform power connectivity in the SINR model. CoRR, abs/0906.2311 (2009)
3. Avin, C., Lotker, Z., Pignolet, Y.A.: On the Power of Uniform Power: Capacity of Wireless Networks with Bounded Resources. In: Proc. 17th Ann. European Symp. on Algorithms, ESA (2009)
4. Clark, B., Colbourn, C., Johnson, D.: Unit disk graphs. Discrete Math. 86, 165–177 (1990)
5. Fanghänel, A., Kesselheim, T., Räcke, H., Vöcking, B.: Oblivious Interference Scheduling. In: Proc. 28th Principles of Distributed Computing, PODC (2009)
6. Goussevskaia, O., Halldorsson, M., Wattenhofer, R., Welzl, E.: Capacity of Arbitrary Wireless Networks. In: Proc. 28th Ann. IEEE Conference on Computer Communications, INFOCOM (2009)
7. Goussevskaia, O., Oswald, Y.A., Wattenhofer, R.: Complexity in Geometric SINR. In: Proc. ACM Intl. Symp. on Mobile Ad Hoc Networking and Computing, MOBIHOC (2007)
8. Grönkvist, J.: Interference-Based Scheduling in Spatial Reuse TDMA. PhD thesis, Royal Institute of Technology, Stockholm, Sweden (2005)
9. Gupta, P., Kumar, P.R.: The Capacity of Wireless Networks. IEEE Trans. Inf. Theory 46(2), 388–404 (2000)
10. Hajek, B., Sasaki, G.: Link Scheduling in Polynomial Time. IEEE Trans. Inf. Theory 34(5), 910–917 (1988)
11. Halldórsson, M.: Wireless Scheduling with Power Control. In: Proc. 17th annual European Symposium on Algorithms (ESA), pp. 368–380 (2009)
12. Halldórsson, M., Wattenhofer, R.: Wireless Communication is in APX. In: Albers, S., et al. (eds.) ICALP 2009, Part I. LNCS, vol. 5555, pp. 525–536. Springer, Heidelberg (2009)
13. Kumar, V.S.A., Marathe, M.V., Parthasarathy, S., Srinivasan, A.: End-to-end packet-scheduling in Wireless Ad-Hoc Networks. In: Proc. 15th Ann. ACM-SIAM Symp. on Discrete Algorithms (SODA), pp. 1021–1030 (2004)
14. Lebhar, E., Lotker, Z.: Unit disk graph and physical interference model: putting pieces together. In: Proc. 23rd IEEE Intl. Parallel and Distributed Processing Symposium, IPDPS (2009)
15. Moscibroda, T., Wattenhofer, R.: The Complexity of Connectivity in Wireless Networks. In: Proc. 25th Ann. Joint Conference of the IEEE Computer and Communications Societies (INFOCOM) (April 2006)
16. Moscibroda, T., Wattenhofer, R.: The Complexity of Connectivity in Wireless Networks. In: Proc. 25th Ann. Joint Conference of the IEEE Computer and Communications Societies, INFOCOM (2006)
17. Moscibroda, T., Wattenhofer, R., Weber, Y.: Protocol Design Beyond Graph-based Models. In: Proc. 5th ACM SIGCOMM Workshop on Hot Topics in Networks, HotNets (2006)
18. Rappaport, T.: Wireless communications. Prentice Hall, Englewood Cliffs (2002)
19. Sharma, G., Mazumdar, R.R., Shroff, N.B.: On the Complexity of Scheduling in Wireless Networks. In: Proc. 12th Ann. Intl. Conference on Mobile computing and networking (MOBICOM), pp. 227–238 (2006)
20. Zander, J.: Performance of optimum transmitter power control in cellular radiosystems. IEEE Trans. Veh. Technol. 41 (1992)

Locating a Black Hole without the Knowledge of Incoming Link*

Peter Glaus

Department of Computer Science, Comenius University, Mlynska Dolina, 84248,
Bratislava, Slovakia

Abstract. We study a group of mobile agents operating on an arbitrary unknown distributed system. One of the nodes of the distributed system is extremely harmful and destroys any incoming agent without notification. The task of exploring the distributed system and locating the harmful node, *Black hole search*, has been studied with various modifications.

We are studying the effects of the *knowledge of incoming link* on the size of the optimal solution. When an agent enters a node, the information which port leads back can be given to it. We refer to this as to the *knowledge of incoming link*. In previous research, it was always assumed that the agent is given this information.

In this paper we study arbitrary, unknown distributed systems without the knowledge of incoming link. Agents are asynchronous and they communicate via whiteboards. We present a lower bound on the size of the optimal solution, proving that at least $\frac{\Delta^2+\Delta}{2}+1$ agents are necessary to locate the black hole, with respect to the degree of the black hole Δ. We provide an algorithm for black hole search without the knowledge of incoming link as well. We prove that this algorithm is correct, and that it uses $\frac{\Delta^2+\Delta}{2}+1$ agents, thus providing optimal solution.

1 Introduction

1.1 Black Hole Search

Agent-based distributed algorithms have been widely studied in various modifications. In most cases though, the distributed system is considered non-faulty. We focus our study on distributed systems containing a *black hole*.

Black hole is a harmful node, which destroys all agents that enter it. It is indistinguishable from the outside and once an agent enters, it is unable to send a message or warn other agents. *Black Hole Search* is a task in which the agents have to create a correct graph representation (*map*) of the distributed system with the location of the black hole pointed out.

---

* Research supported by grant APVV 0433-06.

S. Dolev (Ed.): ALGOSENSORS 2009, LNCS 5804, pp. 128–138, 2009.

1.2   Aim of This Work

The *Black Hole Search Problem* (BHS) is the problem of finding an algorithm for the agents to fulfill the Black Hole Search. The solution to this problem and its efficiency can vary a lot and are dependent on the distributed system and the agent model properties. In unoriented arbitrary unknown graphs of n nodes, with the degree of the black hole Δ the optimal algorithm needs $\Delta + 1$ agents in the worst case[1], whereas in oriented graph scenario, the number of necessary agents can be up to 2^{Δ}[2]. In this work we want to study this gap by proposing a new model which has some restrictions similar to the oriented graph scenario.

In all previous studies of BHS, it was anticipated that when an agent enters a node, it automatically knows from which link it entered the node. We call this information the *knowledge of the incoming link*. This information is not inherently present in all distributed systems. For instance, one can think of a software agent that starts its execution on a host without any information about the incoming port.

We study the effects of the knowledge of incoming link on unoriented arbitrary unknown distributed systems. We show that without this knowledge, the problem solution needs more agents to work correctly. We show that there are $\Theta(n^2)$ agents needed for algorithm that solves BHS on arbitrary unknown graphs, more precisely $\frac{n^2+n}{2} + 1$ agents are necessary and sufficient.

1.3   Related Work

First studies of BHS were focused on asynchronous distributed systems with ring networks with use of whiteboard communication [3]. They proved that in such conditions two agents are sufficient and the black hole can be located in $O(n \log n)$ steps.

Important results about influence of prior knowledge of the network can be found in [1]. In case of no prior knowledge, the size of the optimal solution is $\Delta + 1$ agents and cost is $O(n^2)$ steps. When using a sense of direction, only 2 agents are necessary and they can find the black hole in $O(n^2)$ steps. With the knowledge of map of the distributed system, 2 agents are necessary, the cost of the solution is reduced to $O(n \log n)$ steps.

In [4] authors show that for graphs such as hypercubes, cube-connected-cycles, tori and other a solution with cost of $O(n)$ steps exists. It has been proved later that with the consideration of the graph diameter, the cost of the solution can be improved for arbitrary graphs with known topology to $O(n + d \log d)$[5,6].

The Black hole search problem with agents not starting in the home base, but rather scattered in the graph was considered as well. Results can be found in [7,8,9].

All previously mentioned results use a simple technique called *Cautious walk* which reduces the number of agents that enter the black hole. When entering an unknown port, an agent marks it as dangerous and if it does not die in the black hole, it immediately returns back and marks the port as safe. No other agent enters a dangerous port, because it might possibly lead into the black hole. When considering oriented graphs where this technique is not available, up to 2^Δ agents may be needed [2].

2   Definitions

2.1   Distributed System

Distributed system is a graph $G = (V, E)$ with its port labeling. We mostly denote vertices as *nodes* and edges as *links*. The size of the distributed system is the number of the nodes of the graph $n = |V|$. We assume the nodes to have distinct identifiers, which could be easily assigned by the agents themselves.

We also use the term *port*, which denotes the places where a link is connected to a node. Link (u, v) has two ports, one is in the node u and the other is in the node v.

The graphs we use are simple, without double edges or loops of type (u, u). As we consider only undirected graphs the link (u, v) is the same as (v, u). We expect the graph to be biconnected, otherwise finding the black hole might be impossible[1].

The use of the port labeling is necessary for the purpose of clarity.

Agents. A group of agents is initially placed in an arbitrary node of the distributed system. The node where the agents are at the beginning is called *home base*. The agents are autonomous and proceed according to the same algorithm. We focus on the asynchronous agents only. In general, the agents are unaware of each other, although they can communicate by means of whiteboards. Whiteboard can be interpreted as a piece of memory placed in each node. Agents present in a node have access to its whiteboard. Exclusive access to the whiteboards is assumed, only one agent at a time can read and modify it.

Agents' only prior knowledge of the distributed system is the number of nodes n and the degree of the black hole Δ.

Black Hole. There is a harmful node in the distributed system. Every agent that enters a port of a link leading to such node can be considered dead or not functional any more. We call such node a *black hole*. The degree of the black hole is Δ.

For agents that did not enter the black hole we say that they are alive. On the other hand, we use the term dead or we say that agent died when it entered the black hole.

The Knowledge of Incoming Link. All previously stated results and studies assumed that when an agent enters a new node, the agent automatically knows what port it enter through. We refer to this as to *the knowledge of incoming link*.

We study a model where agents have no knowledge of incoming link.

2.2   The Problem

Agents' task is to explore the graph and locate the black hole. All agents act according to the predefined algorithm. We say that the algorithm ends when all the remaining agents take action *finish*. We use the following definition when considering the correctness of the algorithm:

Definition 1 (Correctness). *The algorithm is correct if for any distributed system the algorithm ends with at least one agent alive and all surviving agents have a correct map of the distributed system with correctly marked location of the black hole.*

Complexity. The first measure of the efficiency is the number of agents needed by the algorithm to work correctly and is denoted as the *size* of the solution. The second measure, the *cost* of the solution, is the number of steps that agents make in total before finishing the task. As in most Bhs related works, we consider the size to be more important than the cost and thus the focus is on using the optimal number of agents first and then improving the number of steps made by the agents.

Adversary. When evaluating solutions, we always consider the worst case scenario. Instead of referring to the worst case we use the concept of adversary. Adversary is a kind of powerful opponent, his goal is either to make algorithm fail the task or to work least efficiently as possible. From all the distributed systems that are indistinguishable from the agents' point of view, he can choose the one that is worst in terms of correctness and complexity of the algorithm. He can do this at any time during the exploration based on agents' behavior. For more detail we advice the reader to [1,3].

3   Lower Bound on the Size of the Optimal Solution

We show that any algorithm solving Bhs for an arbitrary unknown graph needs at least $\frac{\Delta^2+\Delta}{2} + 1$ agents to solve Bhs on the graph G_{lb} shown on the Fig. 1.

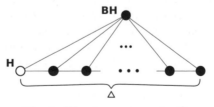

Fig. 1. Worst case scenario: G_{lb}

Let us consider the Fig. 2(b). Agents start in the home base v_1. They see two indistinguishable edges. The algorithm has to send a number of agents through each edge and then other agents wait until some agents come back. If the algorithm sends a different number of agents through each edge, the adversary can make sure that more agents walk through the edge a_1 and thus end up in the

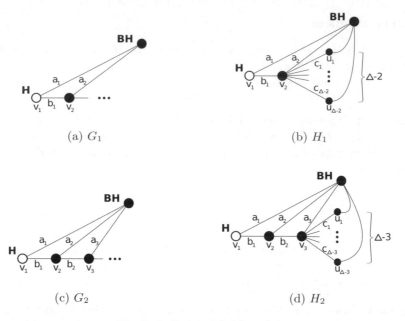

(a) G_1

(b) H_1

(c) G_2

(d) H_2

Fig. 2. Indistinguishable graphs

black hole. This means that an efficient algorithm has to send the same number of agents through the both edges a_1 and b_1.

It can be seen, that there have to be at least Δ agents walking through the edge b_1. If the algorithm sends only $k < \Delta$ agents, the adversary can make sure that none of the agents returns to the home base and thus the algorithm fails. There are Δ edges leading out of v_2. Without loss of generality it can be assumed that no two agents use the same edge, one agent uses the edge a_2 and the other $k - 1$ agents use the edges $c_1 \ldots c_{k-1}$, they get into the nodes $u_1 \ldots u_{k-1}$ and from these they use edges leading into the black hole. All k agents die in the black hole and no agent returns.

For the graph H_1, there have to be at least Δ agents using the edge b_1 and thus Δ agents using the edge a_1. When considering the Fig. 2(a) and the graph G_1 it can be observed that for agents waiting in the home base, the graphs G_1 and H_1 are indistinguishable. This means that the algorithm has to act in the same way in both cases, thus also in the graph G_1 there have to be at least Δ agents traveling through the edges a_1 and b_1.

A very similar situation can be seen in the Fig. 2(d). As stated before, the adversary can make sure that there are at least Δ agents traveling through the edge a_1. Now the edge b_1 is known to be safe and agents can freely move into the node v_2. Let us assume that the algorithm now knows that a_1 leads into the black hole so we do not have to consider it. Once again, there are two indistinguishable edges a_2, b_2 and there is no point for sending more agents into one of them.

Similarly as in the graph H_1, to make sure that at least one agent gets back into the node v_2 we need at least $\Delta - 1$ agents in the node v_3. Otherwise all agents that went into v_3 can end up in the black hole. With the knowledge of v_1 and v_2, the graph G_2 from the Fig. 2(c) is indistinguishable from the graph H_2. This implies that the algorithm, which solves BHS for an arbitrary unknown graph, will in the worst case send Δ agents through the edge a_1 and $\Delta - 1$ agents through the edge a_2 in both, G_2 and H_2.

Extending the previous argument on graphs $G_3 \ldots G_\Delta$, where G_Δ is similar to G_{lb} we can prove that for $i \in \{1, \ldots, \Delta\}$ there are $\Delta - i + 1$ agents traveling through an edge a_i and thus dying in the black hole. Following theorem is thus implied.

Theorem 1 (Lower Bound on the Size of the Optimal Solution). *Any algorithm solving* BHS *problem for an arbitrary unknown graph without the knowledge of incoming link needs at least* $\frac{\Delta^2 + \Delta}{2} + 1$ *agents.*

4   Size-Optimal Algorithm

4.1   Algorithm

We propose the following algorithm as a solution for the Black hole search problem on a distributed system without the knowledge of incoming link.

All ports are classified into four categories, similar to those used in the *cautious walk*, with one extra. Unmarked ports are called *unknown*. When one or more agents have entered a port, it is marked as *dangerous*. If a port is dangerous and it is known that at least one of the agents that entered such port has been alive afterwards, then the port can be marked as *safe*. When a link has both ports safe, then the link is safe as well and both ports of the link are marked as *explored*. Furthermore, for both explored ports the nodes to which they lead are known and are written on the whiteboard.

One or more nodes of the graph that are connected by safe links are called *safe component*. Safe component, which contains the home base is called *main safe component* (MSC). Once an agent marks link safe, it identifies both nodes of the link to be part of the same safe component connected by the safe link. It is done by leaving a special message on the whiteboard. When a safe component is connected to the home base or to MSC by a safe link, agent marks all nodes of the newly connected component as a part of the main safe component.

Every agent searching the graph has a counter of steps it has made. Every time an agent is going to use a port, it leaves a message on the whiteboard stating the port's label, agent's ID and the current state of its counter and it increases its counter as well. Each agent keeps track of how many steps have other agents done. When an agent A enters a node, it looks on the whiteboard and for every agent B that left a message, it updates its information about B's number of steps. An agent always remembers the complete list of agents that visited the current node. The list of counters, known map of the distributed system and a list of agents that entered a dangerous port are kept in the home base as well.

The lists are used as follows. An agent that enters a node u first compares its list of agents in the previous node with the list of agents that left the node u. By comparing the state of their counters, the agent can immediately find out, whether any of the agents went through the same link and it knows by which port as well. If there was such agent, it marks the port explored, goes back to mark the other port as well and returns to the node u.

Second thing an agent has to do when it enters a new node u is to compare its list of all agents and maxima of their counters to the list of agents that left u. If there is a port marked as dangerous and it knows that one of the agents that entered it stayed alive afterwards then it marks this port safe and enters it.

After these two checks, the agent proceeds with its own exploration.

Now we can state rules for the agents, which they obey at all circumstances. We will prove the correctness of this algorithm in the next section.

1. When an agent is in a node that is not part of MSC, it will never enter a dangerous port.
2. When an agent is in a node, it will always make a move, unless the problem is solved or all ports are dangerous. If all ports are dangerous, the agent will wait until one of the ports is made safe and then proceeds with the exploration.
3. When agent is in MSC it can enter a dangerous port under following conditions:
   – There are no unknown or safe ports in MSC.
   – The size of MSC is less than $n - 1$.
   – There are k dangerous ports leading out of MSC and $k \leq \Delta$.
   – There are less than $\Delta - k + 2$ agents, that entered the port it wants to enter.

   This condition ensures that if there are $k \leq \Delta$ dangerous ports at a certain time, then there will be no more than $\Delta - k + 2$ agents entering any of the dangerous ports. Of course, if in some previous state there were k' dangerous ports where $k' < k$ then there might be some ports that were used by $\Delta - k' + 2$ agents which is more than $\Delta - k + 2$. In this case, however, no more agents will enter these ports.
4. An agent has to enter a port when it wants to mark it as safe.
5. An agent moves through an unknown port from node u to node v, upon arrival to the node v it checks its list of agents that visited the node u and compares it with the whiteboard. If it finds out that some agent previously traveled from v through port p and came to u then it has to mark the port p and the whole link as safe[1].

From these rules, it follows that when an agent is not able to reach the home base by a safe path, it does not enter any dangerous ports. The agent does not stop exploring. If all ports are dangerous it waits until some port is marked safe. When the agent discovers that some port/link can be marked as safe, then it is its duty to do so.

---

[1] By marking a link safe, we always mean marking its ports as explored as well.

The general idea of the algorithm is following. Agents working according to the algorithm explore the graph by traversing the nodes. Algorithm can be divided into three parts as follows:

1. An agent starts in the home base and leaves MSC through some available port.
2. It traverses the unknown area outside MSC until it returns to MSC. As the agents do not have information about the area outside MSC, they traverse the nodes in no special order. They remember information about nodes and other agents as was mentioned above, and leave messages about their state. Using the remembered information, algorithm can be easily designed in such way that agents by their behavior obey the rules stated above.
3. When agent returns to MSC it checks for ports it might be able to mark safe. If there are such ports, it marks them and returns to the home base. Afterwards, it updates the information kept in the home base and is ready to leave MSC again.

4.2   Correctness

First we state some supporting lemmas and then prove that MSC will keep expanding until the whole graph except the black hole is explored. Detailed proofs of the lemmas can be found in the Appendix.

Lemma 1. *When an agent A is not in MSC and A is in a node v_D with all ports marked as dangerous, one of the ports will be eventually marked as explored.*

The main idea of this lemma is that if all ports are marked as dangerous then at least one agent left through each port. It is possible to prove that at least one of these agents is able to return and mark the link it passed as safe.

Corollary 1. *When an agent is not in MSC and it is in a safe component with all outgoing ports marked as dangerous, one of the ports will be eventually marked as explored.*

Lemma 2. *A link that has both ports safe will be marked as safe, and the ports as explored. Furthermore, it will be marked safe by one of the agents that marked its ports safe.*

In the following lemma, we focus on the agents exploring outside of MSC. These agents are not allowed to enter any dangerous ports. It is possible to show that there are always enough agents outside MSC, so that at least one does not die in the black hole. The main idea of the proof is the analysis of the rule which allows only $\Delta - k + 2$ agents to enter k dangerous ports.

Lemma 3. *For MSC of size smaller than $n - 1$ the following statement holds. When there are no more agents that could leave MSC according to the third rule, then at least one of the agents outside of MSC does not enter the black hole.*

We use the Lemma 3 for the following statement. At least one agent survives, agents never stop exploring and they cannot be stuck. The fact is that there is only restricted number of nodes and links to be explored thus at some point an agent has to return to MSC.

Lemma 4. *For MSC of size smaller than $n - 1$ the following statement holds. When there are no more agents that could leave MSC according to the third rule, then at least one of the agents that left MSC returns back into MSC.*

We prove that MSC will be expanding until it contains $n-1$ nodes in the following manner. At the beginning, only the home base is a part of MSC and it has all ports marked as unknown. Agents start to explore by entering these ports. They always try to leave MSC until it contains $n - 1$ nodes. Lemma 4 implies that some agent always returns, which further means that at least one agent keeps returning and leaving the MSC.

The agent always leaves MSC by some link and enters a node u outside MSC. Agents act in such way that they always try to enter unknown ports if available, which further means that when an agent enters node u n times, then either the agent or some other agent had to enter also the port leading back to MSC.

Theorem 2 (Correctness). *Agents with their exploration will expand the main safe component until it contains $n-1$ nodes, thus exploring whole the graph except the edges possibly leading into the black hole. By this they finish the black hole search.*

5   Upper Bound on the Size of the Optimal Solution

In the proof of the lower bound value we used the graph G_{lb} on the Fig. 1. Note that our algorithm uses optimal number of agents to fulfill BHS on such graph $\frac{\Delta^2 + \Delta}{2} + 1$.

Even more, let us order all ports leading into the black hole based on the number of agents that used them in descending order, these numbers make a following sequence: $p_1 = \Delta, p_2 = \Delta - 1, \ldots p_{\Delta-1} = 2, p_\Delta = 1$. This corresponds with the claim from the lower bound proof that for each edge a_i leading into the black hole, there had to be $\Delta - i + 1$ agents that passed through this edge.

Theorem 3 (Upper Bound on the Size of the Optimal Solution). *Algorithm for the Black hole search problem obeying conditions stated before will succeed with $\frac{\Delta^2 + \Delta}{2} + 1$ agents in the worst case.*

Proof. Consider a sequence of Δ numbers similar to the one mentioned before, for $i \in \{1, \ldots, \Delta\}; p_i = \Delta - i + 1$.

Let us consider graph G_{ub}, with the degree of the black hole Δ, where our algorithm needs more than $\frac{\Delta^2 + \Delta}{2} + 1$ agents to solve BHS. In other words, there are at least $\frac{\Delta^2 + \Delta}{2} + 1$ agents that die in the black hole. Now again we take the numbers of agents that used a port leading into the black hole and order them in descending order. These numbers form a non-increasing sequence of length Δ:

$q_1, q_2 \ldots, q_\Delta$. We stated previously that there are more agents ending up in the black hole in the graph G_{ub} and thus:

$$\sum_{i=1}^{\Delta} q_i > \sum_{i=1}^{\Delta} p_i = \frac{\Delta^2 + \Delta}{2}$$

Both sequences have the same lengths and thus there must exist index j where $q_j > p_j$. We know that $q_j > p_j = \Delta - j + 1$, and thus $q_j \geq \Delta - j + 2$. Now we have to consider what does this mean in terms of the rules for our algorithm.

In the last rule about the number of agents entering a dangerous port at certain conditions, we state that for $k \leq \Delta$ maximally $\Delta - k + 2$ agents enter. When at least $\Delta - j + 2$ agents enter dangerous ports it means that:

$$\Delta - j + 2 \leq \Delta - k + 2$$
$$j \geq k$$

For all ports corresponding to the numbers $q_1, \ldots q_j$, there is an agent that entered these ports last. For this last agent, some conditions must have been fulfilled. There were no unknown ports in MSC. Number of the nodes in MSC was less than $n - 1$, put in other words, there were still some nodes that were not part of MSC. And at last, there were maximally k dangerous ports at that moment, where $k \leq j$ from above stated equation.

Numbers $q_1, \ldots, q_j$ correspond to j different ports leading **into** the black hole. If the graph is biconnected then we are missing at least one dangerous port, that **did not lead** into the black hole. So the last agent would obviously have to break one of the conditions by entering the dangerous port, which leads us to contradiction. ◻

Corollary 2 (Size Optimal Solution). *Proposed algorithm provides size optimal solution for the Black hole search problem without the knowledge of incoming link.*

6   Conclusion

In this work, we have studied the Black hole search problem without the knowledge of incoming link. We have shown that this modification has effects on the size of the solution.

We provided lower bound on the number of agents that are necessary to locate the black hole. Any correct algorithm solving the Black hole search problem without the knowledge of incoming link needs at least $\frac{\Delta^2 + \Delta}{2} + 1$ agents. The algorithm is presented with the proof of correctness, it uses the optimal number of agents in the worst case. The cost of the algorithm and bounds on the optimal cost of the solution are left for further investigation.

References

1. Dobrev, S., Flocchini, P., Prencipe, G., Santoro, N.: Searching for a black hole in arbitrary networks: optimal mobile agent protocols. In: Proceedings of the twenty-first annual symposium on Principles of distributed computing (PODC 2002), pp. 153–162. ACM, New York (2002)
2. Czyzowicz, J., Dobrev, S., Královič, R., Miklík, S., Pardubská, D.: Black hole search in directed graphs. In: SIROCCO 2009. LNCS, Springer, Heidelberg (to appear, 2009)
3. Dobrev, S., Flocchini, P., Prencipe, G., Santoro, N.: Mobile search for a black hole in an anonymous ring. In: Welch, J.L. (ed.) DISC 2001. LNCS, vol. 2180, pp. 166–179. Springer, Heidelberg (2001)
4. Dobrev, S., Flocchini, P., Královič, R., Prencipe, G., Ružička, P., Santoro, N.: Black hole search in common interconnection networks. Networks 47(2), 61–71 (2006)
5. Dobrev, S., Flocchini, P., Santoro, N.: Improved bounds for optimal black hole search with a network map. In: Kralovic, R., Sýkora, O. (eds.) SIROCCO 2004. LNCS, vol. 3104, pp. 111–122. Springer, Heidelberg (2004)
6. Dobrev, S., Flocchini, P., Santoro, N.: Cycling through a dangerous network: A simple efficient strategy for black hole search. In: 26th IEEE International Conference on Distributed Computing Systems (ICDCS 2006), p. 57. IEEE Computer Society, Los Alamitos (2006)
7. Dobrev, S., Flocchini, P., Prencipe, G., Santoro, N.: Multiple agents rendezvous in a ring in spite of a black hole. In: Papatriantafilou, M., Hunel, P. (eds.) OPODIS 2003. LNCS, vol. 3144, pp. 34–46. Springer, Heidelberg (2004)
8. Chalopin, J., Das, S., Santoro, N.: Rendezvous of Mobile Agents in Unknown Graphs with Faulty Links. In: Pelc, A. (ed.) DISC 2007. LNCS, vol. 4731, pp. 108–122. Springer, Heidelberg (2007)
9. Flocchini, P., Ilcinkas, D., Santoro, N.: Ping pong in dangerous graphs: Optimal black hole search with pure tokens. In: Taubenfeld, G. (ed.) DISC 2008. LNCS, vol. 5218, pp. 227–241. Springer, Heidelberg (2008)

Energy Efficient Alert in Single-Hop Networks of Extremely Weak Devices*

Marek Klonowski, Miroslaw Kutyłowski, and Jan Zatopiański

Institute of Mathematics and Computer Science, Wrocław University of Technology
{Marek.Klonowski,Miroslaw.Kutylowski,
Jan.Zatopianski}@pwr.wroc.pl

Abstract. We present an alert algorithm for single-hop radio networks with polylogarithmic time complexity and sublogarithmic energy complexity. Our algorithm works correctly with high probability independently of the number of sensors that try to broadcast an alert signal. Moreover, we show that it can be made fairly robust against node failures. We show a lower bound for energy cost that matches the energy cost of our algorithm.

Our solution has very weak computing communication and storage requirements and therefore can be applied for a system containing extremely weak devices.

1 Introduction

One of the key applications of sensor networks is monitoring a particular area and alarming when some event occurs. For instance, it might be a system that sets alert when air pollution or fire is detected. We assume that a number of small sensors is spread over a monitored area and they broadcast alert signals when they detect smoke, substantial increase of temperature (or its gradient), and so on. We say that an algorithm terminates successfully, if all sensors are notified when at least one sensor detects that a triggering event has occurred somewhere in the monitored area. Alternatively, we might be interested in informing a given sink node (or nodes) about the event (typically, the sink transmits this information via other networks).

A sensor for which the triggering event has occurred is called *stimulated*. The fact that the number of stimulated sensors is unpredictable requires special handling. We need to take into consideration even extreme cases – when only one or almost all sensors are stimulated. This is difficult since if more than one sensor broadcasts at the same time, a *conflict* occurs – and the message is not heard by other sensors. In this way the sensors block each other by transmitting at the same time.

A crucial aspect that we need to consider are often limited energy resources of wireless sensors. They are usually equipped with batteries that cannot be easily recharged in a target environment (replacing batteries means sending maintenance worker to each single sensor!). However, the sensors are intended to work for a long time. Since wireless communication consumes most energy, we need to minimize the time when sensor's transmitter or receiver is switched on. In this paper we present an algorithm that

---

* Partially supported by Polish Ministry of Science and Higher Education, grant number N N206 1842 33.

S. Dolev (Ed.): ALGOSENSORS 2009, LNCS 5804, pp. 139–150, 2009.

requires sublogarithmic energy (understood as the maximum number of steps when a transmitter or receiver is switched on over all sensors in the network). We show that this algorithm terminates successfully with an overwhelming probability: if there is at least one stimulated sensor, all sensors become notified.

Previous and Related Work. There is a long line of papers on algorithms for ad hoc radio networks. Many different models have been studied, ranging from very limited devices to units comparable to PCs with high bandwidth connections. The alert problem is very similar to the wake up-problem. It was studied for the first time in [3] for single hop networks, and then in [4], as well as in [2,1] for arbitrary networks. In all these papers it was assumed that a subset of all nodes wakes up spontaneously and have to wakes up other nodes. The main difference between wake-up protocols and alert problem is that in wake-up even "sleeping" nodes are informed by an incoming message. In practice such an assumption means that listening does not need significant amount of energy and sensors are permanently in a "listening mode". In practice, listening requires a lot of energy.

[9] is another important paper describing a similar problem. Its authors explicitly assume that listening is energy consuming. The paper [9] presents practical solutions that can applied for general graphs (multi-hop topology). However, the presented algorithms seem to be relatively slow in a single-hop topology. Moreover, the authors of [9] use a different measure of energetic efficiency. To some extent a similar problem was also studied in [6], however not from the point of view of energy consumption.

In our paper we also discuss a model wherein most nodes may have extremely limited capabilities - i.e. they are unable to receive any message.

2   Model Description

We assume that n devices, called *sensors*, are placed in a target environment. All sensors perform their tasks in discrete periods called *slots* as they would have an access to a global clock. In each period, each sensor can be in one of the three possible states - it can be *BROADCASTING a signal*, it can be *LISTENING* to other sensors or it can be *INACTIVE*. We assume the so-called *half–duplex* mode. It means that a sensor can either listen to other sensors or broadcast a signal (but not both) in a single slot. Since we assumed that we use very simple devices, they can broadcast a single kind of signal on one channel. We also assume that if two or more sensors broadcast a signal in the same slot, then all sensors that listen to them cannot distinguish the result from the situation, when no sensor broadcasts. Since we assumed the half-duplex mode, broadcasting sensor is not sure if its signal has been successfully broadcast (i.e. that no other sensor has been transmitting at the same time). Of course, it can be later informed about the transmission status by other sensors listening at this moment.

We also assume that all sensors perform the same underlying algorithm. Of course, their behavior can be different during the runtime of the algorithm due to some interaction with other sensors or as a result of using random number generators working independently on each device. We also assume that each pair of sensors is in the common range of broadcasting. So, our system can be regarded as a kind of ad hoc single–hop radio network with no collision detection (no-CD model) of very weak devices (in terms of communication and storage capabilities).

Let us note that, if we assumed collision detection mechanism, then the solution would be simple - if a collision is detected, then all listening nodes know that there is at least one active node.

Furthermore, tentatively we assume that all sensors are enumerated, i.e. each sensor has a unique label in the set $[n] = \{1, \ldots, n\}$. It requires performing an initialization procedure as a kind of preprocessing (e.g. like in [7]), it is a one-time effort, acceptable for long-living systems. We discuss in Sect. 3.2 how to relax this assumption.

Energy effort of a sensor is a number of slots, in which the sensor is active, i.e. it broadcasts a signal or it is listening. The energy complexity of an algorithm is a maximum of energy effort over all sensors during the runtime of the algorithm. This is a standard measure of energy complexity used among others in [7], motivated by the fact that we need to have all nodes working.

We denote the number of stimulated sensors as n_0. As we already assumed $0 \leq n_0 \leq n$ is not known in advance. In the next section we propose an algorithm that meets the following conditions:

1. its running time $t = \text{poly}(\log n)$ slots,
2. it has sublogarithmic energy complexity,
3. no sensor is notified about the alert if $n_0 = 0$,
4. if $n_0 > 0$, then all sensors are notified about the alert with probability $1 - \Theta(1/n)$.

3 Algorithm Description

Symbols. Let k be a parameter of the algorithm to be fixed later. Parameter t, such that $k|t$ is a number of slots in the algorithm i.e. its runtime. Without important limitations we assume that $\log n$ is an integer and n is divisible by $k \log n$. We also assume that $n > \log^2(n)$, which is true for $n > 16$.

For any natural m, let $[m] = \{1, \ldots, m\}$. For every $i \in [\frac{n}{k}]$ and $j \in [k]$, let $s(i, j)$ denote the sensor labeled with $(i-1)k + j$. The first $k \log n$ sensors (i.e. sensors $s(i, j)$ for $i \in [\log n]$, $j \in [k]$) are called *guarding sensors* or just *guardians*, and play a special role in the algorithm. By analogy, $T[i, j]$ for $i \in [\frac{t}{k}]$ and $j \in [k]$ represents the slot $((i-1)k + j)$. For the sake of clearity the ith group of k consecutive slots $\{T[i, j] \mid j \in [k]\}$ is denoted by $T[i, *]$.

Algorithm Overview. The algorithm consists of four phases. Each of the stimulated sensors broadcasts the signal in randomly chosen slots. Guardian sensors try to catch these signals and propagate them to the rest of the sensors.

The first phase (Phase 1a and 1b) is performed in order to ensure that at least one of the guardians is notified by a stimulated sensor when n_0 is small. For this purpose each active node broadcasts in l randomly chosen slots. The second phase (Phase 2a and 2b) guarantees that one of the guardians is notified of the alert if n_0 is large, e.g. $n_0 \approx n$. So, Phases 1a, 1b and 2a, 2b are in some sense complementary. Phases 3 and 4, by contrast to previous ones, are deterministic.

In Phase 3 guardians, which were notified about alert, distribute their information to some other guardians. For this purpose each notified guardian with number i broadcasts the signal in the ith slot of this phase and the guardian $i + 1$ is listening. In Phase 4 the last guardian broadcasts the signal to all n sensors (or to some subset of devices interested in being informed about the alert).

In fact this idea boils down to making an effective scheduling of behavior of guardian sensors and an unknown number of broadcasting sensors that avoids conflicts. For our purposes it suffices to ensure that there is at least one slot monitored by guardians such that exactly one of the stimulated sensors broadcast the signal in this slot. Note that, in order to guarantee high probability of such an event, we need also to take care of the case when a small number of sensors is stimulated. We can for example imagine a "naive algorithm" for which each stimulated sensor chooses one out of t slots and the remaining sensors are listening. In the case when $n_0 = 2$ the probability of failure for such an algorithm equals $\frac{1}{t}$ which is relatively high in a practical scenario wherein $t = \text{poly}(\log n)$. For that reason, in Pase 1 stimulated sensors choose several slots to broadcast the alert signal.

3.1 The Alert Algorithm

At the beginning of the algorithm n_0 stimulated sensors are, by definition, *notified* about the alert. No of the remaining sensors is notified.

Phase 1a. Each of n_0 stimulated sensors chooses independently at random l distinct slots from the set $\{T[i,j] \mid i \in [\log n], j \in [k]\}$.

Phase 1b. This phase takes all slots $T[i,j]$ for $i \in [\log n], j \in [k]$. In the slot $T[i,j]$:
  1. The guardian $s(i,j)$ listens to other sensors. If it receives the alarm signal, then it becomes notified.
  2. Each stimulated sensor, except guardians, broadcasts alarm signal, if it has chosen this slot in Phase 1a.

Phase 2a. Each of n_0 stimulated sensors chooses independently at random at most one slot $T[i + \log n, j]$ for $i \in [\log n], j \in [k]$. Slot $T[i + \log n, j]$ is chosen with probability $p_{i,j} = 1/(2^i k)$.

Phase 2b. This phase takes all slots $T[i + \log n, j]$ for $i \in [\log n], j \in [k]$.
  In slot $T[i + \log(n), j]$:
  1. The guardian $s(i,j)$ listens to other sensors. If it receives the signal, then it becomes notified.
  2. Each stimulated sensor, except guardians, broadcasts alarm signal, if it has chosen this slot in Phase 2a.

Phase 3. This phase covers slots from $T[2\log(n) + i, j]$ for $i \in [\log n], j \in [k]$. In the slot $T[2\log(n) + i, j]$:
  1. The guardian $s(i,j)$ broadcasts the signal if it is notified about the alert.
  2. The guardian next to $s(i,j)$ (i.e. $s(i, j+1)$ if $j \neq k$ or $s(i+1, 1)$ if otherwise) is listening. If it receives the signal, then it becomes notified.

Phase 4. In the slot $T[3\log(n), k]$:
  1. The last guardian (i.e. $s(\log(n), k)$) broadcasts the alarm signal, if it has been notified about the alert.
  2. All other sensors are listening. If they receive the alarm signal, they become notified.

Example. We demonstrate the algorithm in two cases for $n_0 = 10$ and $n_0 = 2$, in both cases with $k = 3$ and $l = 10$.

In Fig. 1 and 2 a black dot represents a broadcasting sensor and a row of cells represents consecutive slots. Two or more dots in a cell mean that a collision has occurred and the message was not heard by any sensor. Of course, the desired situation is to have *exactly one dot in a cell*.

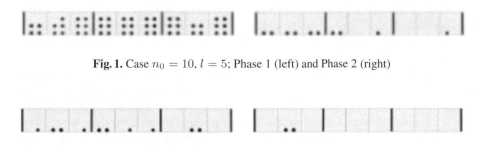

Fig. 1. Case $n_0 = 10$, $l = 5$; Phase 1 (left) and Phase 2 (right)

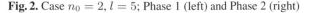

Fig. 2. Case $n_0 = 2$, $l = 5$; Phase 1 (left) and Phase 2 (right)

Case 1: A large number of stimulated sensors. When the number of stimulated sensors is relatively large we expect success of the algorithm (i.e. one dot in a cell) in Phase 2. Phase 1 is depicted in Fig. 1 (left) where there are much more stimulated sensors than slots (so we cannot expect a slot with exactly one broadcasting sensor). Phase 2 of the same experiment is presented in Fig. 1 (right). The sensors broadcast with different probability in different groups of slots. There should be a group of slots with an appropriate number of broadcasting sensors to have a single transmission in a slot with a high probability.

Case 2: A small number of stimulated sensors. When the number of stimulated sensors is small (Fig. 2), in Phase 1 there is a slot with a single transmission with high probability. It is possible even in the case of very small number of stimulated sensors, since each sensor broadcasts the alarm signal l times. In Phase 2 there are too few sensors to have a slot with a single transmission with a high probability.

3.2   Extensions

Detectors. Let us note that in our protocol we have in fact two subsets of nodes - "guardians" (a small subset) and regular nodes (i.e. "detectors') acting in some sense independently. Let us note that guardians have $O(1)$ energetic complexity. On the other hand detectors do not have to receive any information. Indeed, we can use extremely simple devices as detectors. In particular, they do not have to be able to adapt to the behavior of any other sensor. They also do not have to be distinguishable (no unique ID is necessary). Moreover, broadcasted message is a single alert-flag. The only substantial requirement is a simple random bit generator (e.g. based on physical impact of the event to be detected –like temperature). Moreover, since the algorithm guarantees a high success probability for any number of sensors smaller than a fixed n, it is unnecessary to know the exact number of the detectors. It is enough to know a rough upper bound for n. For that reason one can add a number of detectors long after the initial deployment (i.e. for replacing the damaged ones or for increasing network density).

Guardians. Another important issue is an algorithm for the "guardians" collecting the signals from detectors. Such a protocol can be improved in terms of the number of sensors/immunity against node failures for the price of increasing of energetic complexity. We can get various trade-offs tailored for a particular scenario. One of the possible approaches providing robustness is to randomly and independently assign guardians to slots in such a way to have $O(\log(n))$ in each of them w.h.p. After that, a leader is chosen in each group and the leaders are responsible for distributing alert. In such a way we obtain trade-offs between energy use, time and the number of guardians. In such an approach we do not need to know the exact number of guardians in advance or to enumerate them. We analyze the protocol, however, in the basic form with enumerated "guardians", as described above.

Let us also note that even in the case of a fixed set of enumerated guardians they can be periodically changed, i.e if in the T-th run of the algorithm, sensor p performed some special task, then in the run $T + 1$ this task is performed by the sensor $p + F \mod n$, where F is the number of listening sensors participating in the algorithm. We can build an algorithm immune against failures of even a significant number of listening sensors (with high probability). For example, such a strategy can be based on local repairing of enumerated structure. In the simplest approach sensors can be assigned randomly to guarding slots in such a way that we keep the number of "guardian candidates" low in each slots. At Phase 3 guardians are chosen from small sets via leader election. That would of course increase runtime of the procedure.

Division into Phases. Let us note that dividing the algorithm into phases $1a, 1b$ and $2a, 2b$ was motivated by the need to take care of situations when we have, respectively, a small and a large number of stimulated sensors. For that reason it is possible to partially "compress" both phases and improve time complexity. However, the improvement is not substantial while the analysis and description of this algorithm become more difficult. Similarly, some small improvements can be easily applied to limit the number of broadcasts of guarding sensors.

4 Analysis of the Algorithm

In our analysis we use the following parameters: $k = \log^2(n)$, $l = \frac{\log n}{\log \log(n)}$. Such parameters seem to be well motivated by practical reasons and are convenient in calculations. However other choice could also be interesting.

Theorem 1 (Main result). *Our algorithm:*

1. *has time complexity $O(\log^3(n))$,*
2. *has energy complexity $O\left(\frac{\log n}{\log \log(n)}\right)$,*
3. *broadcasts the alert signal to all sensors with probability at least $1 - \frac{3}{n}$.*

4.1 Time and Energy Complexity

Considering the above description one can easily see that this algorithm is performed in deterministic time $3 \log^3(n)$. Slightly more demanding is to analyze energy effort of each sensor. As we assumed before, we treat listening as well as broadcasting in a slot as a unit energy effort.

We need to consider three (possibly overlapping) types of sensors:

Guarding sensors. Let us note that each of these sensors listens exactly once in Phase 1b, exactly once in Phase 2b and exactly once in Phase 3. Moreover, some of these sensors can broadcast in Phase 3 or 4 exactly once. So the energy effort for this type of sensors is exactly 4.

Stimulated sensor. Each stimulated sensor broadcasts exactly $l = \frac{\log n}{\log \log(n)}$ times in Phase 1b. Moreover, it broadcasts exactly once in Phase 2b.

Non stimulated sensors. They listen once in Phase 4.

Thus the maximal energy effort is $l + 4 = \frac{\log n}{\log \log(n)} + 4 = O\left(\frac{\log n}{\log \log(n)}\right)$ as stated in Theorem 1. The most energy demanding case is when a guarding sensor is also a stimulated one.

4.2 Success Probability

The most difficult part of the analysis is to estimate probability of a successful execution of the algorithm. In other words, we need to estimate the probability that all sensors are notified about the alert, if at least one sensor has been stimulated (i.e. $n_0 > 0$). (Obviously, if no sensor has been stimulated, then the allert will not be broadcast.) However, if more than one sensor has been stimulated, then it is possible that they choose the same slots to broadcast the signal. This would cause a failure of the algorithm. Our aim is to estimate the probability of all "bad events" regarding that $n_0 > 0$ is unknown. In our analysis we use two models – Bernoulli trials and balls-and-bins model. (For information regarding them refer for instance to [8].)

Before we start the analysis let us recall some facts from probability theory.

Lemma 1. *Let a random variable X have a binomial distribution with parameters n, p (i.e. $X \sim B(n,p)$). Then for any $n \in \mathbb{N}_+$, $p \in (0,1)$ and $t \geq 0$:*

- $\Pr(X \geq E[X] + t) \leq \exp\left(-E[X]\varphi\left(\frac{t}{E[X]}\right)\right) \leq \exp\left(-\frac{t^2}{2(E[X]+t/3)}\right)$,
- $\Pr(X \leq E[X] - t) \leq \exp\left(-\frac{t^2}{2E[X]}\right)$,

where $\varphi(x) = (1+x)\log(1+x) - x$ for $x > -1$.

Both facts are variants of the classical Chernoff inequality (see [5, Theorem 2.1]).

Balls and Bins Model. We consider m balls that are thrown sequentially into L bins. Each ball is placed in one of m bins with equal probability and its placement is independent from other choices.

Lemma 2. *Let us assume that m balls are thrown independently at random into L bins, where $m < L/2$. Let X denote the number of bins that contain afterwards exactly one ball. Then*
$$\Pr(X = 0) \leq \exp\left(-m\left(1 - \frac{1}{L}\right)^{2m-2}\right).$$

Due to space limitations we skip the proof based on Azuma-Hoeffding Theorem (see [8]) and the fact that each ball changes the value X by at most two (Lipshitz condition).

Lemma 3. *Let us suppose that we have $m = l \cdot n_0 < L$ balls. In each round l balls are placed in l distinct bins chosen at random. Let X denote the number of bins that contain exactly one ball after throwing all n_0 balls. Then*

$$\Pr(X = 0) < \exp\left(-\frac{m}{2}\left(\log\left(\frac{L}{2m} \right) - 1 \right) \right).$$

Proof. Let us define Y_i as a random variable such that $Y_i = 1$, if the ith ball was placed in a non-empty bin (i.e. a bin that was chosen by one of the previous balls) and $Y_i = 0$ otherwise. Let $S = \sum_{i=1}^{m} Y_i$.

Fact 1. *If $S < \frac{m}{2}$,, then there is at least one bin with exactly one ball.*

Indeed, let us note that if $S < \frac{m}{2}$, then more than $\frac{m}{2}$ bins are non empty. However, this implies that at least one bin must have exactly one ball.

Fact 2. *Let $X_1, \ldots, X_n$ be arbitrary random variables with finite first moment. Let $Y_i = Y_i(X_1, \ldots, X_{i-1})$. If $E(Y_i|Y_{i-1}, Y_{i-2}, \ldots, Y_1) \le p$, then for each j:*

$$\Pr\left(\sum_{i=1}^{n} Y_i \ge j \right) \le \Pr\left(B(n, p) \ge j \right).$$

It is easy to see that in our case $E(Y_i|Y_{i-1}, Y_{i-2}, \ldots, Y_1) < \frac{m}{L}$. Indeed, at every step i at most $m - 1$ bins are non–empty. Applying Fact 2 to S we get:

$$\Pr\left(S \ge \frac{m}{2} \right) \le \Pr\left(B\left(m, \frac{m}{L} \right) \ge \frac{m}{2} \right) = \Pr\left(B\left(m, \frac{m}{L} \right) \ge \frac{m^2}{L} + \frac{m}{2} - \frac{m^2}{L} \right).$$

Using Lemma 1 with $t = \frac{m}{2} - \frac{m^2}{L}$ and $\frac{t}{E[X]} = \frac{t}{E[B(m, \frac{m}{L})]} = \frac{L}{2m} - 1$ we finally get

$$\Pr\left(S \ge \frac{m}{2} \right) \le \exp\left(-\frac{m^2}{L}\left(\frac{L}{2m}\log\left(\frac{L}{2m} \right) - \frac{L}{2m} + 1 \right) \right) \le \exp\left(-\frac{m}{2}\left(\log\left(\frac{L}{2m} \right) - 1 \right) \right).$$

Together with Fact 1 it completes the proof of Lemma 3.   □

To prove Theorem 1 we need to show that probability of successful broadcasting is greater or equal $1 - 1/n$ for any $1 \le n_0 \le n$. We consider two cases. In the first case, when n_0 is small, we show that at least one listening sensor in Phase 1b is notified about the alert by one of n_0 stimulated sensors. In other words, we show that there is at least one slot such that exactly one stimulated sensor broadcasts. Then we show that if n_0 is large, then in Phase 2b at least one listening sensor is notified. Of course, if at least one listening sensor is notified in Phase 1b or in Phase 2b, then all sensors will be notified about the alert in Phase 4. So the algorithm is successfully finished.

Case 1: $n_0 \in [1, 2\log^2 n]$. Let us suppose that $n_0 < 2\log^2 n$. In Phase 1a, each of n_0 stimulated sensors tries to broadcast the alert signal in $\frac{\log n}{\log\log(n)}$ randomly chosen out of $\log^3(n)$ slots in Phase 1b. We estimate the probability that at least one of them will be successful. We can use Lemma 3 with parameters $m = n_0 \cdot \frac{\log n}{\log \log(n)}$ and $L = \log^3(n)$. Namely, probability that in none of $\log^3(n)$ slots exactly one sensor broadcasts is smaller than:

$$F(n_0) = \exp\left(-\frac{n_0 \cdot \log(n)}{2 \log \log(n)}\left(\log\left(\frac{\log^2(n) \log \log(n)}{2 n_0}\right) - 1\right)\right) < \frac{1}{n}.$$

One can easily check that for any $n_0 \in [1, 2 \log^2(n)]$ holds $F(n_0) < \frac{1}{n}$. It can be proved by investigating the minimal value of the function $f(x) = x\left(\log\left(\frac{A}{x} - 1\right)\right)$ for a constant A in the interval $[1, 2 \log^2(n)]$.

Corollary 1. *If $n_0 \in [1, 2 \log^2 n]$, then with probability higher than $1 - \frac{1}{n}$ exactly one sensor is broadcasting the alert signal in Phase 1b.*

Case 2: $n_0 \in [2 \log^2 n + 1, n]$. This case, for which we dedicate Phases 2a and 2b, is more difficult. First, let us note that in this case each sensor tries to broadcast the signal in one of groups $T[i + \log n, *]$ with probability $1/2^i$. After a particular group is chosen, a slot $T[i + \log n, j]$ is chosen with probability $1/\log^2(n)$ for each j (i.e. uniformly at random it the group chosen).

Let X_i denote the number of stimulated sensors that decided in Phase 2b to broadcast in the group of slots $T[i + \log(n), *]$. It is easy to see that random variables X_i for $1 \leq i \leq \log(n)$ have binomial distribution with parameters $(n_0, 2^{-i})$. It implies that $E[X_i] = \frac{n_0}{2^i}$.

We show that with high probability there is a group of slots with approximately $\log^2 n$ broadcasting sensors:

Lemma 4. *For any $n_0 \in [2 \log^2 n + 1, n]$ there exists such i_0 that*

$$\Pr(\{X_{i_0} < 0.5 \log^2 n\} \cup \{X_{i_0} > 3 \log^2 n\}) \leq \frac{2}{n}.$$

Proof. Let us note that for assumed values of n_0 there must exist such i_0 that $\log^2 n \leq E[X_{i_0}] = \alpha \log^2 n \leq 2 \log^2 n$. This follows immediately from the fact that $E[X_i] = \frac{n_0}{2^i}$. Of course, X_{i_0} has binomial distribution with parameters $(n_0, 2^{-i_0})$, so for any β such that $\alpha > \beta > 0$, by Lemma 1 we have: $\Pr(X_{i_0} < (\alpha - \beta) \log^2 n) < \exp\left(-\frac{\beta^2 \log^2 n}{2\alpha}\right)$.

Let us substitute $\beta = \alpha - 0.5$. Since $\frac{(\alpha - 0.5)^2}{2\alpha} \geq \frac{1}{8}$ for $\alpha \in [1, 2]$, we get

$$\exp\left(-\frac{(\alpha - 0.5)^2}{2\alpha} \log^2 n\right) \leq \exp\left(-\frac{1}{8} \log^2 n\right) \leq \frac{1}{n}.$$

By analogy, using again Lemma 1 we get

$$\Pr(X_{i_0} > 3 \log^2 n) \leq \Pr(X_{i_0} > \alpha \log^2 n + \log^2 n) \leq \exp\left(-\frac{\log^2 n}{2\alpha + 2/3}\right) < \frac{1}{n}.$$

We conclude that the probability that X_{i_0} *is not* in the interval $[0.5 \log^2 n, 3 \log^2 n]$ is smaller than $\frac{2}{n}$. $\qquad\square$

Let us consider now a group of slots $T[i_0 + \log(n), *]$. We have shown that with a high probability $m \in [0.5 \log^2 n, 3 \log^2 n]$ sensors broadcast in this group of slots. Each slot in this group is chosen with the same probability $(\log^2(n))^{-1}$. By $\mathcal{A}$ let us denote the event that none of the slots in the group $T[i_0 + \log(n), *]$ is chosen by *exactly one* stimulated sensor. We can use Lemma 2 to get:

$$\Pr(\mathcal{A}) \leq \exp\left(-m\left(1 - \frac{1}{\log^2(n)}\right)^{2m-2}\right).$$

We assume that $m \in [0.5 \log^2 n, 3 \log^3 n]$. By investigating $F'(x)$ it can be easily proved that the function $F(x) = x\left(1 - \frac{1}{\log^2(n)}\right)^{2x-2}$ has exactly one local maximum on $[0, \infty)$. Since $F(0.5 \log^2 n) > \log(n)$ and $F(3 \log^2 n) > \log(n)$, we get that $F(x) > \log(n)$ for $x \in [0.5 \log^2 n, 3 \log^3 n]$. On the other hand, we have $\Pr(\mathcal{A}) \leq \exp(-F(m)) \leq \frac{1}{n}$. Finally, with probability $1 - 1/n$ the alert signal is successfully broadcast in at least one slot in the group $T[i_0 + \log(n), *]$, conditioned upon the event that $m \in [0.5 \log^2 n, 3 \log^2 n]$. This holds with probability at least $1 - 2/n - 1/n$.

Corollary 2. *When $n_0 > 2 \log^2 n$, then with probability greater than $1 - \frac{3}{n}$ exactly one sensor broadcasts in Phase 2b.*

From Corollaries 2 and 1 we have that for any number of stimulated sensors at least one sensor successfully broadcasts during Phase 1b or 2b with probability at least $1 - \frac{3}{n}$. This suffices to broadcast the alert signal to other sensors in Phases 3 and 4. This concludes the proof of Theorem 1.   □

5   Lower Bound

In this section we show that there is a trade-off between time and energy cost for alert algorithms. In particular, we show that every polylogarithmic time algorithm has energy cost at least such as our algorithm provided that detectors cannot adapt to behaviour of other sensors (because e.g. they do not have receivers).

Theorem 2. *Every Monte Carlo alert algorithm for a network of n sensors in described model with runtime $t < n$ has energetic complexity $l > \frac{\log(n/2)}{\log t}$.*

Proof. By a *broadcasting pattern* of a particular sensor we understand a string of length t with a 1 on position i ($i \leq t$), if the sensor activates its transmitter at step i. Since we have assumed that each sensor can broadcast at most l times, all broadcasting patterns belong to $P = \{\overline{x} \in (0,1)^t | \text{HAMMING}(\overline{x}) \leq l\}$, i.e. to the set of binary strings of length t having at most l ones. To each pattern we can assign a unique label in $[|P|] = \{1, \ldots, |P|\}$. A strategy of broadcasting for a sensor is a set of rules of choosing a particular broadcasting pattern. In general, strategies can be randomized. We can identify a strategy of a particular sensor with a random variable with values in the set P. So a strategy of the ith sensor can be represented as a vector

$$\mathcal{S}^{(i)} \in \left\{(p_1^{(i)}, \ldots, p_{|P|}^{(i)}) \in [0,1]^{|P|} \,\Big|\, \sum_{i=1}^{|P|} p_i = 1\right\},$$

where $p_j^{(i)}$ is a probability that the jth broadcasting pattern is used by the ith sensor.

For two strategies $\mathcal{S}^{(1)}, \mathcal{S}^{(2)}$ we define their product as

$$\mathcal{S}^{(1)} \circ \mathcal{S}^{(2)} = \sum_{j=1}^{|P|} p_j^{(1)} \cdot p_j^{(2)}$$

and their sum as $\mathcal{S}^{(1)} + \mathcal{S}^{(2)} = \left(p_1^{(1)} + p_1^{(2)}, \ldots, p_{|P|}^{(1)} + p_{|P|}^{(2)} \right)$.

We use following auxiliary fact that can be proved by a simple induction:

Fact 3. *Let us consider a function* $F(\overline{p}) = \sum_{i=1}^{|P|} (p_i)^2$ *for* $\overline{p} = (p_1, \ldots, p_{|P|}) \in [0,1]^{|P|}$ *with* $\sum_{i=1}^{|P|} p_i = A$. *Then:*

1. $F(\overline{p}) \leq A^2$,
2. $F(\overline{p})$ *reaches its minimum* $\frac{A^2}{|P|}$ *for* $\overline{p}_0 = \left(\frac{A}{|P|}, \frac{A}{|P|}, \ldots, \frac{A}{|P|} \right)$.

Let us note that we need to assume that two sensors can have in general two arbitrary strategies. Moreover, these strategies can be strongly correlated in order to maximize probability of successful execution of particular tasks. For example, one can assign strategies to particular sensors in order to avoid conflicts with a high probability and to make a successful transmission. However, we show that there are some limitations of designing strategies aimed at avoiding conflicts.

First of all, let us note that if two sensors choose the same pattern, then it always leads to a failure of the algorithm. Obviously, avoiding this does not guarantee success of the algorithm. If we have for example two sensors it is easy to avoid such a situation by designing appropriate strategies that choose patterns with disjoint slots when sensor broadcast the signal. Let $\mathcal{A}_{i,j}$ denote the probability that sensors i and j choose the same pattern according to their strategies. Of course, $\Pr(\mathcal{A}_{j_1,j_2}) = \mathcal{S}^{(j_1)} \circ \mathcal{S}^{(j_2)}$. To guarantee success of algorithm with an overwhelming probability for an arbitrary choice of stimulated sensors we need to have in particular $\Pr(\mathcal{A}_{j_1,j_2}) < \frac{1}{n}$ for any $j_1 \neq j_2 \in [n]$. This implies that $\mathcal{S}^{(j_1)} \circ \mathcal{S}^{(j_2)} < \frac{1}{n}$ for all $j_1, j_2 \in [n], j_1 \neq j_2$. Thus, $\sum_{j \neq j_2} \left(\mathcal{S}^{(j_1)} \circ \mathcal{S}^{(j_2)} \right) < 2\binom{n}{2}\frac{1}{n}$. Let us note that in such a case

$$\left(\sum_{j \in [n]} \mathcal{S}^{(j)} \right) \circ \left(\sum_{j \in [n]} \mathcal{S}^{(j)} \right) = \sum_{j_1 \neq j_2} \mathcal{S}^{(j_1)} \circ \mathcal{S}^{(j_2)} + \sum_{j \in [n]} \left(\mathcal{S}^{(j)} \circ \mathcal{S}^{(j)} \right)$$

$$\overset{*}{<} 2\binom{n}{2}\frac{1}{n} + \sum_{j \in [n]} \left(\mathcal{S}^{(j)} \circ \mathcal{S}^{(j)} \right) \overset{**}{\leq} n - 1 + n \cdot 1 = 2n - 1.$$

The inequality marked as $(*)$ is due to the assumption that the product of strategies of two different sensors must be smaller than $\frac{1}{n}$; the inequality marked as $(**)$ is a consequence of Fact 3.

On the other hand, we have $\left(\sum_{j \in [n]} \mathcal{S}^{(j)} \right) \circ \left(\sum_{j \in [n]} \mathcal{S}^{(j)} \right) \geq \frac{n^2}{|P|}$ by Fact 3. This

implies in particular that $\frac{n^2}{|P|} \leq 2n - 1$. Thus, $|P| > \frac{n^2}{2n-1} > \frac{n}{2}$. Since $|P| = \sum_{i=0}^{l} \binom{t}{i} < t^l$, for $l < t$, we get the bound $l > \frac{\log(n/2)}{\log t}$. $\qquad\square$

References

1. Chlebus, B., Kowalski, D.: A Better Wake–up in Radio Networks. In: Proc. PODC 2004, pp. 266–274 (2004)
2. Chrobak, M., Gąsieniec, L., Kowalski, D.: The Wake–up Problem in Multi–Hop Radio Networks. In: Proc. ACM–SIAM SODA 2004, pp. 992–1000 (2004)
3. Gąsieniec, L., Pelc, A., Peleg, D.: The Wakeup Problem in Synchronous Broadcast Systems. SIAM J. Discrete Math. 14(2), 207–222 (2001)
4. Jurdziński, T., Stachowiak, G.: Probabilistic Algorithms for the Wakeup Problem in Single-Hop Radio Networks. In: Bose, P., Morin, P. (eds.) ISAAC 2002. LNCS, vol. 2518, pp. 535–549. Springer, Heidelberg (2002)
5. Janson, S., Łuczak, T., Ruciński, A.: Random Graphs. 2000. Wiley and Sons, Chichester (2000)
6. Kowalski, D.R.: On Selection Problem in Radio Networks. In: Proc. PODC 2005, pp. 158–166 (2005)
7. Kutyłowski, M., Rutkowski, W.: Adversary Immune Leader Election in Ad Hoc Radio Networks. In: Di Battista, G., Zwick, U. (eds.) ESA 2003. LNCS, vol. 2832, pp. 397–408. Springer, Heidelberg (2003)
8. Mitzenmacher, M., Upfal, E.: Probability and Computing. Cambridge University Press, Cambridge (2005)
9. Moscibroda, T., von Rickenbach, P., Wattenhofer, R.: Analyzing the Energy-Latency Trade-Off During the Deployment of Sensor Networks. In: INFOCOM 2006 (2006)

Brief Announcement: Universal Data Aggregation Trees for Sensor Networks in Low Doubling Metrics[*]

Srivathsan Srinivasagopalan, Costas Busch, and S. Sitharama Iyengar

Computer Science Department, Louisiana State University, Baton Rouge, USA
{ssrini1,busch,iyengar}@csc.lsu.edu

Abstract. We describe a novel approach for constructing a single spanning tree for data aggregation towards a sink node. The tree is *universal* in the sense that it is static and independent of the number of data sources and fusion-costs at intermediate nodes. The tree construction is in polynomial time, and for *low doubling dimension* topologies it guarantees a $O(\log^2 n)$-approximation of the optimal aggregation cost. With constant fusion-cost functions our aggregation tree gives a $O(\log n)$-approximation for every Steiner tree to the sink.

1   Summary

We consider the fundamental problem of data aggregation in sensor networks towards a sink node s. The motivation comes from the hierarchical matching algorithm in [1] that constructs a data aggregation tree that is *simultaneously* good for all canonical fusion-cost functions f which are concave and non-decreasing. However, every time the data sources change the aggregation tree has to be reconstructed. In order to alleviate this problem, a novel approach in [2] builds a *single* aggregation tree which is independent of the number of data sources. This is for networks formed by randomly distributed nodes over a 2-dimensional plane. Here, we combine the above ideas to build a *universal* aggregation spanning tree for low (constant) doubling-dimension graphs, such that the tree is independent of the data sources, and can accommodate any canonical fusion-cost function. Our approach gives a $O(\log^2 n)$-approximation to the optimal aggregation cost (measured as the total involved communication cost), where n is the number of nodes. For constant fusion-cost we obtain a spanning tree that approximates within a $O(\log n)$ factor every Steiner tree that includes the sink.

Given a graph G, we first construct a *virtual tree* T based on a hierarchical clustering. The performance of T is estimated for low doubling-dimension graphs. We then project T to a real spanning tree that preserves the asymptotic aggregation performance. We provide a hierarchical clustering $Z_0, \ldots, Z_\kappa$ with $\kappa + 1 = O(\log n)$ levels, where each Z_i is a partition of G. Every cluster in Z_i is a connected subgraph of G with diameter $O(2^i)$. Each cluster has a leader; let I_i

---

[*] Supported by PKSFI grant 32-4233-40860-LSU, and NSF grant 0846081.

S. Dolev (Ed.): ALGOSENSORS 2009, LNCS 5804, pp. 151–152, 2009.

denote the leaders at level i. For any $u, v \in I_i$, $\mathrm{dist}_G(u, v) = \Omega(2^i)$. Each cluster at level i (with leader ℓ_i) is completely contained by some cluster at level $i + 1$ (with leader ℓ_{i+1}), with the exception of $i = \kappa$. Virtual tree T consists of $\kappa + 1$ levels and has as nodes the leaders of the clusters, edges of the form $e = (\ell_i, \ell_{i+1})$ (ℓ_i is the child), and weight of e proportional to $\mathrm{dist}_G(\ell_i, \ell_{i+1})$. The root of T is s (which is the leader of the single cluster of Z_κ), while the leaves are the individual nodes of G (partition Z_0 consists of the individual nodes of G).

The data aggregation in tree T is performed level by level in κ phases. In phase i each leader at level i receives data from its children and then fuses the data. The size of the data produced by a node during aggregation depends on the fusion-cost function f. Assume for now a constant function $f(\cdot) = 1$. For the analysis consider an arbitrary set of source nodes A. Let $X_i \subseteq I_i$ be the set of leaders at level i which hold data at the end of phase i. In phase $i + 1$, each leader in X_i sends a message to its parent giving a total communication cost $O(|X_i| \cdot 2^{i+1})$. For every leader $v \in X_i$, there is at least one node in A that belongs to the cluster of v at level i. Let $A_i \subseteq A$ denote the union of such data sources, where $|A_i| = |X_i|$. Using the doubling dimension property of G it can be shown that there is a subset $A_i' \subseteq A_i$ such that $|A_i'| \geq |A_i|/(2^{3\rho} + 1)$ (where ρ is the doubling dimension parameter), and for any pair $u, v \in A_i'$, $\mathrm{dist}_G(u, v) = \Omega(2^i)$. The optimal aggregation cost for A is at least the cost of the Steiner tree connecting the A_i' to the sink which is $\Omega(|A_i'| \cdot 2^i) = \Omega(|A_i| \cdot 2^i) = \Omega(|X_i| \cdot 2^i)$ (for constant ρ). Therefore, the aggregation cost of a phase is optimal within a constant factor. Considering all $\kappa = O(\log n)$ phases, the total aggregation cost is within a factor of $O(\log n)$ from optimal.

For the analysis of non-constant fusion-cost functions, we further divide set X_i into $\lambda = O(\log n)$ classes, $X_i^0, \ldots, X_i^{\lambda-1}$, so that at the end of phase i each node $v \in X_i^j$ contains data of size $f(|A_i^v|) \in [2^j, 2^{j+1})$, where $A_i^v \subseteq A$ is the set of source nodes which belong to the cluster of v at level i. By collapsing all the nodes in A_i^v to a single artificial data source of weight 2^j, the data aggregation problem of each class is reduced to the constant fusion-cost function case (an additional $\Theta(2^j)$ factor appears in both the lower and upper bounds). Thus, the aggregation cost for each class is optimal within a constant factor. By considering all classes and phases we obtain a $\kappa\lambda = O(\log^2 n)$ approximation.

The projection of the virtual tree to a real spanning tree is performed by replacing every edge in T with a shortest path in G. The aggregation performance is maintained by avoiding interference between paths of the same level.

References

[1] Goel, A., Estrin, D.: Simultaneous optimization for concave costs: single sink aggregation or single source buy-at-bulk. In: Proceedings of the fourteenth annual ACM-SIAM Symposium on Discrete Algorithms (SODA 2003), Baltimore, Maryland, pp. 499–505 (2003)

[2] Jia, L., Noubir, G., Rajaraman, R., Sundaram, R.: Gist: Group-independent spanning tree for data aggregation in dense sensor networks. In: Gibbons, P.B., Abdelzaher, T., Aspnes, J., Rao, R. (eds.) DCOSS 2006. LNCS, vol. 4026, pp. 282–304. Springer, Heidelberg (2006)

Brief Announcement on MOGRIBA: Multi-Objective Geographical Routing for Biomedical Applications of WSN

Djamel Djenouri[1] and Ilangko Balasingham[1,2]

[1] Department of Electronics and Telecommunications, NTNU, Trondheim, Norway
djamel.djenouri@iet.ntnu.no
[2] Interventional Center, Rikshospitalet University Hospital, Oslo, Norway
ilangko.balasingham@medisin.uio.no

Abstract. A new routing protocol for wireless sensor networks is proposed in this paper. The proposed protocol focuses on medical applications, by considering its traffic diversity and providing a differentiation routing using quality of service (QoS) metrics. The design is based on modular and scalable approach, where the protocol operates in a distributed, localized, computation and memory efficient way. The main contribution of this paper is data traffic based QoS with regard to all the considered QoS metrics, notably reliability, latency, and energy. To our best knowledge, this protocol is the first that makes use of the diversity in the data traffic while considering latency, reliability, residual energy in the sensor nodes, and transmission power between sensor nodes as QoS metrics of the multi-objective problem. Simulation study comparing the protocol with state-of-the QoS and geographical routing protocols shows that it outperforms all the compared protocols.

1 Solution Overview

The considered application consists of a typical health care scenario. Several biomedical sensors may be embedded in different parts of the patient's body to measure and transmit data either through wired or wireless links to a body sensor mote that acts as a cluster-head of the body sensor network. It collects raw data, makes the required processing if necessary (coding, aggregation, etc.), and sends results to the sink node(s) responsible for covering the patient's area and uploading the information into the health care server. We define two kinds of responsible sinks for each patient; primary sink and secondary sink. A separate copy of each message requiring high reliability is sent to both sinks. This increases reliability as only one correct reception is necessary for the system. We consider in this paper energy efficiency, reliability, and latency, which are all involved in the medical application scenario. Giving these requirements data traffic may be split into: i) regular traffic that has no specific data-related QoS need, ii) reliability-sensitive traffic, which should be delivered without loss, but can tolerate reasonable delay, iii) delay-sensitive traffic, which should be delivered within a deadline, but may tolerate reasonable packet loss, and finally

S. Dolev (Ed.): ALGOSENSORS 2009, LNCS 5804, pp. 153–154, 2009.
© Springer-Verlag Berlin Heidelberg 2009

iv) critical traffic, of high importance and requiring both high reliability and short delay, e.g, physiological parameters of a patient during a surgery. For each packet, the protocol locally selects the most power-efficient node that ensures the required QoS. A deadline for delivery at final recipients is considered together with energy when routing delay-sensitive packets. Best effort is assured for reliability-sensitive packets by selecting the most reliable and energy-efficient routes. The two strategies are combined for critical traffic requiring both high reliability and hard deadline. Regular packets have no specific requirement, hence only energy-efficiency is taken into account for this type of packets. The proposed protocol was designed using a modular approach, and evaluated through a comparative simulation using GloMoSim. The proposed protocol, MOGRIBA, was compared with MMSPEED, DARA, EAGFS, SPEED, and a geographical greedy forwarding. The simulation setup consists of 900 nodes located in a 1800 m^2 area, and 1000 s of simulation time. Results depicted in Figures 1 (a) and (b) show MOGRIBA clearly outperforms all protocols, by ensuring low latency and high reliability. Detailed description of the protocol can be found in [1].

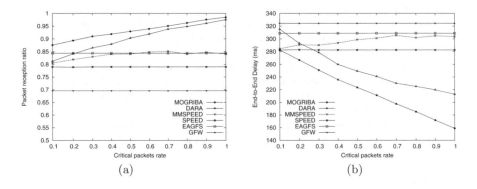

Fig. 1. a) Packet reception ratio, b)End-to-end delay

Acknowledgements

This work was carried out at the Norwegian University of Science and Technology (NTNU), during the tenure of an ERCIM Postdoc, as a part of the MELODY project funded by the Research Council of Norway.

Reference

1. Djenouri, D., Balasingham, I.: New QoS and geographical routing in wireless biomedical sensor networks. In: BROADNETs 2009, Madrid, Spain (accepted 2009)

Routing on Delay Tolerant Sensor Networks

Michael Keane[1], Evangelos Kranakis[2], Danny Krizanc[2], and Lata Narayanan[3]

[1] Department of Mathematics and Computer Science, Wesleyan University,
Middletown CT 06459, USA
[2] School of Computer Science, Carleton University, Ottawa, ON, K1S 5B6, Canada,
Supported by NSERC and MITACS grants
[3] Department of Computer Science and Software Engineering, Concordia University,
Montreal, QC, H3G 1M8, Canada, Supported by NSERC grant

Abstract. Delay (or disruption) tolerant sensor networks may be modeled as Markovian evolving graphs [1]. We present experimental evidence showing that considering multiple (possibly not shortest) paths instead of one fixed (greedy) path can decrease the expected time to deliver a packet on such a network by as much as 65 per cent depending on the probability that an edge exists in a given time interval. We provide theoretical justification for this result by studying a special case of the Markovian evolving grid graph. We analyze a natural algorithm for routing on such networks and show that it is possible to improve the expected time of delivery by up to a factor of two depending upon the probability of an edge being up during a time step and the relative positions of the source and destination. Furthermore we show that this is optimal, i.e., no other algorithm can achieve a better expected running time. As an aside, our results give high probability bounds for Knuth's toilet paper problem [11].

Keywords and Phrases: Ad hoc networks, Delay tolerant, Disruption tolerant, Evolving graphs, Routing, Sensors.

1 Introduction

Delay (or disruption) tolerant networks (DTNs) are characterized by their experiencing frequent, variable and long-duration periods of intermittent connectivity. Examples of such networks include satellite networks, mobile radio networks, energy-constrained sensor networks, etc. Such networks may be captured by Ferreira's *evolving graph* model [6] in which a network is modelled as a sequence of subgraphs of a fixed graph.

Our study is specifically motivated by the case of sensor networks with limited battery power for communication. A standard technique for power saving in such networks is to put sensors to sleep for long periods. Upon waking up the sensor searches among its neighboring sensors for ones that are awake and with which it can establish a communication link. (We assume that the sensors are "location-aware" in that they know their location in some co-ordinate system as well as the co-ordinates of their neighbors.) After transferring what messages it has to send

S. Dolev (Ed.): ALGOSENSORS 2009, LNCS 5804, pp. 155–166, 2009.

along these links the sensor goes back to sleep. The time between waking periods is chosen randomly. A network communicating under these circumstances is modelled well by a special class of geometric Markovian evolving graphs [1]. We assume the graph evolves in time steps. At each time step each potential edge (between neighboring sensors) is up with some fixed probability p, independent of the other potential edges. We are interested in the question of routing packets on such networks.

Experience shows that for sufficiently dense sensor networks (i.e., above the connectivity threshold) the geographic greedy path (i.e., each node chooses the edge that minimizes the geographic distance to the destination) generally minimizes the routing delay for routing between any given source and destination [10]. This suggests the following algorithm for routing in the sensor networks described above. A node attempting to deliver a packet to a given destination, upon waking up checks to see if the neighboring node that is closest to the destination is awake. If yes, it passes the packet to this node and goes to sleep. Otherwise it goes to sleep and waits for the next time it is awake. We call this the *greedy* strategy. If each edge is up with probability p and the greedy path (exists and) is of length l then clearly the expected number of steps required to deliver the packet to its destination is l/p. The question arises if one can do better by considering other (non-greedy) paths.

We provide experimental evidence that the following natural algorithm can improve the expected delivery time by as much as 65 per cent depending upon the value of p and the relative positions of the source and destination. Fix a value k. Upon waking up a node sorts its neighbors by their distance to the destination. If there is at least one neighbor among the top k that is awake and it is closer to the destination, it passes the packet to the best among them and goes to sleep. Otherwise it goes to sleep and waits for the next time it is awake. We call this the k-greedy strategy. (Clearly 1-greedy is the greedy strategy we defined above.) Our experiments are performed on sensor networks consisting of 1000 randomly distributed sensors on a unit square with radius of communication sufficiently above the threshold of connectivity to ensure the greedy path correctly delivers a packet with high probability. They show that as one increases k the improvement achieved increases until a maximum at about $k = 8$ but that most of the improvement (more than 60 percent) comes already from $k = 2$. We also observed a noticeable drop in improvement when considering packets whose greedy path is close to the perimeter of the square versus those in the central region of the square.

In order to study this problem analytically we consider the case of routing on a Markovian $n \times n$ grid where on each time step each edge of the grid exists (i.e., is up) with probability p independent of the other edges. Analogous to the greedy algorithm above, imagine that we fix a shortest path and forward the packet along that path whenever edges are available. Without loss of generality consider the case of a packet starting at node (i, j) and destined for $(0, 0)$ where $i \geq j$. In this case the expected time for delivery will be $(i + j)/p$.

We consider the following algorithm analogous to the 2-greedy strategy above. On a given step, if $i > 0$ and $j > 0$ (recall that $i \geq j$), then if the edge to $(i-1, j)$ is up, take it, i.e., pass the packet across the edge. If the edge to $(i-1, j)$ is down but the edge to $(i, j-1)$ is up, take it. Otherwise wait for the next time step. If i or j is 0 then wait for the unique edge on the shortest path to $(0,0)$ to be up.

Let $r = 1-(1-p)^2$ be the probability that at least one of the edges to $(i-1, j)$ or $(i, j-1)$ is up. We show that the time required to deliver a packet by this algorithm is

$$\max\left\{\frac{i+j}{r}, \frac{\max(i,j)}{p}\right\} + O\left(\sqrt{(i+j)\log(i+j)}\right)$$

with high probability, i.e., with probability at least $1 - \frac{1}{i+j}$. Furthermore we show that this is optimal up to lower order terms. Our results indicate that depending on p, packets following paths closer to the center of the grid (e.g., along the diagonal) can achieve as much as a factor of 2 improvement in their expected delivery time over the simple greedy strategy. For packets closer to the perimeter of the grid, the improvement drops until we reach the case of packets whose shortest path is a straight line where no improvement is possible. Simulations confirm that the behavior of the grid algorithm and the 2-greedy strategy on the unit square are qualitatively very similar.

Finally we note that the analytic problem we are studying is a variant of Knuth's toilet paper problem [11] and that our results can be used to show high probability results for that problem as well.

1.1   Related Work

Since traditional routing protocols make the assumption that the network graph is connected they may fail to route packets if a path from the source to the destination does not exist at all times. To deal with the problem of intermittent connectivity several approaches have been proposed by the networking community. For the most part, these approaches either assume that the graph evolves in a predictable (even repetitive) fashion or that the connectivity of the network is the result of a predictable process such as the (possibly random) movement of the nodes in a given region. Examples of such network include LEO satellite networks where the edges of the graph change in a predictable fashion, vehicular networks where nodes (cars) following predictable paths and MANETs, sometimes modeled as networks of mobile nodes that encounter each other randomly inside a bounded region. Experimental studies along these lines include [3,4,12,13,15,16,18,19]. In the setting where the evolution of the graph is known in advance, the problem can be approached using extensions to standard shortest path calculations. In the random movement setting, most approaches may be described as a variant of controlled flooding, where an effort is made to not overload the network.

The evolving graphs model of delay tolerant networks was introduced by Ferreira [6]. In a series of papers, Ferreira and co-authors experimentally evaluated a variety of standard protocols as well as novel approaches to routing on such graphs [7,8]. In [2] it is shown that when the graph sequence is given in advance, the "best" path under a number of natural metrics can be computed in polynomial time. Several related papers examine properties of the evolving graphs model itself. [9] looks at connectivity in evolving graphs with geometric properties and [1] examines the cover time of random walks in this model.

Related to the analysis of our algorithm is the following problem (generally referred to as the *toilet paper problem*), first described and solved by Knuth [11]. A toilet stall contains two rolls of toilet paper of n sheets each. The stall is used by people of two types: *big choosers* and *little choosers*. They arrive to use the toilet randomly and independently, the former with probability p and the latter with probability $1 - p$. Big (respectively, little) choosers select exactly one sheet of paper from the roll with the most (respectively, least) number of sheets. What is the expected number of toilet sheets remaining just after one of the two rolls has emptied, defined to be the residue $R_n(p)$?

Knuth [11] uses combinatorial techniques to prove that for fixed p and r, which satisfy the condition $4p(1 - p) < r < 1$, we have that

$$
E[R_n(p)] = \begin{cases} \frac{p}{2p-1} + O(r^n) & \text{if } p > 1/2 \\[2mm] 2\sqrt{\frac{n}{\pi}} - \frac{1}{4}\frac{1}{\sqrt{n\pi}} + O(n^{-3/2}) & \text{if } p = 1/2 \\[2mm] \frac{1-2p}{1-p}n + \frac{p}{1-2p} + O(r^n) & \text{if } p < 1/2 \end{cases}
$$

as $n \to \infty$ where the constants implied by the O notation depend on p, r but not on n. The case $p = 1/2$ is identical to Banach's match box problem given in the Scottish book [14]. For a related generalization of this problem using a martingale approach we refer the reader to [17] and [5].

1.2   Outline of the Paper

In the next section we present the results of our simulation of the k-greedy strategy for nodes distributed randomly on the unit square. In Section 3 we prove matching upper and lower bounds on the performance of the 2-greedy strategy on the Markovian grid. Due to space limitations the proofs will be appear in the full version of the paper.

2   Experimental Results for the k-Greedy Strategy

In this section we present experimental results concerning a natural strategy for routing on a special class of geometric Markovian evolving graphs. For this class of graphs, the node set is a set of points on the plane. An edge potentially exists between two nodes if their Euclidean distance is less than a given distance R. The graph evolves in time steps. During each time step each potential edge exists with probability p, independently of the other edges. We assume the nodes are "location aware", i.e., their is a fixed co-ordinate system agreed upon by all nodes and the nodes know their position in this system as well as the positions of their potential neighbors.

We are interested in studying the behavior of the following natural routing strategy for such graphs. Fix a value k. Consider a packet with destination t currently located at a given node other than t. On each step, the current node calculates the distance of all its neighbors to the destination and sorts them in increasing order. If among the first k potential neighbors their exists a node whose distance to t is less than the distance from the current node to t and the edge to that node exists, it forwards the packet along the existing edge to the node that is closest to t. If no such node exists, it waits until the next step. We call this strategy the k-greedy strategy and will refer to 1-greedy as simply the greedy strategy.

Experience has shown that for randomly distributed points on a unit square, if R is chosen sufficiently large, then the greedy strategy results in a path that generally minimizes the number of routing steps required to deliver the packet for most source-destination pairs [10]. Intuition suggests that by considering more paths, e.g., by increasing k in the strategy above, one might improve the performance of the algorithm. We ran a series of experiments to test this hypothesis. A standard experiment involved randomly (uniform in both co-ordinates) distributing 1000 points in a unit square and choosing $R = .1$. Experiments were run for a variety of source-destination pairs but we found there was little loss of generality by fixing the destination to be $(0,0)$. All the results reported below are based upon the average of 1000 runs with a single randomly chosen point set and a fixed parameter set of p, k and source node.

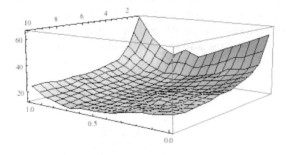

Fig. 1. Effect of k. $p = .2$ and destination is $(0,0)$; k varies from 1 to 10; source is $(x, 1 - x^2)$ where x varies from 0 to 1.0 by .1; z-axis gives the number of steps required.

The effect of k. Figure 1 shows the effect of the parameter k on the strategy. This example is for the case where p is fixed at .2 and we consider an equidistant set of source points equidistant from $(0,0)$ on the curve $y = 1 - x^2$ (with x varying from 0 to 1 by .1). Similar results are obtained for other values of p (not to close to 0 or 1) and choices of source points. The general trend for each source point is that the number of steps required to reach the destination drops as k increases until about $k = 8$ at which point the improvement levels off. Over all values of $k > 1$ and all points the average improvement over straight greedy ($k = 1$) is 49.9 per cent. For $k = 8$ the average improvement is 61.4 per cent with a maximum of 65.6 per cent and a minimum of 54.3 per cent. We note that the majority of the observed savings over greedy occurs by $k = 3$ with 61 per cent explained by $k = 2$ and 79 per cent by $k = 3$.

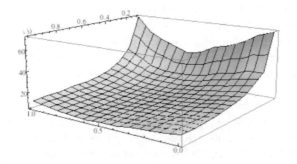

Fig. 2. Effect of p. $k = 2$ and destination is $(0,0)$; p varies from .1 to 1.0 by .1 along the top axis; source is $(x, 1 - x^2)$ where x varies from 0. to 1.0 by .1; z-axis gives the number of steps required.

The effect of p. Figure 2 shows the effect of varying p. This example is for the case where $k = 2$, for p ranging from .1 to 1 by .1 intervals and we again consider a set of equidistant source points. Similar results are obtained for other values of k and choices of source points. As expected the number of steps required increases significantly as p is decreased. At the same time the average savings over greedy increases from 8.4 per cent to 40.0 per cent as p varies from .9 down to .1. A slight effect due to the position of the source is visible in Figure 2 in that nodes closer to the edge of the square require longer to reach the destination even though they are the same Euclidean distance away as the nodes in the center. (Along each fixed p, the curve is slightly concave when moving from x equals 0 to 1.)

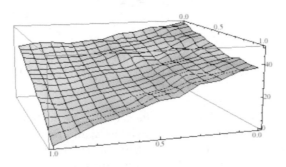

Fig. 3. Effect of source position. $k = 2$ and destination is $(0,0)$; x and y of source vary from 0 to 1.0 by .1; z-axis gives the number of steps required.

The effect of source position. Figure 3 plots for $p = .2$ and $k = 2$ the time required for a uniform grid of points to route to the destination $(0,0)$. Similar results are obtained for other values of k and p. While it is clear that the distance to the destination is a major factor in the number of steps required to reach it, there appears to be a slight increase in the time for points with source near the edge of the square as opposed in the center. (This effect is perhaps more noticeable in figure 2.)

3   Routing on the Grid

In an attempt to explain the observations made in section 2, in this section we study greedy routing on a special case of the Markovian evolving grid. (This might be considered a coarse approximation to the above where one divides the unit square into a uniform grid of subsquares and identifies the points inside each subsquare.) The node set of the $n \times n$ grid is $\{(i,j)|0 \le i,j < n\}$ and the potential edge set is $\{\{(i,j),(k,l)\}||i-k|+|j-l| = 1\}$. On each time step each edge exists with probability p independently of all other edges.

Analogous to the greedy strategy above one might consider a routing algorithm that fixes a shortest path from source to destination and then waits for that edge to be up in order to forward the packet. Without loss of generality consider a packet starting at (i,j) and destined for $(0,0)$. It can expect to take $\frac{i+j}{p}$ steps to reach its destination under this scheme.

Clearly the above does not take advantage of the many possible shortest paths between most source-destination pairs. Again, consider the case of a packet starting at (i,j) destined for $(0,0)$ where neither $i = 0$ nor $j = 0$. In this case there are two possible shortest paths, one starting with the edge to $(i-1,j)$ and one to $(i,j-1)$. In analogy to the 2-greedy strategy above, one might consider taking either one of these *distance-reducing* edges if they exist. Let $r = 1-(1-p)^2$ be the probability that at least one of the two distance-reducing edges exists. Assuming that $0 < p < 1$, we see that $1/2p < 1/r < 1/p$, i.e., the waiting time between moves in this case is always less than waiting for a specific edge and maybe up to 50 per cent less depending on the value of p. A question arises as to what to do if both edges exist. For instance, one might consider flipping a coin in this case. In fact, we show below the optimal strategy is to take the edge which reduces $|i-j|$. (If $i = j$ either a coin flip or a fixed choice can be used to decide.) We call this edge the *equalizing* edge or link. See figure 4.

More formally we study the following algorithm for a node (i,j) holding a packet destined for $(0,0)$:

1. If $i = 0$ and the edge to $(0,j-1)$ exists, forward the packet to $(0,j-1)$.
2. If $j = 0$ and the edge to $(i-1,0)$ exists, forward the packet to $(i-1,0)$.
3. If the edge to $(i-1,j)$ exists and the edge to $(i,j-1)$ does not exist, forward the packet to $(i-1,j)$.
4. If the edge to $(i,j-1)$ exists and the edge to $(i-1,j)$ does not exist, forward the packet to $(i,j-1)$.

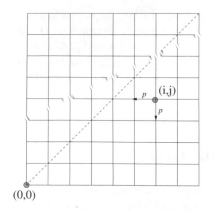

Fig. 4. Either of the two possible distance-reducing links at (i, j) is up independent of the other and with probability p. There are two distance-reducing links at (i, j) while only one is equalizing (the one leading towards the diagonal).

5. If both edges to $(i - 1, j)$ and $(i, j - 1)$ exist and $i > j$ then forward the packet to $(i - 1, j)$, else to $(i, j - 1)$.
6. Otherwise, wait.

Let q be the probability of forwarding a packet on an equalizing link. Consider the event DR that a distance-reducing link exists. Since DR occurs if either exactly one or both distance-reducing edges are up we conclude that $\Pr[DR] = 2p(1 - p) + p^2$. Consider the events BL that both distance-reducing links are up, and OL that only the distance equalizing link is up. Then

$$q = \Pr[BL \mid DR] + \Pr[OL \mid DR]$$
$$= \frac{p^2}{2p(1 - p) + p^2} + \frac{p(1 - p)}{2p(1 - p) + p^2}$$
$$= \frac{1}{2 - p}.$$

Observe that for $0 < p < 1$, $q = 1/(2 - p) > 1/2$.

3.1   Analysis of the Algorithm

We want to compute an upper bound on number of steps to route a packet from the source node (i, j) to the destination node $(0, 0)$. It is clear from the description of the algorithm that the route followed by a packet can be divided into two phases.

- Phase 1: The packet travels from the node (i, j) to a node in the first row (or first column) of the grid.
- Phase 2: The packet travels entirely in the first row (or first column) until the node $(0, 0)$ is reached.

Let X be the random variable that is the distance from the origin at which the packet hits the horizontal or vertical axis, that is, the packet enters the horizontal axis at node $(X, 0)$ (or the vertical axis at node $(0, X)$). In the rest of the paper, we use $m = i + j$ to denote the total number of links traversed by the packet. Therefore, the packet uses $m - X$ links in Phase 1, and X links in Phase 2. In the first phase, every intermediate node has two distance-reducing links available and in the second phase, there is exactly one distance-reducing link available at every node. It follows that the packet waits an expected $1/r$ steps to access a link in the first phase, and an expected $1/p$ steps to access a link in the second phase. Thus the expected time taken by the algorithm is $(m - E(X))/r + E(X)/p$. In this section we prove high probability bounds on X and the number of steps taken by the algorithm. Note that the value X is equivalent to the *residue* analyzed by Knuth in the toilet paper problem. The number of sheets on the two toilet paper rolls represent the x and y co-ordinates and choosing an equalizing link is analogous to being a big-chooser. Our bounds on X may be interpreted as high probability bounds on the residue left at the time one roll becomes empty starting with i sheets on one roll and j sheets on the other.

Since q is the probability that a packet is forwarded along an equalizing link it is natural to conjecture that the route of a packet starting at (i, j) with $i > j$ will be characterized by a line L with slope $\frac{1-q}{q}$ passing through the point (i, j). Two events will change the trajectory of the packet. Either the packet reaches the diagonal line $y = x$ or it reaches the horizontal or vertical axis as shown in Figure 5. Which of these two events occurs depends on the starting position of the packet.

Define by R the region $\{(i, j) \mid i \geq j > i\frac{1-q}{q} \text{ or } i\frac{q}{1-q} < i \leq j\}$ delimited by the two lines $y = \frac{qx}{1-q}$ and $y = \frac{(1-q)x}{q}$ (see shaded region in Figure 5). Without

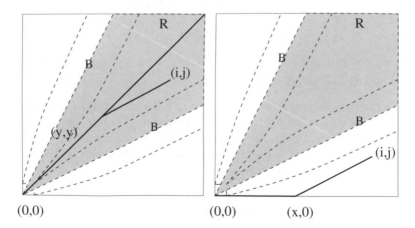

Fig. 5. Possible routes of a packet starting from the source node (i, j), either inside (left) or outside (outside) the shaded region R. When the packet is within the band it may hit either the diagonal or the horizontal.

loss of generality we consider only starting positions on or below the diagonal of the square. (The case when the starting positions are above the diagonal can be handled in a similar manner.) Also let B be the band delimited by two curves (depicted with dashed lines) surrounding the above lines defined by $y = \frac{q}{1-q}x \pm c_0\sqrt{\frac{x}{q}\log\frac{x}{q}}$ and $y = \frac{1-q}{q}x \pm c_0\sqrt{\frac{x}{q}\log\frac{x}{q}}$ where $c_0 = \sqrt{\ln 2(1 + \ln 8)/2}$.

The thrust of the argument is to show that three basic cases may occur depending on the starting position of the packet:

$(i,j) \in R \setminus R$. Phase 1 may be divided into two sub-phases for such a packet. In the first sub-phase, it is routed within the region R, staying "close" to the line L until it hits the diagonal. In the second sub-phase, it stays "close" to the diagonal and hits the horizontal axis at distance $O(\log m)$ from the origin with high probability.

$(i,j) \notin R \cup B$: The packet is routed with high probability outside the region R, staying close to the line L and hits the horizontal axis, at distance $O(\sqrt{m \log m})$ away from the point $(i - jq/(1-q), 0)$.

$(i,j) \in B$: A packet starting in this area may behave either like a packet in the first case or like one in the second case. In other words, the packet may either hit the diagonal, and then continue on to hit the horizontal axis at distance $O(\log m)$ from the origin. Alternatively, it may hit the horizontal axis without hitting the diagonal, but at distance $O(\sqrt{m \log m})$ from the origin.

We make this precise in the following lemma:

Lemma 1. *Consider a packet starting at position (i,j), and let X be the random variable such that the packet enters the horizontal axis at node $(X, 0)$ or the vertical axis at node $(0, X)$. With probability at least $1 - 1/2m$, the value of X is less than:*

$$\begin{cases} i - \frac{jq}{1-q} + c_0\sqrt{m \log m} & \text{if } (i,j) \notin R \cup B \\ c_1 \log m & \text{if } (i,j) \in R \setminus B \\ \max\{c_0 + c_2, c_1\}\sqrt{m \log m} & \text{if } (i,j) \in B \end{cases}$$

for $m = i+j > 2$, where $c_0 = \sqrt{\ln 2(1 + \ln 8)/2}$, $c_1 = -2/\log(1/2 + 2q(1-q)) > 0$ is a constant that depends only on q, and $c_2 = \sqrt{\ln 2(1 + \ln 4)/2}$.

Lemma 1 gives us a bound on the number of links travelled in each phase with high probability. (It also provides high probability bounds on the residue in Knuth's toilet paper problem.) It remains to factor in the number of steps waiting for a link to come up, and compute the number of steps taken by the algorithm. The main result of the paper follows:

Theorem 1. *With probability at least $1 - 1/(i+j)$ the number of steps to route a packet from node (i,j) to node $(0,0)$ is*

$$\begin{cases} \frac{i+j}{r} + O\left(\sqrt{(i+j)\log(i+j)}\right) & \text{if } (i,j) \in R \cup B \\ \frac{\max\{i,j\}}{p} + O\left(\sqrt{(i+j)\log(i+j)}\right) & \text{if } (i,j) \notin R \cup B \end{cases}$$

3.2 Lower Bound

In this section we show that the result of Theorem 1 is tight.

Theorem 2. *The expected number of steps for any routing algorithm to route a packet from* (i, j) *to* $(0, 0)$ *is at least*

$$\max\left\{ \frac{i+j}{r}, \frac{\max\{i, j\}}{p} \right\}.$$

4 Conclusion

In this paper we analyzed a natural algorithm for routing on a delay tolerant grid which improves the expected time of delivery by up to a factor of two over a fixed path algorithm, depending upon the probability of an edge being up during a time step and the relative positions of the source and destination. Furthermore we showed that this is optimal, in the sense that no other algorithm can achieve a better expected running time. We also presented experimental evidence that considering multiple (possibly not shortest) paths instead of one fixed (greedy) path can decrease the expected time to deliver a packet on a randomly deployed Markovian sensor network by as much as 65 per cent depending on the probability that an edge exists in a given time interval.

References

1. Avin, C., Koucky, M., Lotker, Z.: How to Explore a Fast-Changing World. In: Aceto, L., Damgård, I., Goldberg, L.A., Halldórsson, M.M., Ingólfsdóttir, A., Walukiewicz, I. (eds.) ICALP 2008, Part I. LNCS, vol. 5125, pp. 121–132. Springer, Heidelberg (2008)
2. Bui-Xuan, B., Ferreira, A., Jarry, A.: Computing Shortest, Fastest, and Foremost Journeys in Dynamic Networks. International Journal of Foundations of Computer Science 14, 267–285 (2003)
3. Burgess, J., Gallagher, B., Jensen, D., Levine, B.N.: MaxProp: Routing for Vehicle-Based Disruption-Tolerant Networks. In: Proceedings IEEE INFOCOM, pp. 1–11 (2006)
4. Daly, E.M., Haahr, M.: Social network analysis for routing in disconnected delay-tolerant MANETs. In: Proceedings of the 8th ACM international symposium on Mobile ad hoc networking and computing, pp. 32–40 (2007)
5. Duffy, K., Dukes, W.M.B.: On Knuth's Generalisation of Banach'Match Box Problem. Mathematical Proceedings of the Royal Irish Academy 104(1), 107–118 (2004)
6. Ferreira, A.: Building a reference combinatorial model for manets. IEEE Network 18, 24–29 (2004)
7. Ferreira, A., Goldman, A., Monteiro, J., Ferreira, A.: On the Evaluation of Shortest Journeys in Dynamic Networks. In: Sixth IEEE International Symposium on Network Computing and Applications, 1007. NCA 2007, pp. 3–10 (2007)
8. Goldman, A., Monteiro, J., Ferreira, A.: Performance Evaluation of Dynamic Networks using an Evolving Graph Combinatorial Model. In: Proceedings of WiMob, pp. 173–180 (2006)

9. Jarry, A., Lotker, Z.: Connectivity in evolving graph with geometric properties. In: Proceedings of the 2004 joint workshop on Foundations of mobile computing, pp. 24–30 (2004)
10. Karp, B., Kung, H.T.: GPSR: Greedy Perimeter Stateless Routing for Wireless Networks. In: Proceedings of Mobicom, pp. 243–254 (2000)
11. Knuth, D.: The toilet paper problem. American Math Monthly 91(8), 365–370 (1984)
12. Lindgren, A., Doria, A., Schelen, O.: Probabilistic Routing in Intermittently Connected Networks. In: Proceedings of Workshop on Service Assurance with Partial and Intermittent Resources, pp. 239–254 (2004)
13. Liu, C., Wu, J.: Scalable routing in delay tolerant networks. In: Proceedings of the 8th ACM international symposium on Mobile ad hoc networking and computing, pp. 51–60 (2007)
14. Mauldin, R.D. (ed.): The Scottish Book:Mathematics from the Scottish Cafe. Birkheuser (1981)
15. Merugu, S., Ammar, M.H., Zegura, E.W.: Routing in Space and Time in Networks with Predictable Mobility. Technical report, Georgia Institute of Technology, GIT-CC-04-07 (2004)
16. Spyropoulos, T., Psounis, K., Raghavendra, C.S.: Spray and wait: an efficient routing scheme for intermittently connected mobile networks. In: Proceedings of SIGCOMM, pp. 252–259 (2005)
17. Stirzaker, D.: A generalization of the matchbox problem. Mathematical Scientist 13, 104–114 (1988)
18. Vahdat, A., Becker, D.: Epidemic routing for partially connected ad hoc networks. Duke University (2000)
19. Walker, B.D., Glenn, J.K., Clancy, T.C.: Analysis of simple counting protocols for delay-tolerant networks. In: Proceedings of the second workshop on Challenged networks CHANTS, pp. 19–26 (2007)

Better Face Routing Protocols

Xiaoyang Guan

Department of Computer Science, University of Toronto

Abstract. Existing face routing protocols guarantee message delivery on static connected plane graphs. To apply them to real networks, one must maintain a spanning plane subgraph and assume that the network changes only when routing is not being performed. To improve efficiency, they are often used only when greedy approaches fail.

We present protocols for connected quasi unit disk graphs, where nodes which are close to one another (distance at most $\varepsilon \geq 1/\sqrt{2}$) are always neighbors, and nodes which are far apart (distance > 1) are never neighbors. Our protocols do not extract a subgraph of the network, do not store routing information at nodes, and guarantee message delivery under more general conditions that allow unstable edges to repeatedly change between being active and inactive during routing.

1 Introduction

We consider geometric routing, also known as location-based or geographic routing, in wireless ad-hoc networks [3,9,12,13,17]. Given the location of a destination, a node uses its location (obtained via GPS) and the locations of nearby nodes to make routing decisions, instead of using a routing table. There are two general approaches: greedy routing and face routing. In greedy routing, a node forwards the packet to its neighbor that is closest to the destination under some metric, for example, the physical distance to the destination. Greedy routing is very simple, but it does not guarantee message delivery: the packet may reach a node whose neighbors are all farther away from the destination [3]. Face routing uses a plane subgraph of the network to do routing. If this graph is static and connected, face routing guarantees message delivery [3]. Most geometric routing protocols in the literature combine face routing with greedy routing [3,9,13]. They operate in greedy mode until the packet reaches a node where greedy routing cannot proceed. They switch to face routing mode as a recovery mechanism and switch back to greedy mode when possible.

In Sect. 4, we present a new version of face routing that uses a more general rule to decide the face to be traversed. In static graphs, this version of face routing is similar to some protocols that combine greedy routing with face routing, but does not require switching between greedy and face routing modes. Our new version is conceptually simpler and helps to extend face routing to non-static graphs.

Existing face routing protocols need to separately construct a spanning plane subgraph, which may be difficult in real wireless networks due to radio ran

S. Dolev (Ed.): ALGOSENSORS 2009, LNCS 5804, pp. 167–178, 2009.
© Springer-Verlag Berlin Heidelberg 2009

irregularities and imprecise location information [10,16] Problems with the resulting routing graph can lead to failure of face routing protocols.

Experiments show that links in wireless ad-hoc networks are often unstable even when nodes are stationary, such as in rooftop networks [1,4]. However, existing protocols do not have techniques to deal with changes to the network and do not guarantee message delivery unless faces remain static while being traversed. This limits their applicability to real networks.

A (virtual) plane graph can be obtained from any graph by replacing each edge crossing with a virtual node. This idea is used on a sparse spanning subgraph of a static network to obtain a plane graph for routing [14,15]. One of the endpoints of the edges crossing at each virtual node serves as a proxy for that virtual node, sending and receiving messages on its behalf, and maintaining its routing table, which requires extra storage. It may not be easy to adapt this approach to non-static graph models, because nodes need to dynamically maintain the routing subgraph and routing tables.

In Sect. 5, we present techniques to apply face routing on general non-planar network graphs directly, without extracting a subgraph. We conceptually add virtual nodes to obtain a virtual plane graph. However, in our approach, real nodes do not maintain any information about virtual nodes. Instead, we simulate face routing on the virtual graph using only local information, which can be extended to non-static graphs efficiently. While the idea of simulating face routing on virtual plane graphs is simple, developing a provably correct protocol that implements this idea using only a small amount of local information is not straightforward.

For connected quasi unit disk graphs, we present a protocol in Sect. 6 that implements our approach when two-hop neighbor information is available at each node and guarantees message delivery. This protocol distributes the computation by exploiting a geometric property of quasi unit disk graphs. Note that previous protocols for quasi unit disk graphs [2,14] require at least this amount of neighbor information to construct and maintain a routing subgraph (and use extra space for routing tables).

We extend our protocol to edge dynamic networks, i.e., networks with unstable links. In particular, a face might change while it is being traversed. We do this, in Sect. 7, by combining our techniques for quasi unit disk graphs with ideas from our previous protocol for edge dynamic graphs [7], which assumes that the network is always a connected plane graph. The resulting protocol for edge dynamic quasi unit disk graphs with $\varepsilon \geq 1/\sqrt{2}$ guarantees message delivery under general conditions.

Detailed code, expanded descriptions, and complete proofs can be found in [8].

2   Model

We represent networks by graphs embedded in the plane. If no edges cross, it is a *plane* graph and its edges partition the plane into disjoint regions called *faces*.

In a *unit disk graph* (UDG), two vertices are connected by an edge if and only if they are at most distance 1 apart. This simple model for wireless ad-hoc networks is widely employed, but it is unrealistic, because nodes may not have uniform, circular transmission ranges, e.g., due to obstacles.

The *quasi unit disk graph* (QUDG) [2,14] allows the transmission region to be non-circular. In a QUDG, there is a constant ε, $0 \leq \varepsilon \leq 1$, such that two vertices are neighbors if their distance is at most ε, two vertices are not neighbors if their distance is greater than 1, and two vertices whose distance is greater than ε but at most 1 may or may not be neighbors. Both the UDG and QUDG models are static: no changes to the network are allowed during routing.

In an *edge dynamic graph*, nodes remain stationary, but edges may change. An *edge dynamic quasi unit disk graph* (EDQUDG) is a QUDG at all points in time: nodes that are at most distance ε apart are always neighbors and nodes that are more than distance 1 apart are never neighbors. An EDQUDG is different from a QUDG in that an edge whose length is between ε and 1 may repeatedly change between being active and inactive at arbitrary times. An EDQUDG represents a network in which the wireless connections between the nodes that are more than distance ε apart are unstable, e.g., due to moving obstacles.

In previous work, the time to transmit a packet along an edge is assumed to be negligible. Here, we only assume that it is bounded above by some constant. If the edge exists for the entire transmission, the packet arrives successfully. In edge dynamic graphs, if an edge becomes inactive while a packet is being transmitted along it, or if a transmission is taking too long, we assume the data link layer protocols can detect this, and the sender re-routes the packet.

3   Related Work

Face routing, proposed in [12], was the first geometric routing algorithm that guaranteed message delivery without flooding. Several variants [3,9,13] were subsequently proposed. A typical face routing protocol [3] sends the packet in counterclockwise direction along the boundary of each face intersected by the line segment pd between the source p and the destination d. It starts with the first edge following pd in clockwise order around p. After traversing an edge (u, v), the edge after (v, u) in clockwise order around v is traversed next. When the traversal reaches an edge that intersects pd at a point p' closer to d, point p' becomes the new starting point and the traversal switches to the next face. This procedure repeats until d is reached. Although the basic idea of face routing is simple, subtle details can result in delivery failure in certain circumstances [5].

There have been a few papers on geometric routing in QUDGs. For connected QUDGs with $\varepsilon \geq 1/\sqrt{2}$, Barrière et al. [2] add virtual edges corresponding to paths in the network graph to construct a super-graph that has a connected spanning plane subgraph. Nodes exchange information with neighbors to determine which, if any, virtual edges to add. Each node maintains a routing table for its incident virtual edges. It is unclear whether this approach can be extended to EDQUDGs.

For QUDGs with $0 \leq \varepsilon \leq 1$, Kuhn et al. [14] give a distributed algorithm to construct a sparse spanner. Then they apply Barrière et al.'s technique to obtain a sparse spanning plane graph for routing in QUDGs with $\varepsilon \geq 1/\sqrt{2}$.

Both Kuhn et al. [14] and Lillis et al. [15] add virtual nodes to obtain plane graphs and mention that a real node can act as a proxy for a virtual node in face routing. However, they do not explain how proxies are chosen, nor how they behave.

Tethered-Traversal [6,7] works for any edge dynamic graph that is always a plane graph. It uses information about the path followed by a packet, carried in the packet header, to determine whether the next edge along the boundary of the current face should be traversed. The algorithm guarantees message delivery if, during the traversal of each face, the graph contains a stable connected spanning subgraph. Tethered-Traversal does not necessarily guarantee message delivery in an FDQUDG, since it may not be a plane graph.

4   A New Version of Face Routing

We present a new version of face routing that guarantees message delivery while naturally incorporating a greedy approach. The main difference between this version and the classical face routing protocols described in the literature is the rule to choose the new starting point [3,5,9,13]. Specifically, in our new version, starting from the starting point p of a face, a packet destined for d is forwarded along the boundary of the face intersected by the line segment pd, until it reaches a point p' that is closer to d than p is. Then, point p' becomes the new starting point and the packet starts to traverse the face intersected by the line segment $p'd$. This procedure repeats until the packet reaches the destination.

Figure 1 shows an example of the path followed by a packet using our protocol, in which the packet traverses faces F_1, F_2, F_4, and F_5 successively. The traversal does not necessarily switch to another face when a new starting point is found: In our example, each node visited on face F_5 is closer to the destination than its predecessor. For comparison, notice that original face routing protocols would switch from face F_1 to F_3 at node x, where edge (x, y) is found intersecting sd, but our new protocol switches from F_1 to F_2 at node u.

A new starting point can be any point on the boundary of the current face that is closer to the destination than the current starting point is. In our version of face routing, once we reach an edge that contains such a point, we choose the point on that edge closest to the destination as the new starting point. In static graphs, such a point can always be found, as long as the source and the destination are in the same connected component of the graph. Note that, as in the original face routing protocols, a new starting point is not necessarily at a node. In fact, if a face routing protocol only uses nodes as new starting points, it can fail to deliver a packet in certain plane graphs [5].

In static graphs, the *behavior* of our new protocol is similar to some protocols that combine greedy routing with face routing, such as GPSR [9]. However, our protocol is a pure face routing protocol, so that it is not necessary to switch between greedy routing and face routing. It simply uses a different rule to decide when to switch faces, which makes it easier to extend to non-static graph models.

An example where our protocol and GPSR differ is at node u in Fig. 1. GPSR switches to greedy mode at node u and goes from u to w, because node w is

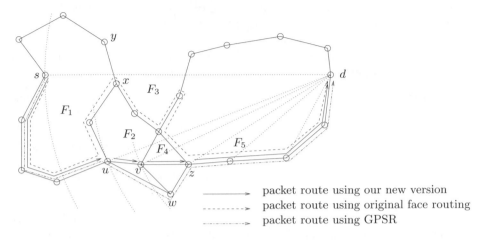

packet route using our new version
packet route using original face routing
packet route using GPSR

Fig. 1. Paths followed by a packet travelling from node s to node d

the neighbor of u that is closest to d. Our protocol switches from face F_1 to F_2 at u and thus goes to node v, instead. Both protocols subsequently forward the packet to node z, and thereafter follow the same path.

Our protocol does not try to minimize the length of the route, although in many cases, it produces good routes. To optimize the length of the route, the techniques in [13] can be applied to our protocol. Specifically, the face traversal is confined to an adaptively resizable region, and a face may be traversed in both directions when necessary to find the optimal path.

5   Virtual Face Routing

There are two problems with using face routing on a non-planar network graph: the graph may not have a connected spanning plane subgraph, and, even if such a subgraph exists, extracting it may be difficult or complicated [2,10,11,16].

A non-planar network graph can be viewed as a virtual plane graph. Conceptually, we add a virtual node at each point where two or more edges cross, and split the edges at these virtual nodes. Thus, we obtain a virtual plane graph that consists of the original network nodes and the virtual nodes. If the original graph is connected, so is the virtual plane graph, and if we apply face routing in this virtual plane graph, we would find a *virtual path* to the destination. Kuhn et al. [14] and Lillis et al. [15] maintain routing tables at real nodes to enable messages to be sent to and from virtual nodes. In our approach, additional routing information does not need to be stored at real nodes. We simply compute a real path in the network graph that *follows* the virtual path. We say that such a protocol *simulates* face routing in the virtual plane graph.

To formally define what it means for a real path to *follow* a virtual path, we first introduce some definitions and notation. We call an edge in the virtual graph a *virtual edge*, which is either an entire edge in the network graph or part of one. We consider the edges in paths to be directed. We use Greek letters α, β, etc., to denote the nodes in a virtual path, which may be virtual or real, and use lowercase letters to denote real nodes.

Given a virtual path whose last node is a real node, we define a function that maps this virtual path to a sequence of real nodes as follows.

Definition 1. *Let* $\pi = \nu_0, \nu_1, \ldots, \nu_k$, *for* $k \geq 1$, *be a virtual path whose last node* ν_k *is a real node. Let* $F(\pi) = u_0, u_1, \ldots, u_{k-1}, \nu_k$, *where* u_i *is the beginning node of the real edge that contains the virtual edge* (ν_i, ν_{i+1}) *for* $i = 0, \ldots, k-1$. *We say that a real path* P *follows a virtual path* π *if* $F(\pi)$ *is a subsequence of* P.

Proposition 2. *A protocol that simulates face routing in all virtual plane graphs guarantees message delivery in static connected graphs.*

Proof. The virtual plane graph of a connected graph is also connected, because adding virtual nodes and splitting an edge at a virtual node do not disconnect any path in the original graph. Because face routing guarantees message delivery in a static connected plane graph [6], the virtual path obtained by applying face routing in the virtual plane graph of a static connected graph leads to the destination node. By definition, a protocol that simulates face routing computes a real path that follows the virtual path and, hence, leads to the destination.   □

In the following, we describe our general approach to simulating face routing in the resulting virtual graph, without assuming any specific graph model. To simulate face routing in a virtual graph, there are two issues to be addressed: to compute the virtual path and to find a real path that follows it. All the computation should be done in a distributed manner and use only local information available at each node, plus the information the protocol puts in the packet header.

The virtual path will be computed one edge at a time. A natural way to do this is to let the beginning node of the real edge that contains the current virtual edge determine the next virtual edge. Given the current virtual edge (α, β), the next virtual edge (β, γ) is the first virtual edge after (β, α) in clockwise order around β, as illustrated in Fig. 2. Suppose (α, β) is contained in the real edge (u, v), and (β, γ) is contained in the real edge (w, x), which intersects (u, v) at β. If node u knows its neighbors, which real edges intersect its incident (real) edges, and which real edges intersect them, then it is easy for u to compute (β, γ). However, if *node* u *only knows its neighbors and the real edges that intersect its incident edges*, node u cannot necessarily determine the ending point γ of the next virtual edge.

With this limited information, the virtual path can still be determined, if we *distribute the computation in a different way*. At each step of the traversal, given the beginning point α of the current virtual edge and the real edge (u, v) that contains the current virtual edge, node u computes the ending point β of the current virtual edge, which is also the beginning point of the next virtual edge, and the real edge (w, x) that contains the next virtual edge. To find a real path that follows the virtual edge, node u computes a real path to w. This is done using only u's local information. Notice that, in this distributed computation of

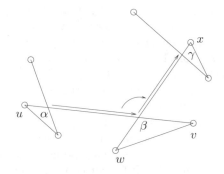

Fig. 2. Computing the next virtual edge

the virtual path, the two ends of a virtual edge may be determined at different real nodes: the beginning point of the virtual edge and its underlying real edge are determined in one step at a node, and its ending point is determined in the next step at a possibly different node.

Once the ending point β of the current virtual edge is determined, node u checks whether (α, β) contains any point that is closer to the destination than the starting point of the current virtual face. If so, the traversal switches to the next virtual face; otherwise, node u forwards the packet to node w, and the traversal is continued.

6 Routing in Quasi Unit Disk Graphs

Now we use the idea of simulating face routing in a virtual graph to obtain routing protocols for QUDGs with $\varepsilon \geq 1/\sqrt{2}$.

First suppose that a node has three-hop neighbor information, i.e. it knows the set of nodes that are at most three-hops away and the locations of these nodes. The following geometric property of QUDGs with $\varepsilon \geq 1/\sqrt{2}$ allows a node to determine all the edges that intersect each of its incident edges [8].

Lemma 3. *In a QUDG with $\varepsilon \geq \frac{1}{\sqrt{2}}$, if (x, y) intersects (u, v) at a point between u and the midpoint of (u, v), then at least one of x and y is a neighbor of u.*

A node can locally perform the computation described at the end of Sect. 5 to compute the starting point of the next virtual edge and the real edge that contains it. Thus, if all nodes have three-hop neighbor information, then it is possible to simulate face routing in the virtual plane graph of a QUDG [8].

Two-hop neighbor information is insufficient for a node to determine all the edges that cross its incident edges. For example, in Fig. 2, with only two-hop neighbor information, node u does not know the existence of edge (w, x). However, by Lemma 3, node v does. More generally, the endpoints of the real edge containing the current virtual edge can jointly determine the ending point of that virtual edge and the real edge that contains the next virtual edge.

Virtual-Face-Traversal is a protocol for QUDGs with $\varepsilon \geq 1/\sqrt{2}$ using two-hop neighbor information. It behaves as follows: Suppose the packet is at node u, and edge (u, v) contains the current virtual edge (α, β). Node u knows v and α from the packet header. From Lemma 3, if β is between α and the midpoint of (u, v), then β and all the edges crossing (α, v) at β can be determined from u's local information. Otherwise, they can be determined from v's local information, so node u forwards the packet to v.

After node u or v finds β, it checks whether any point on (α, β) is closer to the destination than the starting point is. If so, it uses the point on (α, β) that is closest to the destination as the new starting point. This switches the traversal to the next virtual face. Otherwise, it forwards the packet to the beginning node of the network edge containing the next virtual edge. This is done either directly or via the ending node of that edge, because from Lemma 3, at least one of the endpoints of that edge is a neighbor of the current node.

The source node is the first starting point of the traversal. At the source node and when each subsequent starting point is determined, an initialization algorithm is used to compute the network edge that contains the first virtual edge to be traversed and to set up the packet header, which includes the distance from the starting point to the destination, the beginning point of the current virtual edge, and the network edge that contains the current virtual edge.

Pseudo code for Virtual-Face-Traversal can be obtained by removing lines T1–T3 from Algorithm 1 on page 176.

Theorem 4. *With two-hop neighbor information, Virtual-Face-Traversal simulates face routing in the virtual plane graph of any connected QUDG with $\varepsilon \geq \frac{1}{\sqrt{2}}$.*

The proof of correctness of Virtual-Face-Traversal follows by combining this result and Proposition 2:

Corollary 5. *Virtual-Face-Traversal guarantees message delivery in connected QUDGs with $\varepsilon \geq \frac{1}{\sqrt{2}}$, provided nodes have two-hop neighbor information.*

7   Routing in Edge Dynamic Quasi Unit Disk Graphs

In an edge dynamic graph, a new edge may split the face currently being traversed into two. If the packet is travelling on a newly formed virtual face that does not contain a point closer to the destination, the packet could be trapped on that virtual face. To avoid such problems, we use techniques introduced in Tethered-Traversal [7] to extend Virtual-Face-Traversal to EDQUDGs with $\varepsilon \geq 1/\sqrt{2}$. The idea is to store information about the traversal of the current virtual face in a field of the packet header, called the *tether*, and then use this information to determine whether following the next edge would cause the packet to loop back. If so, that edge is ignored by the current node.

Specifically, the tether stores the path followed by the packet on the current virtual face. Each time a new starting point is determined, the tether is also initialized with the first node of the path. As the traversal proceeds, additional nodes are appended to the tether.

The high level structure of this protocol, shown in Algorithm 1, is almost the same as Virtual-Face-Traversal, except for the extra lines T1–T3. These lines use the tether to check whether the network edge that contains the next virtual edge on the current virtual face would cause any problem. More specifically, if that edge intersects the tether and forms a counterclockwise cycle, the current node ignores this edge and re-computes the next edge of the traversal. (Clockwise cycles are not a problem, as discussed in [7].) Otherwise, the packet header is updated and the packet is forwarded to the beginning node of the next edge. Figure 3 shows an example of a counterclockwise cycle formed by a candidate next edge with the tether during the traversal. Tethered-Traversal, which applies these techniques in edge dynamic plane graphs, was proved correct in [7]. The proof of correctness of Virtual-Face-Traversal-with-Tether, which applies these techniques in EDQUDGs with $\varepsilon \geq 1/\sqrt{2}$, appears in [8], but is more difficult.

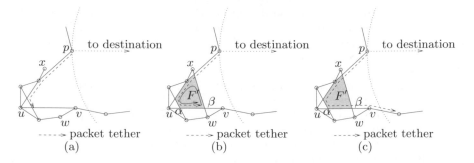

Fig. 3. (a) Traversal of the current virtual face. (b) New edge (w, x) forms a counterclockwise cycle with the tether, and packet is on the new virtual face F'. (c) Traversal continues by ignoring edge (w, x).

Delivery is impossible if part of the graph becomes disconnected from the destination while it contains the packet. Even if the whole graph is always connected, delivery might be prevented if every path between the source and destination is unstable [6]. To guarantee message delivery for Virtual-Face-Traversal-with-Tether, we require the following condition:

Condition 1. *During the entire traversal of each virtual face, there exists a stable connected spanning subgraph of the network graph.*

For Virtual-Face-Traversal-with-Tether to work correctly, it is also necessary that, when an edge is assigned to *packet.next_edge*, it remains connected until *packet.next_edge* is updated. We can bound this time period as follows. Once *packet.next_edge* is determined, the current node sends the packet to the beginning node of *packet.next_edge*, either directly or via the ending node of *packet.next_edge*, and during the computation of the next edge, the packet may be forwarded along *packet.next_edge*. Hence, the time between two successive updates of *packet.next_edge* is at most the time needed for three transmissions plus a small amount for computation. This is assumed to be a small constant.

Algorithm 1. Virtual-Face-Traversal-with-Tether

   ▷ *Performed by node z, the node that currently holds the packet.*

1 **begin**

2   **if** the destination is reached **then** release the packet; return

3   **if** z is the beginning node of *packet.next_edge*

4   **then if** z sees any edge crossing between the beginning point of the current virtual edge and the midpoint of *packet.next_edge*

5   **then** compute the ending point of the current virtual edge and the network edge containing the next virtual edge (based on z's local info)

6   **else** forward the packet to the ending node of *packet.next_edge*; return

7   **else**   ▷ *z is the ending node of packet.next_edge*

8   **if** the packet was not sent from the beginning node of *packet.next_edge*

9   **then** forward the packet to the beginning node of *packet.next_edge*; return

10   **else** compute the ending point of the current virtual edge and the network edge containing the next virtual edge (based on z's local info)

11   **if** the shortest distance from the current virtual edge to the destination is less than the distance from the current starting point to the destination

12   **then** update starting point and call initialization subroutine to compute *packet.next_edge*   ▷ *switch faces*

13   **else**

T1   **if** the edge containing the next virtual edge forms a counterclockwise cycle with the tether

T2   **then** remove that edge from the two-hop neighborhood of node z

T3   Virtual-Face-Traversal-with-Tether; return

14   update *packet.next_edge* and other header fields

15   **if** z is the beginning node of *packet.next_edge*

16   **then** Virtual-Face-Traversal-with-Tether; return

17   **else**   ▷ *route the packet to the beginning node of packet.next_edge*

18   forward the packet to the beginning node of *packet.next_edge* if it is a neighbor of z, otherwise forward it to the ending node of *packet.next_edge*

19 **end**

Condition 2. *If an edge is assigned to packet.next_edge, it remains connected for at least the time needed for three transmissions plus a small amount for computation.*

These conditions are sufficient to guarantee message delivery when Virtual-Face-Traversal-with-Tether is used. Note that these conditions are quite general. In particular, a face can change while it is being traversed.

Theorem 6. *Virtual-Face-Traversal-with-Tether guarantees message delivery in edge dynamic quasi unit disk graphs with $\varepsilon \geq \frac{1}{\sqrt{2}}$, provided nodes have two-hop neighbor information and Conditions 1 and 2 are satisfied.*

8   Conclusions and Future Work

In this paper, we present protocols that simplify and extend the application of face routing. We propose a more general rule to determine when to switch faces and the point at which to start traversing a new face. This can be viewed as a variant of face routing that incorporates a greedy approach. We also explain how to simulate face routing on the network graph directly, without extracting a plane subgraph. This extends face routing to more general graphs and simplifies face routing protocols. Using these ideas, we have developed provably correct protocols that simulate face routing for a variety of different network graph models with different assumptions on the information available at each node [8]. Some of these (including the protocol with three-hop neighbor information mentioned at the beginning of Sect. 6) are straightforward; others (including Virtual-Face-Traversal) are more complicated, but require less information at each node.

Experiments have been performed to evaluate the performance of a variety of face routing protocols and the protocols that combine face routing with greedy routing [3,9,13]. The length of the paths computed by those protocols are compared with the length of the shortest path between a source and a destination. It would be interesting to perform the same experiments for our virtual face traversal protocols. Moreover, we would like to conduct experiments or simulations on networks with unstable links to study how the parameters of the networks, such as the frequency of link failure, affect the performance of the Virtual-Face-Traversal-with-Tether protocol and the likelihood that the conditions under which it guarantees message delivery are satisfied.

The most interesting question that remains is whether our protocols can be extended to network graphs whose nodes may move during the routing process. In the special case where nodes do not move far away from their central locations, it is possible to transform the network graph to an edge dynamic quasi unit disk graph with $\varepsilon \geq 1/\sqrt{2}$, on which Virtual-Face-Traversal-with-Tether can be applied. Details appear in [8]. We hope that our techniques can be applied to obtain face routing protocols on quasi unit disk graphs in which nodes move arbitrarily.

Acknowledgements. This research was performed under the supervision of professors Faith Ellen and Peter Marbach. I am deeply thankful for their invaluable advice. Especially, Faith Ellen has spent an incredible amount of time and effort editing this paper and proofreading the algorithms and their proofs of correctness.

References

1. Aguayo, D., Bicket, J., Biswas, S., Judd, G., Morris, R.: Link-level measurements from an 802.11b mesh network. SIGCOMM Comput. Commun. Rev. 34(4), 121–132 (2004)
2. Barrière, L., Fraigniaud, P., Narayanan, L., Opatrny, J.: Robust position-based routing in wireless ad hoc networks with irregular transmission ranges. Wireless Communications and Mobile Computing 3(2), 141–153 (2003)
3. Bose, P., Morin, P., Stojmenović, I., Urrutia, J.: Routing with guaranteed delivery in ad hoc wireless networks. Wireless Networks 7(6), 609–616 (2001)
4. Chambers, B.A.: The grid roofnet: a rooftop ad hoc wireless network. Master's thesis, EECS Dept., MIT (June 2002)

5. Frey, H., Stojmenovic, I.: On delivery guarantees of face and combined greedy-face routing in ad hoc and sensor networks. In: Proc. MobiCom, pp. 390–401 (2006)
6. Guan, X.: Routing in ad hoc networks using location information. Master's thesis, Department of Computer Science, University of Toronto (2003)
7. Guan, X.: Face traversal routing on edge dynamic graphs. In: Proc. IPDPS - Workshop 12 (WMAN 2005), p. 244.2 (2005)
8. Guan, X.: Face Routing in Wireless Ad-Hoc Networks. PhD thesis, Department of Computer Science, University of Toronto (2009)
9. Karp, B., Kung, H.T.: GPSR: greedy perimeter stateless routing for wireless networks. In: Proc. MobiCom, pp. 243–254 (2000)
10. Kim, Y.-J., Govindan, R., Karp, B., Shenker, S.: On the pitfalls of geographic face routing. In: Proc. DIALM-POMC, pp. 34–43 (2005)
11. Kim, Y.-J., Govindan, R., Karp, B., Shenker, S.: Lazy cross-link removal for geographic routing. In: Proc. SenSys, pp. 112–124 (2006)
12. Kranakis, E., Singh, H., Urrutia, J.: Compass routing on geometric networks. In: Proc. CCCG, pp. 51–54 (1999)
13. Kuhn, F., Wattenhofer, R., Zhang, Y., Zollinger, A.: Geometric ad-hoc routing: of theory and practice. In: Proc. PODC, pp. 63–72 (2003)
14. Kuhn, F., Wattenhofer, R., Zollinger, A.: Ad-hoc networks beyond unit disk graphs. In: Proc. DIALM-POMC, pp. 69–78 (2003)
15. Lillis, K.M., Pemmaraju, S.V., Pirwani, I.: Topology control and geographic routing in realistic wireless networks. In: Kranakis, E., Opatrny, J. (eds.) ADHOC-NOW 2007. LNCS, vol. 4686, pp. 15–31. Springer, Heidelberg (2007)
16. Seada, K., Helmy, A., Govindan, R.: On the effect of localization errors on geographic face routing in sensor networks. In: Proc. IPSN, pp. 71–80 (2004)
17. Stojmenović, I.: Position based routing in ad hoc networks. IEEE Commmunications Magazine 40(7), 128–134 (2002)

Building a Communication Bridge with Mobile Hubs

Onur Tekdas, Yokesh Kumar, Volkan Isler, and Ravi Janardan

Department of Computer Science and Engineering, University of Minnesota,
Minneapolis, MN - 55455, USA

Abstract. We study scenarios where mobile hubs are charged with building a communication bridge between two given points s and t. We introduce a new bi-criteria optimization problem where the objectives are minimizing the number of hubs on the bridge and either the maximum or the total distance traveled by the hubs. For a geometric version of the problem where the hubs must move onto the line segment $[s, t]$, we present algorithms which achieve the minimum number of hubs while remaining within a constant factor of a given motion constraint.

1 Introduction

The task of building a communication bridge connecting two locations arises frequently. For example, when fighting forest fires, a high capacity connection between the command center and a temporary base may be needed. When there is no underlying communication infrastructure (which is typically the case in emergency response scenarios), mobile entities with communication capabilities can be used to build a communication bridge. In particular, with recent advances in robotics, using autonomous agents for this purpose is becoming feasible.

In this work, we address the problem of building a communication bridge in an efficient fashion. Imagine that we are given a source s and a destination t (the two locations that need to be connected), and initial locations of n robots (or *mobile hubs*). The goal is to pick a subset of these robots and determine final locations for them, so that when the robots arrive at their final locations, there is a path between s and t in the underlying communication graph. In this case, we say that a *communication bridge* between s and t has been established. Throughout the paper, we assume that two entities can communicate if and only if they are within a given communication radius r. See also Figure 1(a).

We focus on two measures of efficiency. The first one is the distance traveled by the robots to establish the communication bridge. Relevant objectives are minimizing the maximum or the total Euclidean (L_2) distance traveled. This measure is important when the robots have limited battery power. The maximum distance traveled also determines how quickly the bridge can be established. The second measure is the number of robots required to establish the communication bridge. This is an important parameter because if we use a small number of robots for the given task, then the remaining robots can be used for other tasks.

S. Dolev (Ed.): ALGOSENSORS 2009, LNCS 5804, pp. 179–190, 2009.

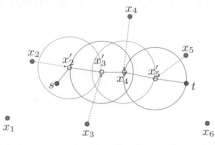
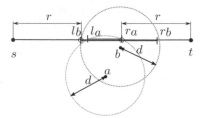

(a) A communication bridge with mobile hubs

(b) An instance where the ordering property does not hold.

Fig. 1. (a): Initial locations of the robots are x_i, $i = 1, \ldots, 6$; s and t cannot communicate. By moving $x_2 \to x_2'$, $x_3 \to x_3'$, $x_4 \to x_4'$ and $x_5 \to x_5'$ a communication bridge with four hubs connecting s and t is established. The circles around the nodes illustrate the communication radius. **(b):** Robot a (resp. robot b) can reach points inside the line segment $[l_a, r_a]$ (resp. segment $[l_b, r_b]$). Although a is to the left of b, a must move to the right of b, to r_a, and b must move to the left of a, to l_b, to establish a communication bridge. The final locations of robots are shown by unfilled circles.

In addition, a communication bridge with a small number of hubs is desirable in order to minimize the delay.

Our results and techniques. We believe that the two metrics mentioned above are equally important. Therefore, we study the resulting bi-criteria optimization problem. Specifically, we present algorithms to minimize the number of hubs in the communication bridge for a given maximum (or total) travel distance in L_2 metric. Surprisingly, these problems have not been studied previously.

In this paper, we focus on a geometric version where the underlying environment is the Euclidean plane, and the chosen robots are required to move onto the straight line segment $[s, t]$ to form a communication bridge. This special case is important from a practical standpoint because moving the robots onto this line segment yields the minimum number of hubs in the communication bridge, as compared to any other curve joining s and t. Another motivation for this model is low power, inexpensive infra-red communication which is becoming a popular choice for small robots: In an extreme case, if each robot is equipped with only two IR receivers/transmitters such that the pairs are placed 180 degrees apart, a straight line communication is necessary to establish a communication bridge between s and t. From a theoretical perspective, these problems turn out to be quite challenging. One of the major sources of difficulty is the lack of an "ordering property" in the optimal solution (We make the ordering property explicit in Section 2.1.). As an example, consider the version where we are given a maximum travel distance for each robot. Suppose robot a (resp. robot b) can reach points inside the line segment $[l_a, r_a]$ (resp. $[l_b, r_b]$). It is possible to build instances where r_a is to the left of r_b but in the optimal solution robot a moves to the right of robot b (Figure 1(b)).

For the maximum distance version (*MaxDist*), we overcome this hurdle by relaxing the distance requirement: if the optimal algorithm can build a communication bridge with at most k hubs by moving each robot at most distance d, we present an approximation algorithm which builds a communication bridge with k hubs by moving each robot at most distance $\sqrt{2}d$ (Section 2.1). The key result enabling the algorithm is the presence of an ordering property for the relaxed version. For the sum version (*SumDist*), we show that there is an ordering property but for the L_1 metric (sum of absolute values of coordinate differences). We present an algorithm which exploits this ordering property and returns the optimal solution for the L_1 metric. This in turn yields a $\sqrt{2}$ approximation plus a small additive error due to discretization (Section 2.2).

The algorithms we present are dynamic programming solutions which exploit the ordering property. However, even with the ordering property, the dynamic programming solutions are not straight-forward. This is mainly because the final locations of the robots must be chosen from the continuous set of points on the line segment $[s, t]$: There are instances in which robots must be placed precisely to achieve the optimal solution, and slightly perturbing the optimal solution (to a finite set of points) breaks connectivity. Therefore, our algorithms avoid an apriori discretization of the line segment.

Finally, we present an interesting property regarding the number of hubs. Let $L > r$ be the distance between s and t. Clearly, at least $n^* = \lceil L/r \rceil - 1$ hubs are required to connect s and t. However, building a bridge with n^* hubs may not be feasible due to the motion constraint. We show that any minimal solution which satisfies the motion constraint uses at most $2n^*$ hubs (Section 3). This means that by removing constraints on distance we gain a factor of at most 2 in the number of hubs.

1.1 Related Work

In the robotics literature, the interactions between robots and a static sensor network have been studied for network repair [1], connectivity [2] and data-collection problems [3]. From a systems perspective, researchers have proposed architectures that exploit controlled mobility [4,5,6,7]. A recent review on the state of the art in exploiting sink mobility can be found in [8].

In [9], Demaine et. al studied the problem of moving pebbles along the edges of a graph (with n vertices) so as to achieve various connectivity objectives while minimizing the number of moves. In particular, they sketch an $O(n)$-approximation algorithm for the problem of creating a path of pebbles between two given vertices. Since connectivity and mobility are coupled in their model, their results do not apply to the problems studied here. In this paper, we present the first results for the problem of building a communication bridge while minimizing the number of hubs and the distance traveled by them for a given communication radius.

2   Building a Bridge with the Minimum Number of Hubs

In this section, we study the problem of building a communication bridge between s and t while optimizing the number of hubs and the movement of the robots. We present solutions to two bi-criteria optimization problems: In the first problem (*MaxDist*), we seek a solution with the minimum number of hubs subject to the constraint that each robot moves at most a given distance d. In the second problem (*SumDist*), the constraint is that the total movement must not exceed B. For the rest of the paper, we will treat d and B as given.

A couple of remarks: When the distance between s and t is less than r, i.e. $|st| \leq r$, there is no need for any intermediate robots. Hence, we consider the case where $|st| > r$. Also, in order to achieve a bridge between s and t, it is both necessary and sufficient that the distance along $[s, t]$ between every consecutive pair in the communication bridge is at most r. Therefore, $|st| \leq (n + 1)r$, which implies that the bridge between s and t is achievable if and only if $n \geq \lceil |st|/r \rceil - 1$. Since this condition is easy to test at the outset, we will assume, without loss of generality, that n satisfies the preceding threshold and the bridge between s and t.

2.1   MaxDist: Minimizing Maximum Distance

In *MaxDist*, we are given points s and t and a set, $\mathcal{P} = \{p_1, p_2, \ldots, p_n\}$, of point-robots in the plane and a maximum traveling distance d. Any two members of $\mathcal{P} \cup \{s, t\}$ can communicate with one another if they are within (Euclidean) distance r of each other. Let $u_i = (x_i, y_i)$ be the initial position of p_i. We wish to select a subset $S \subseteq \mathcal{P}$ and compute a final position $v_i = (x'_i, y'_i)$ on the line segment $[s, t]$ for each $p_i \in S$ such that (i) s and t are connected via point-to-point communication links where points are selected from the final locations of robots in S and link lengths are not greater than the communication distance r, (ii) the distance traveled by each robot p_i is not greater than d (i.e. $\forall_{p_i \in S} |u_i v_i| \leq d$), and (iii) the total number of hubs in the communication bridge (i.e. $|S|$) is minimized.

Let L be the line passing through s and t. We place a coordinate frame where the x-axis is aligned with L, s is at 0 (i.e. $x_s = 0$) and t is at location $x_t > 0$. Without loss of generality, we define *right* as the positive direction of this frame. The final location of robots $p_i \in S$ can be determined as $v_i = (x'_i, 0)$ in this new coordinate frame. Hence, we can use x'_i to denote the final location $v_i = (x'_i, 0)$. Also note that the projection of the initial location $u_i = (x_i, y_i)$ on to L is simply x_i.

We start by pruning the set $\mathcal{P}$ and removing robots which are more than distance d away from L (i.e. if $|y_i| > d$ then p_i is removed). Moreover, we can remove the robots p_i such that $x_i < -d$ or $x_i > x_t + d$. This is because these robots cannot reach the line segment $[s, t]$. Let us call the new set which consist of robots satisfying the above constraints as $\mathcal{P}'$.

For each robot $p_i \in \mathcal{P}'$, we compute a line segment $l_i : [x_i - d, x_i + d]$ (Figure 2). We will pick the final location of p_i from this line segment. Note that this is a relaxation because the robot may have to move more than distance d. But the deviation is bounded as it is stated in the following proposition:

Proposition 1. *For any final location $x'_i \in [x_i - d, x_i + d]$ where $p_i \in \mathcal{P}'$, the distance traveled is not greater than $\sqrt{2}d$, i.e. $|u_i v_i| \leq \sqrt{2}d$.*

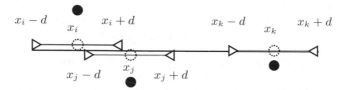

Fig. 2. Let x_i be the projection of the initial location of robot p_i. We relax the final location of p_i to $l_i : [x_i - d, x_i + d]$ which is shown as the left-most line segment.

The number of hubs required for the relaxed version is not more that the number of hubs required for the original problem:

Proposition 2. *Let k^* and k be the number of hubs used in an optimal solution to the original problem and an optimal solution to the relaxed problem, respectively. Then, $k \leq k^*$.*

The relaxed version of the problem satisfies a simple ordering property which allows us to design an efficient algorithm. As mentioned previously (Figure 1(b)) the original problem may not have the ordering property. We now explain the ordering property satisfied in the relaxed version.

Consider a placement of robots on L where the final location of each robot p_i is chosen from the line segment $[x_i - d, x_i + d]$. We order the robots according to x_i values in non-decreasing order. We say that the placement is *well-ordered* if for any two robots p_i and p_j such that $x_i \leq x_j$ we have $x'_i \leq x'_j$.

Lemma 1 (Ordering Property). *There exists a well-ordered optimal solution for the relaxed problem.*

Proof. In an optimal placement, let us call (p_i, p_j) an *unordered consecutive pair* if two robots p_i and p_j which are consecutive in the final bridge, are placed at respective locations x'_i and x'_j with $x_i \leq x_j$ but $x'_i > x'_j$. We claim that there is an optimal solution with zero unordered consecutive pairs. Consider an optimal solution which has the minimum number of unordered pairs. Suppose that this number is non-zero. Let p_i and p_j be two robots forming a consecutive unordered pair (if an unordered pair exists, so does a consecutive one). We show that the final locations of these two robots can be swapped, reducing the number of unordered pairs by one. This contradicts with the minimality of the number of unordered pairs.

First, from the relaxed segment assumption (i) $x'_i \leq x_i + d$ and (ii) $x_j - d \leq x'_j$ holds. Since this is an unordered pair, we have: (iii) $x_i \leq x_j$ and (iv) $x'_i > x'_j$. From (i)-(iv) we have: $x_i - d \leq x_j - d \leq x'_j < x'_i \leq x_i + d$. Observe that $x_i - d \leq x'_j < x_i + d$ holds, hence we can move p_i to x'_j which is in its feasible region.

Similarly, we find that $x_j - d \leq x'_j < x'_i \leq x_i + d \leq x_j + d$. Hence, x'_i is in the feasible region of p_j which makes it possible to move p_j to x'_i.

Finally, we can conclude that we can swap the final locations of p_i and p_j and decrease the number of unordered pairs by one while p_i and p_j remain in their respective feasible regions. Moreover, since p_i and p_j are consecutive, swapping does not introduce additional unordered pairs. This contradicts the fact that the solution has the minimum number of unordered pairs.   □

The ordering property allows us to use dynamic programming to compute an optimal solution.

Before presenting the algorithm, we define the *reach* of a solution $S = \{p_1, p_2, \ldots, p_m\}$. Without lost of generality, let us assume that S is sorted in increasing order. If there is a communication bridge between s and p_m, then we have a reachable region from 0 to $x'_m + r$ where we can place a robot connected to s. As we assume that reach starts from 0, we can define the *reach* of S with a single parameter, i.e. $reach(S) = x'_m + r$.

Let $OPT(k, i)$ be the maximum *reach* which uses k robots from the set $\{p_1, p_2, \ldots, p_i\}$ to form a connected set with s where $\forall_{1 \le j \le i} \, p_j \in \mathcal{P}'$. To simplify the notation, we define the function $conn(k, i)$. This function returns true if and only if $[x_i - d, x_i + d]$ intersects with the *reach* of $OPT(k, i - 1)$. In other words, this function tests whether a robot x_i can extend the *reach* $OPT(k, i - 1)$ by moving inside its feasible region l_i and extend the *reach* of s. This condition is satisfied if the following holds: $OPT(k, i - 1) \ge x_i - d$ and $x_i + d \ge 0$.

We now present the dynamic programming algorithm.

$$OPT(0, i) = r \; \forall_i \tag{1}$$

$$OPT(1, i) = \begin{cases} \min(x_i + d, r) + r \; \forall_i & if \; conn(0, i) \\ 0 & o/w \end{cases} \tag{2}$$

$$OPT(k, i) = 0 \; \forall_{i < k} \tag{3}$$

$$OPT(k, i) = \begin{cases} \min(x_i + d, OPT(k - 1, i - 1)) + r & if \; conn(k - 1, i) \\ OPT(k, i - 1) & o/w \end{cases} \tag{4}$$

The first two equations constitute the base cases. When we do not use any robots (i.e. $k = 0$) then the *reach* is r which is the reachability region of s (first equation). The second equation sets the initial values for $OPT(1, i)$. If feasible region l_i intersects with $[0, r]$ then we put the robot p_i at $\min(x_i + d, r)$ and set the *reach* of $OPT(1, i)$ as $\min(x_i + d, r) + r$. Otherwise since p_i cannot be connected to s we put a 0 value. Since $OPT(k, i)$ uses k robots from the set $\{p_1, p_2, \ldots, p_i\}$ the cardinality of this set cannot be less than k. This condition is addressed by Equation 3.

In the last equation, we compute all remaining entries $OPT(k, i)$. We know that the optimal solution chooses one of the $j \le i$ as the kth hub. We consider two cases: (1) the last hub is p_i: we look up the optimal solution with $k - 1$ hubs which are selected from the set $\{p_1, p_2, \ldots, p_{i-1}\}$. If $[x_i - d, x_i + d]$ intersects with $OPT(k - 1, i - 1)$ then the optimum solution will put p_i to the rightmost possible location which is $x'_i = \min(x_i + d, OPT(k - 1, i - 1))$ and we set the *reach* $OPT(k, i) = x'_i + r$. (2) The last hub is not p_i: Then the kth hub should be selected from set $\{p_1, p_2, \ldots, p_{i-1}\}$ whose maximum value is calculated by $OPT(k, i - 1)$ in the previous iterations. If the first case suffices, we pick it since it extends *reach* more than the second case (due to the ordering property) otherwise we pick the second case and set it to $OPT(k, i)$.

Using the above formula, we calculate the dynamic programming table where both k and i vary between 0 and m where $m \leq n$ is the cardinality of pruned set $\mathcal{P}'$. From this table we find the minimum k such that $OPT(k, m) \geq x_t$. This yields the optimal solution to the relaxed problem. By Proposition 1, our solution gives a $\sqrt{2}$ approximation on the maximum distance traveled by using at most the same number of hubs used in the optimal solution (due to Proposition 2).

The running time of our algorithm is $O(n^2)$. This is because the size of the table is $O(n^2)$ and for each entry we take the maximum of two values (Equation 4).

Theorem 1. *If there exists a solution to MaxDist that uses k hubs such that each robot moves at most distance d, then we can compute a solution where we use at most k hubs and each hub moves at most $\sqrt{2}d$ in $O(n^2)$ time.*

2.2 SumDist: Minimizing the Total Distance

In *SumDist*, we are given points s and t and a set $\mathcal{P} = \{p_1, p_2, \ldots, p_n\}$ of mobile hubs, as well as a budget B on the total distance traveled. Let $u_i = (x_i, y_i)$ be the initial position of p_i on the plane. We wish to select a subset $S \subseteq \mathcal{P}$ and compute a final position $v_i = (x'_i, y'_i)$ on the line segment $[s, t]$ for each $p_i \in S$ such that (i) s and t are connected via point-to-point communication links, (ii) the total L_2 (Euclidean) distance traveled is not greater than B (i.e. $\sum_{p_i \in S} |u_i v_i| \leq B$), and (iii) the total number of hubs in the communication bridge (i.e. $|S|$) is minimized.

Similar to *MaxDist*, we place a coordinate frame where the x-axis is aligned with L (the line passing through s and t), s is at $x = 0$ and t is at $x_t > 0$. The *reach* of a solution is defined as before.

Unfortunately, there exist instances where the ordering property does not hold in the L_2 metric. However, it turns out that when the underlying distance metric is L_1, there is an optimal solution which satisfies an ordering property, which in turn enables a dynamic programming based solution. We say that a placement is *well-ordered* if for any two robots p_i and p_j such that $x_i \leq x_j$ we have $x'_i \leq x'_j$.

Lemma 2. *If the distance metric is L_1, then there exists a well-ordered optimal solution.*

Proof. Let us assume that OPT_1^* is an optimal solution which includes the least number of unordered pairs. Let p_i and p_j be consecutive hubs used in OPT_1^* such that $x_i \leq x_j$ but $x'_i > x'_j$. We will show that swapping p_i and p_j's final locations does not increase the budget, i.e. if $b = |x_i - x'_i| + |x_j - x'_j|$ and $b' = |x_i - x'_j| + |x_j - x'_i|$ then $b \geq b'$ holds. On the other hand, the number of unordered pairs decreases by one. This contradicts the minimality of the number of unordered pairs. Note that, since we only swap the final locations of the hubs, the connectivity is preserved. Further, swapping does not change the total budget used in the y direction. Therefore, the overall budget does not increase as well.

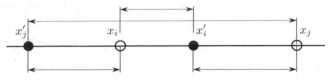

Fig. 3. Figure shows the case: $x'_j \leq x_i < x'_i \leq x_j$. Upper line segments show the total cost for the initial solution and lower line segments show the costs after swapping. When we swap the final locations of robots, we decrease the total cost while satisfying the ordering property.

Assume that we fix the locations of x_i and x_j: we have three "bins" ($x \leq x_i$, $x_i < x \leq x_j$ and $x_j < x$) for possible locations of x'_i and x'_j. The following set of equations correspond to all 6 possible cases. In each case, the claim above holds. In Figure 3, the second statement in the first line is illustrated.

$$x'_j < x'_i \leq x_i \leq x_j \Rightarrow b = b' \quad x'_j \leq x_i < x'_i \leq x_j \Rightarrow b > b'$$

$$x'_j \leq x_i \leq x_j < x'_i \Rightarrow b \geq b' \quad x_i \leq x'_j < x'_i \leq x_j \Rightarrow b > b'$$

$$x_i \leq x'_j \leq x_j < x'_i \Rightarrow b \geq b' \quad x_i \leq x_j \leq x'_j < x'_i \Rightarrow b = b' \qquad \square$$

We now solve *SumDist* optimally for the L_1 metric (up to an arbitrarily small additive cost). We start by building a table $T(k, i, B)$ which stores the maximum *reach* using k hubs subject to: (i) the ith robot is the kth hub, and (ii) the budget for the first k robots is at most B. The entries are computed as follows:

$$T(0, i, B) = r \ \forall_i \tag{5}$$

$$T(k, i, B) = 0 \ \forall_{k>i} \tag{6}$$

$$T(k, i, 0) = \begin{cases} x_i + r & \text{if initially there is a } bridge \text{ with } k \text{ hubs} \\ 0 & \text{o/w} \end{cases} \tag{7}$$

$$T(k+1, i, B) = \max_{k \leq j < i} \max_{b' \in C(x_i)} \min(T(k, j, B - b), x_i + b') + r \tag{8}$$

$$T(k, i, B + \varepsilon) = \max_{k \leq j < i} \max_{b' \in C(x_i)} \min(T(k, j, B + \varepsilon - b), x_i + b') + r \tag{9}$$

where B is discretized by ε, $b' = b - y_i$ and $C(x_i)$ is a set of possible values for b'. We will discuss ε and $C(x_i)$ shortly. The first two equations are the base cases. If initially the robots create a communication bridge between s and p_i with k hubs, then Equation 7 sets the *reach* $T(k, i, 0)$ to $x_i + r$. This can be checked by building a graph G whose vertices are $P' \cup \{s, t\}$ where P' is the set of hubs that are initially on $[s, t]$. There is an edge between two vertices if the distance between them is at most r. If G has a path between s and p_i of length at most k, then a communication bridge from s to p_i can be formed with budget 0.

Here, we discuss only how to extend the first dimension of the dynamic programming formulation (Equation 8). The argument for the other dimension (Equation 9) is similar.

To calculate $T(k+1, i, B)$, we consider the optimal *reach* with k hubs when using the p_j as the kth hub for all $j < i$ (due to the ordering property we do not need to consider the locations of earlier hubs in the optimal solution). Let $R = T(k, j, B - b)$ be the maximum *reach* achievable by using k robots with p_j as the last hub and a total budget of $B - b$. The final location of p_j in this optimal *reach* is $R - r$. We need to compute the *reach* for $k + 1$ hubs where p_i is the last hub and p_i travels at most b units. For this, we consider all possibilities for R.

Note that the distance of the initial location $u_i = (x_i, y_i)$ to L is y_i. Hence, $b \geq y_i$ must hold for p_i to act as a hub. Let $b' = b - y_i$, then, $[x_i - b', x_i + b']$ is the region that robot p_i can be placed on the line L with a budget of b'. Due to the ordering property, p_i must be placed to the right of p_j. Therefore, its location is after $R - r$ and before R (otherwise p_j and p_i cannot communicate). In other words, valid locations for p_i are given by the intersection of $[x_i - b', x_i + b']$ and $[R - r, R]$, and this set should be non-empty.

We now compute the set of valid budgets b for robot p_i. Since the robot has to travel y_i for the vertical component, the remaining budget for the horizontal component is $b' = b - y_i$. Let $C(x_i)$ be the set of possible values for b'. This set is computed as follows:

$$C(x_i) = \{b' | b' \leq B - y_i \wedge Z(x_i, R)\} \tag{10}$$

$$Z(x_i, R) = \begin{cases} R - r - x_i \leq b' \leq R - x_i & \text{if } x_i \leq R - r \\ 0 \leq b' \leq R - x_i & \text{if } R - r < x_i \leq R \\ b' = x_i - R & \text{o/w} \end{cases} \tag{11}$$

For a budget b' to be valid, we must have $b \leq B$. This gives the first condition for b': $b' \leq B - y_i$. We use the function Z to constrain b' as a function of x_i and the current *reach* R. We consider the three cases based on the location of x_i with respect to the location of the last robot (x'_j) and the *reach* $R = x'_j + r$. See Figure 4.

Case 1 ($x_i \leq x'_j$): In this case, we must have $b' \geq R - r - x_i$, (otherwise p_i cannot extend the current *reach*) and $b' \leq R - x_i$ (if p_i moves further to the right, p_j and p_i can't communicate).

Case 2 ($x'_j < x_i \leq R$): Similar to case 1, b' should not be greater than $R - x_i$. The lower bound is obtained by the nonnegativity of b'.

Case 3: When x_i is to the right of the current *reach* R, there is only one value robot p_i should move: the rightmost reachable point.

The new *reach* after placing robot p_i to $min(R, x_i + b)$ is $min(R, x_i + b) + r$. In order to compute $T(k+1, i, B)$, among all possible $j < i$ and all possible budgets $b' \in C(x_i)$, we find the optimal *reach*. Since the size of the set $C(x_i)$ is bounded by r/ε, each entry can be calculated in $O(nr/\varepsilon)$ time.

We now show how this result yields an approximation algorithm for L_2. Let OPT_1^* and OPT_2^* be optimal solutions for L_1 and L_2 metrics, respectively. The following lemma bounds the deviation between OPT_1^* and OPT_2^*.

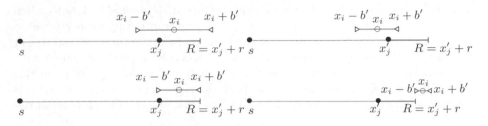

Fig. 4. Let x'_j be the last hub location at the *reach* and p_i be the robot considered at the current iteration. **Top Left:** When b' is too large both end points of feasible region is out of the the region $[x'_j, R]$, hence b' is redundant in this example. **Top Right and Bottom Row:** The three cases considered in Equation 11 are illustrated.

Lemma 3. *Let OPT_2^* be the optimal solution for the L_2 metric with a given budget B. Suppose OPT_2^* can connect s and t using k hubs. There exists optimal solution OPT_1^* for the L_1 metric which can connect s and t by using k hubs and a budget of $\sqrt{2}B$.*

Proof. Let (x_i, y_i) be the initial location of a robot used in OPT_2^* and x'_i be the final location. The L_1 and L_2 distances are $|x_i - x'_i| + y_i$ and $\sqrt{|x_i - x'_i|^2 + y_i^2}$, respectively. Without loss of generality, we scale the distances by $1/y_i$ so that the L_1 and L_2 distances become $a+1$ and $\sqrt{a^2 + 1}$, respectively where $a = |x_i - x'_i|/y_i$. From elementary calculus, it is easy to show that: $f(a) = \frac{a+1}{\sqrt{a^2+1}} \leq \sqrt{2}$. □

To obtain the optimal L_1 solution for budget B, we solve $T(k, i, B)$ for all possible k, i, B (where B is discretized with ε intervals). Due to the discretization, the total budget used here can be at most $k_1^* \varepsilon$ than the budget used by OPT_1^* where k_1^* is the number of hubs used by OPT_1^*. In other words, our dynamic programming algorithm can find a solution with k_1^* hubs by using at most $B_1 + k_1^* \varepsilon$ budget where B_1 is the used budget with L_1 metric. This means that B', the total budget used by our solution will be bounded by $B_1 + n\varepsilon$. Consequently, the total budget used by our algorithm will be at most $\sqrt{2}B + n\varepsilon$ where B is the given budget in L_2 metric. We can choose ε to achieve an arbitrarily small additive error.

We now establish the running time of the algorithm. The size of the table is $O(\frac{n^2 B}{\varepsilon})$ and as we discussed earlier each entry can be calculated in $O(nr/\varepsilon)$ time. Hence, the time complexity of our algorithm is $O(\frac{n^3 Br}{\varepsilon^2})$.

Theorem 2. *If there exists a solution to SumDist that uses k hubs such that the total movement of robots is B in the L_2 (Euclidean) metric, then we can compute a solution where we use at most k hubs and the total movement of robots is at most $\sqrt{2}B + n\varepsilon$ in $O(\frac{n^3 Br}{\varepsilon^2})$ time, where ε is the discretization constant.*

3   Bounds on Number of Hubs

Let $OPT(d)$ be the number of hubs in an optimal solution to *MaxDist* with distance constraint d. How does this constraint affect the number of hubs on the bridge? In other words, if $OPT(\infty) = \lceil |st|/r \rceil - 1$ is the number of hubs required in the unrestricted version, how far is $OPT(d)$ from $OPT(\infty)$? In this section, we show that $OPT(d)/OPT(\infty) \leq 2$.

Assume that $m - 1 < |st|/r \leq m$, for some integer $m > 1$. (The case $m = 1$ is uninteresting, as s and t are then within distance r, hence connected.)

Partition $[s, t]$ into m equal-length intervals, labeled from s to t as $I_1, I_2, \ldots, I_m$. Each interval has length greater than $(1 - 1/m)r$ and at most r. Consider any solution for $OPT(d)$. This solution connects s and t with the fewest number of hubs. In such a solution, we can have at most two hubs inside any $I_j, 2 \leq j \leq m-1$. To see this, note that if there were three or more hubs in I_j, then all but the two extreme ones in I_j could be removed without losing connectivity (since the length of I_j is at most r), thereby obtaining a solution for $OPT(d)$ that has fewer hubs than the original optimal solution—a contradiction. Along similar lines note that I_1 and I_m can each contain at most one sensor; if there was more than one sensor in I_1 (resp. I_m), then all the ones except the one farthest from s (resp. t) can be removed without losing connectivity.

It follows that for any optimal solution, we have $OPT(d) \leq 2(m - 2) + 2 = 2(m - 1)$. Also, $OPT(\infty) = \lceil |st|/r \rceil - 1 = m - 1$. Hence, we have the following.

Lemma 4. $OPT(d)/OPT(\infty) \leq 2$.

It can be shown that the same bound applies for *SumDist* as well. We omit the details.

Next, we show that the bound in Lemma 4 is tight: We claim that, for any finite d, there is an instance of *MaxDist* with the optimal solution $OPT(d)$ for which $OPT(d)/OPT(\infty) = 2$.

Let $|st|/r = m > 1$; thus, each interval $I_1, I_2, \ldots, I_m$ defined above has length r. Let ε be a real number in the (open) interval $(0, \frac{r}{m-1})$. Consider a set $V = \{v_1, v_2, \ldots, v_{2(m-1)}\}$ of points on $[s, t]$, defined as follows: for $j = 2, 4, \ldots, 2(m - 1)$, $v_j = \frac{j}{2}\varepsilon + \frac{j}{2}r$, and for $j = 1, 3, \ldots, 2m - 3$, $v_j = \frac{j+1}{2}\varepsilon + \frac{j-1}{2}r$. See Figure 5.

The set V satisfies the following (easily-verifiable) properties: (i) $v_1 \neq s \in I_1$ and $v_{2(m-1)} \neq t \in I_m$; (ii) successive points in $V \cup \{s,t\}$ are within distance r; and (iii) at least one pair of successive points in $V' \cup \{s,t\}$ is not within distance r for any $V' \subset V$.

Let $\mathcal{P}$ be a set of $n \geq 2(m - 1)$ robots $\{p_1, p_2, \ldots, p_n\}$ and choose their initial positions in $\mathbb{R}^2$ as follows: for $j = 1, 2, \ldots, 2(m - 1)$, place p_j at initial position $u_j = (v_j, d)$. Place any remaining sensor in $\mathcal{P}$ at some distance greater than d from $[s, t]$.

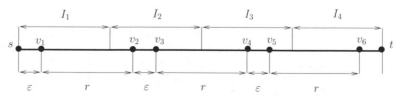

Fig. 5. Selection of points $v_1, v_2, \ldots, v_{2(m-1)}$ on $[s, t]$, with $m = 4$

Observe that only $p_1, p_2, \ldots, p_{2(m-1)}$ can move onto $[s, t]$ and, moreover, each such p_j can move only to the location v_j. By properties (ii) and (iii) above, it follows that $p_1, p_2, \ldots, p_{2(m-1)}$ are necessary and sufficient to establish a communication bridge between s and t. Therefore, $OPT(d) = 2(m-1)$ and the claim follows.

4 Conclusion

In this paper, we introduced the problem of building a communication bridge between two points s and t while minimizing the number of hubs on the bridge and satisfying a maximum (or total) distance constraint for the hubs. For both versions we presented constant factor approximation algorithms for the geometric version where the hubs must move onto $[s, t]$.

There are many interesting directions for future work. It is not clear whether the $\sqrt{2}$ approximation factor for the geometric version can be improved. The general version in which the final locations of hubs can be anywhere on the plane seems difficult. Solving the version where there are multiple source and destination pairs seems to be even harder.

Acknowledgment

This work is supported in part by NSF IIS-0917676, NSF CCF-0907658, NSF CNS-0936710, NCF INT-0422775 and NCF CCF-0514950. Volkan Isler thanks Jie Gao and Sanjeev Khanna for useful discussions.

References

1. Corke, P., Hrabar, S., Peterson, R., Rus, D., Saripalli, S., Sukhatme, G.: Autonomous deployment and repair of a sensor network using an unmanned aerial vehicle. ICRA 2004 (2004)
2. Atay, N., Bayazit, B.: Mobile wireless sensor network connectivity repair with k-redundancy. In: WAFR (2008)
3. Tekdas, O., Lim, J., Terzis, A., Isler, V.: Using mobile robots to harvest data from sensor fields. IEEE Wireless Communications (2009)
4. Kansal, A., Somasundara, A.A., Jea, D.D., Srivastava, M.B., Estrin, D.: Intelligent fluid infrastructure for embedded networks. In: MobiSys 2004, pp. 111–124. ACM, New York (2004)
5. Chatzigiannakis, I., Kinalis, A., Nikoletseas, S.: Efficient data propagation strategies in wireless sensor networks using a single mobile sink. Comput. Commun. 31(5), 896–914 (2008)
6. Wang, W., Srinivasan, V., Chua, K.C.: Using mobile relays to prolong the lifetime of wireless sensor networks. In: MobiCom 2005, pp. 270–283. ACM, New York (2005)
7. Tariq, M.M.B., Ammar, M., Zegura, E.: Message ferry route design for sparse ad hoc networks with mobile nodes. In: MobiHoc 2006, pp. 37–48 (2006)
8. Ma, J., Chen, C., Salomaa, J.P.: mWSN for large scale mobile sensing. J. Signal Process. Syst. 51(2), 195–206 (2008)
9. Demaine, E.D., Hajiaghayi, M., Mahini, H., Sayedi-Roshkhar, A.S., Oveisgharan, S., Zadimoghaddam, M.: Minimizing movement. In: SODA 2007, pp. 258–267 (2007)

Compressing Kinetic Data
from Sensor Networks

Sorelle A. Friedler* and David M. Mount**

Dept. of Computer Science, University of Maryland, College Park, MD 20742, USA
sorelle@cs.umd.edu
http://www.cs.umd.edu/~sorelle
mount@cs.umd.edu
http://www.cs.umd.edu/~mount

Abstract. We introduce a framework for storing and processing kinetic data observed by sensor networks. These sensor networks generate vast quantities of data, which motivates a significant need for data compression. We are given a set of sensors, each of which continuously monitors some region of space. We are interested in the kinetic data generated by a finite set of objects moving through space, as observed by these sensors. Our model relies purely on sensor observations; it allows points to move freely and requires no advance notification of motion plans. Sensor outputs are represented as random processes, where nearby sensors may be statistically dependent. We model the local nature of sensor networks by assuming that two sensor outputs are statistically dependent only if the two sensors are among the k nearest neighbors of each other. We present an algorithm for the lossless compression of the data produced by the network. We show that, under the statistical dependence and locality assumptions of our framework, asymptotically this compression algorithm encodes the data to within a constant factor of the information-theoretic lower bound optimum dictated by the joint entropy of the system.

1 Introduction

There is a growing appreciation of the importance of algorithms and data structures for processing large data sets arising from the use of sensor networks, particularly for the statistical analysis of objects in motion. Large wireless sensor networks are used in areas such as road-traffic monitoring [1], environment surveillance [2], and wildlife tracking [3, 4]. With the development of sensors of lower cost and higher reliability, the prevalence of applications and the need for efficient processing will increase.

Wireless sensor networks record vast amounts of data. For example, road-traffic camera systems [1] that videotape congestion produce many hours of video

---

* The work of Sorelle Friedler has been supported in part by the AT&T Labs Fellowship Program.
** The work of David Mount has been supported in part by the National Science Foundation under grant CCR-0635099 and the Office of Naval Research under grant N00014-08-1-1015.

S. Dolev (Ed.): ALGOSENSORS 2009, LNCS 5804, pp. 191–202, 2009.

or gigabytes of data for analysis even if the video itself is never stored and is instead represented by its numeric content. In order to analyze trends in the data, perhaps representing the daily rush hour or weekend change in traffic patterns, many weeks or months of data from many cities may need to be stored. As the observation time or number of sensors increases, so does the total data that needs to be stored in order to perform later queries, which may not be known in advance.

In this paper we consider the problem of compressing the massive quantities of data that are streamed from large sensor networks. Compression methods can be broadly categorized as being either *lossless* (the original data is fully recoverable), or *lossy* (information may be lost through approximation). Since lossy compression provides much higher compression rates, it is by far the more commonly studied approach in sensor networks. Our ultimate interest is in scientific applications involving the monitoring of the motion of objects in space, where the loss of any data may be harmful to the subsequent analysis. For this reason, we focus on the less studied problem of lossless compression of sensor network data. Virtually all lossless compression techniques that operate on a single stream rely on the statistical redundancy present in the stream in order to achieve high compression rates [5, 6, 7]. In the context of sensor networks, this redundancy arises naturally due to correlations in the outputs of sensors that are spatially close to each other. As with existing methods for lossy compression [8, 9], our approach is based on aggregating correlated streams and compressing these aggregated streams.

A significant amount of research to date has focused on the efficient collection and processing of sensor network data within the network itself, for example, through the minimization of power consumption or communication costs [10, 11, 12]. We focus on losslessly compressing the data locally and then downloading it to traditional computer systems for analysis. Clustering the stationary sensors is a strategy that has been previously used to improve the scalability as well as the energy and communication efficiency of the sensor network [13]. Compressing the data before transmission additionally improves the communication efficiency.

We are particularly interested in *kinetic data*, by which we mean data arising from the observation of a discrete set of objects moving in time (as opposed to continuous phenomena such as temperature). We explore how best to store and process these assembled data sets for the purposes of efficient retrieval, visualization, and statistical analysis of the information contained within them. We assume that we do not get to choose the sensor deployment based on object motion (as done in [14]), but instead use sensors at given locations to observe the motion of a discrete set of objects over some domain of interest. Thus, it is to be expected that the entities observed by one sensor will also likely be observed by nearby sensors, albeit at a slightly different time. Well-designed storage and processing systems should capitalize on this redundancy to optimize space and processing times. In this paper we propose a statistical model of kinetic data as observed by a collection of fixed sensors. We will present a method for the lossless compression of the resulting data sets and will show that this method is within a constant factor of the asymptotically optimal bit rate, subject to the assumptions of our model.

Although we address the problem of compression here, we are more generally interested in the storage and processing of large data sets arising from sensor networks [8,15,16,17,18]. This will involve the retrieval and statistical analysis of the information contained within them. Thus, we will discuss compression within the broader context of a framework for processing large kinetic data sets arising from a collection of fixed sensors. We feel that this framework may provide a useful context within which to design and analyze efficient data structures and algorithms for kinetic sensor data.

The problem of processing kinetic data has been well studied in the field of computational geometry in a standard computational setting [19,20,21,22,23,24]. A survey of practical and theoretical aspects of modeling motion can be found in [25]. Many of these apply in an online context and rely on *a priori* information about point motion. The most successful of these frameworks is the *kinetic data structures* (KDS) model proposed by Basch, Guibas, and Hershberger [23], which models objects as points in motion, where the motion is expressed as piecewise algebraic flight plans. Although KDS has been valuable for developing theoretical analyses of points in motion (see [26] for a survey), it is unsuitable in many real-world contexts due to these strong assumptions. Similarly, a framework for sensor placement by Nikoleteas and Spirakis assumes that possible object trajectories are modeled by a set of 3D curves over space and time [14]. Our framework makes no *a priori* assumptions about the motion of the objects.

Algorithms that involve the distributed online processing of sensor-network data have also been studied and successfully applied to the maintenance of a number of statistics online [10, 11, 27, 28]. Efficiency is typically expressed as a trade-off between communication complexity and accuracy or by the amount of communication between a tracker and an observer. The idea of the tracker and observer is reminiscent of an earlier model for incremental motion by Mount *et al.* [29]. Unlike these models, our framework applies in a traditional (non-distributed) computational setting.

Here is a high-level overview of our framework, which will be described in greater detail in Section 2. We assume we are given a fixed set of sensors, which are modeled as points in some metric space. (An approach based on metric spaces, in contrast to standard Euclidean space, offers greater flexibility in how distances are defined between objects. This is useful in wireless settings, where transmission distance may be a function of non-Euclidean considerations, such as topography and the presence of buildings and other structures.) Each sensor is associated with a region of space, which it monitors. The moving entities are modeled as points that move over time. At regular time intervals, each sensor computes statistical information about the points within its region, which are streamed as output. For the purposes of this paper, we assume that this information is simply an *occupancy count* of the number of points that lie within the sensor's region at the given time instant. In other words, we follow the minimal assumptions made by Gandhi *et al.* [30] and do not rely on a sensor's ability to accurately record distance, angle, etc.

Again, our objective is to compress this data in a lossless manner by exploiting statistical dependencies between the sensor streams. There are known lossless compression algorithms, such as Lempel-Ziv [7], that achieve the optimal lower bound encoding bit rate (as established by Shannon [31]) asymptotically. It would be infeasible to apply this observation *en masse* to the entire joint system of all the sensor streams. Instead, we would like to partition the streams into small subsets, and compress each subset independently. In our context, the problem is bounding the loss of efficiency due to the partitioning process.

In order to overcome this problem we need to impose limits on the degree of statistical dependence among the sensors. Our approach is based on a locality assumption. Given a parameter k, we say that a sensor system is k-*local* if each sensor's output is statistically dependent on only its k-nearest sensors. In Section 3, we prove that any k-local system that resides in a space of fixed dimension can be partitioned so that joint compressions involve groups of at most $k+1$ sensors. We show that the final compression is within a factor c of the information-theoretic lower bound, where c is independent of k, and depends only on the dimension of the space. In Section 4, we give experimental justification for our k-local model.

2   Data Framework

In this section we present a formal model of the essential features of the sensor networks to which our results will apply. Our main goal is that it realistically model the data sets arising in typical wireless sensor-networks when observing kinetic data while also allowing for a clean theoretical analysis. We assume a fixed set of S sensors operating over a total time period of length T. The sensors are modeled as points in some metric space. We may think of the space as $\mathbb{R}^d$ for some fixed d, but our results apply in any metric space of bounded doubling dimension [32]. We model the objects of our system as points moving continuously in this space, and we make no assumptions *a priori* about the nature of this motion. Each sensor observes some *region* surrounding it. Our framework makes no assumptions about the size, shape, or density of these regions. The sensor regions need not be disjoint, nor do they need to cover all the moving points at any given time.

Each sensor continually collects statistical information about the points lying within its region, and it outputs this information at synchronized time steps. As mentioned above, we assume throughout that this information is simply an *occupancy count* of the number of points that lie within the region. (The assumption of synchronization is mostly for the sake of convenience of notation. As we shall see, our compression algorithm operates jointly on local groups of a fixed size, and hence it is required only that the sensors of each group behave synchronously.)

As mentioned in the introduction, our framework is based on an information-theoretic approach. Let us begin with a few basic definitions (see, e.g., [33]). We assume that the sensor outputs can be modeled by a stationary, ergodic random process. Since the streams are synchronized and the cardinality of the moving point set is finite, we can think of the S sensor streams as a collection of S strings, each of length T, over a finite alphabet. Letting lg denote the logarithm base-2, the *entropy* of a discrete random variable X, denoted $H(X)$, is defined to be $-\sum_x p_x \lg p_x$, where the sum is over the possible values x of X, and p_x is the probability of x.

We generalize entropy to random processes as follows. Given a stationary, ergodic random process X, consider the limit of the entropy of arbitrarily long sequences of X, normalized by the sequence length. This leads to the notion of *normalized entropy*, which is defined to be $H(X) = \lim_{T\to\infty} -\frac{1}{T} \sum_{x,|x|=T} p_x \lg p_x$, where the sum is over sequences x of length T, and p_x denotes the probability of this sequence. Normalized entropy considers not only the distribution of individual characters, but the tendencies for certain patterns of characters to repeat.

We also generalize the entropy to collections of random variables. Given a sequence $X = \langle X_1, X_2, \ldots, X_S \rangle$ of (possibly statistically correlated) random variables, the *joint entropy* is defined to be $H(X) = -\sum_x p_x \lg p_x$, where the sum is taken over all S-tuples $x = \langle x_1, x_2, \ldots, x_S \rangle$ of possible values, and p_x is the probability of this joint outcome [33]. The generalization to *normalized joint entropy* is straightforward and further strengthens normalized entropy by considering correlations and statistical dependencies between the various streams.

In this paper we are interested in the lossless compression of the joint sensor stream. Shannon's source coding theorem states that in the limit, as the length of a stream of independent, identically distributed (i.i.d.) random variables goes to infinity, the minimum number of required bits to allow lossless compression of each character of the stream is equal to the entropy of the stream [31]. In our case, Shannon's theorem implies that the optimum bit rate of a lossless encoding of the joint sensor system cannot be less than the normalized joint entropy of the system. Thus, the normalized joint entropy is the gold standard for the asymptotic efficiency of any compression method. Henceforth, all references to "joint entropy" and "entropy" should be understood to mean the normalized versions of each.

As mentioned above, joint compression of all the sensor streams is not feasible. Our approach will be to assume a limit on statistical dependencies among the observed sensor outputs based on geometric locality. It is reasonable to expect that the outputs of nearby sensors will exhibit a higher degree of statistical dependence with each other than more distant ones. Although statistical dependence would be expected to decrease gradually with increasing distance, in order to keep our model as simple and clean as possible, we will assume that beyond some threshold, the statistical dependence between sensors is so small that it may be treated as zero. There are a number of natural ways to define such a threshold distance. One is an *absolute approach*, which is given a threshold distance parameter r, and in which it is assumed that any two sensors that lie at distance greater than r from each other have statistically independent output streams. The second is a *relative approach* in which an integer k is provided, and it is assumed that two sensor output streams are statistically dependent only if each is among the k nearest sensors of the other. In this paper we will take the latter approach, which we will justify after introducing some definitions.

Formally, let $P = \{p_1, p_2, \ldots, p_S\}$ denote the sensor positions. Given some integer parameter k, we assume that each sensor's output can be statistically dependent on only its k nearest sensors. Since statistical dependence is a symmetric relation, two sensors can exhibit dependence only if each is among the k nearest neighbors of the other. More precisely, let $NN_k(i)$ denote the set of k closest sensors to p_i (not including sensor i itself). We say that two sensors i and j are *mutually k-close* if $p_i \in NN_k(j)$ and $p_j \in NN_k(i)$. A system of sensors is said to be *k-local* if for any two sensors that are not mutually k-close, their observations are statistically independent. (Thus, 0-locality means that the sensor observations are mutually independent.) Let $\boldsymbol{X} = \langle X_1, X_2, \ldots, X_S \rangle$ be a system of random streams associated with by S sensors, and let $H(\boldsymbol{X})$ denote its joint entropy. Given two random processes X and Y, define the *conditional entropy* of X given Y to be $H(X \mid Y) = -\sum_{x \in X, y \in Y} p(x, y) \log p(y \mid x)$. Note that $H(X \mid Y) \leq H(X)$, and if X and Y are statistically independent, then $H(X \mid Y) = H(X)$. By the chain rule for conditional entropy [33], we have $H(\boldsymbol{X}) = H(X_1) + H(X_2 \mid X_1) + \ldots + H(X_S \mid X_1, \ldots, X_{S-1})$. Letting $D_i(k) = \{j : 1 \leq j < i$ and x_i and x_j are mutually k-close$\}$ we define the *k-local entropy*, denoted $H_k(\boldsymbol{X})$, to be $\sum_{i=1}^{S} H(X_i \mid D_i(k))$. Note that $H(\boldsymbol{X}) \leq H_k(\boldsymbol{X})$ and equality holds when $k = S$. By definition of k-locality, $H(X_i \mid X_1, X_2, \ldots, X_{i-1}) = H(X_i \mid D_k(i))$. By applying the chain rule for joint entropy, we have the following easy consequence, which states that, under our locality assumption, k-local entropy is the same as the joint entropy of the entire system.

Lemma 1. *Given a k-local system with set of observations $\boldsymbol{X}$, $H(\boldsymbol{X}) = H_k(\boldsymbol{X})$.*

We show in the full version of this paper that if KDS is used to observe a system in which the sensor regions are modeled as a sparse collection of unit disks and objects change their trajectories relatively frequently, KDS requires on the order of $H_k(\boldsymbol{X})$ bits of storage [34]. Thus, since KDS has full knowledge of the system, $H_k(\boldsymbol{X})$ is a reasonable measure of optimality.

One advantage of our relative characterization of mutually dependent sensor outputs is that it naturally adapts to the distribution of sensors. It is not dependent on messy metric quantities, such as the absolute distances between sensors or the degree of overlap between sensed regions. Another reason arises by observing that, in an absolute model, all the sensors might lie within distance r of each other. This would imply that all the sensors could be mutually statistically dependent on each other, which would render optimal compression based on joint entropy intractable. Nonetheless, by imposing a relatively weak density assumption, our model can be applied in such contexts. For example, consider a setting in which each sensor monitors a region of radius r. Given two positive parameters α and β, suppose that we were to assume that the number of sensors whose centers lie within any ball of radius r is at most α, and (instead of our k-local assumption) we were to assume that the outputs of any two sensors can be statistically dependent only if they are within distance βr of each other. Then, by a simple packing argument, it follows that such a system is k-local for $k = O(\alpha \beta^{O(1)})$ in any space of constant doubling dimension. Thus, our model would be applicable in this context.

3   Compression Results

Before presenting the main result of this section, we present a lemma which is combinatorially interesting in its own right. This partitioning lemma combined with a compression algorithm allows us to compress the motion of points as recorded by sensors to an encoding size which is c times the optimal, where c is an integral constant to be specified in the proof of Lemma 2.

3.1   Partitioning Lemma

First, we present some definitions about properties of the static point set representing sensor locations. Let $r_k(p)$ be the distance from some sensor at location p to its kth nearest neighbor. Recall that points are mutually k-close if they are in each other's k nearest neighbors. We say that a point set $P \in \mathbb{R}^d$ is k-clusterable if it can be partitioned into subsets $C_{i1}, C_{i2}, \ldots$ such that $|C_{ij}| \le k+1$ and if p and q are mutually k-close then p and q are in the same subset of the partition. Intuitively, this means that naturally defined clusters in the set are separated enough so that points within the same cluster are closer to each other than they are

partition(point set P, k)

```
for all p ∈ P
    determine NN_k(p) and r_k(p)
i = 1
while P ≠ ∅
    unmarked(P) = P
    P_i = ∅
    while unmarked(P) ≠ ∅
        r = min_{p∈unmarked(P)} r_k(p)
        p' = p ∈ P : r = r_k(p)
        P_i = P_i ∪ {p ∈ P : ‖pp'‖ ≤ r}
        P = P \ {p ∈ P : ‖pp'‖ ≤ r}
        unmarked(P) = unmarked(P) \
            {p ∈ unmarked(P) : ‖pp'‖ ≤ 3r}
    increment i
return {P_1, P_2, ..., P_c}
```

Fig. 1. The partitioning algorithm that implements Lemma 2

to points outside of the cluster. The following lemma holds for all metrics with constant *doubling dimension*, where these metrics are defined to limit to a constant the number of balls that cover a ball with twice their radius [32]. Euclidean spaces are of constant doubling dimension.

Lemma 2. *In any doubling space there exists an integral constant c such that for all integral $k > 0$ given any set P in the doubling space, P can be partitioned into $P_1, P_2, \ldots, P_c$ such that for $1 \le i \le c$, P_i is k-clusterable.*

The partitioning algorithm that implements Lemma 2 is shown in Figure 1. It proceeds by iteratively finding the unmarked point p with minimum $r = r_k(p)$, moving all points within r, henceforth called a *cluster*, to the current partition, and marking all points within $3r$ of p. A new partition is created whenever all remaining points have been marked. The marked points are used to create a buffer zone which separates clusters so that all points are closer to points within their cluster than they are to any other points in the partition. The algorithm's inner loop creates these clusters, and the outer loop creates the c partitions.

Proof (Sketch). (See the full version of this paper for a detailed proof [34].)
By the construction of the marking process, each partition is k-clusterable. We
will show that at most c partitions P_i are created by the partitioning algorithm of
Figure 1. We refer to each iteration of the outer while loop as a *round*. First note
that at the end of the first round all points are either marked or removed from P.
Each point that remains after the first round was marked by some point during
the first round. By a packing argument based on the minimum nearest neighbor
radius and the radius of the marked region around a point we show that points
can be marked by at most $c = O(1+12^{O(1)}) = O(1)$ rounds, creating c partitions.

Note that a cluster centered at p' with less than $k+1$ points does not violate
the k-clusterable property since this cluster would have been created by clustering $NN_k(p')$ together as originally identified before any points were partitioned.
Such a cluster is formed because some of the original points in $NN_k(p')$ were
previously added to a different partition. Since being mutual k-close is based on
the entire set, smaller clusters are still mutually k-close within that partition.

3.2 Compression Theorem

We now present the main
compression algorithm and
analysis. The algorithm,
presented in Figure 2, compresses each cluster formed
by the partitioning algo-
rithm (Figure 1) separately
and returns the union of
these. Each cluster is compressed by creating a new
stream in which the tth
character is a new character
which is the concatenation
of the tth character of every
stream in that cluster. This
new stream is then com-
pressed using an entropy-

---

compress (stream set X, sensor set P, k)

$\{P_1, P_2, \ldots, P_c\}$ = partition (P, k)
for $i = 1$ to c
    for all clusters j in P_i
        containing streams X_{ij1} through $X_{ijh_{ij}}$
        $\widehat{X}_{ij} = \bigcup_{t=1}^{T} X_{ij1t} \& X_{ij2t} \& \ldots \& X_{ijh_{ij}t}$
        where X_{ijht} is the tth character of X_{ijh}
    return $\bigcup_{ij}$ entropy_compress$(\widehat{X}_{ij})$

Fig. 2. The compression algorithm, which takes a set
X of streams of length T and the associated set P of
sensors which recorded them and returns a compressed
encoding of length $c \cdot H(X)$. The partitioning algorithm of Figure 1 is called and determines the constant
c. entropy_compress is an entropy-based compression
algorithm that returns an encoded stream.

---

based compression algorithm which achieves the optimal encoding length in the
limit. For example, the Lempel-Ziv sliding-window compression algorithm could
be used [7]. We reason about the size of the resulting stream set encoding.

First, we introduce some notation. Let X be the set of streams containing the
information recorded by the sensors of set P where $|X| = |P|$. Given the set of
partitions $\{P_i\}$ resulting from the partitioning lemma in Section 3.1, $\{X_i\}$ is the
set of associated streams. Let $\{C_{ij}\}$ be the set of clusters that are created by
the partitioning algorithm, we call $\{X_{ij}\}$ the set of streams in cluster C_{ij} and
X_{ijh} is the hth stream in cluster C_{ij} with cardinality h_{ij}.

Theorem 1. *A stream set which represents observations from a k-local sensor
system can be compressed to an encoded string which has length at most c times*

the optimal, where c is a constant depending on the doubling dimension of the underlying point set.

Proof. First, we show that each cluster C_{ij} is compressed to a string whose length is equal to the joint entropy of the component streams of that cluster. Each cluster consists of streams $\{X_{ij}\}$ which are merged into one new stream by concatenating the tth character of all the streams to create the tth character of the new stream. This new stream, $\widehat{X}_{ij}$, is then compressed using an optimal compression algorithm. By construction of the streams $\widehat{X}_{ij}$, the entropy $H(\widehat{X}_{ij})$ of a single stream is equal to the joint entropy of its component streams $H(X_{ij1}, X_{ij2}, \ldots, X_{ijh_{ij}})$. The entropy-based encoding algorithm compresses each $\widehat{X}_{ij}$ to an encoded string the length of the stream's entropy and that compression is optimal [35], so $H(X_{ij1}, X_{ij2}, \ldots, X_{ijh_{ij}})$ is the optimal encoding length for cluster C_{ij}.

Our local dependence assumptions, explained in Section 2, say that the stream of data from a sensor is only dependent on the streams of its k nearest neighbors. Additionally, recall that in Section 2 we defined being mutually k-close to require that streams are only dependent if they come from sensors who are in each other's k nearest neighbor sets. By the partitioning lemma from Section 3.1, we know that each cluster C_{ij} is independent of all other clusters in partition P_i. From standard information theoretic results [33] we know that for a collection of streams $Y_1, \ldots, Y_S$, $H(Y_1, Y_2, \ldots, Y_S) = \sum_{i=1}^{S} H(Y_i)$ if and only if the Y_i are independent. Since the elements of $\{\{X_{i1}\}, \{X_{i2}\}, \ldots, \{X_{i|\{C_{ij}\}|}\}\}$ are independent, $H(X_i) = \sum_j H(\{X_{ij}\})$. Combining this with the fact that $H(\widehat{X}_{ij})$ is equal to the joint entropy of its component streams, we have that $H(X_i) = \sum_j H(\widehat{X}_{ij})$. $H(X_i)$ is the optimal compression bound for partition P_i, so we achieve the optimal compression for each partition.

Finally, we show that our compression algorithm is a c-approximation of the optimal. We say that a compression algorithm provides a γ-*approximation* if the length of the compressed streams is no more than γ times the optimal length. Recall that c partitions are generated by the partitioning algorithm from Section 3.1. Each of these partitions is encoded by a string of length $H(X_i)$ in the limit, so the total encoding size is $\sum_{i=1}^{c} H(X_i) \leq c \cdot \max_i H(X_i) \leq c \cdot H(\mathbf{X})$, where $H(\mathbf{X})$ is the joint entropy, which is a lower bound on the optimal encoding size, and the last inequality follows since $|\mathbf{X}| \geq |X_i|$ for all i. So our algorithm provides a c-approximation of the optimal compression.

Note that using the same method we used to compress the members of individual clusters, we could have combined the characters of all streams and compressed these together. This method would have optimal compression to the joint entropy of the streams. For demonstration of the problem with this method, consider the Lempel-Ziv sliding-window algorithm [7]. The algorithm proceeds by looking for matches between the current time position and some previous time within a given window into the past. The length and position of these matches are then recorded, which saves the space of encoding each character. The window moves forward as time progresses. Larger window sizes yield better results since matches are more likely to be found. The optimal encoded length is achiev by taking the limit as the window size tends to infinity [35]. If all streams are compressed at once, the optimal compression rate is only achieved in the limit as the window size becomes large and in practice compressing all streams at once requires a much larger window before the compression benefits begin. By only compressing k streams together we limit the effect of this problem.

4   Locality Results

In order to justify our claim that sensor outputs exhibit higher statistical dependence on their nearest neighbors, we analyze experimental data recorded by sensors operating under assumptions similar to our framework. The data we analyze was collected at the Mitsubishi Electric Research Laboratory [36]. It consists of sensor activation times for over 200 sensors observing the hallways of a building. Each sensor records times of nearby motion in coordinated universal time. For our analysis, we group activations into *time steps* consisting of the count of all activations for a single sensor over 0.1 second. These serve as the sensor counts over which we find the normalized joint entropy of data for sensor pairs, and we consider these counts only in terms of the presence or absence of motion during a given time step. We consider one minute of this data, or 600 data points.

Joint entropy values

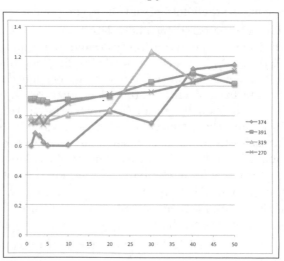

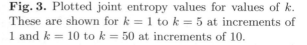

Fig. 3. Plotted joint entropy values for values of k. These are shown for $k = 1$ to $k = 5$ at increments of 1 and $k = 10$ to $k = 50$ at increments of 10.

Recall that the normalized joint entropy of two sequences generated by a common process is defined in Section 2. For our experiment, we consider the value $T = 3$. Probabilities are determined based on the observed outputs of the two sensors whose pairwise joint entropy is being calculated over the sensor streams containing 600 activation status values. The results shown in Figure 3 plot the combinatorial neighbor distances for four sensors against the normalized joint entropy values found. These neighbor distances are calculated based on the sensor locations and do not take walls into account, so some seemingly close sensors turn out not to be statistically dependent on each other. While each sensor's plot starts at a different initial value, there are few low entropy values (relative to the start value) after $k = 10$, showing that as sensors become farther apart they are less likely to be statistically dependent on each other.

In order to justify our claim on the value of compressing sensor outputs, and further, jointly compressing neighboring sensor outputs, we consider eight sensor outputs from a single hallway. The activation status was considered for these sensors for 70,000 0.1 second intervals (or approximately 2 hours). The raw data used 286.7 MB. These eight streams compressed separately with `gzip` (which uses the sliding-window Lempel-Ziv algorithm) used a total of 15.5 MB or 5.4% of the original space. Compressing the eight streams merged together character by character (as described in the compression algorithm in Figure 2), used 7.1 MB, or an additional 45.7% of the separately compressed space.

References

1. Saunier, N., Sayed, T.: Automated analysis of road safety with video data. In: Transportation Research Record, pp. 57–64 (2007)
2. Mainwaring, A., Culler, D., Polastre, J., Szewczyk, R., Anderson, J.: Wireless sensor networks for habitat monitoring. In: ACM international workshop on wireless sensor networks and applications, pp. 88–97 (2002)
3. MIT Media Lab: The owl project, http://owlproject.media.mit.edu/
4. Stutchbury, B.J.M., Tarof, S.A., Done, T., Gow, E., Kramer, P.M., Tautin, J., Fox, J.W., Afanasyev, V.: Tracking long-distance songbird migration by using geolocators. Science, 896 (February 2009)
5. Huffman, D.A.: A method for the construction of minimum-redundancy codes. In: Proc. of the IRE, vol. 40 (September 1952)
6. Rissanen, J.: Generalized Kraft inequality and arithmetic coding. IBM Jour. of Research and Dev. 20 (1976)
7. Ziv, J., Lempel, A.: A universal algorithm for sequential data compression. IEEE Transactions on Information Theory IT-23(3) (May 1977)
8. Deligiannakis, A., Kotidis, Y., Roussopoulos, N.: Processing approximate aggregate queries in wireless sensor networks. Inf. Syst. 31(8), 770–792 (2006)
9. Gandhi, S., Nath, S., Suri, S., Liu, J.: Gamps: Compressing multi sensor data by grouping and amplitude scaling. In: ACM SIGMOD (2009)
10. Cormode, G., Muthukrishnan, S., Zhuang, W.: Conquering the divide: Continuous clustering of distributed data streams. In: IEEE 23rd International Conference on Data Engineering, pp. 1036–1045 (2007)
11. Cormode, G., Muthukrishnan, S., Yi, K.: Algorithms for distributed functional monitoring. In: SODA, pp. 1076–1085 (2008)
12. Soroush, E., Wu, K., Pei, J.: Fast and quality-guaranteed data streaming in resource-constrained sensor networks. In: ACM Symp. on Mobile ad hoc networking and computing, pp. 391–400 (2008)
13. Johnen, C., Nguyen, L.H.: Self-stabilizing weight-based clustering algorithm for ad hoc sensor networks. In: Workshop on Algorithmic Aspects of Wireless Sensor Networks (AlgoSensors), pp. 83–94 (2006)
14. Nikoletseas, S., Spirakis, P.G.: Efficient sensor network design for continuous monitoring of moving objects. Theoretical Computer Science 402(1), 56–66 (2008)
15. Deligiannakis, A., Kotidis, Y., Roussopoulos, N.: Dissemination of compressed historical information in sensor networks. VLDB Journal 16(4), 439–461 (2007)
16. Sadler, C.M., Martonosi, M.: Data compression algorithms for energy-constrained devices in delay tolerant networks. In: SENSYS (November 2006)

17. Guibas, L.J.: Sensing, tracking and reasoning with relations. IEEE Signal Processing Mag. 19(2) (March 2002)
18. Guitton, A., Trigoni, N., Helmer, S.: Fault-tolerant compression algorithms for sensor networks with unreliable links. Technical Report BBKCS-08-01, Birkbeck, University of London (2008)
19. Gupta, P., Janardan, R., Smid, M.: Fast algorithms for collision and proximity problems involving moving geometric objects. Comput. Geom. Theory Appl. 6, 371–391 (1996)
20. Atallah, M.J.: Some dynamic computational geometry poblems. Comput. Math. Appl. 11(12), 1171–1181 (1985)
21. Schomer, E., Theil, C.: Efficient collision detection for moving polyhedra. In: Proc. 11th Annu. ACM Sympos. Comput. Geom., pp. 51–60 (1995)
22. Schomer, E., Theil, C.: Subquadratic algorithms for the general collision detection problem. In: European Workshop Comput. Geom., pp. 95–101 (1996)
23. Basch, J., Guibas, L.J., Hershberger, J.: Data structures for mobile data. In: SODA (1997)
24. Kahan, S.: A model for data in motion. In: STOC 1991: Proc. of the 23rd ACM Symp. on Theory of Computing, pp. 265–277 (1991)
25. Agarwal, P.K., Guibas, L.J., Edelsbrunner, H., Erickson, J., Isard, M., Har-Peled, S., Hershberger, J., Jensen, C., Kavraki, L., Koehl, P., Lin, M., Manocha, D., Metaxas, D., Mirtich, B., Mount, D.M., Muthukrishnan, S., Pai, D., Sacks, E., Snoeyink, J., Suri, S., Wolefson, O.: Algorithmic issues in modeling motion. ACM Computing Surveys 34, 550–572 (2002)
26. Guibas, L.: Kinetic data structures. In: Mehta, D., Sahni, S. (eds.) Handbook of Data Structures and App., pp. 23–1–23–18. Chapman and Hall/CRC (2004)
27. Babcock, B., Olston, C.: Distributed top-k monitoring. In: SIGMOD, pp. 28–39 (2003)
28. Yi, K., Zhang, Q.: Multi-dimensional online tracking. In: SODA (2009)
29. Mount, D.M., Netanyahu, N.S., Piatko, C., Silverman, R., Wu, A.Y.: A computational framework for incremental motion. In: Proc. 20th Annu. ACM Sympos. Comput. Geom., pp. 200–209 (2004)
30. Gandhi, S., Kumar, R., Suri, S.: Target counting under minimal sensing: Complexity and approximations. In: Workshop on Algorithmic Aspects of Wireless Sensor Networks (AlgoSensors), pp. 30–42 (2008)
31. Shannon, C.E.: A mathematical theory of communication. The Bell System Technical Journal 27, 379–423, 623–656 (1948)
32. Krauthgamer, R., Lee, J.R.: Navigating nets: Simple algorithms for proximity search. In: SODA (2004)
33. Cover, T.M., Thomas, J.A.: Elements of Information Theory, 2nd edn. Wiley-IEEE (2006)
34. Friedler, S.A., Mount, D.M.: Compressing kinetic data from sensor networks. Technical Report CS-TR-4941, UMIACS-TR-2009-10, University of Maryland, College Park (2009)
35. Wyner, A.D., Ziv, J.: The sliding-window lempel-ziv algorithm is asymptotically optimal. In: Proceedings of the IEEE, June 1994, pp. 872–877 (1994)
36. Wren, C.R., Ivanov, Y.A., Leigh, D., Westbues, J.: The MERL motion detector dataset: 2007 workshop on massive datasets. Technical Report TR2007-069, Mitsubishi Electric Research Laboratories, Cambridge, MA, USA (August 2007)

Relocation Analysis of Stabilizing MAC Algorithms for Large-Scale Mobile Ad Hoc Networks⋆
(Extended Abstract)

Pierre Leone[1], Marina Papatriantafilou[2], and Elad M. Schiller[2]

[1] Computer Science Department, University of Geneva, Geneva Switzerland
pierre.leone@cui.unige.ch
[2] Chalmers University of Technology, Göteborg Sweden
{ptrianta,elad}@chalmers.se

Abstract. *Throughput* is a basic measure for communication efficiency. It is defined as the average fraction of time that the channel is employed for useful data propagation. This work considers the problem of analytically estimating the throughput of protocols for media access control (MAC) in mobile ad hoc networks (MANETs). The dynamic and difficult to predict nature of MANETs complicates the analysis of MAC algorithms. We use simple extensions to the interleaving model and evolving graphs, for defining the settings that model the location of mobile nodes.

This work improves the understanding on impossibility results, the possible trade-offs and the analysis of fault-tolerant algorithms in MANETs. As the first result in the paper and as motivation for the ones that follow, we show that there is no efficient deterministic MAC algorithm for MANETs. Moreover, we prove a lower bound of the throughput in the radical settings of complete random relocation between every two steps of the algorithm. The lower bound matches the throughput of a strategy that is oblivious to the history of wireless broadcasts.

Subsequently, we focus on the analysis of non-oblivious strategies and assume a bound on the rate by which mobile nodes relocate, i.e., randomly changing their neighborhoods. Our analysis is the first to demonstrate a novel throughput-related trade-off between oblivious and non-oblivious strategies of MAC algorithms that depends on the relocation rate of mobile nodes. We present a non-oblivious strategy that yields a randomized, fault-tolerant algorithm that can balance between the trade-offs. The studied algorithm is the first of is kind because it is a "stateful" one that quickly converges to a guaranteed throughput.

1 Introduction

The designers of media access control (MAC) protocols often do not consider the relocation of mobile nodes. Alternatively, when they do assume that the nodes are not stationary, designers tend to assume that some nodes temporarily do not change their location and coordinate the communications among mobile nodes. An understanding is needed of the relationship between the performances of MAC algorithms and the

---

⋆ Partially supported by the ICT Programme of the European Union under contract numb⸮ ICT-2008-215270 (FRONT'S).

S. Dolev (Ed.): ALGOSENSORS 2009, LNCS 5804, pp. 203–217, 2009.

different settings by which the location of the mobile nodes is modeled. We study this relationship with an emphasis on stabilization concepts, which are imperative in mobile ad hoc networks (MANETs). The study reveals that efficient MAC algorithms are randomized. Moreover, they must balance a trade-off between two strategies; one that is oblivious to the history of wireless broadcasts and one that is not.[1]

A Case for Stabilization as a Design Goal. The dynamic and difficult-to-predict nature of mobile networks gives rise to many fault-tolerance issues and requires efficient solutions. MANETs, for example, are subject to transient faults due to hardware/software temporal malfunctions or short-lived violations of the assumed settings for modeling the location of the mobile nodes. Fault tolerant systems that are *self-stabilizing* [6] can recover after the occurrence of transient faults, which can cause an arbitrary corruption of the system state (so long as the program's code is still intact).

We show how concepts from self-stabilization are useful for practical problems in MANETs. The research takes into account several practical details, such as broadcast collisions, which are difficult to detect or avoid. The concept of *random* starting state of the system allows us to overcome the inherent difficulties that broadcast collisions impose in MANETs. The studied algorithms have natural self-stabilizing versions that guarantee system recovery after an *arbitrary* corruption of the system state (by using periodic restarts, see extensions in [14] and related approaches in [23, and references therein]).

Stabilizing MAC Algorithms. ALOHAnet and its synchronized version Slotted ALOHA [1] are a pioneering wireless systems that employs an oblivious strategy of "random access".[1] Time division multiple access (TDMA) [17] is another early approach where nodes broadcast one after the other, each using its own timeslot. Herman and Tixeuil [11] present a self-stabilizing TDMA algorithm for stationary settings,[2] which is based on distributed vertex-coloring. Jhumka and Kulkarni [13] use the algorithm in [11] and implicitly assume that the rate at which mobile nodes relocate is sufficiently slow to allow (stationary) leaders to be elected for coordinating the timeslot allocation of their neighboring nodes. However, there are no guarantees for successful leader election when the relocation of mobile nodes occurs between every two steps of the algorithm, because the temporarily stationary nodes are not a priori known.

Modeling the Location of Mobile Nodes. Let us look into scenarios in which each mobile node randomly moves in the Euclidian plane $[0, 1]^2$ [similar to 5] and in which two mobile nodes can directly communicate if their distance is less than a threshold $\chi \in [0, 1]$ [as in 16]. This scenario can be modeled by a sequence of evolving communication graphs [8], $\mathfrak{G} = (G_0, G_1, \ldots)$, such that at time instant t, the communication graph, $G_t = (V, E_t)$, includes the set of mobile nodes, V, and the set of edges, E_t, which represents pairs of processors that can directly communicate at time t. (For simplicity, we assume that time is discrete.)

---

[1] The oblivious strategy refers to protocols that keep no information about the history of broadcasts received. The non-oblivious strategy refers to protocols that does keep such information.

[2] By stationary settings we mean that the mobile nodes do not move. Do not confuse with stationary processes/points/sets.

Let us consider two consecutive communication graphs, $G_t, G_{t+1} \in \mathfrak{G}$. In this short run, it can be expected that many of the mobile nodes have *similar neighborhoods* in G_t and G_{t+1}, say, when the threshold $\chi \rightarrow 1$. In the long run, this similarity may disappear because there are *(independent) random relocations* of the mobile nodes due to their random motion, e.g., G_t and G_{t+x} are independent when $x \rightarrow \infty$. These properties of neighborhood similarity and (independent) random relocation motivate the studied system settings in the context of MAC algorithms.

To model the evolution of the communication graphs, we assume that between every two consecutive communication graphs, $G_t, G_{t+1} \in \mathfrak{G}$, a fraction of the mobile nodes, α, relocates from their neighborhood, where $\alpha \in [0, 1]$ is the relocation rate. The relocating nodes and their new neighborhoods are chosen randomly. This leads to a mixed property of *short-term* (independent) random relocation and *long-term* neighborhood similarity. The mix is defined by the relocation rate, α, that can be viewed as the ratio of non-stationary nodes over (temporarily) stationary ones.

Our settings can model scenarios typical to vehicular ad hoc networks. For example, consider a one-way road with cars whose speed distribution has some variance. In such settings, the relocation rate is typically bounded (cf. Remark 1 in Section 5). When the car velocities have high variance and different directions, it is difficult to tightly bound the relocation rate (because the broadcasting timeslots of cars in opposite lanes are not a priori known).

When the relocation rate is unbounded, the property of *short-term* (independent) random relocation can be more dominating than the property of *long-term* neighborhood similarity. We show that in this case, efficient MAC algorithms should employ an oblivious strategy that ignores the history of broadcasts among neighbors (because this dominating property stands in the algorithm's way of effectively learning the broadcasting timeslots of neighbors).[1] Thus, in the context of MAC algorithms, our settings have a clear advantage that facilitates the throughput analysis; a single parameter defines the algorithm's behavior.

Our assumptions on the evolution of the communication graphs are different from: (1) random walks [5], which do not consider *short-term* (independent) random relocations, and (2) population protocols [2], which do not consider *long-term* neighborhood similarity. Moreover, in the scope of MANETs and evolving graphs [8], the literature presents the analytical study of problems and algorithms that are fundamentally different from the one at hand [e.g. 3, 5, 12]. These algorithms are "stateless" and implement Markovian processes that are executed over evolving graphs.[3] The analysis of "stateful" algorithms is important in the context of fault-tolerant algorithms for MANETs, because "stateless" algorithms are inherently self-stabilizing.

Our Contribution. While MAC algorithms have been studied extensively, both numerically and empirically, the analytical study has been neglected thus far. Until now, it has been speculated that existing MAC algorithms (that were designed for stationary settings) would perform well in MANETs.[2] Alternatively, algebraic equations are used for modeling the Kinetics of mobile nodes [4].

---

[3] We use the terms "stateless" and "stateful" to describe those properties of stochastic proces~ and algorithms whose implementations have storage or have no storage, respectively.

Expressive models facilitate the formal demonstration of lower bounds, impossibility results and other limitations, such as trade-offs. It is hard to discover negative results by employing approaches that perform numerical or empirical studies. In addition, Kinetic models [4] can be restrictive and difficult to analyze; it is hard to consider arbitrary behavior of mobile nodes and transient faults.

We use an expressive model that allows taking a different analytical approach and yields:

- **Concise Proofs of an Impossibility Result and a Lower Bound.** We start by considering arbitrary values of the relocation rate and before focusing on bounded values. For arbitrary relocation rate, we show that the best that you can hope for is a randomized oblivious strategy that ignores the history of broadcasts.[1] The proofs is simpler than the ones that can be demonstrated in Kinetic models [4]; it considers the extreme scenario in which the communication graph can drastically change between any two algorithm steps.

- **Improved Understanding of Limitations and Critical Situations.** We focus on demonstrating a throughput-related trade-off between oblivious and non-oblivious strategies of MAC algorithms.[1] We view the relocation rate as the ratio of non-stationary mobile nodes over (temporarily) stationary ones. We identify a critical threshold of the relocation rate and we show that above this critical threshold, it is best to employ an oblivious strategy.[1] The non-oblivious algorithm is a fault-tolerant MAC algorithm for which we analytically estimate the throughput in a large set of settings that model the location of mobile nodes, and wireless communications in which broadcasts can collide.

- **An Insight to "Stateful" and Fault-Tolerant Algorithms.** We analytically estimate the eventual throughput of the non-oblivious strategy as a function of the relocation rate, α.[1] We verify that the algorithm is expected to converge to a guaranteed throughput, within $\mathcal{O}(\log n)$ broadcasting rounds, where n is the number of mobile nodes. The algorithm is the first of its kind in the context of MANETs and evolving graphs, because it is "stateful" and fault-tolerant. We note that it can be extended to consider self-stabilization as well as other trade-offs [see 14].

In the context of MANETs, we expect that the analysis of other trade-offs, self-stabilizing algorithms, as well as negative results, can be simplified by the expressive model that appears in this paper.

2 Preliminaries

The system consists of a set of communicating entities, which we call *processors* or *(mobile) nodes*. Denote the set of processors by P and every processor $p_i \in P$ with a unique index, i, that p_i can access.

Synchronization. Each processor has fine-grained, real-time clock hardware, and all node clocks are synchronized to a common, global time (e.g., using a GPS). We assume that the MAC protocol is invoked periodically by synchronized *common pulses*. The term *(broadcasting) timeslot* refers to the period between two consecutive common pulses, t_x and t_{x+1}, such that $t_{x+1} = (t_x \bmod T) + 1$, where T is a predefined constant named the *frame size*. In our pseudo-code, we use the event timeslot (t) that is triggered by the common pulse. The event raises the execution of its associated subroutine.

Communications. At any instance of time, the ability of any pair of processors to directly communicate is defined by the set, $N_i \subseteq P$, of *neighbors* that processor $p_i \in P$ can communicate with directly. We assume that at any time, N_i are symmetrical; for any pair of processors, $p_i, p_j \in P$ it holds that $p_j \in N_i$ implies that $p_i \in N_j$. Given a particular instance of time, we define the *communication graph* as $G = (V, E)$, where $V = P$ is the set of nodes, and $E = \cup_{i \in P}\{(p_i, p_j) : p_j \in N_i\}$ represents the communication relationships among processors. Throughout this paper, we assume that G is connected.

Interferences. Wireless transmissions are subject to collisions and we consider the potential of processors to interfere with each others' communications. We say that processors $A \subseteq P$ *broadcast simultaneously* if the processors in A broadcast within the same timeslot. We denote by $\mathcal{N}_i = \{p_k \in N_j : p_j \in N_i \cup \{p_i\}\} \setminus \{p_i\}$ the set of processors that may interfere with p_i's communications when any nonempty subset of them, $A \subseteq \mathcal{N}_i : A \neq \emptyset$, transmit simultaneously with p_i. We call $\mathcal{N}_i$ the (symmetrical) *extended neighborhood* of node $p_i \in P$, and $|\mathcal{N}_i|$ the *extended degree* of node $p_i \in P$. Given a particular instance of time, we define the (connected) *collision graph* as $\mathcal{G} = (V, \mathcal{E})$, where $V = P$ is the set of nodes and $\mathcal{E} = \cup_{p_i \in P}\{(p_i, p_j) : p_j \in \mathcal{N}_i\}$. We assume that there is a known constant, D that is strictly greater than the extended degree of any node, i.e., $\forall p_i \in P : |\mathcal{N}_i \cup \{p_i\}| \leq D$. Throughout this paper, we assume that the network is large, i.e., $D \ll |P|$. Moreover, we assume that the frame size is sufficiently large to avoid collisions in any fixed communication graph, i.e., $T \geq D$.[4] Extensions for settings in which $T < D$ are considered in [14].

Communication Primitives. The non-oblivious strategy (Fig. 6) uses existing schemes for packet transmission. The *exposure time*, ϵ, is the period during which a transmitted packet might be intercepted by other transmissions in the sender's extended neighborhood. Such an interception can cause the corruption of the DATA packet in a way that does not allow the sender to detect the disruption.

The non-oblivious strategy (Fig. 6) uses the communications primitives of short exposure time (SET): SET_broadcast(), SET_receive(), SET_carrier_sense() and SET_reception_error(). Requirement 1 implies that messages are received from processors whose broadcasts are not interfered. The procedure SET_ broadcast(m) and the event SET_ receive() allow the transmission of message m with an effectively short exposure time, ϵ. We assume that any processor that calls the procedure SET_broadcast(), does so in an aligned manner. Namely, every timeslot, t, is divided into shorter periods, $[t, t+\epsilon), \ldots [t\epsilon(MaxRnd-1), t+\epsilon MaxRnd), [t\epsilon MaxRnd, t+1)$ and the processor starts calling the procedure $[t\epsilon(k-1), t+\epsilon k)$, where $1 \leq k \leq MaxRnd$ and $MaxRnd \geq 2$ is a predefined constant (see Fig. 1). What the new algorithm requires from the assumed underlying primitives is explained by requirements 1 and 3.

---

[4] Vizing [21] shows that a graph is $(\Delta + 1)$-colorable if Δ is the maximal degree.

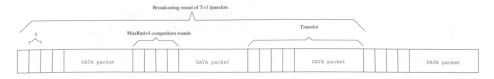

Fig. 1. An example of broadcasting rounds, with 3 timeslots and 4 competition rounds of size ϵ (exposure time)

Requirement 1. *Let $p_i \in P$ be a processor that calls the procedure* **SET_broadcast** *(m) during (and throughout) the period $[t_i^s, t_i^e]$ (starting at time t_i^s and ending at time t_i^e). Suppose that there is no neighboring processor, $p_j \in \mathcal{N}_i$, that calls the procedure* **SET_broadcast**(m) *during (and throughout) the period $[t_j^s, t_j^e]$, where $t_j^s \in [t_i^s, t_i^s + \epsilon]$. Then, all p_i's neighbors, $p_k \in \mathcal{N}_i$, raise the event* **SET_receive**(m) *during the period $[t_k^s, t_k^e]$, where $t_k^s \in [t_i^s, t_i^s + \epsilon]$ and $t_k^e \in [t_i^e, t_i^e + \epsilon]$.*

Requirement 2 implies that processors can sense the carrier whenever there is at least one processor that broadcasts in their extended neighborhoods. The event SET_carrier_sense() is raised upon detecting that there is at least one transmission in the extended neighborhood. We allow the delay of carrier sensing for an effective period of at most ϵ.

Requirement 2. *Let $p_i \in P$ be a processor that calls the procedure* **SET_broadcast** *(m) during (and throughout) the period $[t_i^s, t_i^e]$. Then, any, $p_k \in \mathcal{N}_i$, extended neighbor of p_i raises the event* **SET_carrier_ sense**() *during the period $[t_k^s, t_k^e]$, where $t_k^s \in [t_i^s, t_i^s + \epsilon]$ and $t_k^e \in [t_i^e, t_i^e + \epsilon]$.*

Requirement 3 implies that processors *can* raise the event SET_reception_error() when their neighbors are concurrently attempting to transmit (and their broadcasts collide).[5]

Requirement 3. *Let $p_k \in P$ be a processor and $p_i, p_j \in \mathcal{N}_k$ be two processors in its extended neighborhood, such that $i \neq k$ (possibly $j = k$). Suppose that processors, p_i and p_j, call the procedure* **SET_broadcast**(m) *during (and throughout) the periods, $[t_i^s, t_i^e]$, and respectively, $[t_j^s, t_j^e]$. Suppose that processor p_k raises the event* **SET_reception_error**(), *then the event is raised during the period $[t_k^s, t_k^e]$, where $t_k^s \in [\max(t_i^s, t_j^s), \max(t_i^s, t_j^s) + \epsilon]$ and $t_k^e \in [\min(t_i^e, t_j^e), \min(t_i^e, t_j^e) + \epsilon]$.*

One way to implement the above requirements is to use existing packet transmission schemes that have short exposure time, such as BTMA [20], DBTMA [10] and FAMA [9], to name a few. One may wish to consider an implementation in which requirements 2 and 3 might not occur with a probability of at most p. For the sake of presentation simplicity, we assume that $p = 0$. We note that for any $p > 0$, our proofs hold by taking $T \geq D(1 + \frac{1}{p})$ and waiting for a longer convergence period, where T is the frame size D that is strictly greater than the extended degree of any node (defined above).

---

[5] We note that we do not require that the event SET_reception_error() is indeed raised whenever concurrent broadcasts occur – not even eventually! The event SET_reception_error() is an abstraction for a set of error notifications, such as bad checksum and failure to lock on the carrier single.

- R_{all}. Relocation is unrestricted as long as the communication and the interference graphs are connected.

- R_{rlc}. In any configuration, the communication graph is d-regular and the interference graph is D-regular, where d and D are constants. Every relocation step, r, is a complete random change of the communication and interference graphs. Namely, let $c = (G = (V, E), \mathcal{G} = (V, \mathcal{E}), \{st_i\}_{i=1}^{|P|})$ and $c' = (G' = (V, E'), \mathcal{G}' = (V, \mathcal{E}'), \{st_i\}_{i=1}^{|P|})$ be the two configurations that immediately precede, and respectively, follow the relocation step r. We require that G' can be obtained from G and $\mathcal{G}'$ can be obtained from $\mathcal{G}$ by replacing the indices and states of the nodes in V according to a random (uniform) permutation.

- $R_{rlc}(\alpha)$. Let us consider the graphs $G = (V, E), \mathcal{G} = (V, \mathcal{E}), G' = (V, E')$ and $\mathcal{G}' = (V, \mathcal{E}')$ as they are defined for R_{rlc}. Let $M \subseteq V$ (mobile) be a subset of the vertices in V that are selected uniformly at random, such that $|M| = \alpha|V|$, where $0 \le \alpha \le 1$ is named the *relocation rate*. We require that G' can be obtained from G and $\mathcal{G}'$ can be obtained from $\mathcal{G}$ by replacing the indices and states of nodes in M according to a random (uniform) permutation. For simplicity, we assume that in every execution $R \in R_{rlc}(\alpha)$ and every broadcasting round R' of R, the set M is fixed throughout R' (and can change in other broadcasting rounds of R).[a]

---

[a] We note that in every (extended) neighborhood in the communication graph G (respectively, interference graph $\mathcal{G}$), the expected number of nodes that do not join or leave the (extended) neighborhood is $(1 - \alpha)d$ (respectively, $(1 - \alpha)D$).

Fig. 2. The different classes of settings for modeling the location of the mobile nodes

Modeling the Locations of Mobile Nodes. We simplify the analysis of MANETs by considering simple extensions to the interleaving model [6] in which the communication and the interference graphs are modeled by evolving graphs that represent the condition of bounded relocation rates.

Every processor, $p_i \in P$, executes a program that is a sequence of *atomic steps*. The *state* st_i of a processor p_i consists of the value of all the variables of the processor (including messages in transit for p_i). The term *configuration* is used for a tuple of the form $(G, \mathcal{G}, \{st_i\}_{i=1}^{|P|})$, where G is the communication graph, $\mathcal{G}$ is the interference graph, and $\{st_i\}_{i=1}^{|P|}$ are the processors' states (including the set of all incoming communications). For ease of description, we assume that an adversary controls the location of the mobile nodes and may relocate them. Given configuration $c = (G, \mathcal{G}, \{st_i\}_{i=1}^{|P|})$, a *relocation step*, r, modifies c by changing the communication graph, G, and the interference graph, $\mathcal{G}$. An *execution* (run) $R = (c(0), c(1), \dots)$ is an unbounded sequence of system configurations $c(x)$, such that each configuration $c(x + 1)$ (except the initial configuration $c(0)$) is obtained from the preceding configuration $c(x)$ by the execution of steps, $\{a_i(x)\}_{p_i \in P}$, taken by all processors or by a relocation step, $r(x)$, which the adversity forces. We assume that there is no configuration, $c(k + 1) \in R$ that is immediately preceded and followed by the relocation steps, $r(k)$, and respectively $r(k + 1)$. Namely, the algorithm takes at least one step between any two relocation steps. This does not restrain the generality since the composition of two relocation steps is equivalent to a single relocation step in our setting. Moreover, the system settings imply th mobile nodes do not relocate while the algorithm takes a step, e.g., sends a message

Note that it is possible to describe execution R as an unbounded sequence of finite sequences, $(c(x), \ldots c(x'))$, named *broadcasting rounds*, such that configuration $c(x)$ immediately precedes the atomic step in which the clock value, t, is 0 and configuration $c(x')$ is the first configuration after $c(x)$ that immediately precedes the atomic step in which the clock value is maximal, i.e., $t = T - 1$ (see Section 2).

3   Bounded Rate and Unbounded Rate of Relocations

We start by considering arbitrary values of the relocation rate and then focus on bounded values. The proofs consider classes of executions that encode the locations of mobile nodes (see Fig. 2).

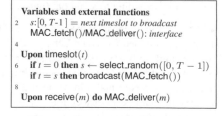

```
Variables and external functions
2  s:[0, T-1] = next timeslot to broadcast
   MAC_fetch()/MAC_deliver(): interface
4
   Upon timeslot(t)
6    if t = 0 then s ← select_random([0, T − 1])
     if t = s then broadcast(MAC_fetch())
8
   Upon receive(m) do MAC_deliver(m)
```

Unbounded Rate of Relocations. Claim 1 considers the extreme scenario in which the communication graph is always connected, but can drastically change between any two

Fig. 3. The oblivious strategy

algorithm steps. The proof is simpler than the ones that can be demonstrated in Kinetic models [4] since it only considers the encounters of mobile nodes.

Claim 1 ([14]). *For arbitrary relocation rate, the best that we can hope for is a randomized and oblivious strategy that ignores the history of received broadcasts.*[1]

Claim 1 demonstrates a lower bound on the throughput that matches the throughput of the oblivious strategy (Fig. 3), which has the throughput of $\frac{1}{e}$ when T is close to D [same as 1].

Bounded Rates of Relocations. The class $R_{rlc}(\alpha)$ acts as a bridge between the scenarios of the class R_{rlc} and stationary settings.[2] This relationship is illustrated in Fig. 4. In $R_{rlc}(\alpha)$, a bounded number of relocations exists between any two consecutive steps of the algorithm; the parameter $0 \leq \alpha \leq 1$ sets the rate by which mobile nodes relocate.

Generally in networks involving mobile nodes and in particular in MANETs, there are many tradeoffs that are related to "delay, throughput, energy-efficiency, locality, dynamics, fairness, [to name a few, which] are still not understood" [Wattenhofer 22]. In order to highlight throughput-related factors that are unique to non-stationary settings, we must exclude tradeoffs that are known to effect the throughput in stationary settings. One of the known trade-offs is the one between the throughput and contention, i.e., the expected number of neighboring nodes that wish to transmit at any time [19]. Therefore, we choose the focal point of saturation situations in which each node always wishes to transmit. The studied algorithm allocates timeslots [as in 11], rather than continuous radio time [as in 19]. Therefore, we assume that the number of nodes in every neighborhood is a constant (rather than expected). Our assumptions model scenarios in which the interference graph always has bounded

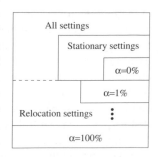

Fig. 4.   Class relationships: $R_{rlc}(0) \subset \ldots \subset R_{rlc}(1) \subset R_{rlc} \subset R_{all}$

vertex-degree of at most the number of timeslots in a broadcasting round. In [14] we suggest extensions to the studied algorithm that relax the above assumptions and can balance the trade-off between throughput and contention using the technique of p-persistent random delay before transmission [19].

4   The Non-oblivious Strategy for Bounded Rate of Relocations

In the previous section, we looked into settings in which the relocation rate is un-bounded and therefore the adversary can stand in the algorithm's way of learning the broadcasting timeslots of its neighbors. We now turn to consider settings in which nodes are able to learn some information about the success of the neighbors' broadcasts. We take a non-oblivious approach for timeslot allocation; nodes avoid broadcasting in the timeslots for which they learn that their neighbors successfully broadcast.[1]

Keeping track of broadcast history is complicated in non-stationary settings because of node relocations and broadcast collations. We present a randomized algorithm that respects the recent history of neighbors' broadcasts. This information is inaccurate. However, when the relocation rate is not to high, the timeslots can be allocated by a distributed vertex-coloring algorithm. Section 5 shows that this non-oblivious approach has higher throughput when the relocation rate is lower than a critical threshold because the ratio of timeslots that are safe to broadcast becomes greater than the one of oblivious approaches, e.g., $\frac{1}{e}$ in the oblivious strategy (Fig. 3).[1]

Vertex-Coloring in Stationary Settings Using Reliable Broadcasts. Vertex-coloring allows nodes to map colors to timeslots and to safely broadcast without collisions. Each node uses a broadcasting timeslot that is unique to its extended neighborhood [as in 11]. Observe that in Luby's algorithm (described in Fig. 5), the colors do not explicitly encode the identity of the neighboring nodes, rather they query about colors that are unused in their

```
let palette := colors; (∗ all colors ∗)
2 repeat
     c := choose(palette); (∗ tentative ∗)
4    inform neighbors about c;
     if c was not chosen by a neighbor then
6       output c; (∗ use c permanently ∗)
        palette := the set of colors that are
8          not permanently used by neighbors;
     until palette = = ∅;
```

Fig. 5. Luby's algorithm [15]

neighborhood. The non-oblivious strategy also queries about the set of timeslots that are not successfully used and choose among them.[1]

Challenges in Non-stationary Settings. In non-stationary settings, topological changes have no end, because node relocations disrupt the broadcasts in "safe" timeslots (i.e., the choice of permanent colors in Luby's algorithm might not last forever in non-stationary settings). Therefore, each node has to continuously be alert for changes in its book-keeping of the set of unused timeslots (cf. palette in Luby's algorithm) and possibly to re-choose its broadcasting timeslot (cf. permanent colors in Luby's algorithm). Moreover, it is not simple to provide feedback for message arrivals when broadcasts may collide (even in stationary settings).[2] In other words, the uniqueness property of colors (broadcasting timeslots) can be violated due to the transient errors in message delivery and the ongoing node relocations.[6]

[6] The uniqueness property: We say that processor $p_i \in P$ has a unique color (broadcasti•• timeslot), if there is no processor $p_j \in \mathcal{N}_i$, such that $s_i = s_j$, where $s_i \in [0, T - 1]$ is value of p_i's timeslot.

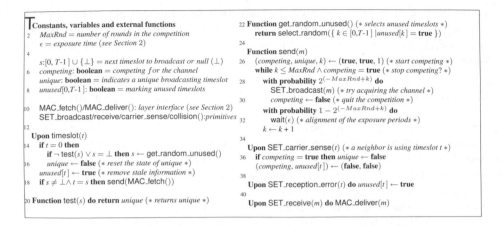

Fig. 6. The non-oblivious strategy, code of processor p_i. We note that SET_carrier_sense() is followed either by SET_reception_error() or (exclusive) by SET_receive() within the same timeslot.

Opportunities. A non-oblivious strategy can be illustrated by a variation on Luby's algorithm that uses inaccurate operations. Namely, nodes might be misinformed on the broadcasting timeslots of their neighbors and miscalculate the set of unused timeslots in their extended neighborhood. Nevertheless, when the relocation rate is lower than a critical threshold, the ratio of timeslots that are safe to broadcast becomes greater than that of an oblivious approach, e.g., $\frac{1}{e}$ in the oblivious strategy.[1]

Inaccurate (Yet Useful) Operations. We consider a randomized algorithm that facilitates the inaccurate operations using the timeslots themselves; each node p_i can possibly inform its neighbors about its chosen timeslot s, by *using it*, i.e., by calling the procedure SET_broadcast() and broadcasting during s in the coming broadcasting round. In parallel, each node can pay attention to the events that may be raised by the lower layer, i.e., the events SET_carrier_sense(), SET_reception_error() and SET_receive(). A timeslot s during which a message successfully arrives to p_i, is marked in p_i's bookkeeping variables as an occupied timeslot. A timeslot t during which a reception error is reported to p_i, is marked in p_i's bookkeeping variables as unused, because there was no successful transmission in t and the transmitting nodes should choose among the unused timeslots. We note that the statements above do not imply that nodes are required to detect the collision of their own broadcasts nor do they expect to receive feedback on their message arrivals.

The Non-oblivious Strategy. This strategy is facilitated by a randomized construction that lets every node inform its extended neighborhood on its broadcasting timeslot and allows the neighbors to record this timeslot as an occupied/unused one. The construction is based on a competition among neighboring nodes that attempt to broadcast within the same timeslot (cf. among nodes that chose the same tentative color in Luby's ~orithm). When there is a single competing node, that node is guaranteed to win. ~ely, the node succeeds in informing its extended neighborhood on its broadcasting timeslot and letting the extended neighborhood to mark its broadcasting timeslot as an occupied one. In the case where there are $x > 1$ competing nodes, there might be more than one winner in the competition. However, most of the competitors are expected to lose. The nodes that have lost, mark their broadcasting timeslot as an unused one when there is more than one winner. Thus, on the next broadcasting, it is expected that only a few of the losing nodes will compete for the same timeslot again; they are expected to re-choose their timeslots. How this works is explained in more detail below.

Informing on the Chosen timeslot: The **send**(m) *Function.* We define the construction in Fig. 6 as a competition among nodes that are attempting to broadcast in a particular timeslot, s. The competition's objective is to allow a single node to be the first to broadcast.

By Requirement 1 (Section 2), when a node that calls the procedure **SET_broadcast**() is the only one to do so within its extended neighborhood and the period ϵ, the broadcast succeeds, where ϵ is the exposure time (see Section 2). Therefore, we consider $MaxRnd$ synchronized competition rounds and let each round to be of length ϵ (cf. lines 27 to 33 and Fig. 1), where $MaxRnd$ is a predefined constant. A node leaves the competition either because it decides to broadcast (cf. line 29) or because it notices that a neighboring node has (cf. line 37).

Each node randomly decides on the exact time within the timeslot in which it starts broadcasting. The processors call the procedure **SET_broadcast**() with probability $p(k) = 2^{(-MaxRnd+k)}$, where $k \in [1, MaxRnd]$ is the round number of the competition (cf. line 27). Namely, the probability for at least one node to broadcast is increased exponentially in every loop iteration (cf. lines 27 to 33). Moreover, for any number of competitors, it can be shown that most of them are expected to lose. The losing nodes are expected to distinguish correctly between the cases of a single winner and all other cases, because they do not call the procedure **SET_broadcast**() (see requirements 2 and 3, Section 2). The correct distinction between these cases facilitates the correct bookkeeping of unused timeslots.

Recording Success of Own Broadcast: The Function **test**(s). A broadcast is said to be successful if its **DATA** packet is not transmitted concurrently with the transmission of another node in the extended neighborhood. The objective of the function is to indicate the possible success of the node's last attempt to broadcast. The variable $unique$, which is stored at each node, holds the state of the indication for the previous broadcasting round. Before starting the competition, the node presumes that it will prevail the competition (cf. line 26). In case the node loses, the state is updated accordingly (cf. line 36). Suppose that during the previous broadcasting round the node broadcasts (cf. line 37) as part of the node's attempt to access the media in timeslot s. Moreover, suppose that in s, there is no indication that a neighboring node broadcasts (cf. line 35). In this case, the function **test**(s) returns **true** if no collision was reported (cf. line 37), and in any other case, the function returns **false** (cf. line 20).

Recording Unused timeslots: The Array $unused$ *and the Function* **get_random_unused**(). During the broadcasting round that follows the t-th timeslot, t it is said to be unused if there were no successful broadcasts in t. A node maintains information on unused timeslots in the array $unused$. Immediately before any broadcast in timeslo

t, the node presumes that t is an unused one (cf. line 17). When the node receives an indication that a neighboring node has accessed the channel in t, it marks t as occupied, i.e., not unused (cf. line 37). However, in case there is an indication of a disruption in the transmission, the timeslot is marked as an unused one (cf. line 39). We note that the technique of reservoir sampling [7, 14] allows uniform sampling of an unused timeslot from an unbounded sequence using a single index for storing the broadcasting timeslot.

5   Analyzing the Non-oblivious Strategy

The analysis of the algorithm is simplified by assuming that the broadcasting timeslots initially hold uniformly random values, i.e., equivalent to executing the algorithm with a "wrapper" (see Fig. 7). The convergence time and the throughput are estimated before

> **Let** s be a uniformly random value in $[0, T\text{-}1]$
> 2 **do forever**
> > run the non-oblivious strategy (Fig. 6)

Fig. 7. "Wrapper"-structure for simplicity

suggesting the critical threshold of relocation rate. Theorem 1 estimates the throughput of the non-oblivious strategy by bounding its value from below, $\underline{x}$, and above, $\overline{x}$. These bounds depend merely on the relocation rate, α, and $\frac{\overline{x}}{\underline{x}} \in \mathcal{O}(\frac{1}{1-\alpha^2})$.

Theorem 1 ([14]). *Suppose that $R \in R_{rlc}(\alpha)$ is an execution of the non-oblivious algorithm (Fig. 7). Within $\ell \in \mathcal{O}(\frac{\log n}{-\log \gamma})$ broadcasting rounds in R, the system reaches a suffix, R', such that the expected throughput of processor $p_i \in P$ in any broadcasting round in R' is $x_\ell \in [\underline{x_\ell} - \delta_\ell, \overline{x_\ell} + \delta_\ell]$, where $\underline{x_\ell} = D(1 - 1/(\frac{\sigma}{\alpha} + (1 - \sigma)))$, $\overline{x_\ell} = D\frac{1}{e\alpha + 1}$, $\delta_\ell \in \mathcal{O}(\gamma^\ell)$, $\gamma = (1 - \alpha)(1 - \sigma)$ and $\sigma \in (0, 1)$.*

Proof outline: The proof is followed by considering the ℓ-th broadcasting round. We define the numbers, x_ℓ and y_ℓ, as the expected number of mobile nodes in an extended neighborhood that have, and respectively, do not have unique timeslots on the ℓ-th broadcasting round. [6] Propositions 1 and 2 below, estimate the ratios, $\alpha, (1-\beta) \in [0, 1]$, of processors that stop having, and respectively, start having unique timeslots in every broadcasting round. Given x_ℓ and y_ℓ, Equations 1 estimate the values of $x_{\ell+1}$ and $y_{\ell+1}$.

$$D = x_\ell + y_\ell; \qquad x_\ell = (1 - \alpha)x_{\ell-1} + (1 - \beta)y_{\ell-1}; \qquad y_\ell = \alpha x_{\ell-1} + \beta y_{\ell-1} \quad (1)$$

Proposition 1 considers Property 1 below, and estimates the number of nodes that stop having unique timeslots.

Property 1. Let $s \in [0, T - 1]$ be the broadcasting timeslot of node $p_i \in P$ in broadcasting round $(c(x), \ldots c(x'))$ in which a MAC algorithm is executed. The value of s is a random variable of a uniform distribution in $[0, T - 1]$.

Proposition 1. *Suppose that Property 1 holds in execution $R \in R_{rlc}(\alpha)$ of the non-oblivious strategy. Let us consider p_i's extended neighborhood, $\mathcal{N}_i$, and a broadcasting round, $R'' = (c(x), \ldots c(x'))$, such that in R'' there are y mobile nodes with unique broadcasting timeslots. [6] Then, during R'' the expected number of mobile nodes whose timeslots become non-unique due to the relocation steps, $r \in R''$, is at most αy.*

It can be shown that Property 1 holds throughput R [see 14]. Therefore, Proposition 1 is implied by the definition of $R_{rlc}(\alpha)$. Proposition 2 considers the number of processors whose timeslots become unique on the first step of the ℓ-th broadcasting round.

Proposition 2. *Let $R' = (c(x), \ldots c(x'))$ be a broadcasting round in R and define the (timeslot) recovery ratio, $(1 - \beta) \in [0, 1]$, in R' as follows: Let $\mathcal{N}_i$ be p_i's extended neighborhood and y the number of processors, $p_j \in \mathcal{N}_i$, that do not have a unique timeslot in configuration $c(x)$.* [6] *Let βy be the expected number of processors, $p_j \in \mathcal{N}_i$, whose timeslots do not become unique in $c(x' + 1)$. Then $\sigma(1 - \alpha) \le (1 - \beta) \le \frac{1}{e}$, where $\sigma = \frac{5+3/e}{32}$.*

By linearizing equations 1, we have that $\underline{x}_\ell + \Theta((1 - (\alpha + \sigma(1 - \alpha)))^\ell) \le x_\ell \le \overline{x}_\ell + \Theta((1 - (\alpha + \frac{1}{e}))^\ell)$ [see 14]. Therefore, within $\ell \in \mathcal{O}(\frac{\log n}{-\log \gamma})$ broadcasting round, the value of the terms $\Theta((1 - (\alpha + \sigma(1 - \alpha)))^\ell)$ and $\Theta((1 - (\alpha + \frac{1}{e}))^\ell)$ can be bounded; $x_\ell \in [\underline{x}_\ell - \delta_\ell, \overline{x}_\ell + \delta_\ell]$, where $\delta_\ell \in \mathcal{O}(\gamma^\ell)$. ∎

Suggesting a Critical Threshold. The non-oblivious algorithm (Fig. 7) should not be used when the relocation rate, α, is greater than the critical threshold, $\alpha_c \in [0, 1]$, which we now suggest. The eventual values of the throughput are presented in Fig. 8 and together with Theorem 1 allow us to discover that the non-oblivious strategy has a lower throughput than the oblivious strategy for any relocation rate that is higher than $1/(1 + \frac{1}{\sigma(e-1)}) > 0.24$. By letting $\alpha_c < 0.24$, we assure that, within $\ell \in \mathcal{O}(\frac{\log n}{-\log \gamma})$ broadcasting rounds, the throughput of the non-oblivious algorithm is higher than $\frac{1}{e}$, which is the throughput of the oblivious strategy (see Claim 1). Moreover, the non-oblivious algorithm should be used, when $\alpha < \alpha_c - \delta_\ell$, because when $\alpha_c - \alpha < \delta_\ell$, the factor, γ, of the convergence rate might be low and cause a long convergence period, where $\delta_\ell \in O(\gamma^\ell)$ is a predefined safety constant (cf. Theorem 1).

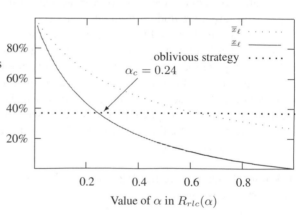

Fig. 8. Throughput of oblivious and non-oblivious strategies; $[\underline{x}, \overline{x}]$ bounds the latter

Remark 1 (**Typical settings of a one-way road**). Let us assume that 75% of the cars have the same velocity, say, a cruising speed of 90 kn/h. Moreover, 25% of the cars go in the same direction, but at a speed that is at most $\pm 20\%$ of the speed limit, i.e., 18 km/h slower or faster. Suppose that there are at most 2 lanes, a car takes 7.5 m of a lane, the timeslot period is 5 ms, the communication range is 25 m, the interference range is 75 m, which implies at most $13.3\dot{}$ (40) cars in any neighborhood (respectively, extended neighborhood) and allows 5 frames (broadcasting rounds) per second. Suppose that 75% of the cars have the same velocity, that 25% of them go 5 m/s (18 km slower or faster, and that a uniform distribution of cars exists in the stream. Namely, the neighborhoods change: 25% of the cars have at most 2 different cars in their (extended) neighborhoods in every $\frac{7.5}{5}$ s, which is $(2\frac{7.5}{5})/5 = \frac{3}{5}$ cars per frame; 75% of the cars have a new car within their communication and interference ranges that stays for 25, and respectively, 75 frames, which is less than $\frac{3}{5}$ cars per frame. I.e., $\alpha = \frac{3}{5}/13.3^{\cdot} = 5\%$, which is about 5 times smaller than the critical threshold, α_c, and yields a throughput that is about twice that of the oblivious strategy (see Fig. 8).

6 Conclusions

This work is an analytical study of the relationship between a fundamental protocol for MANETs and the settings that model the location of mobile nodes. The study focuses on a novel throughput-related trade-off between oblivious and non-oblivious strategies of MAC algorithms. The trade-off depends on the relocation rate of mobile nodes. The non-oblivious algorithm can balance such trade-offs and can be extended to consider stronger requirements of fault tolerance as well as other tradeoffs. The studied algorithm is the first of its kind, because it is a "stateful" and fault-tolerant one. Thus, our methods can simplify the design of "stateful" self-stabilizing algorithms for MANETs, because we explain how to consider practical details, such as broadcast collisions and the location of mobile nodes. Moreover, we expect that the methodology used in this paper can study more trade-offs and new algorithms [18] in this context.

Expressive models facilitate the demonstration of lower bounds, impossibility results and other limitations, such as trade-offs. It is difficult to discover negative results by employing approaches that perform numerical or empirical studies. In addition, Kinetic models [1] can be restrictive and difficult to analyze; it is hard to consider arbitrary behavior of mobile nodes and transient faults when algebraic equations are used. Interestingly, the simpler analytical model is more expressive than the existing approaches; in the context of MANETs, it is the first to facilitate the analysis of "stateful" algorithms as well as negative results.

Acknowledgments. We thank Zvi Lotker, Sébastien Tixeuil and Philippas Tsigas for important discussions.

References

[1] Abramson, N.: Development of the ALOHANET. IEEE Information Theory 31(2), 119–123 (1985)

[2] Angluin, D., Aspnes, J., Fischer, M.J., Jiang, H.: Self-stabilizing population protocols. ACM Transactions on Autonomous and Adaptive Systems (TAAS) 3(4) (2008)

[3] Avin, C., Koucký, M., Lotker, Z.: How to explore a fast-changing world (cover time of a simple random walk on evolving graphs). In: Aceto, L., Damgård, I., Goldberg, L.A., Halldórsson, M.M., Ingólfsdóttir, A., Walukiewicz, I. (eds.) ICALP 2008, Part I. LNCS, vol. 5125, pp. 121–132. Springer, Heidelberg (2008)

[4] Bettstetter, C.: Smooth is better than sharp: a random mobility model for simulation of wireless networks. In: Meo, M., Dahlberg, T.A., Donatiello, L. (eds.) MSWiM, pp. 19–27. ACM, New York (2001)

[5] Díaz, J., Mitsche, D., Pérez-Giménez, X.: On the connectivity of dynamic random geometric graphs. In: SODA 2008, pp. 601–610 (2008)

[6] Dolev, S.: Self-Stabilization. MIT Press, Cambridge (2000)

[7] Efraimidis, P., Spirakis, P.G.: Weighted random sampling with a reservoir. Inf. Process. Lett. 97(5), 181–185 (2006)

[8] Ferreira, A.: Building a reference combinatorial model for MANETs. Network 18(5), 24–29 (2004)

[9] Fullmer, C.L., Garcia-Luna-Aceves, J.J.: Solutions to hidden terminal problems in wireless networks. In: SIGCOMM, pp. 39–49 (1997)

[10] Haas, Z.J., Deng, J.: Dual busy tone multiple access (DBTMA)-a multiple access controlscheme for ad hoc networks. IEEE Transactions on Communications 50(6), 975–985 (2002)

[11] Herman, T., Tixeuil, S.: A distributed TDMA slot assignment algorithm for wireless sensor networks. In: Nikoletseas, S.E., Rolim, J.D.P. (eds.) ALGOSENSORS 2004. LNCS, vol. 3121, pp. 45–58. Springer, Heidelberg (2004)

[12] Jarry, A., Lotker, Z.: Connectivity in evolving graph with geometric properties. In: Basagni, S., Phillips, C.A. (eds.) DIALM-POMC, pp. 24–30. ACM, New York (2004)

[13] Jhumka, A., Kulkarni, S.S.: On the design of mobility-tolerant TDMA-based media access control (MAC) protocol for mobile sensor networks. In: Janowski, T., Mohanty, H. (eds.) ICDCIT 2007. LNCS, vol. 4882, pp. 42–53. Springer, Heidelberg (2007)

[14] Leone, P., Papatriantafilou, M., Schiller, E.M.: Relocation adaptive and stable MAC algorithm for large-scale and highly mobile ad hoc networks. Technical Report 2008:23, Department of Computer Science, and Engineering, Chalmers University of Technology (Sweden) (September 2008)

[15] Luby, M.: Removing randomness in parallel computation without a processor penalty. J. Comput. Syst. Sci. 47(2), 250–286 (1993)

[16] Penrose, M.D.: Random Geometric Graphs. Oxford University Press, Oxford (2003)

[17] Schmidt, W.G.: Satellite time-division multiple access systems: Past, present and future. Telecommunications 7, 21–24 (1974)

[18] Schneider, J., Wattenhofer, R.: Coloring Unstructured Wireless Multi-Hop Networks. In: 28th ACM Symposium on Principles of Distributed Computing (PODC), Calgary, Canada (August 2009)

[19] Takagi, H., Kleinrock, L.: Throughput analysis for persistent CSMA systems. IEEE Transactions on Communications 33(7), 627–638 (1985)

[20] Tobagi, F.A., Kleinrock, L.: Packet Switching in Radio Channels: Part II–The Hidden Terminal Problem in CSMA and the Busy-Tone Solution. IEEE Transactions on Communications 23(12), 1417–1433 (1975)

[21] Vizing, V.G.: On an estimate of the chromatic class of a p-graph. Diskret. Analiz 3(7), 25–30 (1964)

[22] Wattenhofer, R.: Ad hoc and sensor networks (hs 2008). Lecture notes/slides (October 2008), http://www.dcg.ethz.ch/lectures/hs08/asn/lecture/6/chapter06mediaaccess.ppt

[23] Yuichi Sudo, J.N., Yamauchi, Y., Ooshita, F., Kakugawa, H., Masuzawa, T.: Loosely-stabilizing Leader Election in Population Protocol Model. In: SIROCCO (to appear, 2009)

Deterministic Collision Free Communication Despite Continuous Motion

Saira Viqar and Jennifer L. Welch

Texas A&M University, USA

Abstract. We present a deterministic solution for nodes in a mobile wireless ad hoc network to communicate reliably and maintain local neighborhood information. The nodes are located on a two-dimensional plane and may be in continuous motion. In our solution we tile the plane with hexagons. Each hexagon is assigned a color from a finite set of colors. Two hexagons of the same color are located sufficiently far apart so that nodes in these two hexagons cannot interfere with each other's broadcasts. Based on this partitioning we develop a periodic deterministic schedule for mobile nodes to broadcast. This schedule guarantees collision avoidance. Broadcast slots are tied to geographic locations instead of nodes and the schedule for a node changes dynamically as it moves from tile to tile. The schedule allows nodes to maintain information about their local neighborhood. This information in turn is used to keep the schedule collision-free. We demonstrate the correctness of our algorithm, and discuss how the periodic schedule can be adapted for different scenarios.

1 Introduction

A mobile ad hoc network (MANET) consists of autonomous mobile computing nodes which communicate with each other through wireless transmissions. The nodes do not have access to a centralized communication infrastructure and have to coordinate their activities in a distributed fashion. The communication medium is shared and hence, only one mobile node in a local neighborhood may broadcast at a particular time. If multiple neighboring nodes broadcast simultaneously then a collision might occur at the receiving node, disrupting the message transmission. Coordinating the broadcasts of such mobile nodes in a distributed way is a non-trivial task. The problem is further complicated by the fact that the nodes may be in continuous motion and hence the local neighborhood topology never stabilizes.

Existing solutions to the problem adopt a probabilistic approach, including the hello protocols (cf. [5]) and reservation based MAC protocols (cf. [4,12]). All of these protocols experience some probability of error, due to collisions in the wireless communication caused by two or more nodes broadcasting at the same time and thus disrupting the receipt of the message. Many applications can tolerate such errors. However, for some real time, mission critical applications, even a small probability of error might have severe penalties. We present

...lev (Ed.): ALGOSENSORS 2009, LNCS 5804, pp. 218–229, 2009.

...ringer-Verlag Berlin Heidelberg 2009

a deterministic collision-free protocol which guarantees reliable communication despite the inherent drawbacks of a wireless ad hoc environment where nodes may be continuously in motion. Our protocol can be used to build a reliable communication infrastructure to meet the requirements of such mission critical applications.

Such a reliable communication infrastructure is of particular importance in applications for vehicular ad hoc networks (VANETs). These applications ensure the safety of drivers by warning them about collisions with other vehicles (cf. [16]) or advising drivers about adverse traffic conditions (e.g., rain, snow and fog). A protocol with deterministic guarantees is essential under such conditions since human life is at stake. It can also be used to relay information from the anti-skid systems and fog-probing radars already present in vehicles to police cars, ambulances, and snowplows (cf. [22]). Our system model which consists of nodes moving arbitrarily on the plane with bounded speed is in accordance with the motion of vehicles on highways, as well as on parallel roads and intersections in urban areas. In addition to VANETs our protocol also has applications in the area of robotic sensor networks [19] used for rescue and reconnaissance missions.

We also address the issue of deterministically maintaining up-to-date information about the local neighborhood of a node. The maintenance of this neighborhood knowledge is a part of our proposed solution and is interleaved with the collision-free schedule. It is also a significant problem in its own right–information about nearby nodes is required for numerous tasks in a mobile ad hoc network. For instance, neighborhood knowledge is needed for routing (cf. [5,18,17]), broadcasting (cf. [6,21,3]), distributed token circulation (cf. [15]), etc.

The main contributions of this research are as follows

1. We develop a reliable communication scheme for mobile nodes which is collision-free.
2. We develop a deterministic technique for mobile nodes to maintain neighborhood knowledge as they move in and out of each others' broadcast range.

The two parts of our scheme mentioned above are interdependent of each other. Thus in our scheme, it is necessary for nodes to possess local neighborhood knowledge to broadcast in a collision-free way. Since nodes can broadcast without having collisions, they can maintain information about their local neighborhood in a timely and efficient way.

Our work focuses on *maintaining* information about neighboring nodes and learning about neighbors as they enter communication range. We do not handle the *initial discovery* of nodes already present in communication range when a node starts up. We assume that nodes acquire this knowledge during an initialization period which is not part of our protocol.

Our work is inspired by that of Ellen *et al.* [7], in which a collision-free schedule is presented for nodes that are restricted to moving along a one-dimensional line (such as along a highway). Their work is particularly relevant for Vehicular Ad Hoc Networks (VANETs) since vehicles often move along highways laid ou* in straight lines. Their results, however, are not applicable to two-dimensior VANETs with multiple lanes, parallel roads and intersections since the nodes

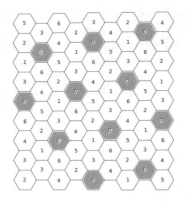

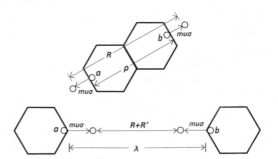

Fig. 1. An example of a partitioning. Hexagons are partitioned into seven classes. Hexagons of the same color or partition broadcast at the same time.

Fig. 2. If a and b are in adjacent hexagons at the beginning of a phase they can receive each other's broadcasts since $\rho + 2mu\sigma \leq R$. On the other hand if c and d are in hexagons allocated the same slot they can broadcast without collision since $\lambda - 2mu\sigma \geq R + R'$.

restricted to one dimension. In this paper we no longer restrict nodes to moving on a one-dimensional straight line and consider the general case of nodes moving arbitrarily on a two-dimensional plane. Hence our work is not only applicable to two-dimensional VANETs but also any other type of two-dimensional MANETs.

In our solution we use a combination of Space Division Multiplexing (SDM) and Time Division Multiplexing (TDMA). For the SDM part of our algorithm we consider the plane to be tiled with hexagons. We partition the hexagons into a finite set of colors such that nodes in different hexagons of the same color cannot interfere with each other's broadcasts. The partitioning is shown in a simple example in Figure 1. The partitioning allows nodes in different geographic locations to broadcast simultaneously without collisions. We also take into consideration the fact that nodes may be in motion as they broadcast. Based on this partitioning, we develop an efficient periodic deterministic schedule for mobile nodes to transmit which guarantees collision avoidance. The schedule is based on TDMA and ensures that nodes in different colored hexagons never broadcast at the same time. The schedule ensures that every node learns about other nodes before they have entered a certain distance inside its broadcast radius.

2   Related Work

Much of the previous work on collision-free broadcasting in wireless ad hoc networks assumes static nodes. The algorithm of Gandhi *et al.* constructs a broadcast tree [8] and uses it to schedule transmissions without collisions in a static wireless network; however in dynamic network topologies, construction and maintenance of a broadcast tree is not efficient. Prabh *et al.* also present a distributed scheduling algorithm for hexagonal wireless ad hoc networks in which nodes remain static [20]. The algorithm provides network-wide conflict-free packet transmission with guaranteed transmission latency. They assume that there is a base station or sink at the center of the network and focus on many to one communication.

Certain protocols which handle node mobility rely on the presence of centralized infrastructure. For example Arumugam *et al.* give a self-stabilizing, deterministic TDMA algorithm for sensor networks [1]. The addition and removal of sensors is allowed, however, they assume the presence of a base station which maintains a spanning tree of the network and is responsible for token circulation. There is no discussion of how the algorithm would behave if the nodes were in continuous motion. Like our work they also assume that time synchronization is present during token circulation. Local neighborhood knowledge is also assumed.

In [13] the authors assume that the sensors are located exactly at the points of a regular lattice. For mobile sensors they suggest that the lattice points should be spaced finely enough so that just one sensor is within the Voronoi region of a single lattice point. However they do not consider the case of sensors crossing the boundaries of Voronoi regions while they transmit. Furthermore, making the lattice points closer together would lead to a highly inefficient schedule with a very large number of transmission slots. In [2] Baldoni *et al.* consider a model in which nodes can move arbitrarily on the plane with a bound on the speed. They present bounds for the speed of nodes in relation to the speed of information propagation. However, they do not give a constructive solution to the problem of collision-free communication among mobile nodes. In [11] Ioannidou presents a model for mobile ad hoc networks based on tiling the plane with hexagons, and use it to implement dynamic quorum systems. The hexagons are assumed to be surrounded by circles called camases, which represent bounds on how far nodes can travel within a particular interval of time. However, the authors assume that there is no interference in the network, that is, collision avoidance is performed by a lower layer of the network.

3   Definitions

We consider a set of n nodes which move on a two-dimensional plane. Each mobile node has a unique identifier from a set I. This set is bounded in size. The mobile nodes may fail at any time. We only consider crash failures. For each node there is a trajectory function which specifies the motion of the node by giving the location of the node on the plane at every time. We assume that a node's trajectory remains constant for a certain fixed interval of time (this interval is defined in the next section). The maximum speed of the nodes has an upper bound given by σ.

Communication between nodes takes place through wireless broadcast. The transmission radius of the wireless network is given by R and the interference radius is given by R'. If we consider two nodes p and p' such that p broadcasts and p' remains within distance R of p during the broadcast, then the message sent by p will *arrive* at p'. If there is no other transmitting node within interference radius R' of p' during the broadcast slot of p the message will be *received* by p' and p' successfully learns the contents of the message.

Each node has access to the current time (through GPS etc.). Hence, its location at a particular time can be determined from its trajectory function. Notice that the presence of a GPS device is a realistic assumption for vehicular ad hoc networks. Nodes begin transmitting at fixed intervals of time. A *broadcast slot* is the time it takes for a node to complete its transmission so that its message arrives at all nodes in broadcast range.

We assume there exists an upper bound on the number of nodes per unit area. This upper bound on the density of nodes is realistic since nodes cannot be infinitely small in size.

3.1   Problem Definition

The aim of this work is to provide a deterministic collision-free schedule for mobile nodes such that every node gets infinitely many opportunities to broadcast. This schedule can serve as the Medium Access Control (MAC) layer for mobile ad hoc networks where nodes may be in continuous motion for long periods of time.

4   Algorithm Overview

In our solution we assume that the plane is tiled with hexagons. Our choice of hexagons is based on two factors. Hexagons can form a regular tiling of the plane, and they give a good approximation of the circular broadcast range of wireless nodes.

In our algorithm mobile nodes are dynamically scheduled to broadcast depending on the geographic location of the tile they occupy at a particular instant of time. The size of these hexagonal tiles depends on the broadcast radius R of the mobile nodes. Roughly we require that R spans a little more than two tiles. This ensures that nodes in adjacent hexagons are within each others' broadcast radius.

A set of m contiguous hexagonal tiles are grouped together to form a *supertile*. Each tile in a supertile is assigned a different color. These supertiles also tile the plane. Corresponding hexagons which lie at the same position in two different supertiles share the same color and are scheduled to broadcast simultaneously. By carefully selecting the number of tiles m in a supertile and its shape, we ensure that tiles of the same color in adjacent supertiles are located far enough apart, so that nodes in these tiles can broadcast simultaneously without causing a collision at any receiving node. Note that collision-freedom is ensured despite the fact that the nodes maybe in continuous motion while they broadcast.

The choice of m depends on the actual values of the broadcast radius R, the interference radius R', and the upper bound σ on the maximum speed of the nodes. Roughly, the supertile should be large enough so that nodes in tiles assigned the same color remain more than $R + R'$ apart, even if they are moving straight toward each other. We assume that the tiling of the plane and the assignment of colors to tiles is predetermined and known to all the mobile nodes advance. Tiling the plane in this way is a form of space division multiplexing

(SDM) since the mobile nodes are separated in space to prevent interference. In addition to this, we perform Time Division Multiplexing inside the hexagons and the supertiles. A fixed number of broadcast slots (given by u) are grouped together to form a *round*. Each round corresponds to one hexagon, and is the time allocated to all the nodes in one hexagon to schedule their broadcasts. In order to cover all the hexagons in one supertile we then require m rounds; one for each color. We define this as one *phase*. The length of one phase is then equal to mu broadcast slots. The assignment of the m rounds in a phase to different colored tiles forms an ordering of the colors with respect to time. Note that the ordering of colors can change from phase to phase depending on the *schedule*. In Section 6 we discuss different types of schedules.

Slots are allocated to mobile nodes only at the beginning of every phase. Hence at the start of every phase a mobile node determines the color of the hexagonal tile it is located in. It can then determine which one of the m rounds in that phase it should broadcast in. Furthermore, at the start of every phase, a mobile node possesses knowledge about all other nodes present in its own tile (owing to the maintenance of local neighborhood knowledge). Specifically it is aware of the identifiers of these nodes. Based on the rank of its own identifier in this set of identifiers, it can select one of the u slots in its round, to carry out its broadcast. Hence, at the start of a phase, every node in every tile knows exactly which slot to broadcast in. Note that we assume that the maximum number of nodes that can occupy a tile at any instant is bounded by $v < u$. This allows us to have fixed length rounds and phases. The first v slots of a round are used by the nodes to perform broadcasts. The remaining $u - v$ slots can be used by other protocols or applications.

As mentioned earlier, the size of the tiles and supertiles is also influenced by σ, the upper bound on node speed, because σ determines the maximum distance that a node can travel in one phase. Since the length of a phase is mu slots, this distance is given by $mu\sigma$. We require that R should be larger than the diameter of two tiles by at least $2mu\sigma$. We also require that tiles of the same color be separated at least by $R + R'$ in addition to $2mu\sigma$. Suppose that a node moves out of its tile before its turn to broadcast in a phase. These constraints will ensure that its broadcast still reaches its neighbors, without causing a collision. In essence, the broadcasts of all the nodes in one supertile are separated in time and cannot interfere. Only nodes present in all tiles of the same color throughout the plane broadcast simultaneously. However, these nodes are always sufficiently separated and cannot interfere with each others' broadcasts.

The pseudocode for the algorithm is given below. The function *clock*() returns the current time, and *location*() returns the current location of the node. The function *findColor*() takes as argument the location of the node. It uses the fixed division of the plane into tiles and supertiles to determine which color tile the node is located in. A node includes its trajectory function in its broadcast packet so that neighbors can calculate the location of the node at the beginning of the next phase. We assume that a node's trajectory remains unchanged for the duration of at least one phases. This is to ensure that neighbors can have up t date information about a node's trajectory until it broadcasts new informatic

---

Algorithm 1. Code for node p

---

id {node p's id}

$trajectory$ {p's trajectory}

N {set of "neighboring" nodes; initially contains all nodes within p's broadcast radius; each entry q consists of $q.id$ and $q.trajectory$}

S {set of nodes that might become neighbors; initially empty; candidates are collected during each phase}

when $receive\ a\ message(id, trajectory)\ from\ node\ q$
    $S := S \cup < id, trajectory >$

when $clock() = \pi mu$, for some integer π {the beginning of phase π}
    $N := \emptyset$ {N is the set of neighbors of a node}
    $loc := location()$ {(x, y) coordinates, based on p's trajectory and current time}
    $hex := findHex(loc)$ {calculate hexagon containing loc}
    $color := findColor(hex)$ {calculate color of hexagon(expressed as an integer)}
    $\forall p \in S$ {update neighbor set}
        if $(p.trajectory(\pi mu) \in Hex(loc))$ {determine neighbors}
            $N := N \cup p$ {N is the set of neighbors}
    $i := getRank(N)$ {get rank of p's id in set N; smallest id in N has rank 1, etc.}
    $slot := color + (i - 1)$ {this is the slot to broadcast in}
    $S := \emptyset$

when $clock()\ mod\ mu = slot$ {time to broadcast}
    $broadcast(id, trajectory)$

---

5   Analysis

5.1   Collision Avoidance

We require the following constraint (C1) for collision avoidance (see Figure 2).

C1. Let the minimum distance between simultaneously transmitting hexagons be λ. Then we require $\lambda - 2mu\sigma \geq R + R'$.

The following lemma (whose proof is omitted due to space constraints) shows that under constraint (C1) the algorithm ensures collision avoidance. Consider two nodes present right at the boundary of different hexagons of the same color at the beginning of a phase. They are separated only by the minimum possible distance (λ). Even if they are moving directly toward each other throughout the current phase, their broadcasts will not cause a collision. Hence, a node can cross the boundary of its original hexagon during a phase safely (without causing collisions). This property is maintained from phase to phase.

Lemma 1. *If (C1) holds then every broadcast that arrives at a node is received.*

5.2   Maintenance of Neighborhood Knowledge

We assume that at start-up all nodes have information about nodes within their ⁓oadcast radius, that is all nodes know the trajectory function of nodes that within their broadcast radius. This is stated in assumption (A1).

A1. At the beginning of phase 0, every node knows about every other node within distance R of itself.

We introduce constraint (C2) in order to ensure the maintenance of neighborhood knowledge (see Figure 2). Lemma 2 shows that nodes maintain knowledge about nodes in their own and adjacent hexagons. The proof is omitted due to limited space.

C2. Let the distance between the farthest points on the boundary of adjacent hexagons be equal to ρ. We require that $\rho + 2mu\sigma \leq R$.

Lemma 2. *If assumption (A1) and constraints (C1) and (C2) hold, then at the beginning of each phase π ($\pi \geq 0$) of Algorithm 1 every node knows about every node that is in its own or an adjacent hexagon.*

6   Schedules

A *schedule* defines the order in which the rounds are allocated to different colored tiles in a supertile. A schedule can span multiple phases, and each phase can have a different ordering of the m colors. We define a schedule to be *periodic* if the sequence of colors repeats after a fixed number of phases. For a particular execution of the algorithm the schedule for all supertiles is the same and known *a priori*. In this section we present a general framework for schedules in terms of liveness, fairness, and directional bias; these terms are defined subsequently. We also discuss the advantages of particular schedules through examples.

A particular execution of the algorithm is defined to be *safe* if no collisions occur during the entire execution. The constraints that we have discussed so far ensure safety. In particular the distribution of colors on the plane avoids inter-tile collisions, whereas neighborhood knowledge together with the TDMA performed in each round prevents intra-tile collisions. In order to ensure *liveness* during an execution we require the following condition: *Every color present in a supertile is allocated at least one round in the schedule.* Furthermore in order to ensure *fairness* we require the following: *Each color is allocated the same number of rounds in the schedule.*

A schedule is defined to have *directional bias* if it favors the propagation of information in one particular direction. We start by considering schedules with a time period equal to one phase. In such schedules each color is allocated exactly one round during one phase and the sequence of colors is the same for every phase. However, such schedules can suffer from directional bias. The following example illustrates this. Suppose that we have a schedule in which slots are allocated from left to right and top to bottom in a supertile in one phase. This schedule is biased in favor of propagating information rightwards. A similar argument holds for information traveling downwards. Consider the horizontal *path* b shown in Figure 3. Suppose that information has to travel on this path from one node to another in the rightward direction. The information will propagate at a rate of one supertile per phase. Now suppose that the information has

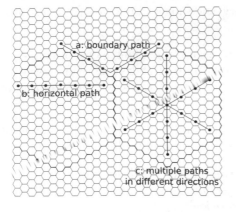

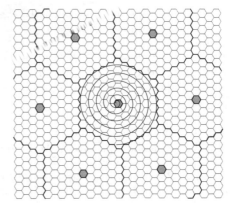

Fig. 3. Information should flow on all paths without directional bias

Fig. 4. An example of the network division into regions where $m=91$

travel leftwards. This will occur at a rate of only one hop per phase which is considerably slower. So the schedule is biased in favor of the information traveling rightwards and downwards. This shows that a schedule which is optimal for a certain path may perform poorly for some other path.

We can modify the schedule depending on the requirements of the application. For example for VANETs with parallel roads we can have alternating left to right and right to left allocation of rounds along each road, depending how the road traverses a supertile. Instead of delving into the requirements of particular applications, however, we construct a generalized schedule which is neutral in terms of directional bias.

In order to avoid the above mentioned directional bias we consider cases where the time period is more than one phase. Hence, the order in which rounds are allocated to colors can change from phase to phase. We seek a schedule that is efficient and that is not biased toward speeding up information propagation in one direction at the expense of another direction. From the above examples it is clear that we should alternate between all directions in order to have an unbiased schedule. Consider the paths in example c shown in Figure 3. The schedule should favor propagation along all six paths from the center equally. The most obvious way this can be achieved is if we allocate slots in a circular fashion. We can allocate slots in a supertile in concentric circles, starting from the center of the supertile going toward its boundaries, in one phase. This enables the propagation of information from the center of the supertile toward its boundaries. In the next phase we can allocate slots starting at the boundaries of the supertile, going toward the center. This will facilitate the propagation of information toward the center of the supertile. The reason that we alternate between inward and outward phases is to allow information to pass quickly along paths such as *path a* in Figure 3. If we did not alternate and had only inwards phases then the first half of this path would take one phase, whereas as the second half would require ne phase for every hop and vice versa.

Finally the phases alternate between anticlockwise phases and clockwise phases. The motivation for this is demonstrated by *path b* in Figure 3. The clockwise phase will allow efficient propagation from left to right whereas the anticlockwise phase will allow efficient propagation from right to left. The resulting schedule consists of a allocation of broadcast slots in concentric circles in which the hexagons take turns in one phase going in a clockwise manner outwards and in the next phase going anticlockwise inwards. The next two phases follow an anticlockwise outwards pattern and a clockwise inwards pattern. The periodicity of this final schedule is four phases. This schedule is depicted in Figure 4.

6.1   An Example of the Network Tiling

In this section we show that the schedule developed above is practically feasible, under the given constraints. We use the default values for R (the broadcast radius) and R'(the interference radius) given in the IEEE 802.11 standard [10] which are 250 meters and 550 meters respectively. Suppose we take the duration of a phase to be equal to 100 milliseconds, and σ to be equal to 200 km per hour. This is a reasonable assumption for VANETs. Using these values, we can show that the maximum distance that a node can travel in one phase is 5.55 meters ≤ 6 meters, which we take as the value of $mu\sigma$. We want to maximize the size of the hexagons so that we can have fewer hexagons in between two hexagons which are allocated slots at the same time. This will allow us to minimize m and have fewer broadcast slots in one phase. Hence, taking $\rho + 2mu\sigma = 250$ meters we calculate the side of a hexagon (given by s) to be equal to 65.8 meters. From constraint (C1) we know that $\lambda \geq R + R' + 2mu\sigma = 250 + 550 + 12 = 812$ meters. The distance between two hexagons of the same color has to be greater than or equal to $\lambda = 812$ meters. To calculate the distance in terms of s the side of a hexagon, we divide by $s = 65.8$, hence $\lceil 812/65.8 \rceil = 13$. Therefore the distance between hexagons of the same color should be greater than or equal to 13 times the side of a hexagon. An example of such a tiling of the network is given in Figure 4. Here each region consists of 91 hexagons, hence $m = 91$. This tiling is formed with regions which consist of concentric rings of hexagons and may not be optimal in terms of m for the given values of R and R'. However, the shape of the regions is relatively regular, which makes it easier to formulate a schedule and perform analysis. Note that using the final schedule given in Section 6 each node gets to transmit once during a phase.

7   Conclusions

In this paper we have presented a deterministic schedule for nodes in a MANET, which avoids collisions and allows nodes to maintain information about neighboring nodes. It remains open to analyze the rate of information propagation in our schedule. Our scheme does not provide a means for nodes to gain knowledge about neighbors already inside the broadcast radius when a node starts up. This would be a slow and expensive process, as shown by the $(N - n)A$ lo bound in [14] (here N is the size of the namespace of node identifiers, n is the number of nodes, and A is the maximum size of the channel set available to a node). For vehicular ad hoc networks using vehicle identification numbers as identifiers, the size of the name space is prohibitively large. We are also assuming that the nodes are mobile, which raises further issues. Whether it is possible to gain knowledge efficiently about neighbors deterministically for mobile nodes remains an open question. In the context of vehicular networks, surrounding roadside infrastructure could be used to provide knowledge about neighbors at startup. It would be of interest to incorporate an initialization period into the scheme during which a node discovers existing neighbors and from which a node could transition into the above schedule without causing disruptions. Perhaps it is possible to quantify the trade off between the amount of initial knowledge required and the time needed to get started. More generally, it would be of interest to explore the fundamental limitations of deterministic solutions through lower bounds on performance or impossibility results.

Acknowledgments

We thank Hyun-Chul Chung, Srikanth Sastry, and the reviewers for helpful comments. This work was supported in part by NSF grant 0500265 and THECB grants 00512-0007-2006 and 000512-0130-2007.

References

1. Arumugam, M., Kulkarni, S.S.: Self-Stabilizing Deterministic TDMA for Sensor Networks. In: International Conference on Distributed Computing and Internet Technologies, pp. 69–81 (2005)
2. Baldoni, R., Ioannidou, K., Milani, A.: Mobility Versus the Cost of Geocasting in Mobile Ad-Hoc Networks. In: Pelc, A. (ed.) DISC 2007. LNCS, vol. 4731, pp. 48–62. Springer, Heidelberg (2007)
3. Bar-Yehuda, R., Goldreich, O., Itai, A.: On the Time Complexity of Broadcast in Multi-Hop Radio Networks: An Exponential Gap Between Determinism and Randomization. J. Computer Systems and Sciences 45(1), 104–126 (1992)
4. Bharghavan, V., Demers, A., Shenker, S., Zhang, L.: MACAW: A Media Access Protocol for Wireless LANs. In: ACM SIGCOMM, Conference on Communications Architectures, Protocols, and Applications, pp. 212–225 (1994)
5. Broch, J., Maltz, D.A., Johnson, D.B., Hu, Y.C., Jetcheva, J.: A Performance Comparison of Multi-Hop Wireless Ad Hoc Network Routing Protocols. In: ACM/IEEE International Conference on Mobile Computing and Networking, pp. 85–97 (1998)
6. Bruschi, D., Pinto, M.D.: Lower Bounds for the Broadcast Problem in Mobile Radio Networks. Distributed Computing 10(3), 129–135 (1997)
7. Ellen, F., Subramanian, S., Welch, J.L.: Maintaining Information About Nearby Processors in a Mobile Environment. In: Chaudhuri, S., Das, S.R., Paul, H.S., Tirthapura, S. (eds.) ICDCN 2006. LNCS, vol. 4308, pp. 193–202. Springer, Heidelberg (2006)
8. Gandhi, R., Parthasarathy, S., Mishra, A.: Minimizing Broadcast Latency and Redundancy in Ad Hoc Networks. In: 4th ACM International Symposium on Mobile Ad Hoc Networking and Computing, pp. 222–232 (2003)

9. Greenberg, A.G., Winograd, S.: A Lower Bound on the Time Needed to Resolve Conflicts Deterministically in Multiple Access Channels. Journal of the ACM 32(3), 589–596 (1985)
10. IEEE 802.11, IEEE Standard for Information technology-Telecommunications and information exchange between systems-Local and metropolitan area networks-Specific requirements - Part 11: Wireless LAN MAC and PHY Specifications (2007)
11. Ioannidou, K.: Dynamic Quorum Systems in Mobile Ad-Hoc Networks. PhD. Thesis, Department of Computer Science, University of Toronto (2006)
12. Karn, P.: MACA - A New Channel Access Method for Packet Radio. In: ARRL/CRRL Amateur Radio 9th Computer Networking Conference, pp. 134–140 (1990)
13. Klappenecker, A., Lee, H., Welch, J.L.: Scheduling Sensors by Tiling Lattices. submitted for publication
14. Krishnamurthy, S., Thoppian, M.R., Kuppa, S., Chandrasekaran, R., Mittal, N., Venkatesan, S., Prakash, R.: Time-efficient distributed layer-2 auto-configuration for cognitive radio networks. Computer Networks: The International Journal of Computer and Telecommunications Networking 52(4), 831–849 (2008)
15. Malpani, N., Chen, Y., Vaidya, N., Welch, J.L.: Distributed Token Circulation in Mobile Ad Hoc Networks. IEEE Transactions on Mobile Computing 4(2), 154–165 (2005)
16. Misener, J., Sengupta, R., Krishnan, H.: Cooperative Collision Warning: Enabling Crash Avoidance with Wireless Technology. In: 12th World Congress on ITS (2005)
17. Park, V., Corson, M.: A Highly Adaptive Distributed Routing Algorithm for Mobile Ad Hoc Networks. In: IEEE INFOCOM, The Conference on Computer Communications, Sixteenth Annual Joint Conference of the IEEE Computer and Communications Societies, Driving the Information Revolution, pp. 1405–1413 (1997)
18. Perkins, C., Royer, E.: Ad-hoc On-Demand Distance Vector Routing. In: 2nd Workshop on Mobile Computing Systems and Applications, pp. 90–100 (1999)
19. Petriu, E., Whalen, T., Abielmona, R., Stewart, A.: Robotic Sensor Agents: a New Generation of Intelligent Agents for Complex Environment Monitoring. IEEE Magazine on Instrumentation and Measurement 7(3), 46–51 (2004)
20. Prabh, K., Abdelzaher, T.: On Scheduling and Real-Time Capacity of Hexagonal Wireless Sensor Networks. In: 19th Euromicro Conference on Real-Time Systems, pp. 136–145 (2007)
21. Prakash, R., Schiper, A., Mohsin, M., Cavin, D., Sasson, Y.: A Lower Bound for Broadcasting in Mobile Ad Hoc Networks. EPFL Technical report, IC/2004/37 (2004)
22. Wald, L.: When the Roads Talk, Your Car Can Listen. The New York Times, October 30 (2008)

Self-stabilizing Deterministic Gathering

Yoann Dieudonné[1] and Franck Petit[2]

[1] MIS CNRS, Université de Picardie Jules Verne Amiens, France
[2] INRIA, LIP UMR 5668, Université de Lyon / ENS Lyon, France

Abstract. In this paper, we investigate the possibility to deterministically solve the gathering problem (GP) with weak robots (anonymous, autonomous, disoriented, oblivious, deaf, and dumb). We introduce strong multiplicity detection as the ability for the robots to detect the exact number of robots located at a given position. We show that with strong multiplicity detection, there exists a deterministic self-stabilizing algorithm solving GP for n robots if, and only if, n is odd.

Keywords: Distributed Coordination, Gathering, Mobile Robot Networks, Self-stabilization.

1 Introduction

The distributed systems considered in this paper are teams (or swarms) of *mobile robots* (sensors or agents). Such systems supply the ability to collect (to sense) environmental data such as temperature, sound, vibration, pressure, motion, etc. The robots use these sensory data as an input in order to act in a given (sometimes dangerous) physical environment. Numerous potential applications exist for such multi-robot systems, *e.g.*, environmental monitoring, large-scale construction, risky area surrounding, exploration of an unknown area. All these applications involve basic cooperative tasks such as pattern formation, gathering, scatter, leader election, flocking, etc.

Among the above fundamental coordination tasks, we address the *gathering* (or *Rendez-Vous*) problem. This problem can be stated as follows: robots, initially located at various positions, gather at the same position in finite time and remain at this position thereafter. The difficulty to solve this problem greatly depends on the system settings, *e.g.*, whether the robots can remember past events or not, their means of communication, their ability to share a global property like observable IDs, sense of direction, global coordinate, etc. For instance, assuming that the robots share a common global coordinate system or have (observable) IDs allowing to differentiate any of them, it is easy to come up with a deterministic distributed algorithm for that problem. Gathering turns out to be very difficult to solve with *weak* robots, *i.e.*, devoid of (1) any (observable) IDs allowing to differentiate any of them (*anonymous*), (2) any central coordination mechanism or scheduler (*autonomous*), (3) any common coordinate mechanism or common sense of direction (*disoriented*), (4) means of communication allowing them to communicate directly, *e.g.*, by radio frequency (*deaf and dumb*), and (5) any way to remember any previous observation nor computation performed

S. Dolev (Ed.): ALGOSENSORS 2009, LNCS 5804, pp. 230–241, 2009.
© Springer-Verlag Berlin Heidelberg 2009

in any previous step (*oblivious*). Every movement made by a robot is then the result of a computation having observed positions of the other robots as a only possible input. With such settings, assuming that robots are points evolving on the plane, no solution exists for the gathering problem if the system contains two robots only [19]. It is also shown in [15] that gathering can be solved only if the robots have the capability to know whether several robots are located at the same position (*multiplicity detection*). Note that a *strong* form of such an ability is that the robot are able to count the exact number of robots located at the same position. A *weaker* form consists in considering the detector as an abstract device able to say if any robot location contains either exactly one or more than one robot.

In this paper, we investigate the possibility to *deterministically* solve the gathering problem with *weak robots* (*i.e.*, anonymous, autonomous, disoriented, oblivious, deaf, and dumb). This problem has been extensively studied in the literature assuming various settings. For instance, the robots move either among the nodes of a graph [11,13], or in the plane [1,2,4,12,14,15,19], their visibility can be limited (visibility sensors are supposed to be accurate within a constant range, and sense nothing beyond this range) [12,17], robots are prone to faults [1,7].

In this paper, we address the stabilization aspect of the gathering problem. A deterministic system is (self-)stabilizing if, regardless of the initial states of the computing units, it is guaranteed to converge to the intended behavior in a finite number of steps [9]. To our best knowledge, all the above solutions assume that in the initial configuration, no two robots are located at the same position. So, effectively, as already noticed in [6,8], this implies that none of them is "truly" self-stabilizing—initial configurations where robots are located at the same positions are avoided. Note that surprisingly, such an assumption prevents to initiate the system where the problem is solved, *i.e.*, initially all the robots occupy the same position.

In this paper, we study the gathering problem assuming any arbitrary initial configurations, that is in which some robots can share the same positions. Clearly, assuming weak multiplicity detection (each robot location contains either exactly one or more than one robot), the problem cannot be solved deterministically. Informally, if all the robots are at exactly two positions, then there is no way to maintain a particular position as an invariant. So, there are some executions where the system behaves as if it contains exactly two robots, leading to the impossibility result in [19]. We introduce the concept of strong multiplicity detection—the robot are able to count the exact number of robots located at the same position. Even with such capability, the problem cannot be solved deterministically, if the number of robots is even. The proof is similar as above: If initially the robots occupy exactly two positions, then there is no way to maintain a particular position as an invariant. Again, the impossibility result in [19] holds. By contrast, we show that with an odd number of robots, the problem is solvable. Our proof is constructive, as we present and prove a deterministic algorithm for that problem. The proposed solution has the nice property of being self-stabilizing since no initial configuration is excluded.

In the next section (Section 2), we describe the distributed system and the problem we consider in this paper. Our main result with its proof is given in Section 3 — due to the lack of space, some of the proofs are omitted. We conclude this paper in Section 4. Due to the lack of space, some proofs have been moved in the Annexes section.

Preliminaries

In this section, we define the distributed system and the problem considered in this paper.

2.1   Distributed Model

We adopt the semi-synchronous model introduced in [18], below referred to as *SSM*. The *distributed system* considered in this paper consists of n robots $r_1, r_2, \cdots, r_n$—the subscripts $1, \ldots, n$ are used for notational purpose only. Each robot r_i, viewed as a point in the Euclidean plane, moves on this two-dimensional space unbounded and devoid of any landmark. It is assumed that two or more robots may simultaneously occupy the same physical location.

Any robot can observe, compute and move with infinite decimal precision. The robots are equipped with sensors enabling to detect the instantaneous position of the other robots in the plane. In particular, we distinguish two types of multiplicity detection: *weak multiplicity detection* and *strong multiplicity detection*.

Definition 1 (Weak multiplicity detection). *[4,10] The robots have weak multiplicity detection if, for every point p, their sensors can detect if there is no robot, there is one robot, or there are more than one robot. In the latter case, the robot might not be capable of determining the exact number of robots.*

Definition 2 (Strong multiplicity detection). *The robots have strong multiplicity detection if, for every point p, their sensors can detect the number of robots on p.*

Each robot has its own local coordinate system and unit measure. The robots do not agree on the orientation of the axes of their local coordinate system, nor on the unit measure. They are *uniform* and *anonymous*, i.e, they all have the same program using no local parameter (such that an identity) allowing to differentiate any of them. They communicate only by observing the position of the others and they are *oblivious*, i.e., none of them can remember any previous observation nor computation performed in any previous step.

Time is represented as an infinite sequence of time instants $0, 1, \ldots, j, \ldots$ Let $\mathcal{P}(t)$ be the set of the positions in the plane occupied by the n robots at time t. For every t, $\mathcal{P}(t)$ is called the *configuration* of the distributed system in t. Given any point p, $|p|$ denotes the number of robots located at p. $\mathcal{P}(t)$ expressed in the local coordinate system of any robot r_i is called a *view*. At each time instant t, each robot r_i is either *active* or *inactive*. The former means that, during the computation *step* $(t, t+1)$, using a given algorithm, r_i computes in its local coordinate system a position $p_i(t+1)$ depending only on the system configuration at t, and moves towards $p_i(t+1)$—$p_i(t+1)$ can be equal to $p_i(t)$, making the location of r_i unchanged. In the latter case, r_i does not perform any local computation and remains at the same position. In every single activation, the distance traveled by any robot r is bounded by σ_r. So, if the destination point computed by r is farther than σ_r, then r moves toward a point of at most σ_r. This distance may be different between two robots.

The concurrent activation of robots is modeled by the interleaving model in which the robot activations are driven by a *fair scheduler*. At each instant t, the scheduler arbitrarily activates a (non empty) set of robots. Fairness means that every robot is infinitely often activated by the scheduler.

2.2   Specification

The *Gathering Problem* ($\mathcal{GP}$) is to design a distributed protocol P for n mobile robots so that the following properties are true :

- *Convergence*: Regardless of the initial positions of the robots on the plane, all the robots are located at the same position in finite time.
- *Closure*: Starting from a configuration where all the robots are located at the same position, all the robots are located at the same position thereafter.

3   Gathering with Strong Multiplicity Detection

In this section, we prove the following theorem:

Theorem 1. *With strong multiplicity detection, there exists a deterministic self-stabilizing algorithm solving $\mathcal{GP}$ for n robots if, and only if, n is odd.*

As mentioned in the introduction, even with strong multiplicity detection there do not exist any deterministic algorithm solving $\mathcal{GP}$ for an even number of robots. So, to prove Theorem 1 we first give a deterministic self-stabilizing algorithm solving $\mathcal{GP}$ for an odd number of robots having the strong multiplicity detection. Then, we prove the correctness of the algorithm.

3.1   Deterministic Self-stabilizing Algorithm for an Odd Number of Robots

In this subsection, we give a deterministic self-stabilizing algorithm solving $\mathcal{GP}$ for an odd number of robots. We first provide particular notations, basic definitions and properties. Next, the protocol is presented.

Notations, Basic Definitions and Properties. Given a configuration $\mathcal{P}$, $Max\mathcal{P}$ indicates the set of all the points p such that $|p|$ is maximal. In other terms, $\forall p_i \in Max\mathcal{P}$ and $\forall p_j \in \mathcal{P}$, we have $|p_i| \geq |p_j|$. $|Max\mathcal{P}|$ will be the cardinality of $Max\mathcal{P}$.

Remark 1. Since the robots have the strong multiplicity detection, then they are able to compute $|p|$ for every point $p \in \mathcal{P}$. In particular, all the robots can determine $Max\mathcal{P}(t)$ at each time instant t.

Given three distinct points r, r' and c in the plane, we say that the two half-lines $[c, r)$ and $[c, r')$ divide the plane into two *sectors* if and only if

- either r, r' and c are not collinear,
- or r, r' and c are collinear and c is between r and r' on the segment $[r, r']$.

If it exists then this pair of sectors is denoted by $\{\underline{rcr'}, \overline{rcr'}\}$ and we assume that the two half-lines $[c, r)$ and $[c, r')$ do not belong to any sector in $\{\underline{rcr'}, \overline{rcr'}\}$. Note that, if the three points r, r' and c are not collinear then one of two sectors is *convex* (angle centered at c between r and $r' \leq 180^{\circ}$) and the other one is *concave* (angle centered at c between r and $r' > 180^{\circ}$). Otherwise, the three points r, r' and c are collinear and the two sectors are convex and more precisely they are *straight* (both conjugate angles centered at c between r and r' are equal to 180°).

Definition 3 (Smallest enclosing circle). *[6] Given a set $\mathcal{P}$ of $n \geq 2$ points $p_1, p_2, \cdots, p_n$ on the plane, the smallest enclosing circle of $\mathcal{P}$, called $SEC(\mathcal{P})$, is the smallest circle enclosing all the positions in $\mathcal{P}$. It passes either through two of the positions that are on the same diameter (opposite positions), or through at least three of the positions in $\mathcal{P}$.*

When no ambiguity arises, $SEC(\mathcal{P})$ will be shortly denoted by SEC and $SEC(\mathcal{P}) \cap \mathcal{P}$ will indicate the set of all the points both on $SEC(\mathcal{P})$ and $\mathcal{P}$. Besides, we will say that a robot r is inside SEC if, and only if, there is not located on the circumference of SEC. In any configuration $\mathcal{P}$, SEC is unique and can be computed in linear time [3].

Given a set $\mathcal{P}$ of $n \geq 2$ points $p_1, p_2, \cdots, p_n$ on the plane and $SEC(\mathcal{P})$ its smallest enclosing circle, $\mathcal{R}ad(SEC(\mathcal{P}))$ will indicate the length of the radius of $SEC(\mathcal{P})$.

The next lemma contains a simple fact.

Lemma 1. *Let $\mathcal{P}_1$ be an arbitrary configuration of n points. Let $\mathcal{P}_2$ be a configuration obtained by pushing inside $SEC(\mathcal{P}_1)$ all the points which are in $\mathcal{P}_1 \cap SEC(\mathcal{P}_1)$. We have $\mathcal{R}ad(SEC(\mathcal{P}_2)) < \mathcal{R}ad(SEC(\mathcal{P}_1))$.*

Let $\mathcal{S}$ and C be respectively a sector in $\{\underline{pcp'}, \overline{pcp'}\}$ and a circle centered at c. We denote by $arc(C, \mathcal{S})$ the arc of the circle C inside $\mathcal{S}$. Given a set $\mathcal{P}$ of $n \geq 2$ points $p_1, p_2, \cdots, p_n$ on the plane and $SEC(\mathcal{P})$ its smallest enclosing circle centered at c, we say that p and p' are *adjacent on $SEC(\mathcal{P})$* if, and only if, p and p' are in $\mathcal{P}$ and there exists one sector $\mathcal{S} \in \{\underline{pcp'}, \overline{pcp'}\}$ such that there is no point in $arc(SEC(\mathcal{P}), \mathcal{S}) \cap \mathcal{P}$.

The following property is fundamental about smallest enclosing circles

Property 1. [5] Let $\mathcal{P}$ and c be respectively a set of $n \geq 2$ points $p_1, p_2, \cdots, p_n$ on the plane and the center of $SEC(\mathcal{P})$. If p and p' are *adjacent on $SEC(\mathcal{P})$* then, there does not exist a concave sector $\mathcal{S}$ in $\{\underline{pcp'}, \overline{pcp'}\}$ such that there is no point in $arc(SEC(\mathcal{P}), \mathcal{S}) \cap \mathcal{P}$.

Property 2 is more general than Property 1

Property 2. Let $\mathcal{P}$ and c be respectively a set of $n \geq 2$ points $p_1, p_2, \cdots, p_n$ o
the plane and the center of $SEC(\mathcal{P})$. If p and p' are in $\mathcal{P}$ then, there does not
exist a concave sector $\mathcal{S}$ in $\{\underline{pcp'}, \overline{pcp'}\}$ such that there is no point in $\mathcal{S} \cap \mathcal{P}$.

Proof. Assume by contradiction that p and p' are in $\mathcal{P}$ and, there exists a
concave sector $\mathcal{S}$ in $\{\underline{pcp'}, \overline{pcp'}\}$ such that there is no point in $\mathcal{S} \cap \mathcal{P}$. So, there is
no point in $arc(SEC(\mathcal{P}), \mathcal{S}) \cap \mathcal{P}$. We deduce that there exists a concave sector
$\mathcal{S}'$ in $\{\underline{qcq'}, \overline{qcq'}\}$ such that q and q' are adjacent on $SEC(\mathcal{P})$ and there is no
point in $arc(SEC(\mathcal{P}), \mathcal{S}') \cap \mathcal{P}$. Contradiction with Property 1. □

Figure 1 illustrates Property 2.

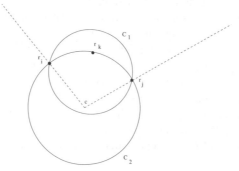

Fig. 1. C_2 is an enclosing circle for the three points r_i, r_j and r_k. However, there is no
point in the intersection between C_2 and the concave sector formed by r_i, r_j and the
center c of C_2. So, C_2 can be replace by a smaller enclosing circle, here C_1, even if all
the points are on the circumference of C_2.

Observation 1. *Given three collinear points, c,r,r'. If c is on the segment $[r, r']$,
then c cannot be on the circumference of a circle enclosing r and r'.*

Definition 4 (Convex Hull). *[16] Given a set $\mathcal{P}$ of $n \geq 2$ points $p_1, p_2, \cdots, p_n$
on the plane, the convex hull of $\mathcal{P}$, denoted $H(\mathcal{P})$, is the smallest polygon such
that every point in $\mathcal{P}$ is either on an edge of $H(\mathcal{P})$ or inside it.*

Informally, it is the shape of a rubber-band stretched around $p_1, p_2, \cdots, p_n$. The
convex hull is unique and can be computed with time complexity $O(n \log n)$ [16].
When no ambiguity arises, $H(\mathcal{P})$ will be shortly denoted by H and $H(\mathcal{P}) \cap \mathcal{P}$
will indicate the set of the positions both on $H(\mathcal{P})$ and $\mathcal{P}$.

From Definition 4, we deduce the following property :

Property 3. Let $\mathcal{P}$ be respectively a set of $n \geq 2$ points that are not on the same
line and let $H(\mathcal{P})$ be a convex hull. The two following properties are equivalent

1. Any point c, not necessarily in $\mathcal{P}$, is located on H (either on a vertex or an
   edge)
2. there is a concave or a straight sector $\mathcal{S}$ in $\{\underline{rcr'}, \overline{rcr'}\}$ such that r and r' are
   in $\mathcal{P}$ and there exists no point $\in \mathcal{P} \cap \mathcal{S}$.

he relationship between the smallest enclosing circle and the convex hull is iven by the following property

Property 4. [3] Given a set $\mathcal{P}$ of $n \geq 2$ points on the plane. We have

$$SEC(\mathcal{P}) \cap \mathcal{P} \subseteq H(\mathcal{P}) \cap \mathcal{P}$$

The Algorithm. Based on the definitions and basic properties introduced above, we are now ready to present a deterministic self-stabilizing algorithm that allows n robots (n odd) to gather in a point, regardless of the initial positions of the robots on the plane. The idea of our algorithm is as follows : It consists in transforming an arbitrary configuration $\mathcal{P}$ into one where there is exactly one point $p_{max} \in Max\mathcal{P}$. When such a configuration is reached, all the robots which are not located at p_{max} move towards p_{max} avoiding to create another point q than p_{max} such that $|q| \geq p_{max}$.

When $|Max\mathcal{P}| \neq 1$, we will distinguish two cases: $|Max\mathcal{P}| = 2$ and $|Max\mathcal{P}| \geq 3$.

If $Max\mathcal{P} = \{p_{max1}; p_{max2}\}$, then each robot which is not located neither at p_{max1} nor at p_{max2} moves towards its closest position $\in Max\mathcal{P}$ by avoiding to create an adding maximal point. Since the number of robots is odd, we have eventually either $|p_{max1}| > |p_{max2}|$ or $|p_{max1}| > |p_{max2}|$ and then, $|Max\mathcal{P}| = 1$.

For the case $|Max\mathcal{P}| \geq 3$, our strategy consists in trying to create a unique maximal point inside SEC. To reach such a configuration, we distinguish three cases :

1. If there is no robot inside SEC, then all the robots are allowed to move towards the center of SEC.
2. If all the robots inside SEC are located at the center of SEC, then only the robots located in $SEC \cap Max\mathcal{P}$ are allowed to move towards the center of SEC.
3. If some robots inside SEC are not located at the center of SEC, then only the robots inside SEC are allowed to move towards the center of SEC.

The algorithm is shown in Algorithm 1. It uses two subroutines: *move_to_carefully(p)* and *choose_closest_position(p_1, p_2)*. The former allows a robot r, located at q, to move towards p only if there is no robot on the segment $[q, p]$, except the robots located at p or the robots located at q. The latter one returns the closest position to r among $\{p_1, p_2\}$. If the distance between r and p_1 is equal to the distance between r and p_2, then the function returns p_1.

Proof of Closure

Lemma 2 (Closure). *According to Algorithm 1, if all the robots are located at the same position p, then all the robots are located at the same position thereafter.*

Proof of Convergence

Cases $|Max\mathcal{P}| = 1$ and $|Max\mathcal{P}| = 2$.

Algorithm 1. Gathering for an odd number of robots, executed by each rob

$\mathcal{P} :=$ the set of all the positions;
$Max\mathcal{P} :=$ the set of all the points $p \in \mathcal{P}$ such that $|p|$ is maximal;
if $|Max\mathcal{P}| = 1$
then $p_{max} :=$ the unique point in $Max\mathcal{P}$;
      if I am not on p_{max};
      then $move\_to\_carefully(p_{max})$;
      endif
endif
if $|Max\mathcal{P}| = 2$
then $p_{max1} :=$ the first point in $Max\mathcal{P}$;
      $p_{max2} :=$ the second point in $Max\mathcal{P}$;
      if I am not neither on p_{max1} nor p_{max2}
      then $q := choose\_closest\_position(p_{max1}, p_{max2})$;
          $move\_to\_carefully(q)$;
      endif
endif
if $|Max\mathcal{P}| \geq 3$
then $SEC :=$ the smallest circle enclosing all the points in $\mathcal{P}$;
      $c :=$ the center of SEC;
      $Boundary := SEC \cap \mathcal{P}$;
      $Inside := \mathcal{P} \setminus Boundary$;
      if $Inside \neq \emptyset$
      then if All the robots $\in Inside$ are located at c
          then if I am in $(Boundary \cap Max\mathcal{P})$
             then $move\_to(c)$;
             endif
          else if I am in $Inside$
             then $move\_to(c)$;
             endif
          endif
      else $move\_to(c)$;
      endif
endif

Lemma 3. *Let $\mathcal{P}$ be an arbitrary configuration for an odd number of n robots. According to Algorithm 1, if $|Max\mathcal{P}| = 1$ then all the robots are located at the same position in finite time.*

Lemma 4. *Let $\mathcal{P}$ be an arbitrary configuration for an odd number of n robots. According to Algorithm 1, if $|Max\mathcal{P}| = 2$ then all the robots are located at the same position in finite time.*

Case $|Max\mathcal{P}| \geq 3$. In this paragraph, we prove that starting from a configuration where $|Max\mathcal{P}| \geq 3$, all the robots are located at the same position in finite time. More precisely, we consider the case where there exists at least one robot inside

$C(\mathcal{P}(t))$ (refer to Lemma 7) and the case where there is no robot inside $\exists C(\mathcal{P}(t))$ (refer to Lemma 8).

In order to prove Lemma 7, we use Lemmas 5 and 6. In particular, Lemmas 5 shows that, under specific conditions, the center of $SEC(\mathcal{P}(t))$ is inside $SEC(\mathcal{P}(t+1))$ even if $SEC(\mathcal{P}(t)) \neq SEC(\mathcal{P}(t+1))$ or the center of $SEC(\mathcal{P}(t))$ is not the center of $SEC(\mathcal{P}(t+1))$.

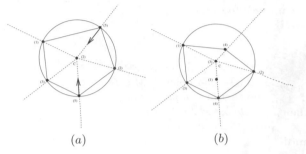

(a)   (b)

Fig. 2. The numbers between parenthesis indicate the multiplicity. In Figure a, we have a configuration $\mathcal{P}(t)$ where the center c of $SEC(\mathcal{P}(t))$ is inside the convex hull. Figure b, we have configuration $\mathcal{P}(t+1)$ where some robots have moved toward c and c is inside the new convex hull.

Lemma 5. *Let $\mathcal{P}(t)$ be a configuration such that $|Max\mathcal{P}| \geq 3$ and there exists at least one robot inside $SEC(\mathcal{P}(t))$.*

According to Algorithm 1, if both conditions are true :

1. *some robots $\in \mathcal{P}(t) \cap SEC(\mathcal{P}(t))$ move in straight line toward the center c of $SEC(t)$ and,*
2. *for every $p \in \mathcal{P}(t) \cap SEC(\mathcal{P}(t))$ there exists at least one robot in p which does not reach c at time $t+1$,*

then, the center of $SEC(\mathcal{P}(t))$ is inside $SEC(\mathcal{P}(t+1))$ at time $t+1$.

Proof. Let c be the center of $SEC(t)$ at time t. We consider two cases, depending on whether c is on the convex hull $H(\mathcal{P}(t))$ or not, at time t.

- c **is on** $H(\mathcal{P}(t))$ **at time** t. From Property 3, there exists a concave or a straight sector $\mathcal{S}$ in $\{xcy, \overline{xcy}\}$ such that x and y are in $\mathcal{P}(t)$ and there is no point $\in \mathcal{P}(t) \cap \mathcal{S}$. However, from Property 2, we know that there exists no pair of points x and y in $\mathcal{P}(t)$ such that there exists a concave sector $\mathcal{S}$ in $\{xcy, \overline{xcy}\}$ and $\mathcal{P}(t) \cap \mathcal{S} = \emptyset$. So, there exists **only** a straight sector $\mathcal{S}$ in $\{xcy, \overline{xcy}\}$ such that x and y are in $\mathcal{P}(t)$ and there is no point $\in \mathcal{P}(t) \cap \mathcal{S}$. Consequently, c is on the segment $[x, y]$ at time t. Since the robots move in straight line towards c and since there exist some robots located at x and some robot located at y which do not reach c at time $t+1$ then, c is on the segment $[r, s]$ at time $t+1$ with r and $s \in \mathcal{P}(t+1)$. From Observation 1, we deduce that c is inside $SEC(\mathcal{P}(t+1))$ at time $t+1$.

  – c **is not on** $H(\mathcal{P}(t))$ **at time** t. In this case, all the points in
    not on the same line otherwise c would have been on $H(\mathcal{P}(t))$. S
    Property 3 we know that there does not exist a concave or a straight se
    in $\{\overline{xcy}, \overline{\overline{xcy}}\}$ such that x and y are in $\mathcal{P}(t)$ and there is no point $\in \mathcal{P}(t$
    Since the robots move in straight line towards c and since for each p
    $p \in \mathcal{P}(t)$ there exists at least one robot located at p which does not reac.
    at time $t+1$ then, we deduce that there does not exist a concave or a straigh
    sector $\mathcal{S}$ in $\{\overline{rcs}, \overline{\overline{rcs}}\}$ such that r and s are in $\mathcal{P}(t+1)$ and there is no point
    $\in \mathcal{P}(t+1) \cap \mathcal{S}$ (Figures 2.a and 2.b illustrate this fact). So, from Property 3
    c is inside $H(\mathcal{P}(t+1))$ at time $t+1$, and from Lemma 4 we deduce that c
    is inside $SEC(\mathcal{P}(t+1))$.   □

Lemma 6. *Let $\mathcal{P}(t)$ be a configuration such that $|Max\mathcal{P}| \geq 3$ and there exists at least one robot inside $SEC(\mathcal{P}(t))$. If any robot r is inside $SEC(\mathcal{P}(t))$ and r is located on the boundary of $SEC(\mathcal{P}(t+1))$ then $|Max\mathcal{P}(t+1)| \leq 2$.*

Proof. By contradiction assume that r is inside $SEC(\mathcal{P}(t))$ and r is located on the boundary of $SEC(\mathcal{P}(t+1))$ and $|Max\mathcal{P}(t+1)| > 2$. Let c be the center of $SEC(\mathcal{P}(t))$ at time t. From assumption, some robots on the boundary of $SEC(\mathcal{P}(t))$ have moved toward the center of $SEC(\mathcal{P}(t))$. According to Algorithm 1, that implies that all the robots inside $SEC(\mathcal{P}(t))$, notably r, are located at the center of $SEC(\mathcal{P}(t))$ at time t. So, c is on the boundary of $SEC(\mathcal{P}(t+1))$. From Lemma 5, we deduce that there exists a point $p \in \mathcal{P}(t) \cap SEC(\mathcal{P}(t))$ such that all the robots in p have reached c at time $t+1$. However, according to Algorithm 1 only the robots located in $\in Max\mathcal{P}(t) \cap SEC(\mathcal{P}(t))$ are allowed to move at time t. Therefore, for every point $p \neq c$ we have $|c| > |p|$ at time $t+1$. Hence, $|Max\mathcal{P}(t+1)| = \{c\}$ i.e., $|Max\mathcal{P}(t+1)| = 1$. A contradiction.   □

Lemma 7. *Let $\mathcal{P}(t)$ a configuration such that $|Max\mathcal{P}| \geq 3$ and there exists at least one robot inside $SEC(\mathcal{P}(t))$. According to Algorithm 1, all the robots are located at the same position in finite time.*

Proof. Assume by contradiction $|Max\mathcal{P}| \geq 3$ forever. From Lemma 1, fairness and because of the fact that each robot r can move to at least a constant distance $\sigma_r > 0$ in one step, we know that there exists a time instant t_k where the radius of $SEC(t_k)$ becomes at most σ_r. From t_k on, each time a robot r moves toward c, the center of SEC, r reaches c in one step. From Lemma 6, we know that, for every $k' \geq k$, the robots inside $SEC(\mathcal{P}(t_k))$ are inside $SEC(\mathcal{P}(t_{k'}))$. Furthermore, for some $k' \geq k$, some robots that are inside $SEC(t_{k'})$ can be no longer located at c, the center of $SEC(t_{k'})$ because $SEC(t_{k'})$ is different as it was previously. But in that case, no robot located on $SEC(t_{k'})$ can move until each robot inside $SEC(t_{k'})$ reaches c. Thus, by induction, there exists $k' \geq k$ such that the number of robots located at c, the center of $SEC(t_{k'})$, is greater than the number of robots which are not located at c, *i.e.,* eventually $|Max\mathcal{P}| = 1$. A contradiction. So, $|Max\mathcal{P}| \leq 2$ in finite time and from Lemmas 3 and 4 all the robots are located at the same position in finite time.   □

8. *Let $\mathcal{P}(t)$ be a configuration such that $|Max\mathcal{P}| \geq 3$ and there exists ι inside $SEC(\mathcal{P}(t))$. According to Algorithm 1, all the robots are located same position in finite time.*

f. According to Algorithm 1, all the robots may decide to move toward center of SEC. Since each robot r can move to at least a constant distance $r > 0$ in one step, if all the robots are always on the boundary of $SEC(\mathcal{P})$ then, by fairness, the gathering problem is solved in finite time. Otherwise,

- either, there exists $t_k > t$ such that $|Max\mathcal{P}(t_k)| \geq 3$ and there exists at least one robot inside $SEC(\mathcal{P}(t))$: From Lemma 7, we deduce that all the robots are located at the same position in finite time,
- or, there exists $t_k > t$ such that $|Max\mathcal{P}(t_k)| \leq 2$ from Lemmas 3 and 4 all the robots are located at the same position in finite time. $\square$

4 Conclusion

Assuming strong multiplicity detection, we provided a complete characterization (necessary and sufficient conditions) to solve the gathering problem. Note that we do not know whether strong multiplicity detection is a necessary condition to solve the gathering problem. In future works, we would like to address this problem in the fully asynchronous model (Corda).

References

1. Agmon, N., Peleg, D.: Fault-tolerant gathering algorithms for autonomous mobile robots. SIAM J. Comput. 36(1), 56–82 (2006)
2. Ando, H., Oasa, Y., Suzuki, I., Yamashita, M.: A distributed memoryless point convergence algorithm for mobile robots with limited visibility. IEEE Transaction on Robotics and Automation 15(5), 818–828 (1999)
3. Chrystal, P.: On the problem to construct the minimum circle enclosing n given points in a plane. The Edinburgh Mathematical Society, Third Meeting, page 30 (1885)
4. Cieliebak, M., Flocchini, P., Prencipe, G., Santoro, N.: Solving the robots gathering problem. In: Baeten, J.C.M., Lenstra, J.K., Parrow, J., Woeginger, G.J. (eds.) ICALP 2003. LNCS, vol. 2719, pp. 1181–1196. Springer, Heidelberg (2003)
5. Cieliebak, M.: Gathering non-oblivious mobile robots. In: Farach-Colton, M. (ed.) LATIN 2004. LNCS, vol. 2976, pp. 577–588. Springer, Heidelberg (2004)
6. Defago, X., Konagaya, A.: Circle formation for oblivious anonymous mobile robots with no common sense of orientation. In: 2nd ACM International Annual Workshop on Principles of Mobile Computing (POMC 2002), pp. 97–104 (2002)
7. Défago, X., Gradinariu, M., Messika, S., Raipin-Parvédy, P.: Fault-tolerant and self-stabilizing mobile robots gathering. In: Dolev, S. (ed.) DISC 2006. LNCS, vol. 4167, pp. 46–60. Springer, Heidelberg (2006)
8. Dieudoné, Y., Petit, F.: Scatter of robots. Parallel Processing Letters 19(1), 175–184 (2009)
9. Dolev, S.: Self-Stabilization. MIT Press, Cambridge (2000)

10. Flocchini, P., Ilcinkas, D., Pelc, A., Santoro, N.: Remembering without me. Tree exploration by asynchronous oblivious robots. In: Shvartsman, A.A., Fe P. (eds.) SIROCCO 2008. LNCS, vol. 5058, pp. 33–47. Springer, Heidelberg (2C

11. Flocchini, P., Kranakis, E., Krizanc, D., Santoro, N., Sawchuk, C.: Multiple n bile agent rendezvous in a ring. In: Farach-Colton, M. (ed.) LATIN 2004. LNC. vol. 2976, pp. 599–608. Springer, Heidelberg (2004)

12. Flocchini, P., Prencipe, G., Santoro, N., Widmayer, P.: Gathering of asynchronous robots with limited visibility. Theor. Comput. Sci. 337(1-3), 147–168 (2005)

13. Klasing, R., Markou, E., Pelc, A.: Gathering asynchronous oblivious mobile robots in a ring. Theor. Comput. Sci. 390(1), 27–39 (2008)

14. Prencipe, G.: Corda: Distributed coordination of a set of autonomous mobile robots. In: Proceedings of the Fourth European Research Seminar on Advances in Distributed Systems (ERSADS 2001), pp. 185–190 (2001)

15. Prencipe, G.: Impossibility of gathering by a set of autonomous mobile robots. Theor. Comput. Sci. 384(2-3), 222–231 (2007)

16. Preparata, F.P., Hong, S.J.: Convex hulls of finite sets of poin ts in two and three dimensions. Commun. ACM 20(2), 87–93 (1977)

17. Souissi, S., Défago, X., Yamashita, M.: Using eventually consistent compasses to gather memory-less mobile robots with limited visibility. ACM Trans. Auton. Adapt. Syst. 4(1), 1–27 (2009)

18. Suzuki, I., Yamashita, M.: Agreement on a common x-y coordinate system by a group of mobile robots. In: Intelligent Robots: Modeling and Planning, pp. 305–321 (1996)

19. Suzuki, I., Yamashita, M.: Distributed anonymous mobile robots - formation of geometric patterns. SIAM Journal of Computing 28(4), 1347–1363 (1999)

Gossiping in Jail

Avery Miller

University of Toronto, Toronto ON, Canada
a4miller@cs.toronto.edu

Abstract. Consider a set of prisoners that want to gossip with one another, and suppose that these prisoners are located at fixed locations (e.g., in jail cells) along a corridor. Each prisoner has a way to broadcast messages (e.g. by voice or contraband radio) with transmission radius R and interference radius $R' \geq R$. We study synchronous algorithms for this problem (that is, prisoners are allowed to speak at regulated intervals) including two restricted subclasses. We prove exact upper and lower bounds on the gossiping completion time for all three classes. We demonstrate that each restriction placed on the algorithm results in decreasing performance.

1 Introduction

Gossiping is a fundamental task for any radio sensor network. Each processor p_i in the network has a message m_i that it wishes to share with all processors in the network. When each process terminates, it has all of the messages. Gossiping can be used for performing any aggregate computation that requires information from each processor, such as discovering the network topology or reaching consensus.

We define several natural classes of deterministic algorithms by placing restrictions on which processors transmit simultaneously. The most restrictive of these are the *singleton* algorithms, in which only one processor may transmit during each transmission slot. Such algorithms are of interest when there is a collection of processors whose physical distance from one another is at most the interference radius R'. In this case, allowing two or more processors to transmit simultaneously would result in a wasted transmission slot: all processors found within the transmission radius of one transmitting processor are also found within the interference radius of another transmitting processor, so no message is received by any processor. In *collision-free* algorithms, more than one processor is allowed to transmit during a single transmission slot, unless the transmissions result in a collision. One benefit of designing a collision-free algorithm is that each transmitted message is received by all neighbours of the processor that transmitted it. This can make the correctness proof and running-time analysis of the algorithm much easier. *Unrestricted* algorithms have no restrictions on which processors may transmit during a single transmission slot.

We restrict our attention to static networks located in physical environments that can be modelled in one dimension, for example: roadways, sidewalks, or

S. Dolev (Ed.): ALGOSENSORS 2009, LNCS 5804, pp. 242–251, 2009.

corridors. We proceed by defining our formal model of such networks, and derive exact upper and lower bounds on the time complexity of gossiping each of the three classes defined above. Using these bounds, we will show t₁ each restriction placed on the algorithm negatively affects performance for sor networks. Full details and proofs can be found in [7].

2 Related Work

Gossiping in static ad hoc radio networks has been thoroughly studied in networks where the transmission radius of each processor's radio is equal to its interference radius. Most of the results in the literature assume that the transmission radius is not necessarily the same for all processors and that processors do not initially know the network topology.

The simplest gossiping algorithm consists of repeating the Round Robin protocol for D rounds, where D is the network diameter. During each round, each processor transmits during the time slot corresponding to its unique ID number. The time complexity of this singleton algorithm is quadratic (or worse if the ID numbers are from a large domain). The first subquadratic algorithm was proposed by Chrobak, Gąsieniec and Rytter [3]. They presented a technique to extend any broadcasting algorithm with any time complexity $f(n)$ to an algorithm for gossiping which has time complexity $O(n\sqrt{f(n)}\log n)$. Applying the technique to a constructive broadcasting algorithm with time complexity $O(n^{3/2})$ (from Chlebus et al. [1]), the authors proved an upper bound of $O(n^{7/4}\log n)$ for constructive gossiping algorithms. Gąsieniec, Radzik and Xin [6] presented a non-constructive algorithm that solves gossiping in time $O(n^{4/3}\log^4 n)$. Chlebus, Gąsieniec, Lingas and Pagourtzis [2] showed several upper and lower bounds on the time complexity of gossiping by non-adaptive algorithms. An algorithm is *non-adaptive* if processors only use their ID and the total number of processors for deciding when to transmit. In contrast, an *adaptive* algorithm can use other information, such as detected collisions or the contents of received messages, to decide when processors will transmit. The authors gave a singleton algorithm that completes the gossiping task in ad hoc radio networks in time $(n-1)(n-2)+4$. They showed that there exists a family of networks for which any singleton algorithm takes at least $n^2 - O(n^{7/4+\epsilon})$ steps, for any $\epsilon > 0$. Further, they gave a non-constructive proof that there exists a non-adaptive deterministic algorithm for gossiping that completes in time $n^2 - \omega(n)$. They also proved a lower bound of $n^2/2 - O(n)$ time slots for any deterministic non-adaptive algorithm. Their lower bounds were proven for networks that are modelled by arbitrary neighbourhood graphs, that is, they do not restrict to networks that exist in a physical space. Real-world solutions to the gossiping task may not be subject to these lower bounds.

For networks in which the transmission radius is the same for all processors, Chlebus, Gąsieniec, Lingas and Pagourtzis [2] demonstrated a deterministic non-adaptive algorithm that completes the gossiping task in time $O(n^{3/2})$. When all processors are aware of the network topology, Gąsieniec, Potapov, and Xin [5] provided a deterministic algorithm for the gossiping task that uses at most ...ne slots. The best known algorithm, especially useful for networks with small ...meter, is presented by Cicalese, Manne, and Xin [4]. Their algorithm com- ...etes in $O(D + \frac{\Delta \log n}{\log \Delta - \log \log n})$ time if no processor has more than Δ neighbours.

The gossiping task can be solved using a randomized algorithm in which, at each step, a small subset of processors is randomly chosen to exchange infor- mation with its neighbours. This technique, which can be used to solve various tasks in mobile networks, is, confusingly, also called gossiping. We restrict our attention to deterministic solutions to the gossiping task.

3   Model

A static ad hoc radio network consists of a set P of n processors $p_1, \ldots, p_n$, in order from left to right, arranged at fixed arbitrary locations in one-dimensional space. Each processor runs a locally-stored deterministic algorithm. We assume that time is slotted and that each processor knows when each slot begins. Each time slot is long enough so that each message is completely transmitted, even in the case of a large message that contains all of the m_i's. So we assume that each processor always transmits all of the gossiping messages that it knows. The topology of the network is known by all processors. This is not an unrealistic assumption for static networks, since one can first execute a gossiping algorithm that is designed to discover the network topology, and then subsequently use a gossiping algorithm that assumes that the topology is known. We assume that the network is *connected*. The *diameter* D of the network is the length of the shortest sequence of processor transmissions such that a message originating from p_1 reaches p_n.

During the course of an algorithm, processors may perform wireless trans- missions by broadcasting messages in both directions. A transmitted message is assumed to reach only those points within *transmission radius* R of the transmit- ting processor's location. Processors found within the transmission radius of p are p's *neighbours*. The signal sent by a transmitting processor reaches all points within distance $R' \geq R$ of the transmitting processor's location. The parame- ter R' is called the *interference radius*, since a processor q that is found within distance R' of a transmitting processor p cannot, at the same time, receive a message from a transmitting processor p' that is within distance R due to the signals interfering with one another. The occurrence of such signal interference is known as a *collision*. For our upper bounds, we assume that a processor cannot detect collisions, whereas for our lower bounds, we allow processors to detect collisions. Hence, our bounds apply both in the presence or absence of collision detectors.

4   Singleton Algorithms

In any gossiping algorithm, each processor must transmit at least once, since a processor that never transmits can never share its message. This implies that

any singleton algorithm requires at least n transmission slots. When D
the processors transmitting in order of increasing index is a straightforw
algorithm that uses exactly n slots. When each processor transmits, all otr
processors in the network receive the transmitted message. In the remainder
this section, we assume that $D \geq 2$, and prove that $n + D - 2$ transmission slot
are necessary and sufficient for singleton algorithms solving the gossiping task.

We present a singleton algorithm, `SingletonGossip`, that completes the gossiping task in a connected network using at most $n + D - 2$ transmission slots.
When a processor transmits, it transmits all of the messages that it knows. First,
all processors that are not neighbours of p_1 transmit in order from right to left.
Note that, when p_{n-i} transmits, the set of messages $\{m_{n-i}, \ldots, m_n\}$ arrives at
p_{n-i-1}. Let p_r be the rightmost neighbour of p_1. Next, each of the processors
$p_1, p_2, \ldots, p_r$ transmit in order from left to right. Just before it transmits, p_r knows
all of the messages, so all neighbours of p_r (which include $p_1, \ldots, p_{r-1}$) receive
all of the messages. Finally, the complete set of messages is sent rightwards to p_n
as fast as possible: the processor to transmit in a given transmission slot is the
rightmost processor that received a transmission in the previous transmission
slot. The pseudocode for this protocol is listed in Figure 1.

```
r  =  label of rightmost neighbour of p₁
for k  =  n downto (r + 1)
        pₖ transmits
for k  =  1 to r
        pₖ transmits
next  =  label of rightmost neighbour of pᵣ
while (next < n)
        pₙₑₓₜ transmits
        next  =  label of rightmost neighbour of pₙₑₓₜ
```

Fig. 1. Pseudocode for `SingletonGossip`

The `while` loop executes exactly $D - 2$ times, which leads to the following
result.

Theorem 1. *The total number of slots used by* `SingletonGossip` *is* $n + D - 2$.

Next, we prove a matching lower bound for any singleton algorithm that solves
the gossiping task.

Lemma 2. *At least* $n + D - 2$ *transmission slots are required by any singleton
algorithm for gossiping among n processors.*

Proof. For each processor p_i, let t_i be the transmission slot during which p_i
transmits for the first time. Suppose $t_{last} = \max\{t_1, \ldots, t_n\}$. Since at most one
processor may transmit per transmission slot, and every processor must transmit
at least once, we have $t_{last} \geq n$.

et P' be the sequence of transmissions that occur after the first transmission p_{last}. After p_{last} transmits, message m_{last} reaches p_1 by some (possibly empty) subsequence of transmissions B of P' by processors to the left of p_{last}. Similarly, m_{last} reaches p_n by some (possibly empty) subsequence of transmissions C of P' by processors to the right of p_{last}. Note that B and C are disjoint, so $|B| + |C| \leq |P'|$. Let B' be obtained from sequence B by reversing the order of transmission. Then, performing the sequence $A = (p_1, B', p_{last}, C)$ results in m_1 reaching p_n. Hence, $|A| \geq D$ and $|P'| \geq |B'| + |C| = |A| - 2 \geq D - 2$. Therefore, at least $n + |P'| \geq n + D - 2$ transmission slots are used.   □

5   Collision-Free Algorithms

We describe a collision-free algorithm, CFGossip, that solves the gossiping task. It divides the network into segments of size $R + R' + 1$. The processors in each segment transmit in order from left to right (as much as possible in parallel), and then send messages from each end of the network to the opposite end. The algorithm ensures that no collisions occur.

A subset P' of $D - 1$ processors is designated as the set of *forwarding* processors, and these processors are not scheduled to transmit during the first phase of the algorithm. Consecutive elements of P' are at most distance R apart and every non-forwarding processor is within distance R from some processor in P'.

During the first phase, the non-forwarding processors in each segment transmit in order from left to right. The length of each segment is sufficiently large to ensure that transmitting processors in non-neighbouring segments can never cause a transmission collision. To avoid collisions between transmitting processors in neighbouring segments, we schedule processors found in even-numbered segments during even-numbered slots, and processors in odd-numbered segments during odd-numbered slots. Additional processors may transmit if collisions do not result.

During the second phase of the algorithm, the forwarding processors share the messages that they received during the first phase. More specifically, the messages received during phase 1 by the leftmost processor in P' are transmitted by processors in P', in order from left to right. These transmissions are called *right-transmissions*. Simultaneously, the messages received during phase 1 by the rightmost processor in P' get forwarded by processors in P', in order from right to left. These transmissions are called *left-transmissions*. These can be done in parallel, except when a right-transmission and a left-transmission will cause a collision. In this case, two slots are used. Since the message of each non-forwarding processor is received by some processor in P' during the first phase, the messages of all processors get collected and forwarded during this process.

Let $k \leq 2\lceil R'/R \rceil + 2$ be the smallest integer such that the ith and $(i + k)^{th}$ processors in P' can transmit simultaneously without causing a collision, for $1 \leq i \leq D - 1 - k$. The first phase uses at most $n - D$ slots. Two processors transmit during each slot of the first and last $\lfloor (D - k)/2 \rfloor$ slots of the second phase. When the processors performing right- and left-transmissions are close to one another, $D - 2\lfloor(D-k)/2\rfloor - 2$ right-transmissions are performed, followed by a single transmission which acts as both a right- and left-transmission, followed by $D - 2\lfloor(D - k)/2\rfloor - 2$ left-transmissions. In total, CFGossip algorithm uses at most $n + 2\lceil R'/R\rceil$ transmission slots.

By Lemma 2, in any network with $D > 2\lceil R'/R\rceil + 2$, a singleton algorithm requires at least $n + D - 2 > n + 2\lceil R'/R\rceil$ transmission slots. It follows that CFGossip is better than any singleton algorithm for the gossiping task in such a network.

Next, we find a lower bound for the number of transmission slots required by any collision-free gossiping algorithm. Consider a network N where the processors are equally spaced distance $R/2 + \epsilon$ apart, where $0 < \epsilon < R/(4R'/R - 2) \le R/2$. This network is connected, since the distance between consecutive processors is $R/2 + \epsilon < R$. Since $\epsilon > 0$, the distance between p_i and p_{i+2} is greater than R, which implies the following.

Proposition 3. *For any $i \in \{1, \ldots, n - 1\}$, a transmission by p_i is received by p_{i+1}, but not by any processor to the right of p_{i+1}. Similarly, for any $i \in \{2, \ldots, n\}$, a transmission by p_i is received by p_{i-1}, but not by any processor to the left of p_{i-1}.*

From Proposition 3, it follows that the number of hops between two processors p_a and p_b is equal to $|b - a|$, so the diameter of the network N is $n - 1$. The distance $d(p_a, p_b)$ between two processors p_a and p_b is $|b - a|(R/2 + \epsilon)$. Using the fact that $\epsilon < R/(4R'/R - 2)$, we show that a collision occurs (at processor p_{j+1}) if there exists $1 < \ell \le 2\lfloor R'/R\rfloor$ such that p_j and $p_{j+\ell}$ transmit during the same slot.

Proposition 4. *If $1 \le \ell \le 2\lfloor R'/R\rfloor$ and $1 \le j \le n - \ell$, then $d(p_{j+1}, p_{j+\ell}) \le R'$.*

Let B be a sequence of sets of collision-free transmissions, and let B_t be the prefix of B of length t (where B_0 is the empty sequence). We denote by $RM(B, i)$ the rightmost processor that knows m_i after executing the transmission sequence B. We define $LM(B, i)$ analogously as the leftmost processor that knows m_i after executing the transmission sequence B. Proposition 3 implies the following two facts.

Proposition 5. *Suppose that $RM(B_t, 1) = p_i$. Then, $RM(B_{t+1}, 1) = p_{i+1}$, if p_i transmits during transmission slot $t + 1$, and $RM(B_{t+1}, 1) = p_i$ otherwise.*

Proposition 6. *Suppose that $LM(B_t, n) = p_i$. Then, $LM(B_{t+1}, n) = p_{i-1}$ if p_i transmits during transmission slot $t + 1$, and $LM(B_{t+1}, n) = p_i$ otherwise.*

To produce the desired lower bound, we consider the total number of transmission slots required for both m_1 to reach p_n and m_n to reach p_1. As a measure of progress, we consider the minimum number of transmissions needed to send a message between the leftmost processor that has received m_n and the rightmost processor that has received m_1. More formally, for any transmission slot t, let $p_a = RM(B_t, 1)$ and $p_b = LM(B_t, n)$, and define $h(B_t) = b - a$. Then,

$(B_0) = n - 1$, and, for any t after which gossiping is complete, $h(B_t) = 1 - n$. From Propositions 5 and 6, it follows that, for any transmission slot t before gossiping is complete, $h(B_t) = h(B_{t-1})$ if and only if neither $RM(B_{t-1}, 1)$ nor $LM(B_{t-1}, n)$ transmit. Further, it follows that $h(B_t) = h(B_{t-1}) - 1$ if exactly one of $RM(B_{t-1}, 1)$ or $LM(B_{t-1}, n)$ transmits, and $h(B_t) = h(B_{t-1}) - 2$ if both $RM(B_{t-1}, 1)$ and $LM(B_{t-1}, n)$ transmit. Along with Proposition 4, we get the following useful result.

Lemma 7. *For every transmission slot t, $h(B_t) \geq h(B_{t-1}) - 2$. If $0 < |h(B_{t-1})| \leq 2 \lfloor R'/R \rfloor$, then $h(B_t) \geq h(B_{t-1}) - 1$.*

Theorem 8. *In any collision-free gossiping algorithm, for $n > 2\lfloor R'/R \rfloor$ processors, at least $2(\lceil n/2 \rceil + \lfloor R'/R \rfloor - 1)$ transmission slots are required before p_1 knows m_n and p_n knows m_1.*

Proof. Let B be the sequence of sets of collision-free transmissions performed by the algorithm and let B' be obtained from B by removing the sets in which no progress is made. Let t_4 be the length of B'. Then $h(B'_0) = n - 1$, $h(B'_{t_4}) = 1 - n$, and $h(B'_0), h(B'_1), \ldots, h(B'_{t_4})$ is a decreasing sequence.

By Lemma 7, $h(B'_t) = h(B'_{t-1}) - 1$ if $0 < |h(B'_{t-1})| \leq 2 \lfloor R'/R \rfloor$. It follows that there exist transmission slots $0 < t_1 < t_2 < t_3 \leq t_4$ such that $h(B'_{t_1}) = 2 \lfloor R'/R \rfloor - 1$, $h(B'_{t_2}) = 0$, and $h(B'_{t_3}) = -2 \lfloor R'/R \rfloor - 1$. Hence, $t_2 - t_1 = h(B'_{t_1}) - h(B'_{t_2})$ and $t_3 - (t_2 + 1) = h(B'_{t_2+1}) - h(B'_{t_3})$.

By Lemma 7, for all slots t, $h(B'_{t-1}) - h(B'_t) \leq 2$. Hence, $h(B'_0) - h(B'_{t_1}) \leq 2t_1$, $h(B'_{t_2+1}) \geq h(B'_{t_2}) - 2$, and $h(B'_{t_3}) - h(B'_{t_4}) \leq 2(t_4 - t_3)$. By rearranging, we get $t_1 \geq \lceil (h(B'_0) - h(B'_{t_1}))/2 \rceil$ and $t_4 - t_3 \geq \lceil (h(B'_{t_3}) - h(B'_{t_4}))/2 \rceil$.

Therefore, the length of B' is $t_4 = (t_4 - t_3) + (t_3 - (t_2 + 1)) + (t_2 - t_1) + t_1 + 1 \geq 2(\lceil n/2 \rceil + \lfloor R'/R \rfloor - 1)$. $\square$

Our upper and lower bounds for gossiping by collision-free algorithms differ by at most 4.

6 Unrestricted Algorithms

We modify the `CFGossip` algorithm presented in Section 5 to create a more efficient gossiping algorithm called `Gossip`. The idea is to increase the number of parallel transmissions, while making sure that any processor affected by a transmission collision has already received the full set of messages to be gossiped. The first phase of `Gossip` is identical to the first phase of `CFGossip`. The second phase of `Gossip` is very similar to the second phase of `CFGossip`: the messages received during phase 1 by the leftmost processor in P' get forwarded by processors in P', in order from left to right, towards the rightmost processor in P' via right-transmissions. Simultaneously, the messages received during phase 1 by the rightmost processor in P' get forwarded by processors in P', in order from right to left, towards the leftmost processor in P' via left-transmissions. However, in the case of `Gossip`, after these messages 'cross', there are more slots in which exactly two processors transmit. More specifically, consider a processor p

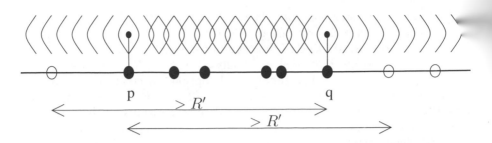

Fig. 2. A situation where p and q are scheduled to transmit during the same slot despite causing transmission collisions

performing a right-transmission and a processor q performing a left-transmission such that any processor the right of q is more than distance R' from p and that any processor to the left of p is more than distance R' from q. We can show that all processors located between p and q have already received the full set of messages to be gossiped. Our `Gossip` algorithm schedules p and q to transmit during the same slot even if collisions occur, since these collisions do not hinder the completion of gossiping. This situation is depicted in Figure 2. The processors represented by filled circles have already received all of the gossiping messages.

Our `Gossip` algorithm uses at most $n + 2\lceil R'/R \rceil - 1$ transmission slots. The analysis of `Gossip` is similar to that of `CFGossip`, but with special attention paid to the slots after the single transmission which acts as both a right- and left-transmission. A more careful analysis shows an upper bound of $n + 2\lceil R'/R \rceil - 2$ for networks in which $D + k$ is even, for example, the network N in section 5, when the number of processors is odd and R' is a multiple of R. For this network, Theorem 8 implies that any collision-free gossiping algorithm requires at least $n + 2\lceil R'/R \rceil - 1$ transmission slots, and, thus, `Gossip` performs better than any collision-free algorithm.

The proof of the following result is similar to the proof of Theorem 8.

Theorem 9. *In any gossiping algorithm, for $n > 2\lfloor R'/R \rfloor$ processors, at least $2\lceil n/2 \rceil + 2\lfloor R'/R \rfloor - 3$ transmission slots are required before p_1 knows m_n and p_n knows m_1.*

The upper bound for `Gossip` differs from the lower bound in Theorem 9 by at most 4.

7 Conclusion

All of the gossiping algorithms in the literature assume that the transmission radius R is equal to the interference radius R'. Our upper bounds consider the more general case, where $R' \geq R$. For one-dimensional static ad hoc radio networks, we have presented a gossiping algorithm that requires no more than

$-2\lceil R'/R\rceil - 1$ transmission slots. We prove that this algorithm is close to optimal by creating a network for which any algorithm requires $2\lceil n/2\rceil + 2\lfloor R'/R\rfloor - 3$
transmission slots. Restricting to the class of collision-free algorithms, we have
presented an algorithm that requires at most $n + 2\lceil R'/R\rceil$ transmission slots,
and have proven that this algorithm is nearly optimal by creating a network for
which any collision-free algorithm requires $2\lceil n/2\rceil + 2\lfloor R'/R\rfloor - 2$ transmission
slots. Restricting further to the class of singleton algorithms, we have provided
an algorithm that takes no more than $n - D + 2$ transmission slots for any network with diameter $D \geq 2$. We prove that this algorithm is optimal by providing
a matching lower bound.

We have also demonstrated separations between the classes of singleton,
collision-free, and unrestricted algorithms. We have proven that, for any one-
dimensional radio network with diameter $D > 2\lceil R'/R\rceil + 2$, our collision-free
algorithm uses less than $n + D - 2$ transmission slots while any singleton algorithm would require at least $n + D - 2$ transmission slots. We also demonstrate
that there exist one-dimensional radio networks for which any collision-free algorithm requires at least $n + 2\lceil R'/R\rceil - 1$ transmission slots while our algorithm
uses less than $n + 2\lceil R'/R\rceil - 1$ transmission slots.

All of the previous lower bounds for gossiping algorithms in static ad hoc
networks assume that $R = R'$ and that the network topology is not known. To
derive lower bounds when the network topology is not known, an adversary can
be created that chooses the network topology based on the algorithm. As we
assume that all of the processors know the network topology, we cannot use this
kind of adversarial argument. We provide the first non-trivial lower bounds for
gossiping in the more difficult setting in which the network topology is known
in advance.

Our results also apply to the transmission complexity of the gossiping task,
that is, the total number of transmissions performed by processors during an
algorithm's execution. Characterizing the transmission complexity can be useful
in situations where processors have a limited amount of battery power and must
conserve energy. We note that two transmitting processors, p and p', contribute
two transmissions to the transmission complexity, regardless of whether or not
the transmissions by p and p' occur during the same transmission slot. Thus,
any algorithm A can be converted into a singleton algorithm A' with the same
transmission complexity as A. It follows that our matching upper and lower
bounds for the time complexity of singleton gossiping algorithms completely
describe the transmission complexity for gossiping in our network model.

For the classes of collision-free and unrestricted algorithms, our upper and
lower bounds differ by a small additive constant. Further, for these two classes, we
have only provided lower bounds on the time to complete gossiping in particular
networks in which gossiping is difficult, rather than providing lower bounds that
depend on various properties (such as the diameter) of an arbitrary network.
Extending these bounds is left as an open problem. We may also consider the
same problem in different networks models, such as: asynchronous networks,
networks that exist in two or three dimensions, mobile networks, or, networks in

which the network topology is not initially known by all processors. Some results for deterministic gossiping in one-dimensional networks with mobile processors can be found in [7].

Acknowledgements

The author wishes to thank his advisor, Faith Ellen, whose helpful insights and guidance led to a vastly improved presentation of this research. Also, the author appreciates the invaluable comments and suggestions from the anonymous reviewers of this paper. The author was supported by the Natural Sciences and Engineering Research Council of Canada.

References

[1] Chlebus, B., Gąsieniec, L., Östlin, A., Robson, J.M.: Deterministic radio broadcasting. In: Welzl, E., Montanari, U., Rolim, J.D.P. (eds.) ICALP 2000. LNCS, vol. 1853, pp. 717–728. Springer, Heidelberg (2000)

[2] Chlebus, B., Gąsieniec, L., Lingas, A., Pagourtzis, A.: Oblivious gossiping in ad-hoc radio networks. In: Proc. 5th International Workshop on Discrete Algorithms and Methods for Mobile Computing and Communications (DIALM 2001), pp. 44–51 (2001)

[3] Chrobak, M., Gąsieniec, L., Rytter, W.: Fast broadcasting and gossiping in radio networks. In: IEEE Symposium on Foundations of Computer Science, pp. 575–581 (2000)

[4] Cicalese, F., Manne, F., Xin, Q.: Faster centralized communication in radio networks. In: International Symposium on Algorithms and Computation, pp. 339–348 (2006)

[5] Gąsieniec, L., Potapov, I., Xin, Q.: Time efficient gossiping in known radio networks. In: Kralovic, R., Sýkora, O. (eds.) SIROCCO 2004. LNCS, vol. 3104, pp. 173–184. Springer, Heidelberg (2004)

[6] Gąsieniec, L., Radzik, T., Xin, Q.: Faster deterministic gossiping in directed ad-hoc radio networks. In: 9th Scandinavian Workshop on Algorithm Theory, pp. 397–407 (2004)

[7] Miller, A.: Gossiping in one-dimensional synchronous ad hoc radio networks. Master's thesis, University of Toronto (2009),
http://www.cs.toronto.edu/~a4miller

Complexity and Approximation of a Geometric Local Robot Assignment Problem*

Olaf Bonorden, Bastian Degener, Barbara Kempkes, and Peter Pietrzyk

Heinz Nixdorf Institute, CS Department, University of Paderborn, 33098 Paderborn, Germany
bono@uni-paderborn.de, degener@uni-paderborn.de,
barbaras@uni-paderborn.de, toon@uni-paderborn.de

Abstract. We introduce a geometric multi-robot assignment problem. Robots positioned in a Euclidean space have to be assigned to treasures in such a way that their joint strength is sufficient to unearth a treasure with a given weight. The robots have a limited range and thus can only be assigned to treasures in their proximity. The objective is to unearth as many treasures as possible. We investigate the complexity of several variants of this problem and show whether they are in $\mathcal{P}$ or are $\mathcal{NP}$-complete. Furthermore, we provide a distributed and local constant-factor approximation algorithm using constant-factor resource augmentation for the two-dimensional setting with $\mathcal{O}(\log^* n)$ communication rounds.

1 Introduction

We consider a large group of tiny robots deployed arbitrarily to a Euclidean space, in which treasures are hidden. Being equipped with sensors, the robots are able to detect treasures positioned within their viewing range. The treasures can have different weights and the robots can have different amounts of strength. The task is to assign the robots to treasures in such a way that the number of unearthed treasures is maximized. A treasure is unearthed if the amount of strength of the robots assigned to it sums up to at least its weight. One constraint must be kept: A robot may only be assigned to a treasure if the treasure is within the robot's viewing range. Note that the robots do not move before the assignment is calculated. Hence, we are dealing with a static scenario.

We will adhere to the figurative description of treasures to be unearthed. In an application these treasures could for example also be tasks which have to be handled by teams of robots or mobile robotic sensor nodes. Another application is the assignment of mobile robotic sensors to objects that need a certain number of guards to be properly monitored. Our main challenge is that all acting entities have only their own local view and no knowledge about the global state of the environment. This is natural for robot teams deployed to areas unaccessible to humans.

We distinguish two scenarios: In the *heterogeneous* scenario the robots can have different strengths, while in the *homogeneous* one every robot has a strength of 1.

---

* Partially supported by the EU within FP7-ICT-2007-1 under contract no. 215270 (FRONTS) and DFG-project "Smart Teams" within the SPP 1183 "Organic Computing" and International Graduate School Dynamic Intelligent Systems.

S. Dolev (Ed.): ALGOSENSORS 2009, LNCS 5804, pp. 252–262, 2009.

Our contribution. To be as general as possible, we explore the complexity of calculating the optimal solution for both scenarios with all knowledge at hand in a traditional global fashion and in two dimensions. We capture the hardness of locality by letting robots only be assigned to treasures in their viewing range. Since we show that most variants are $\mathcal{NP}$-complete, the calculation of the optimal solution is also impracticable in a local and distributed way. So we present a local, distributed approximation algorithm using *resource augmentation*. This is an established tool for algorithmic analysis: An algorithm is provided with additional resources, but is still compared to an optimal algorithm without these. Our algorithm provides a constant factor approximation of the optimal solution and has a runtime of $\mathcal{O}(\log^* n)$ synchronous local broadcast communication rounds. As a building block, we present the first distributed local algorithm for the weighted independent set problem on Δ-bounded degree graphs. It has a Δ^Δ-approximation ratio, which is constant in our case. Due to space limitations we omit some of the proofs. They can be found in the long version of this paper [1].

Related work. This paper deals with allocating robots to points in a Euclidean space. A related area is the one of Multi-Robot Coordination, especially Multi-Robot Task Allocation (MRTA). For an overview, see [2]. Most approaches use experiments or simulations for evaluation ([3], [4], [5], [6]), but some theoretical results exist as well [7].

For our approximation algorithm, we need to compute a maximal independent set on unit disk graphs locally. This has just been shown to be possible in optimal time $\mathcal{O}(\log^* n)$ [8]. We also use a local variant of an approximation algorithm for the maximal independent set problem on bounded degree graphs using $\mathcal{O}(\log^* n)$ time [9].

While our algorithm for the weighted maximum independent set problem yields a Δ^Δ-approximation, the best global algorithm computes a Δ-approximation [10]. We assume that global coordinates are not available to the robots. Our complexity results would still be valid, but our algorithm would be a lot simpler and it would run in constant time using the approach of [11] for computing a maximal independent set.

For a detailed description of related work, see the long version of this paper [1].

Formal problem definition. We define different variants of the UNEARTH TREASURES (UT) problem. All variants accept the same input modeled by two sets T and R and an integer v. $T = \{t_1, \ldots t_n\}$ represents n treasures, $R = \{r_1, \ldots r_m\}$ m robots. v is the viewing range of the robots. Since v is equal for all robots, exactly those robots positioned in the sphere of radius v around a treasure t can be assigned to t. We call this the viewing range v of the treasure. With every treasure $t_i \in T$ and every robot $r_j \in R$ a position $p(t_i)$ resp. $p(r_j)$ in the d-dimensional Euclidean space is associated. Additionally, we associate an integer $w(t_i)$ with treasure t_i representing its weight and an integer $s(r_i)$ with robot r_i representing its strength. The function $assign : R \to T$ is defined in such a way that for all $r_i \in R$ the implication $(assign(r_i) = t_j \Rightarrow \|p(r_i) - p(t_j)\| \leq v)$ is true. The function $unearth : (T, R, assign) \to \mathbb{N}$ computes the number of treasures that are unearthed if the assignment $assign$ is employed. A treasure t_j is unearthed under $assign$ if $\sum_{i|assign(r_i)=t_j} s(r_i) \geq w(t_j)$.

We define the decision problem UT by a function $k : \mathbb{N} \to \mathbb{R}$, $k(n) \leq n$, telling us how many of the n treasures are supposed to be unearthed. In general, the decision problem is formulated as follows: Given two arbitrary sets T and R and an integer v as defined above, does a function *assign* exist with $unearth(T, R, assign) \geq k(n)$? We only consider k which are computable in polynomial time and which are monotonically increasing. In Section 3 we consider the optimization variant of the problem.

2   The Complexity of Robot Assignment

2.1   The Heterogeneous Scenario

To decide whether one treasure can be unearthed ($k(n) = 1$) is in $\mathcal{P}$, since it can be checked for each treasure if the robots in its viewing range suffice to unearth it. This is not the case for $k(n) = c$, $c > 1$ constant, which we show to be weak $\mathcal{NP}$-complete. Then we analyze a class of variants: for each $0 < \varepsilon \leq 1$ and each $k(n) \in \Omega(n^\varepsilon)$ we show that deciding whether $k(n)$ treasures can be unearthed is strongly $\mathcal{NP}$-complete.

Unearthing a Constant Number of Treasures ($k(n) = c$, $c > 1$). Unearthing a constant number of treasures is $\mathcal{NP}$-complete. However, a pseudo-polynomial dynamic program similar as for PARTITION can be found in the long version of this paper [1].

Theorem 1. *The variant of* UT *with* $k(n) = c$ *in the heterogeneous setting is* $\mathcal{NP}$-*complete for any constant* $c > 1$.

Proof. It is easy to see that all variants of UT are in $\mathcal{NP}$. To show the $\mathcal{NP}$-hardness we reduce the $\mathcal{NP}$-complete PARTITION (see [12]) to UT with $k(n) = 2$. We only need to consider $k(n) = 2$, since deciding if $k(n) = c$ with $c > 2$ treasures can be unearthed is at least as difficult as deciding whether two treasures can be unearthed.

   In the PARTITION problem we are given a finite set $A = \{a_1, a_2, \ldots, a_m\}$ of m positive integers which sum up to $2b$, $b \in \mathbb{N}$. Using A, we construct an instance of UT in the following way: We position two treasures t_1 and t_2 with $w(t_1) = w(t_2) = b$ in the plane so that their viewing ranges intersect. Into this intersection we place m robots $r_1, r_2, \ldots, r_m$ with $s(r_i) = a_i$ for all $1 \leq i \leq m$. An assignment for the robots yields a solution for the PARTITION problem and the reduction takes polynomial time in m.   □

Unearthing at Least a Polynomial Number of Treasures ($k(n) \in \Omega(n^\varepsilon), (0 < \varepsilon \leq 1)$). Now we are not dealing with a single problem, but with an infinite set of problems and therefore with a range of special cases. We first prove that UT is $\mathcal{NP}$-complete for $k(n) = n$ and then we reduce this variant to the class of variants were $k(n) \in \Omega(n^\varepsilon)$.

Theorem 2. *The variant of* UT *with* $k(n) = n$ *in the heterogeneous scenario is strong* $\mathcal{NP}$-*complete.*

We reduce the strongly $\mathcal{NP}$-complete problem 3-SATISFIABILITY to UT with $k(n) = n$. Due to space limitations, we omit the proof and refer to [1].

Theorem 3. *The variant of* UT *with fixed* $k(n) \in \Omega(n^\varepsilon), (0 < \varepsilon \leq 1)$ *in the heterogeneous scenario is strongly* $\mathcal{NP}$-*complete.*

Proof. We reduce the UT problem with $k(n) = n$ to the variant where only $f(n) \in \Omega(n^{\varepsilon})$ treasures have to be unearthed. We are given an instance I of UT with n treasures and are asked whether it is possible to unearth $k(n) = n$ of them. For a constant $0 < \varepsilon \leq 1$, we create an instance $\bar{I}$ with $\bar{n}$ treasures from I such that iff it is possible to unearth $f(\bar{n})$ of the treasures in $\bar{I}$ it is possible to unearth $k(n) = n$ of the treasures in I. To achieve this, we extend I with t treasures which cannot be reached by any robot. This means that in $\bar{I}$ we have $\bar{n} = n + t$ treasures. If we choose t in a way that $f(\bar{n}) = k(n)$ and therefore $f(n + t) = n$, $f(\bar{n})$ treasures in $\bar{I}$ can be unearthed if and only if $f(n)$ treasures can be unearthed in I. Moreover, t must be greater than or equal to 0 (we cannot add a negative number of treasures) and polynomial in n, because otherwise the reduction would not be polynomial (since f is computable in polynomial time, this also holds for a t polynomial in n). So now we prove that such a t exists.

There exists a t' such that $f(n + t) = f(n) + t'$, where $t \geq 0$ if and only if $t' \geq 0$, because f is monotonically increasing. Since $f(n) \leq n$ (we cannot unearth more than all treasures) and $f(n) + t' = k(n) = n$, $t' \geq 0$ and therefore also $t \geq 0$. Moreover, because $f(n) \geq 0$, $t' \leq n$. To see that t is polynomial in n, note that $f(n + t) \geq c \cdot (n + t)^{\varepsilon}$ for large n and a constant c, because $f(n) \in \Omega(n^{\varepsilon})$. Additionally, $f(n + t) = f(n) + t' \leq 2n$. Putting these two inequalities together, $c \cdot (n + t)^{\varepsilon} \leq 2n$ and therefore $t \leq (\frac{2n}{c})^{\frac{1}{\varepsilon}} - n$. Since c and ε are constants, it follows that t is polynomial in n.   □

2.2   The Homogeneous Scenario

In the homogeneous scenario, all robots have a strength of 1. We analyze whether adding this constraint simplifies the problem in some of the variants for the function k. This is the case: The problem is in $\mathcal{P}$ if $k(n)$ or $n - k(n)$ is constant (where the case $k(n) = 1$ follows directly from the heterogeneous setting, but not for other c). It is strongly $\mathcal{NP}$-complete for general k and for every k with $k(n) \in \Omega(n^{\varepsilon_1}) \wedge k(n) \in \mathcal{O}(n^{\varepsilon_2})$, $0 < \varepsilon_1 \leq \varepsilon_2 < 1$. Note that the homogeneous scenario is equivalent to a scenario where robots are splittable resources and can be allocated to treasures partially. We first show the algorithms with polynomial runtime, then we prove the $\mathcal{NP}$-hardness claims.

Variants of UT Which Are in $\mathcal{P}$

Theorem 4. *The variants of* UT *with* $k(n) = n$ *(can all treasures be unearthed?), with* $k(n) = n - c$ *(can all but c treasures be unearthed?), and with* $k(n) = c$ *in the homogeneous setting are in* $\mathcal{P}$ *for all* $c \geq 0$.

Proof. We model an instance of UT for $k(n) = n$ as a flow network with one source and one sink. We create one node for each robot and each treasure, and an edge from the source to each robot node (*robot edges*) with an upper bound of 1 for the flow on this edge. There is also an edge from each robot node to those treasure nodes reachable from the respective robot (*assignment edges*). From each treasure node we create an edge to the sink (*treasure edges*) with a capacity of the weight of the treasure.

The maximum flow f of this network can be computed in polynomial time by a standard maximum flow algorithm. Moreover, this maximum flow is integer on each edge [13]. Due to the capacities on the robot edges, in a maximum flow there is at most one assignment edge from each robot node with a flow of 1. All other assignment edges have a flow of 0. So the flow on the assignment edges corresponds to an assignment of robots to treasures. All treasures can be unearthed iff in a maximum flow all treasure edges are saturated, which can be checked in polynomial time. For the other cases, delete all $\binom{n}{c}$ resp. $n - \binom{n}{c}$ possible combinations of c resp. $n - c$ treasures ($\binom{n}{c}$ is polynomial in n) and formulate the corresponding network for each combination. $\qquad\square$

Unearthing an Arbitrary Number of Treasures (General $k(n)$). Now we show that deciding whether the UT problem with an arbitrary $k(n)$ is also $\mathcal{NP}$-complete in the homogeneous setting. We can assume that the function $k(n)$ is part of the input. This is equivalent to getting an integer k as input and being asked whether at least k treasures can be unearthed.

Theorem 5. *The general variant of* UT *with an integer k as part of the input is strongly $\mathcal{NP}$-complete in the homogeneous setting.*

Proof. It is obvious that the problem is in $\mathcal{NP}$, thus we just prove that it is strongly $\mathcal{NP}$-hard by reducing the $\mathcal{NP}$-complete problem PLANAR INDEPENDENT SET to it. Given a planar graph G and an integer k', we construct the input for UT: For each node in G we create a treasure and set its weight to the node's degree, while for each edge e, we create a robot which can only reach the treasures corresponding to the nodes adjacent to e. If these have to be placed too far apart from each other, we use the construction of a connection-gadget, a chain of treasures and robots placed alternatingly in such a way that each robot is in the intersection of exactly two treasures, to link them (see the long version [1]). Thus, a set of treasures T and a set of robots R is constructed. To make things easier to explain, we assume that for every connection-gadget only one of its robots is assigned to unearth a treasure corresponding to a node, while the remaining robots unearth the treasures which belong to the connection-gadget. Therefore, unearthing the treasure corresponding to u makes unearthing treasures which correspond to u's neighbor nodes impossible. Thus, unearthing treasures that correspond to a node is the same as building an independent set in G. Let l be the number of treasures in all created connection-gadgets and $k := l + k'$. This means that an algorithm with input T and R which can decide whether k treasures can be unearthed also decides whether an independent set with cardinality k' exists in G.

Note that allowing the robots to behave in a different way than we assumed above (i.e assigning two robots belonging to the same connection-gadget to treasures corresponding to nodes) does not increase the number of treasures that can be unearthed, since for every treasure corresponding to a node that is additionally unearthed due to this behavior, at least one treasure belonging to a connection-gadget cannot be unearthed. $\qquad\square$

A similar theorem as Theorem 3 applies in the homogeneous setting. Its proof is similar to the one in the heterogeneous setting, but we omit it here and refer to [1].

Theorem 6. *The variant of* UT *in the homogeneous setting is strongly $\mathcal{NP}$-complete for any fixed function k with $k(n) \in \Omega(n^{\varepsilon_1})$ and $k(n) \in \mathcal{O}(n^{\varepsilon_2}), 0 < \varepsilon_1 \leq \varepsilon_2 < 1$.*

3   A Local Approximation Algorithm with Resource Augmentation

This section describes a local, distributed algorithm which uses resource augmentation and computes a constant factor approximation for the UT problem. Robots executing the algorithm must be able to communicate with other robots in their vicinity and posses a unique ID. We assume that treasures have the same capabilities as robots (each treasure was located by a robot which now shares a position with the treasure and performs its communication). The constant factor resource augmentation allows robots and treasures to communicate with each other if the distance between them is at most $\mu \cdot v$ with $\mu = 6$, and permits assigning a robot to a treasure if they are within distance $\mu \cdot v$ of each other. Moreover, every robot has exact information about the relative local position and strength/weight of every robot/treasure within distance $\mu \cdot v$. The communication is performed in $\mathcal{O}(\log^* n)$ synchronous rounds, in which every robot can send $\mathcal{O}(\log n)$ bits as a broadcast to all robots within distance $\mu \cdot v$. Only after a round is finished, a robot can react to the information it received. To avoid trivialities, we demand that each robot has a treasure within its viewing range. Our algorithm is uniform in the sense that no information about the total number of nodes n is required. Furthermore, standard techniques are available to apply our synchronous algorithm to an asynchronous setting via α synchronizers [14]. Since our algorithm is deterministic and the time complexity is low, an efficient roll back compiler mechanism can be used to handle transient failures [15].

Basic Definitions. Given an instance (T,R,v) of UT, we construct the *treasure graph* $\bar{G} = (\bar{V},\bar{E})$ by inserting a node $\bar{v}_i$ to $\bar{V}$ for each $t_i \in T$ and adding an edge $\{\bar{v}_i,\bar{v}_j\}$ to $\bar{E}$, if $t_i, t_j \in T$ (corresponding to $\bar{v}_i, \bar{v}_j \in \bar{V}$) are within distance $2v$ of each other. A *valid clustering* of a UT instance is a set of subsets $C_i \subseteq R \cup T$ which we call *clusters* such that (1) each treasure and each robot is in at least one cluster, (2) in each C_i, exactly one treasure is marked as cluster-center c_i, (3) robots belong to a cluster C_i, iff they are in at most distance $3v$ from c_i, (4) treasures belong to a cluster C_i, iff they are in at most distance $2v$ from c_i and (5) each c_i is contained only in its own cluster C_i.

The *cluster-graph* $\widehat{G} = (\widehat{V},\widehat{E},w)$ with $w : \widehat{V} \to \mathbb{N}$ contains one node $\widehat{v}_i$ for each cluster-center c_i of a fixed valid clustering of an instance of UT. Each node $\widehat{v}_i$ has a weight w_i, which is the value of an approximation for UT in its cluster. Iff there is a robot in the considered instance that can reach two cluster-centers c_i and c_j, there is an edge $\{\widehat{v}_i,\widehat{v}_j\}$ in $\widehat{E}$. Given a graph $G = (V,E)$, a subset V' of V is called *independent*, iff there are no two nodes n_i, n_j in V' such that $(n_i, n_j) \in E$. V' is called an *inclusion-maximal* independent set, iff there is no independent V'' with $V' \subsetneq V''$. For a graph $G = (V,E)$ and a function *weight* that assigns a real number to each node, a subset V' of V is called *maximum weighted independent set*, iff V' is independent and there is no independent set V'' with $\sum_{v' \in V'} \text{weight}(v') < \sum_{v'' \in V''} \text{weight}(v'')$.

Description of the algorithm. The pseudocode in Algorithm 3.1 is written from the view of a single treasure, so that the input for the algorithm is the set of robots and treasures which are within the augmented viewing range of the treasure. At the time of the algorithm's termination, each robot knows the treasure it is assigned to.

Algorithm 3.1. LOCALUT(INPUT: treasures and robots within distance $6v$ of me)

1:   $\bar{G}_{local}$:= treasure-graph induced by treasures within distance $2v$
2:   Use $\bar{G}_{local}$ to compute whether I am in INCLUSION-MAXIMAL INDEPENDENT SET (MIS) of $\bar{G}$
3:   **if** NOT in MIS {*I am no cluster-center*} **then**
4:       wait for assignment by cluster-center
5:   **else**
6:       *myCluster* := robots within distance $3v$ and treasures within distance $2v$ of me
7:       T_c := treasures in *myCluster*; R_c := robots in *myCluster*
8:       *assignment* := ALLTOALL(T_c, R_c) in *myCluster*
9:       *myWeight* := number of unearthed treasures in *assignment*
10:      $\widehat{G}_{local}$:= cluster-graph induced by cluster-centers in local $6v$-neighborhood with resp. weights
11:      *inFinalSet* := LOCALMWIS($\widehat{G}_{local}$)
12:      **if** *inFinalSet* **then**
13:          tell robots in cluster to use *assignment* (OUTPUT)

Algorithm 3.2. ALLTOALL(INPUT: T, R)

1:   L_1 := treasures sorted by weight, lowest first, L_2 := robots sorted by strength, lowest first
2:   **for all** treasures t_i in L_1 **do**
3:       **if** a single robot r_j can satisfy t_i **then**
4:           satisfy t_i by assigning r_j to t_i and delete r_j from L_2 and t_i from L_1
5:   **while** there are treasures in L_1 **do**
6:       take first treasure t from L_1
7:       **while** t is not satisfied AND there are robots in L_2 **do**
8:           assign first robot from L_2 to t
9:           **if** t is satisfied **then**
10:              delete t from L_1
11: **return** assignment of robots to treasures

First, a valid clustering of the robots and treasures is built by computing an inclusion-maximal independent set on the treasure-graph. Each treasure which is in the independent set marks itself as cluster-center. Since this results in a valid clustering (see paragraph *Constructing a valid clustering*), a treasure and a robot belonging to the same cluster have distance of at most $5 \cdot v$. This means that if we use resource augmentation to increase the viewing range by a factor of five, each robot can reach each treasure in the same cluster and therefore each cluster-center can apply ALLTOALL to compute a solution for its cluster which is at most twice as bad as the optimal solution (see paragraph *Correctness of* ALLTOALL). Since robots can be in more than one cluster and two different cluster-centers might therefore assign these robots to different treasures, we need to decide which clusters to keep in the final solution. This is done by computing an approximation of a maximum weighted independent set on the cluster-graph (Algorithm 3.3) and keeping the clusters in this independent set.

Constructing a valid clustering. We need to prove that any inclusion-maximal independent set on the treasure-graph $\bar{G}$ computed by our algorithm yields a valid clustering.

Algorithm 3.3. LOCALMWIS(INPUT: $G_{local} = (V, E, w)$)

1: **while** (NOT marked as deleted) and (NOT assigned to MWIS) **do**
2: Use G_{local} to compute if I am in UNW. INCLUSION-MAXIMAL INDEPENDENT SET(MIS)
   of G
3: **if** NOT in MIS **then**
4:   wait this round
5: **else**
6:   **if** (for all neighbors in cluster-graph) *myWeight* > neighbors.*myweight* **then**
7:    assign myself to MWIS and mark neighboring nodes as deleted
8:   **else**
9:    mark myself as deleted
10: **return** whether assigned to MWIS

To see that this is the case, we have to show that each treasure and each robot is in at least one cluster (Proposition 1) and that each cluster-center is only in its own cluster (Proposition 2).

For the first proposition, assume that there is one treasure t which is not in a cluster. It therefore exists no cluster-center within distance $2v$ of t. Therefore, there is no edge between t and a cluster-center in the treasure-graph. So adding t to the independent set increases the size of it and therefore the independent set was not inclusion-maximal. Now assume that there is one robot r which is not in a cluster. It therefore exists no cluster-center within distance $3v$ of r. Since there is at least one treasure in the viewing range v of r, this treasure cannot be within distance $2v$ of a cluster-center. This constitutes the contradiction.

For the second proposition, consider two cluster-centers c_1 and c_2. Since they both are in the inclusion-maximal independent set of the treasure-graph $\bar{G}$, there is no edge $\{c_i, c_j\}$ in $\bar{G}$. This means that c_i and c_j are in distance more than $2v$ of each other and therefore neither of them is in the other's cluster.

Constant degree of the cluster graph. To be able to compute a maximum weighted independent set on the cluster-graph efficiently, we need the cluster-graph to have a constant degree. This follows from a valid clustering: Since each cluster-center is only in its own cluster, the distance between two cluster-centers is more than $2v$. This implies that each cluster-center has a circle with a radius v surrounding itself which does not intersect with the according circles of other cluster-centers. We call this circle the *exclusive area* of a cluster-center. Furthermore, two cluster-centers which share an edge in the cluster-graph can be at most in distance $6v$ of each other. Now consider a cluster-center c. All its neighbors in the cluster-graph must be in distance $6v$ around c. This means that the exclusive areas of the neighbors of c are in distance at most $7v$ and therefore in an area of size $\pi \cdot (7v)^2 = \pi \cdot 49v^2$ around c. Since each cluster-center has an exclusive area of size πv^2, there can be no more than $\frac{\pi \cdot 49v^2}{\pi v^2} = 49$ cluster-centers and therefore 48 neighbors of c in this area. Thus, a valid clustering of a UT instance results in a cluster-graph with at most degree $\Delta = 48$.

Correctness of ALLTOALL. As soon as the cluster-centers have been defined, each cluster-center computes an approximation for its own cluster. To achieve that each robot can be assigned to each treasure and thus ALLTOALL can be executed, the viewing range of each robot and treasure is increased by a factor of 6. Now we have to show that in an instance of UT where each robot can reach all treasures, ALLTOALL computes a 2-approximation. To see this, we compare the solution computed by ALLTOALL with an optimal solution: We show that for each treasure satisfied by ALLTOALL, there is at most one additional treasure satisfied in the optimal solution.

In the first loop, each satisfied treasure is satisfied by a single robot. In an optimal solution this robot might have been assigned to another treasure, which is the only one which might become unsatisfiable by this action. The second loop iterates over all treasures. There are only two possibilities for how the loop can be left. Either all treasures are satisfied, leading to an optimal solution, or there are no robots left to assign. In this case, observe that the treasures with the smallest values are satisfied. We claim that the algorithm assigns at most twice the needed amount of robot strength to each of these treasures, thus the total power of the robots can at most satisfy the double number of treasures in an optimal solution. This follows from the fact that all wasted robot power belongs to a single robot, because no robots are assigned after the treasure is satisfied. Assume for the sake of contradiction that this robot has more power than is needed to satisfy this single treasure. Then it would have been assigned to the treasure in the first loop of the algorithm.

Correctness of the algorithm. Note that by increasing the viewing range of cluster-centers by a factor of 6 to $6 \cdot v$, we can construct the cluster graph G, where two clusters are connected by an edge only if they are less than $6 \cdot v$ apart from each other. Computing a Δ^Δ-approximation of the maximum weighted independent set of G, where the node weights are the solutions computed by the cluster-centers and Δ the maximum degree of G, allows us to choose the clusters that will be part of the final solution. In oder to see that LOCALMWIS computes such a Δ^Δ-approximation, we have to prove that the while-loop terminates after at most $\Delta + 1$ rounds, where Δ is the degree of the graph. If a node u is in the inclusion-maximal independent set (MIS) in one round, either u will mark itself or all its neighbors as deleted. If u is not in the MIS, one of its neighbors is. So either u will be marked as deleted by its neighbor or one of its neighbors will be marked as deleted. This leaves no neighbors for deletion after Δ rounds. Furthermore, note that the final set is indeed independent: In each round the nodes that are chosen to the maximal independent set are independent by definition. If they assign themselves to the final set, they mark their neighbors as deleted, which subsequently cannot be assigned to the final set in later rounds.

To show that we get a Δ^Δ-approximation, note that from each node which is not in the final set we can define a path of *dominating nodes* to a node chosen to the final set. A dominating node of a node u is a neighbor of u with a larger weight. For any given node which is not in the final set, the next node on the path of dominating nodes is either the one that marked it as deleted or, if the node marked itself as deleted, a neighboring node with a higher value. This neighbor must exist, since otherwise the node would not have marked itself as deleted. After at most Δ hops from each node, a node in the final set is reached, because there are at most $\Delta + 1$ rounds and all remaining nodes in the last round (with no degree) are chosen to the final set. Now consider an arbitrary node u in the final set and all nodes which are not in the final set whose paths lead to

u. These are at most Δ^Δ nodes, because this is an upper bound on the number of nodes in a Δ-neighborhood of a Δ-degree graph. All those nodes have a smaller value than u. Therefore the value of u is at least $\frac{1}{\Delta^\Delta}$ times the value of a set to which all other nodes would have been chosen. This applies to all nodes in the final set. Now we have all preliminaries for proving the correctness of the algorithm.

As shown above, the weight of a cluster is a two-approximation of an optimal solution in the cluster, and the choice of clusters for a final solution is a constant approximation. Furthermore, each robot is only assigned to one treasure within its cluster and therefore travels at most distance $5v$. Thus, Theorem 7 follows.

Theorem 7. *Algorithm* LOCALUNEARTHTREASURES *computes a constant-factor approximation of* UT *using factor-6 resource augmentation.*

Complexity. In a wireless network, the costly part concerning time and energy consumption is the communication between robots and therefore we use the number of communication rounds for measuring the complexity of our algorithms. This leads to a complexity of $\mathcal{O}(1)$ of the algorithm ALLTOALL, since this algorithm uses no communication besides the final broadcast of the solution. However, it is worth noting that the local computation the robots need to perform for ALLTOALL is still efficient in the worst-case: If all treasures and robots are in one cluster, our algorithm takes $\mathcal{O}(n\log n + m\log m)$ local computations. Since the runtime of ALLTOALL dominates the runtime of all local computations, this is also an upper bound on the total local processing time. Furthermore, note that in each communication round at most $\mathcal{O}(\log n)$ bits are transmitted.

The while-loop in LOCALMWIS is executed at most $\Delta + 1$ times. In each round of the loop, an inclusion-maximal independent set is computed. This can be done using the algorithm from [9] in $\mathcal{O}(\log^* n)$ rounds. Line 7 can again take Δ time, the remaining of the loop takes constant time. Since Δ is also constant, the running time of LOCALMWIS is $\mathcal{O}(\log^* n)$.

In line 3 of the algorithm LOCALUNEARTHTREASURES, an inclusion-maximal independent set on a unit disk graph is computed. This can be done using [8] in $\mathcal{O}(\log^* n)$ communication rounds. Since LOCALMWIS also takes $\mathcal{O}(\log^* n)$ communication rounds and the remaining of the algorithm takes constant time, the overall running time is $\mathcal{O}(\log^* n)$ and the following theorem follows.

Theorem 8. *Algorithm* LOCALUNEARTHTREASURES *terminates in* $\mathcal{O}(\log^* n)$ *communication rounds.*

4 Open Questions and Final Comment

There are still some functions $k(n)$ left, for which the complexity of the corresponding variant of the UT problem was not covered. Moreover, we do not know yet whether resource augmentation is needed to be able to compute a constant factor approximation for the UT problem in polynomial time. If this is the case, it is reasonable to improve the factor for resource augmentation. Even a $(1 + \varepsilon)$-augmentation might be possible. This is not the case for the approximation factor: Here, the analysis of the PARTITION problem shows a lower bound of 2. Further open questions are: Can our algorithm be applied directly to an asynchronous setting? Is explicit communication crucial? How far can the constants of our algorithm be improved? Especially the approximation factor of Δ^Δ for the local weighted maximum independent set problem should be significantly improved, since a Δ-approximation for global algorithms is known. Extensions to higher dimensions seem straight forward.

References

1. Bonorden, O., Degener, B., Kempkes, B., Pietrzyk, P.: Complexity and approximation of a geometric local robot assignment problem. Technical Report tr-ri-09-299, University of Paderborn (2009),
   http://wwwhni.uni-paderborn.de/en/alg/publications/
2. Gerkey, B.P., Mataric, M.J.: A Formal Analysis and Taxonomy of Task Allocation in Multi-Robot Systems. The International Journal of Robotics Research 23(9), 939–954 (2004)
3. Lin, L., Zheng, Z.: Combinatorial bids based multi-robot task allocation method. In: Proceedings of the 2005 IEEE International Conference on Robotics and Automation (IRCA), pp. 1145–1150 (2005)
4. Burgard, W., Moors, M., Stachniss, C., Schneider, F.: Coordinated multi-robot exploration. IEEE Transactions on Robotics 21(3), 376–386 (2005)
5. Ostergaard, E., Mataric, M., Sukhatme, G.: Distributed multi-robot task allocation for emergency handling. In: Proceedings of IEEE/RSJ International Conference on Intelligent Robots and Systems, vol. 2, pp. 821–826 (2001)
6. Tang, F., Parker, L.: A complete methodology for generating multi-robot task solutions using ASyMTRe-D and market-based task allocation. In: IEEE International Conference on Robotics and Automation, pp. 3351–3358 (2007)
7. Lagoudakis, M.G., Berhault, M., Koenig, S., Keskinocak, P., Kleywegt, A.J.: Simple auctions with performance guarantees for multi-robot task allocation. In: Multi-Robot Systems. From Swarms to Intelligent Automata, vol. III, pp. 27–38. Springer, Netherlands (2005)
8. Schneider, J., Wattenhofer, R.: A log-star distributed maximal independent set algorithm for growth-bounded graphs. In: Proceedings of the 27th Annual ACM Symposium on Principles of Distributed Computing, PODC (2008)
9. Goldberg, A., Plotkin, S., Shannon, G.: Parallel symmetry-breaking in sparse graphs. In: STOC 1987: Proceedings of the nineteenth annual ACM symposium on Theory of computing, pp. 315–324. ACM, New York (1987)
10. Sakai, S., Togasaki, M., Yamazaki, K.: A note on greedy algorithms for the maximum weighted independent set problem. Discrete Applied Mathematics 126(2-3), 313–322 (2003)
11. Kuhn, F., Moscibroda, T., Wattenhofer, R.: On the locality of bounded growth. In: PODC 2005: Proceedings of the twenty-fourth annual ACM symposium on Principles of distributed computing, pp. 60–68. ACM, New York (2005)
12. Karp, R.M.: Reducibility Among Combinatorial Problems. In: Miller, R.E., Thatcher, J.W. (eds.) Complexity of Computer Computations, pp. 85–103. Plenum, New York (1972)
13. Cormen, T.H., Leiserson, C.E., Rivest, R.L., Stein, C.: Introduction to Algorithms, 2nd edn. MIT Press, Cambridge (2001)
14. Awerbuch, B.: Complexity of network synchronization. J. ACM 32(4), 804–823 (1985)
15. Awerbuch, B., Varghese, G.: Distributed program checking: a paradigm for building self-stabilizing distributed protocols (extended abstract). In: SFCS 1991: Proceedings of the 32nd annual symposium on Foundations of computer science, pp. 258–267. IEEE Computer Society, Los Alamitos (1991)

Author Index

Printing: Mercedes-Druck, Berlin
Binding: Stein+Lehmann, Berlin